To the Arctic!

TO
THE ARCTIC!

The Story
of Northern Exploration
from Earliest Times

by Jeannette Mirsky

WITH AN INTRODUCTION BY
Vilhjalmur Stefansson

THE UNIVERSITY OF CHICAGO PRESS
Chicago and London

THE UNIVERSITY OF CHICAGO PRESS, CHICAGO 60637
THE UNIVERSITY OF CHICAGO PRESS, LTD., LONDON
Published 1970
Printed in the United States of America

02 01 00 99 98 97   7 6 5 4 3
ISBN: 0-226-53179-1 (paperback)
LCN: 72-121386

⊗ The paper used in this publication meets the minimum requirements of
the American National Standard for Information Sciences—Permanence of
Paper for Printed Library Materials, ANSI Z39.48—1984.

*To the memory
of my Mother, who loved to travel,
and
of my Father, whose passion was books*

Contents

Contents

Ross and the success of Parry—Parry's first voyage and the start of modern Arctic exploration—Parry's second voyage to Hudson Bay—Parry's last voyage for the Northwest Passage—Ross's four years in the Arctic—The discovery of the North Magnetic Pole—Back's experience aboard the Terror.

BY LAND: *John Franklin's overland journey to the Frozen Sea—His terrible hardships—Starvation—The cannibalism of Michel—Franklin's second journey along Mackenzie's route—Mapping the Arctic coast of America—Back's descent of the Great Fish River.*

THE HUDSON'S BAY COMPANY: *Simpson's work along the Arctic coast—His tragic death—Rae, the first explorer at home in the Arctic—His explorations—Vast area charted between 1818 and 1847.*

Contents

Contents

Illustrations & Maps

Illustrations & Maps

MAPS

Introduction by
Vilhjalmur Stefansson

To the Arctic! is both fascinating to read and the best history of northern exploration so far written. The fascination steals over you as you read; your approval of the work as a history will follow if you make comparisons, as I have done.

During the collection of a polar library, which now has more than seventeen thousand titles, I have segregated under "Histories of Polar Exploration" about a hundred books published during the last two hundred years. As mere collections of travel tales, some of these are good. From the historian's point of view, if I can judge it, not one of the Arctic volumes approaches the satisfactory.

There are histories of northern exploration where the author's criticism, when applied, is obviously perverted, for instance by nationalism. Perhaps worse are those where the bias is prevailingly moral or moralizing. Sometimes the author tells you in the preface, and in other cases he might as well have told you, that the purpose is neither historical nor scientific, but to mold character. By holding up before our youth the glorious example of "heroes who conquered the Frozen North," these writers expect to fit the rising generation for the Waterloos of peace and war. They seem to feel that a reading of biased narratives, more deceptive than fiction through being partly true, will stiffen moral fiber and lead to a variety of good results.

Close seconds to the ennobling histories are books like Markham's *Lands of Silence*. Their angle of vision is even narrower than either the nationalistic or the moralizing. They are nationalist, they are moral, but their chief bias is for the aggrandizement of a particular class—in Markham's case that of sailors, or, even more narrowly, naval officers. His admiration, and yours if you follow him, are for the sturdy seamen who differed from beasts of draft chiefly in that they were harnessed by themselves rather than by their masters to sledges that they dragged over snow-covered lands and winter seas. Even more admirable, you gather, were the officers who walked light behind the sledges, burdened perhaps with a spyglass or fowling piece.

The first step, then, in my admiration for Jeannette Mirsky is that in *To the Arctic!* she has written a history not for the aggrandizement of a nation or the ennobling of youth but rather to get at and state facts. Her messages, when any, are those of the characters themselves. Those messages may conflict, for the explorers contradict each other and sometimes themselves. So the meaning you get from her book will be your own rather than that of the historian.

Now and then our author does underscore a belief to which she has been converted by a study of the sources. Occasionally during the book you can watch her being converted. For instance, in more than one place she seems inclined to feel, with the majority of her witnesses, that the Arctic is barren and desolate; but eventually a persuasive minority of explorers succeed in leading her to surmise that, in the north as elsewhere, such qualities may lie chiefly in the eye of the beholder.

As remarked, our author's clear purpose is to let her characters speak for themselves. I feel in disagreement with some of these characters; and so there are in this book things with which I disagree. But the trouble, if any, is not with the writer of the history but with the men who thought, planned, and acted out these matters which the historian must chronicle.

As the good historian, Miss Mirsky generally uses first-hand journals and sticks to them. Columbus, for instance, describes a mermaid he observed. I have no quarrel with a historian who quotes the discoverer of San Salvador and Cuba verbatim on mermaids and leaves it at that. It is for the reader better fun, and in the end more instructive, not to be handed a cut and dried verdict on mermaids and Columbus, but to be allowed instead to form his own opinion of what it was the Admiral saw, or thought he saw, and as to what light the episode throws on the ability and reliability of the explorer.

The first edition of *To the Arctic!* (*To the North!*, 1934) was ahead of its time, for in men's minds the Arctic was then still remote and was thought of as being at the top or end of the world. Those who did read the work became its apostles; but they had little success in proselytizing, for not many knew enough about the Arctic to realize that if they read more they would become more interested.

This has all been changed. The times have caught up with our book, largely because men who command press and radio have begun telling us that the Arctic is really at the center of our world and that, in North America for instance, our northern frontier on the Arctic is in many significant respects more important than our eastern frontier upon the Atlantic or our western upon the Pacific.

So this second edition has been brought about through events sufficiently world-shaking to impress newsmen and commentators, chiefly the development of aviation and the conflagration of war. A large fraction of the public has at last come to realize (instead of just saying it, parrot fashion) that the earth is a sphere; a hundred are now talking and reading about the Arctic against one who did when the first edition of this book was published. We devotees of that first edition are glad of the revival, though we feel that it ought to have come about through the sheer merits of the book itself—as with *Arabia Deserta* and *Moby Dick*, which their backers succeeded in reviving without the help of a new interest in deserts or in whaling.

Preface to the 1970 Edition

I T IS, truth to tell, exhilarating to have *To the Arctic!* reissued. Not many nonfiction books of the 1930s have been so fortunate. First appearing as *To the North!* in 1934, its title was changed for the 1948 edition to avoid confusion in the shipping room—the new publisher had brought out Elizabeth Bowen's novel *To the North* in 1932. The change in titles indicates few differences in the text: in addition to correcting typographical errors, I brought the account up to date—augmenting the text by some fifteen thousand words. Since then nothing basically new in geographical exploration has occurred. Thus *To the Arctic!* remains complete, viable, and, mirabile dictu, publishable in 1970. Such continuing grace is not granted to many books.

To the Arctic! has had an unusual history; it began when the book first appeared. As I see it, the theme is one familiar from the fairy-tale genre: a Wicked Fairy appears unexpectedly just as a host of Good Fairies are showering a newborn infant with gifts of health, wealth, long life, and happiness. Usually this happens to a princess; when it happens to a book it makes an interesting story.

To the North! was greeted with, as the phrase goes, paeans of praise: the reviews were all an author could hope for—prominent, lengthy, and most enthusiastic. The publisher was gratified; I was ecstatic. Such a reception seemed like an accolade, a kind of public benediction for the years spent working on the book—three and a half years reading, reading, reading through everything a fine library provided about men's experiences in the Arctic; organizing the millions of words, the thousands of miles, the hundreds of years, the words and deeds of the explorers into a coherent order. And, when finally the manuscript was finished, I sent it for comments to a friend, the late Dorothy J. Teall (remembered as a girl wonder in the publishing world). "I have read your *opus*," she wrote; "now sit down and write the story." She was right. The grandeur of the adventure had disappeared in a thicket of details and in the notes. The praise the book received fully vindicated the long effort that went into its making.

My euphoria was short-lived. It ended with the beginning of what I call l'affaire Cook.

One night while I was having dinner with guests, I was served with a legal paper: Dr. Frederick Albert Cook, a practicing physician in the state of New York, was suing me for fifty thousand dollars, alleging that I had libeled him by stating that he had not reached the North Pole and that by so writing I had hurt his reputation. The two friends with me read the paper still warm from the process server's hand. One was a friend of long standing, the late Dr. Harold Rypins, secretary of the state board of medical examiners; the other was Austin MacCormack, whom I had recently met through a Washington friend when La Guardia brought him to the city to revamp its penal institutions. Dr. Rypins said: "Cook is *not* a practicing physician. I issued no license to him." And Mr. MacCormack said: "This is really very strange. I know Cook. I met him when I was head of the federal parole board. In 1930 when Cook had served five years of a fourteen-year sentence for mail fraud, he was put on parole for five years. I got to know him during those years. I felt he trusted me. Some weeks ago he came to see me, and out of a clear sky he asked me if I knew a Jeannette Mirsky. I told him that as a matter of fact I did. From his reactions I would say that Cook thinks your name is a pseudonym for Marie Stafford, Peary's daughter." At the time it seemed fantastic, even amusing.

Libel, I soon learned, is something lawyers eschew—it is treacherous, unpredictable, and can entrap even the innocent. I listened to the publisher's lawyers who were handling the case. They gave me examples of what could happen and urged caution. I countered by telling them that Peter Freuchen would testify for me: the Eskimos who had accompanied Cook had told him precisely where they had gone when on that trip and would give sworn statements if asked. The lawyers, weighing this and that, the hows and what-have-yous, the ifs and buts, decided the safest thing was to delay a trial hoping that Cook, then eighty, would die and with him his suit. Then, as now, I felt that it was foolish to be sensible and that if the case had gone to trial it would have given the book fabulous publicity. Cook lived until August 1940, lived for three months after receiving a presidential pardon. The book, alas, struggled to survive; its sales—a sad case of malnutrition—were poor; *To the North!* quietly went out of print.

But happily a book has a life of its own: mine gradually made friends, some of whom became my friends. One was instrumental in having it published: another, although praising the book—he considered it "somewhat of a Polar bible"—took exception to my treatment and evaluation of Cook. The sixty-year-old Cook-Peary controversy continues—did one, did both, did neither clearly and demonstrably stand at ninety degrees north latitude, the North Pole? —and is getting not heated but tepid. There is a small, persistent group that insists that Cook, a man of strong determination and modest means, was indeed the first to reach the pole: variously, they depict him as the victim of the establishment (Peary, made an admiral in the United States Navy, was liberally financed and had the backing of the American Geographical Society), or as an enigma for whom answers must be found; they see him as a kind of martyr and liken him to Captain Dreyfus. Plausibility is not proof; their arguments boil down to a simple matter of faith: do you believe or do you not? Cook, Peary—their footsteps are as untraceable as their names would be if written in water.

This book invites you back to a simpler—one might almost say primitive—time when brave explorers did not remain attached to their home bases by umbilici of radio, TV, and computerized decisions; when airplanes did not make routine daily flights across the Arctic; when the Arctic's huge oil deposits had not raised its economic dimensions to a new order of magnitude. These new efforts will, in time, be seen as the beginning of the new era of exploration.

To the Arctic! is about the earthbound days when Arctic explorers were isolated for years by silence and distance, when transportation was by dogsledge and ship, on foot and in frail craft, when the wealth of the north was in fish and furs and whales. In those earthbound days if the odds were greater, so were the opportunities: to be an explorer was a choice open to all. The story, then, told in this book has a beginning, a middle, and an end. The saga is finished—it is a chapter in our past that we can still understand.

J. M.

Princeton, New Jersey, 1970

Preface to the 1948 Edition

Y EARS AGO when I set myself the task of telling between the covers of one book the story of Arctic exploration, I was possessed of great energy, ignorance of the subject, and bravado. I am almost persuaded that those qualities were needed for me to have attempted such a task, for knowingly I would not lightly have commenced a project so complex and sizable. Having stumbled into a subject where the existing histories failed to answer satisfactorily the whos and whys and wherefores, I sat down to do a job that would fill in this void. I read my way through volumes that, if stood side by side, must be measured in city blocks. *To the North!* as this book was first called, was first published in 1934, and I am glad that now, after all these years, it is to be reissued. Thus I have had an opportunity to make emendations and add relevant material so that this new, revised edition would be at once current and better.

Exploration of the Arctic in its pure geographical sense—that is, the process of searching and examining unfamiliar or previously unknown regions—is completed. That is why my additions are quantitatively slight; except for minor refinements of discoveries the great work had already been finished. It is now possible to say that this book attempts to tell the whole story of an adventure that, for Europeans, began with the Greeks and was finished in our day.

Having said what the book contains, I should also like to tell what, among many other things, the book does not contain. It does not trace the movements of Arctic peoples who have left no written record— the Eskimos, the Lapps, the Samoyeds, the Chukchis, and so forth. It does not include everything on Arctic aviation or anything about Arctic warfare, since they are but regional extensions of those activities and belong only secondarily to the Arctic. It does not include every expedition dedicated to scientific problems: the study of ocean currents, weather conditions, flora and fauna, experimentation with crops and domesticated animals, settlements, transportation routes, mining, lumbering, and so on. In brief, this book has self-imposed limitations, but I hope it will serve as a prelude to or background for all those special subjects as their sphere of inquiry is extended into the Arctic.

Before the war and before transatlantic plane service was a commonplace, the Arctic was a region unknown to most people. It was all ice and snow, it was inaccessible, it was "at the top of the map"; it was confused with the Antarctic, which is a continent, and peopled with penguins as well as Eskimos. To be interested in the Arctic in those days demanded explanations and apologies. The war and interhemispheric aviation have enlarged our horizons. Today people know that the shortest lines connecting the great cities of the world fall within the Arctic Circle. The Arctic Ocean is no longer remote: it is the modern Mediterranean, for around it stretch the great powers, the United States of America, the Union of Soviet Socialist Republics, and the British Commonwealth. For good or evil, for war or peace, the Arctic has become part of our world. More than ever before it seems appropriate to tell the story of the long-sustained search that brought it into our world.

In telling this story my object has been to see the problems set by the Arctic and the labors their solution entailed. In this telling I have tried to avoid bias and prejudice. I use the words of the explorers. I have not sought to impose my ideas; I have tried only to find the threads that connect the separate efforts, to give form and clarity to a bewildering amount of seemingly unrelated and isolated incident. I have tried to tell this wonderfully flavored story so that the many episodes are seen in proper perspective.

I advise the reader to make constant use of the maps. Besides making the details of the particular achievements more intelligible, they will help clarify nomenclature. Victoria Island, for example, is variously referred to as Victoria Land, Wollaston Land, and Prince Albert Land, depending on the date of the exploration and the particular region touched at; the words "Sound" and "Channel" are sometimes used interchangeably; and the spelling of proper names varies.

During the three and a half years I spent writing this book I was the recipient of many courtesies, and I wish to thank again all those who helped me. In this revised edition I have incurred further obligations. I am grateful to Alfred A. Knopf for his desire to make the book available once again and to Herbert Weinstock for the friendship that expressed itself in an understanding assistance with the contents. To Professor Theodosius Dobzhansky and his family I am indebted for providing me with articles dealing with seventeenth-century Siberian explorations made by the Russians, and to Anuta Feigin and my sister, Miriam Ittelson, for their translations from the Russian. I should like to thank Commander Donald B. Macmillan for pointing out to me many small errors that crept into the text. I should also like to acknowledge the generosity with which Vilhjalmur Stefansson placed his fine library at my disposal and for his and Peter Freuchen's aid in giving me unpublished data in the Cook-Peary controversy.

My largest single obligation is to my husband, Edward B. Ginsburg, for his staunch belief in this book and his constant helpfulness to me while I was engrossed in it.

J. M.

New York, 1947

To the Arctic!

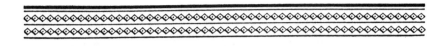

I

Arctic Scenery

NOT SO LONG AGO there was a custom among sailors that accorded to all those who had sailed round Cape Horn the right to put one foot on the table after dinner, while those who had crossed the Arctic Circle could put both feet on the table. Here will be found the stories told by those men who have both feet on the table, told whenever possible in their own words.

The Arctic Circle was first so named by the Greeks. They it was wno first noticed that as they went northward the circles that girdle the stars became larger and that all had their fixed orbits about a fixed point—a pole in the heavens. In addition they noted that there were some stars that were always visible and some that came and went with the seasons. These two groups could be separated by drawing a circle through the constellation of the Great Bear—Arktos. The circle of Arktos runs parallel with the equator at 66° 32′ North, holding, like a great bowl, six million square miles of land and water. The Arctic Ocean is almost completely landlocked by the northern coasts of Europe, Asia, and America, their numerous clusters of islands, and the large island of Greenland. The Arctic Ocean is to the important centers of population what the Mediterranean was to the famed cities of the ancient and medieval worlds, for across it lie the shortest air routes that connect New York, London, Moscow, Peiping.

Were you to travel northward in Asia or America, you would soon leave behind the great northern timberlands. Unevenly the trees thin out, becoming sparse and stunted save where in sheltered valleys they still grow tall and straight. You pass the last outpost of the birch, the cottonwood, the black and white spruce, and before you lies a vast grassy plain, beyond that the sea.

The woodless, nearly level tundra is a low-lying land composed, in some places, of alternate bands of earth and solid ice reaching to a depth of several hundred feet. From October to May it is covered by snow, and when that melts, a haggard-looking land appears, lined with streams and lakes, flabby with bogs and swamps. It is the home of clouds of mosquitoes, the breeding-place for millions of birds. Then suddenly, like an exotic quilt thrown over a slept-in bed, spreads the gaudy, brilliant flora of moss and grass and flowers. This region knows but two seasons: winter and August. * Such for the most part is the coast that America and Asia turn to the Arctic Ocean. Into it empty great rivers that flow northward between banks precipitously carved, draining the floods annually made by melting snow, carrying to the ocean huge harvests of ice. It is in the interior of these plains—not at the North Pole—that the greatest cold is found. (The greatest cold ever recorded—minus 93°—was at Verkhoyansk, Siberia, on the Yana River. That is the region where milk is sold in pieces.) And yet in the summertime these plains are rich grazing-lands, the annual goal for armies of migrating caribou.

Arctic scenery is not limited to the tundra. There are the fiords of Norway and the Alpine grandeurs of Spitsbergen and Franz Josef Land. There are the fantastic islands north of Siberia where lie the graveyards of animals of an extinct age—the mammoth, the fossil ox, the woolly rhinoceros—and where the soil is literally a mixture of sand and ice and ivory and the petrified remains of giant trees. There is the tiny island of Jan Mayen, from which rises Mount Esk, the most northerly of active volcanoes. There is Greenland, a mighty stronghold of the Glacial Age. Look at the map, at Greenland, just short of continental size, and you will see that in all its 830,000 square miles there is a little more than ten per cent that is naked soil; you will see a green thread of ice-free land running sweetly between the sea that crashes on its rocks and an outspread mantle of ice enveloped in the absolute silence of death, the inland Ice-Cap, the white Sahara, a solid frozen expanse. It sends out glaciers, some of which are a thousand feet thick, move at the incredible rate of almost a hundred feet a day, and calve "with the large utterance of the early gods." These offspring, known as icebergs, drift down Baffin Bay to haunt the waters of the North Atlantic, where, though their original strength has been wasted by sun and water and collision, they are still instinct with the power to annihilate a titan of steel and wood built by man.

But the dominion of the ice is not complete. Even in the most northerly of Arctic lands there is a flora of amazing variety. Neither the

* Of course, such generalizations are never true for the whole of the Arctic. There are places well within the Circle where the summer season lasts for three to four months.

4

long period of cold nor the four months of sunlessness can discourage the vigorous plant life, and vegetation exists wherever roots can establish themselves. Several hundreds of species of flowering plants alone have been counted, including many of the common ones found in our meadows—buttercups, dandelions, poppies, bluebells; there are various grasses and ferns and many berry-bearing bushes. There butterflies dance and bees drone, and there man is found.

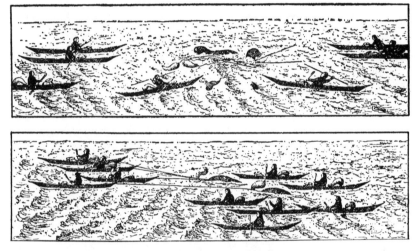

Eskimos Hunting Walrus

THE UPPER PICTURE SHOWS THE ESKIMOS HARPOONING THE HUGE ANIMALS, THE LOWER TOWING THE BODIES TO SHORE. *A native woodcut in Rink's* DAN-ISH GREENLAND (*London, 1877*).

Man is found beyond the tree-line, beyond the crop-line, along the Arctic coasts of Europe, Asia, and America and in some of the ice-free sections of Greenland. The Lapps and Finns, the Samoyeds and Chukchis, and the Eskimos have existed for centuries within these regions. The last are the most distinctive in their mode of life and the most successful in the way they have adapted themselves to Arctic conditions. *Eskimo* is our corruption of the Indian name meaning "eaters of raw flesh," given to these people who call themselves Innuit. Facetiously they have been classified as a "link between Saxons and seals—hybrids, putting the seals' bodies into their own and then encasing their skin in the seals'."[1] * Though they cover a great area, from the Aleutian Islands in Bering Strait a third of the way around

* The superior numeral indicates a reference to the source of the quotation so marked. See "References," pp. 329 ff.

the globe to the east coast of Greenland, they number in all but 33,000 souls. Their material culture is of a high order. Explorers of today have adopted their snow igloo as offering the most suitable shelter. The Eskimos are a people of great skill and ingenuity and have utilized their limited resources for clothing, transportation, heat, and weapons. Out of the bone and skin and blubber and sinew of the animals they hunt they make their sledges, kayaks, umiaks, harpoons, cordage, sewing-gear, and clothes. And it is interesting to note that the methods of Arctic exploration have become better and better as the explorers have gradually adopted Eskimo ways.

From the sixteenth century European explorers have had contacts with these people; expedition after expedition has demanded help of them and never vainly. Robert E. Peary enlisted in his service a whole community. Rasmussen has pointed out that "without their help Peary's name might have been less famous than it is now; for they followed him on all his expeditions, left home and country and kind and put their whole existence at stake, in realizing the fantastic travelling notions of a foreign man." [2] Eskimo women made clothes for him, and Eskimo men drove his sledges, built his shelters, and hunted for him. The foundation of the Peary method was Eskimo assistance.

Strange as may be the land, varied as are the peoples within the Arctic Circle, it is not entirely foreign to what lies around us, not alien to ourselves. In both peoples and place are seen regional variations of a universal theme. The marvelous, the inconceivable, the strange world undreamed of by dwellers to the south is the ice that in a multitude of forms and noises challenges the intruder who wanders there. It is new, it is baffling. It is a white, silent shroud that on a sudden changes and thunders and charges. It is a thing alive with moods, treacherous with whims. It delights in a thousand shapes, which men have labeled with robust names as if thus to limit its capriciousness. There is *young ice*, a thin film that first covers the sea in autumn and soon thickens to *bay ice*. This is churned by rough seas to form *pancake ice*. There is a *field*, fifteen or twenty feet thick, whose surface stretches to the horizon, that sometimes starts spinning—a gigantic mass more than ten thousand million tons in weight, smashing into another field of equal size. A *pack* is a mass of small pieces extensive as a field. There is *sludge*, fragmentary remains of the wreckage of all sorts of ice that has become saturated by the sea. Ice that is badly melted and honeycombed is *rotten*. A *calf* is a piece of ice that breaks away from the lower part of a field or berg and shoots violently to the surface. There are *icebergs*, mountains of ice, sometimes the color of sapphires or emeralds, endlessly different in form—the compelling source of great beauty, great terror. The *ice blink* is a peculiar whitish glow in the sky that denotes the presence of extended ice; the *land blink* is a yellow light, and a blue streak, which spells open water, is a *water sky*. A ship can go through a *lane*, a narrow channel between pack ice, or through a *lead*, a direct line of water; it can be *beset*, immovably held by surrounding ice; it can be *nipped*, its sides forcibly pressed in by the ice; it can be cut in two, crushed, buried.

Again and again the ice has shown its malevolent power. It seems almost human in the variety of methods it uses to repel the explorers who would invade the secret places it guards. Sometimes it is like a wary general who stages a shameful retreat in order to ambush the intruder; or it is like an enchantress, a grim, golden Circe, whose song ensnares. It became the too eager grave for a host of gallant men: Barents, Franklin, Andrée. From these tragedies and defeats it has been learned that this stunning force is not ruled by local evil deities, but is governed by the flow of waters around the whole earth.

It is in terms of the movement of ice and water, currents and tides, that the course of Arctic exploration can best be understood. This explains why the eastern part of the North Atlantic is better for navigation than the banks of Newfoundland, where the East Greenland current with its dangerous cargo of icebergs "signs off." It is the reason why certain Arctic lands and waters were early and easily discovered, why others remained unknown until quite recently. In good measure the success or failure of the explorers depended on being with or against the underlying forces in control there. This fact determined the triumph of Barents in the far north along western Spitsbergen, the impossibility of Pet and Jackman's penetrating the ice-clogged Kara Sea, the tantalizing glimpses of East Greenland, past which streams a procession of pack ice; it explains the lucky drift of the *Tegetthoff* and the ghastly wanderings of the *Jeannette*.

There is a constant integrated flow of currents of water over the whole earth like currents of air in a room. From the other end of the globe, from the Antarctic, a vast cold body of water rises toward the overheated oceans of the torrid zone. Eventually, after long wanderings, called by many names, this current flows into the Gulf of Mexico. Here its energies are restored and accelerated, and it pours out again into the Atlantic. The Gulf Stream, as it is now known, is isolated so completely from the ocean that it is a "river in the ocean," mightier than the Mississippi or the Amazon. It brings the heat of the tropics wherever it touches, making Ireland emerald, softening the polar rigors of Norway. It arrives off the North Cape exhausted and there meets and struggles for supremacy with a cold stream that, born within the Arctic, seeks a warmer home. A truce is called, a compromise effected, and the Gulf Stream bifurcates, one branch turning east to the Lapp coast and Novaya Zemlya, the other keeping northward to the west coast of Spifsbergen. Into the angle of the bifurcation pour masses of ice that have covered the two million square miles of Arctic Ocean, giant harvests of ice that the swollen rivers of America and Asia have dumped at their mouths, mountains of ice that have broken off from the glaciers of Spitsbergen and Greenland—ice extending unbroken to the horizon, ice jammed into high pressure-ridges, ice, ice, ice nagged by shrill winds, moved by inexorable currents, frantically seeking an outlet.

Blocked by the Siberian coast, whose forceful rivers drive the ice offshore, blocked by the many islands of the American coast, the ice has but three exits. There is Baffin Bay, which drains a little of the Melville Sound accumulation and most of the icebergs discharged by the Greenland glaciers; there is Bering Strait, whose principal current is tidal and intermittent; and there is Denmark Strait, a narrow channel between Iceland and Greenland. Into this niggardly opening jams the ice brought by a westward current from Siberia.

Men braved the icy Siberian waters because they hoped there to find an alternative route to the East, a shorter, more direct path to India and China. This was the motive behind the search for the Northeast and Northwest Passages. On the American side the task was the same. From the time of Frobisher, who sailed for Queen Elizabeth, the problem was to seek out and chart a waterway to the East across the top of the Americas. This became England's special problem. Some seasons were favorable and some were not; there were months when ships sailed swiftly, there were months when men toiled doggedly over barriers. There was always the success of a Baffin to efface the tragedy of a Hudson. It was a long parade of men and ships that sought to find a way through the maze of islands of Arctic America. The climax came when Sir John Franklin and one hundred and twenty-nine picked men were defeated as they were about to achieve the long-sought Northwest Passage. They sailed away and were never seen again. Then for a decade Arctic exploration became the search for a person. A grimness and a determination sharpened the keen edge of the searchers' desire to leave no corner unexplored. By then the hope and need and romance of reaching the East had passed. They toiled along a dreary web of coastlines though the hunger for immediate gain was gone. The search persisted and the explorers were sustained by an emotion intangible, but worthy enough to demand the best of mind and strength, and even life itself.

2

Quest and Conquest

O NLY THE VERY STRONGEST of motives could induce men to undertake Arctic voyages during the period just following the discovery of the New World. Men were as fearful of the dangers of the Arctic as they were of the terrors of hell. They dreaded its terrible ice and its terrifying darkness. They ventured within the Arctic only in the hope of finding there a short, direct route to the Spice Islands of the East. The Northeast and Northwest Passages were pictured as possible alternatives to the long voyages round Cape Horn and the Cape of Good Hope. This initial phase had two results: the wealth of the north was noted and exploited, and the romantic strangeness of its regions was broadcast. Monetary gain and adventure sent ships northward in increasing numbers. The age of dread passed as men grew accustomed to the scene around them. The age of exploitation— of whaling—lasted for a long while. Not until the beginning of the nineteenth century did men seek the unknown Arctic regions solely for exploration's sake. Exploration for its own sake was carried on by "professional explorers," men who went time after time to the Arctic regions, who made it their life task to extend the limits of the known, who were completely captivated by the lure of the Arctic.

As the motives for Arctic exploration have changed, so have its methods of travel. At first, during the search for the passages and the hunt for whales, only ships were used. Men went as far as they could sail. Not until "exploration" became the slogan was there a change. Then voyages by ship were supplemented and extended by journeys over the land and ice. The ship became the headquarters for land parties. Immediately the explorers were confronted with a host of problems. They had to have special clothes and special food, they had to cook and they had to have fuel, and they had to carry everything with them as they advanced over land and water and ice. It is extraordinary how long it took the white explorers to admit that the Eskimos

9

had found the best answers to all these problems. Some quirk prevented them from adopting the Eskimo methods—from taking over the dog-drawn sledge, the kayak, the fur clothes, the native diet of fresh meat. They exhausted themselves hauling massive sledges built to carry cumbersome whaleboats. Their provisions included a number of antiscorbutics, but hundreds died of scurvy. "The greatest sledger of that period was Leopold McClintock, and reference to his narratives will show the kind of difficulties and the ceaseless experimenting by which alone he was able to accomplish the extraordinary journeys which he made." [1] It was not sporting to use dogs, and this attitude held until very recently. It was the gallant Captain Scott who wrote that "no journey made with dogs can approach the height of that fine conception which is realized when a party of men go forth to face hardships, dangers, and difficulties by their own unaided efforts." [2] A hundred years passed, blundering, groping years, from the time when Parry first pulled a hand-cart across Melville Island to the time when Stefansson deliberately set about proving his theory of "living off the land."

In the annals of the north we find the start of the new era of Elizabethan expansion, the bursting of times that were "narrow and needy" into the spaciousness of a new age. It was the age of discovery. All around Europe lay virgin lands, trembling to be touched. Discovery was the key that opened the doors to trade. It was the age of new, undreamed-of wealth. Trade, which in the southern zones led to the "plunder of helpless peoples possessed of mineral wealth," [3] in the northern regions was characterized by the ruthless robbing of lands and waters of valuable animals. It was soon evident that the pelts became finer and finer the farther north they were found, and so men went northward following the fur-bearing animals. It was the age that gave birth to great trading-companies, whose moneys were consistently used to promote and advance further exploration. In England the Company of Merchant Adventurers promoted the Russia Company, "which may be called the parent of England overseas," [3] and annually sent ships to Archangel for Russian furs and timber. The profit thus made financed Hudson's voyages of discovery, and these in turn were incredibly well repaid by the exploitation of the Spitsbergen waters, which Hudson reported seething with whales. When these whale-fisheries were exhausted, a new territory was tapped, a new enterprise formed—the Hudson's Bay Company—which gathered in millions of pounds from the animal skins of northern Canada. And always there were the great staple harvests of fish from the Newfoundland banks. It is little wonder that the north was to have such a hold upon the imagination of the English—they who fed and grew upon its bounty.

Like the nursery lamb, everywhere the English went the Dutch were sure to go. They followed them in the Russian trade, establishing rival posts in Archangel. In Spitsbergen the Dutch arrived within a year or two after the English and by their energy and efficiency proved so formidable as to provoke hostilities, so resourceful as to bring home the greater cargoes. The sum realized by these cargoes in the seventeenth century added close to ninety million dollars to the purses of the proud burghers of Amsterdam, Rotterdam, Zaandam, Hoorn, and Enkhuizen. In America the Dutch joined in the search for the Northwest Passage and hired Hudson, the English navigator, for that purpose. He failed in his objective, but found instead the river that bears his name and the pleasant island of Manhattan. Both the English and the Dutch were fresh from their victories over Spain, whose maritime supremacy they were rapidly overtaking, and their ships prowled and poked into all the waters of the world, sailing merrily, boldly, like a child that has suddenly learned to walk. The ledgers of both Dutch and English trading-companies were jubilant hosannas in praise of oil and whalebone, cod and herring; sable, mink, ermine, beaver, muskrat; red, white, and silver fox.

That same century saw Russian traders spurred on to secure the furry wealth for which England and the Netherlands were so eager. Russian hunters went out farther and farther until they roamed as far east as Alaska, as far north as Spitsbergen; Russian traders piled up for their own glory and that of the Czar fortunes in the skins of princely sables and regal ermine, in the ivory of walrus and mammoth tusks. They looted the waters of Bering Sea of its herds of seal and sea-otters to the tune of one hundred million dollars. On all, the North showered her dowry of skins, fish, oil.

Oil, fish, skins still are found there. Today the list is much longer. It includes gold, silver, copper, iron and coal, lumber, petroleum, uranium,* water power, grazing-lands, dairy farms. More and more the north has come into its own, asserting its importance by virtue of immense natural resources. In other intangible, but clearly manifested ways the Arctic has enriched us. Its unfolding is shot through and through with the glittering thread of romance that colors even the most "pedestrian account of perils and profits." [3] Whether man went for adventure or for business, he returned to tell of the marvels of sea and sky and water, to open fresh fields where fancy might feed.

---

*A major source for the manufacture by the United States of atomic bombs used in World War II was the Great Bear Lake region of Canada.

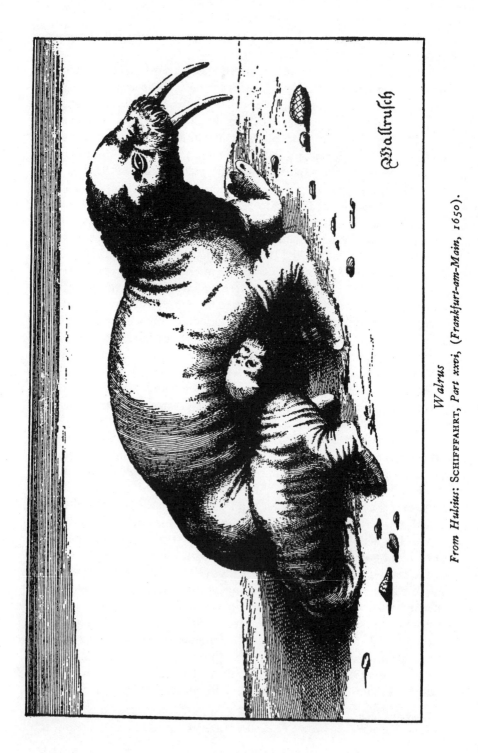

Wallrusch

Walrus

From Hulsius: SCHIFFFAHRT, *Part xxvi, (Frankfurt-am-Main, 1650).*

Just as the Buddhists were able to chart the complicated routes and forms of life that the soul of man must take in its inevitable journey towards Nirvana, so the gorgeous stuff in which the imagination of the early mariners was draped is found, reduced to two dimensions, in old cosmographies and mappemondes. Here, in terms laconic and lapidary, are labeled oceans and islands wherein "nature breeds, Perverse, all monstrous, all prodigious things, Abominable, inutterable, and worse Than fables yet have feigned or fear conceived, Gorgons and Hydras, and Chimæras dire." [4] And sailing to the north, the eyes of those brazen sailors saw sights so incredible that the luster of truth dimmed their gaudiest pigments of lies. As they climbed nearer and nearer the enchanted Circle, time itself was no longer divided into paltry divisions of a day and a night. It assumed a more majestic aspect. In the summer, daylight lasted throughout the twenty-four hours, and those who lingered through a winter found that it was "dark, dark, dark . . . without all hope of day." [5] In Arctic waters were strange animals, the narwhal, akin to the mythical unicorn, tusked walruses, and mammoth spouting whales. The boreal seas were armed with moving fortresses of ice, the sky trembled with sustained miracles of light and form. In the attic of the world were the paraphernalia for those who dressed up everything in the glittering garments of their imagination, who peered delightedly into an icy inferno of perverse wonders, who glimpsed a paradise of "new suns on new horizons." [6]

In the accounts of these regions given by worthy mariners and set down by Hakluyt and Purchas were the raw ingredients from which many poets—Shakespeare, Milton, Keats, Coleridge—brewed a heady drink.

Through the language of the poets, which strikes surely to the emotional core of the mind, we can best understand the mental processes of those in whom the nomadic, the wanderlust, is the imperious force. "The history of Polar exploration is a single mighty manifestation of the power of the unknown over the mind of man, perhaps greater and more evident here than in any other phase of human life. Nowhere else have we won our way more slowly, nowhere else has every new step cost us so much trouble, so many privations and sufferings, and certainly nowhere have the resulting discoveries promised fewer material advantages—and nevertheless, new forces have always been found ready to carry the attack further, to stretch once more the limits of the earth." [7] For from its very start Arctic exploration has been a series of victorious defeats. The struggle to explore the north has lasted for twenty-two centuries, from the time when the adventurous galley of Pytheas of Massilia, about 330 B.C., first brought back tales of a frozen ocean in the north, to the present-day era of flying.

A graph of this "long, slow process, old as the race, through which the frontiers of the known have steadily encroached upon the territory of the unexplored," [6] would show a wavering line with high points when interest in it was quickened and low points that signify apathy, plotted on an ascending line as the youth of each new generation sought out those northern frontiers with "the unquenchable spirit of adventure and the insatiable desire to know." [6] It is interesting to see how the compelling motive of such exploration has changed with the times. In past centuries men understood those who went for the romantic adventure of it, which in itself was a solid, acceptable explanation; whereas today those who go must rationalize that honest, primitive urge, must enlist the aid of science, allying themselves with those who sincerely and without fanfare give to science the devotion it has the right to ask, finding in those far-off places facts that are profoundly linked to phenomena close at home. The true explorer needs no explanations, makes no attempt to justify himself to his fellow men. His is a quixotic nature, living to the fullest in denying what is most dear, obeying a voice that commands him to cut short his ease, abandon his native land, and take the road, like a pilgrim, to accomplish something that will take years in the doing. Should he die on the way, some nameless, lonely spot will at long last hold him. To know all corners of the globe is his need. Man is man by virtue of his coercive curiosity.

3

Earliest Recorded Northern Explorers: the Greeks and the Vikings

THE STAGE is set, the curtain rises, for polar exploration as for so many other dramas of our civilization, in ancient Greece. The first precise information about the Britons, the most northerly people known to antiquity, and the earliest tidings of the Arctic regions were brought to the warm civilization of the Mediterranean by one Pytheas, who was born in the Greek colony at Massilia, now known as Marseille.

He was a great navigator and an able astronomer, but above all else a remarkable observer. His writings, unfortunately, have mostly disappeared; they have come down to us only as fragments "on the stream of time, as chance wreckage, partly distorted and perverted by hostile forces." [1] From them three impressive facts emerge: Pytheas introduced a method for determining geographical location exactly by astronomical measurement; he noted the relation between the moon and the tides; and he was chosen to head an elaborately equipped expedition sent to find the remote sources of tin and amber. The imagination and energy of those Greek merchants of Massilia who organized the quest were stirred by a desire to know from what lands came the strange and valuable products that were finding their way to the southern market.

At a time when Aristotle was meeting his classes under the ilex trees and Alexander the Great was marching toward India, Pytheas, "one of the most intrepid explorers the world has seen," [2] set sail to the north. Between the Pillars of Hercules he went, out into the unknown.

Sailing northward, he passed Cape Finisterre, the extreme point that Himilco, the Carthaginian, had probably reached a century before, and this course brought him to the island of the Britons. He stayed a long while in this land he had discovered. Making extensive trips into the interior, he noted that only on the hills could people escape the forests and swamps that filled the valleys, that they raised wheat and corn and barley and made a "wine" from fermented grain, that they had domestic animals, that they had tools and weapons of iron and adorned their wooden chariots with bronze and gold. He visited the tin mines. Coasting farther north, he saw how agriculture diminished and finally disappeared. He skirted the coast of Scotland and passed the last straggling skerry of the Orkneys. Still he sailed on, eager to verify the information he had received of the land that lay beyond all these—Thule, where night did not exist during the summer, where the winter never knew of daylight. But a barrier stopped further progress. It is impossible to say whether Thule was one of the Shetlands and this obstruction a thick fog that seemed "neither earth, air, nor sky, but a compound of all three"; [3] or whether it was Iceland and this barricade sludge ice, "which can neither be traversed on foot nor by boat." [1]Pytheas was absent almost six years from his home by the blue Rhone. When he died, his work died with him. Only Britain remained connected to the Mediterranean world; its discoverer was considered a liar by the Romans. His detractors had their way and made of his capable and intrepid work a nonsensical hash that persisted as long as men "chewed the cud of knowledge that had been collected in antiquity." [1] It is only in the light of our present-day knowledge that Pytheas emerges as a great man wearing the sober habit of courage and truth.

When Rome disintegrated, the geographical researches of the Greeks disappeared. The concept of the earth as a globe and all the precious lines of exploration that had been traced across its surface were gone. The world was as clean as a schoolroom blackboard in the morning. Then little by little new starts were made. Naïve early maps show Europe and northern Africa as a little island of the known surrounded by monsters and devils and anchored in unnavigable oceans. Fables and myths were put forward in the garb of fact, while facts could be felt under heavy draperies of imaginative presentation.

The first modern gesture toward sifting the truth from the mass of superstition and fancy that for centuries had been lumped together as geography was the doing of that wise and enlightened monarch Alfred the Great of England. Eager for his people to know the *Latin History* of Orosius (417), the geographer, he ordered it translated into Anglo-Saxon; then, dissatisfied with its vague account of the northern countries, he annotated it with a first-hand report of a contemporary trip into the Arctic. Twelve hundred years after Pytheas crossed the threshold of the Arctic, Ottar, a Viking nobleman, first rounded the black table mountain that marks the North Cape and sailed round the Kola Peninsula into the White Sea. He tells of the tribes he met with and their mode of life. So straightforward is the narrative, so clear and precise, that it is possible to trace his exact course. And every minute detail that Ottar noticed had been faithfully recorded by King Alfred.

The Vikings! the Norsemen! a tribe of stalwart men and women to whom conquest was an integral part of living. From the time—two centuries before Christ—when they appeared on the Scandinavian peninsula, subjugated the native Finns, and learned to love that northern arm of Europe as home, on till their ships had mastered the open seas and carried them to Russia, France, England, and Italy, there to rule, their story is consistently one of splendor and wild freedom.

Faced with the difficulty of communicating with the settlements that dotted the winding fiords by overland route, the Vikings were forced to build ships and to perfect them, that they might be safe in northern seas. And the pattern they evolved of the rigging and sails is still so excellent as to be used today, eleven hundred years later. They were the first of whom there is any record who left the comparative security of coastwise sailing for the danger and peril of venturing across wide waters out of sight of land. Out into the huge, empty, unknown ocean they went in boats seventy-eight feet long, sixteen feet wide, and only four feet deep. They had no compass, nor any instrument with which to take their position. They had to depend upon their own guesswork, had to reckon by the sun, the moon, the stars, the winds. Yet in those open square-sailed boats they ranged from Novaya Zemlya and Spitsbergen to Greenland and Newfoundland. The outspread limits of their courageous seafaring—their discoveries, their pioneering, and their colonizations—are immortalized in the stirring cadences of the Icelandic sagas. In skill and daring and achievements the Vikings were five hundred years ahead of the rest of Europe.

The legends tell us that a little after the middle of the ninth century a man set out from Norway to the northwest in search of new lands. Lacking a compass, he took three consecrated ravens. When he had sailed awhile, he let loose the first raven. Without hesitation it flew back to shore, and from this the man knew that he had not gone far enough. He sailed on and then let loose the second raven. It circled over the ship as though undecided whether to go back or forward to the nearest land and then flew home. This told the man that he must have gone about halfway. On he sailed and then gave the third its liberty. The raven flew straight forward. Following in its direction, the man made the new land in triumph. His name was Rabna Floki, or Floki of the Ravens. He had come to Iceland.

The real colonists did not follow immediately. Colonization began during the long reign (860–930) of Harold Haarfager (Fairhair), who, completing a task that his father, Halfdan the Black, had begun, "murdered, burnt, and otherwise exterminated all his brother kings who at that time grew as thick as blackberries in Norway, first consolidated their dominions into one realm . . . and then proceeded to invade the udal rights of the landholders." [3] Rather than submit to this invasion of their liberty, some of the more powerful nobles preferred to look for a new home and, trusting to the vague, whispered report of land to the northwest, forsook the dear hills of their native land and set out across the icy seas. It was by men "with possessions to be taxed, and a spirit too haughty to endure taxation" [3] that Iceland was settled. They sent word to those chafing at home that cattle could live the year round in the new land and that its encircling waters abounded with fish. The flow of newcomers increased. They were men who had tasted the refinements of life, who were conversant with the pleasures of learning. Their isolation safeguarded their culture from being swamped by the bloody convulsions that in ensuing centuries swept over a distracted Europe. "They were the first of any European nation to create for themselves a native literature. . . . Almost all the ancient Scandinavian manuscripts are in Icelandic; the negotiations between the Courts of the North were conducted by Icelandic diplomatists; the earliest topographical survey with which we are acquainted was Icelandic; the cosmogony of the Odin religion was formulated, and its doctrinal traditions and ritual reduced to a system, by Icelandic archæologists; and the first historical composition ever written by any European in the vernacular, was the product of Icelandic genius." [3] Thanks to these indefatigable and delightful chroniclers, two of man's most impressive deeds have been preserved for us: the colonization of Greenland in the tenth century and the discovery of America at the start of the eleventh.

The Saga of Ara Frode (1067–1148) says: "The land which is called Greenland was discovered and settled from Iceland. Eric the Red was the name of the man from Breidafjord, who sailed thither from thence and there took land at the place which is since called Eiriksfjord. He gave the land a name and called it Greenland, and said that having a good name would entice men to go thither." [1]

From the tales Erik the Red emerges from a mere name to the full stature of a man. Besides being as fierce and lawless as any of the warlike and hard Vikings, he had the necessary requirements of the true explorer, the born leader. In addition he possessed the shrewdness of a successful realtor. His was a stormy life. Born in Norway about 950, he was twenty when he and his father were forced to flee for having committed murder. They went to Iceland, where his father died. Here Erik hoped to settle, for he married, cleared land, and knew some peaceful years. But then he quarreled and killed, lay low for a time, and then quarreled and killed again. Erik was declared an outlaw. Where should he go? He could not return to Norway, he could not stay in Iceland. His escape, his one path of hope, lay to the west; always to the west, where new lands beckoned, lay hope. He was thirty-three when, with his family and retainers, he set out.

This first voyage of Erik the Red is outstanding in the history of Arctic expeditions. With a masterly hand he loaded his scanty equipment and provisions into the open Viking ships and set out for an unknown land almost within the Arctic Circle, beyond the ice. There he lived for three years and found time for reconnoitering the new country. He coasted along the southwestern shore from the "outermost belt of the skerries to the head of the long fjords." [1] He noted that the shores of the fiords in the summertime bore a rich vegetation, that there were groves of dwarf willow and birch and bushes thick with berries, that there was pasturage for cattle and sheep. It looked very good to him. He decided that it was a land worthy of colonists. He gave it an alluring name, hoping thus to induce men to leave an Iceland for a Greenland. He returned to Iceland under the protection of a strong friend and succeeded in finding families to emigrate. In 985 the path that his few ships had taken was retraced. Now there were many ships, filled with brave, eager people, laden with horses, cattle, goats, sheep, and with the most precious of their household goods. In Greenland Erik the Red was a great leader, the chief of a new free state. They called the southwestern stretch East Bygd.

Years passed, the settlement grew larger, more people came. It throve with the miraculous speed of a healthy infant. Erik the Red's son grew to manhood. He was a match for his father in fearlessness, in skill, but above all he was lucky. Leif Eriksson is the man who brought Christianity to Greenland. They called him Leif the Lucky when he found more good land to the west.

His trip to Wineland the Good—identified as the eastern coast of Newfoundland—is debatable ground. It is a matter that has claimed the attention and research of able and learned scholars—some saying he made it, others of the opinion that he could have but did not. It is safer to steer a middle course and say that, because of his birth, his daring, and his association with the introduction of the White Christ to Greenland, Leif became the outstanding figure, the hero on whom the saga-writers could fasten the mighty epic of that voyage of discovery. "Leif Eriksson becomes the personification of the first ocean voyager in history, who deliberately and with a settled plan steered straight across the Atlantic, without seeking to avail himself of harbours on the way. . . . It must be remembered that the compass was unknown and that all ships of that time were without fixed decks. This was an exploit equal to the greatest in history; it is the beginning of ocean voyages." [1]

In 999 Leif sailed directly from Greenland to Norway. There the masterful King, Olaf Tryggvesson, was busy forcing Christianity upon his people. Leif was commanded to embrace the new faith and to take back with him a priest who would spread the new gospel. It was on this return voyage that, meeting with foul weather from the start, he was carried far to the west, to a strange country, a beautiful country with fields of grain, large trees, wild grapes—Vinland—where he and his party wintered. The next summer he reached home, bringing the priest with him. Leif the Lucky was the man of the hour.

By 1055 the Greenland colony of East Bygd had spread beyond its northern limit, Frederikshaab, into new settlements—West Bygd. Together they were large and important enough to support their own bishop and a flock of new priests. At their height there were two hundred and eighty homesteads containing about two thousand persons, boasting seventeen churches. The life of these colonists, while not luxurious, was not precarious. They had stables filled with horses, cattle, sheep, and goats, and big barns filled with hay. They fished, caught seals, walrus, and whales. They could pay for necessaries and luxuries imported from Europe. They even explored along the coast toward the north.

The northernmost boundary of West Bygd was at Disko Bay, but beyond that, at 72° 55', was a whaling-station where in 1834 the following runic inscription was found:

Erling Sigvasson and Bjarne Tortarsson and Eindrid Odsson on the seventh day before the day of Victory * erected these stones mcxxxv.

It was from there that they went still farther north and hunted in Wolstenholme Sound, which they called "the Heights of the Winding Fiord." A Greenland priest, in a letter written thirty years after the three friends had carved their names, speaks of a voyage made far up Smith Sound, beyond the eightieth parallel. "Seven hundred years

* A Norse holiday, the 28th of April 1135.

afterwards, a lofty cairn, built by unknown hands, was found on Washington Irving Island in Smith Sound."[2] Might we not in all fairness ascribe this mark, this abiding monument, to the hands of those Vikings, as just tribute to their magnificent courage and enterprise?

The eleventh, the twelfth, the thirteenth centuries saw the colonies flourish and prosper; and then quickly, mortally, they declined, so rapidly that by 1400 the colonies of Greenland, with their bishops and priests, the many people who composed the one hundred and ninety townships, the fine churches and spreading homesteads, were completely gone, like rain in deep snow. Gone suddenly like a note cut short. Gone the very memory of their existence. And the sagas that sing of them came to be regarded less as history, than as the recitals of happy dreams of a never-never land, pleasant, pious lies. No one knows what calamity befell, whether they died in the Black Plague of 1349, whether the ice overwhelmed them, or whether they were killed by armies of Eskimos. No one will ever know, so mysteriously, so utterly did they perish. By the close of the fourteenth century the Scandinavian maritime supremacy had been completely superseded by that of the Hanseatic League. Less and less did the Norsemen's ships rove the northern seas. Soon it was as if the very knowledge of Greenland had disappeared. The well-known routes were deserted and lost, and those northern lands and seas that had been familiar were again desolate. Once more the "perilous edges of the world [were] invested with strangeness, and mystery, and romance."[4]

"The standing-stone on the mound bears no mark,
and Saga has forgotten what she knew."[1]

4

The Paths to Cathay

O F ALL that the Vikings had found, everything except Iceland
was lost again. Iceland alone remained part of the known,
chiefly because fishing-ships from Bristol continued to reach its coastal
banks annually and to return to enrich that growing port with ship-
loads of cod and silver herring. Nearly all that the Vikings had discovered was lost again, but the Viking blood, with its heritage of
daring and fortitude and its tradition of restless and seafaring quest,
was not lost. Carried south by conquest, it created a Norman France,
a Norman England; as far south as Italy its strain went. Five centuries after the Vikings found and lost an Arctic world, the Viking
spirit went north to rediscover it.

"Nothing is harder to translate into terms of our own blasé experience than the pregnant fact that the little pre-Columbian world was
literally islanded in the unknown. East, West, North, and South were
all electrical with premonitions of continents to be, whose looming
shapes were the stuff of dreams, till dreams daringly followed where
they led became more amazing actuality." [1]

More than a century before Columbus steered to the west, two
voyages to the north were made, one by an Englishman, Nicholas of
Lynn, the other by a Venetian, Zeno. While they are of interest to us,
they had no immediate results, for the knowledge of Nicholas's expedition was confined to a very few persons, and the Zeno venture was
not written down until 1558, when the account of it began to spread
abroad. Both voyages were made around 1360. Chaucer, who wrote
of his friend Nicholas in his essay on the astrolabe, gives us some of
the very few facts we know of this man. The task of acquainting ourselves with Nicholas and his work, from meager scattered references,
is similar to that of reconstructing a whole prehistoric animal from a
solitary shin-bone. He was a monk, a mathematician, who sailed for
Norway and points farther north to determine their latitude by means

of an astrolabe. He is said to have made five trips in all and written two books, *Inventio Fortunata* and *De Mundi Revolutione*, in which he incorporated his findings. But everything of the man is lost, and this loss assumes larger and more tragic proportions when we realize that he was the first of the many Englishmen who gave their lives to furthering Arctic exploration and that his precise work might have been an antidote to the malicious tale of the two Zenos, whose book had widespread and prolonged influence.

In 1558 the brothers Niccolò and Antonio Zeno published a transcription of a journal kept by an ancestor who, two hundred years before, had made a wonderful voyage to the north in the service of a northern king, Zichmni. The charming and exciting narrative was accompanied by a map on which the eastern coast of Greenland swings around to meet Norway, while in the great bend lie the islands of Iceland and Icaria, and between Greenland and Estotiland and Drogeo, which lie to the west are Friesland, Estland, and other lands. So clear and precise was this map, so cleverly was the unknown joined to the known, and so far from the minds of those eminent cartographers Mercator and Ortelius and Ramusio was a conscious deception, that they incorporated this map with its whole legend in their maps of the world. Because of it men for years sailed on vain errands to confirm its location of places; as late as the nineteenth century authorities such as Sir John Barrow said: "the more the narrative . . . has been scrutinized, the stronger has the internal evidence appeared in favour of its general veracity." All exploration to the northwest was affected by the Zeno map, which, though repeatedly shown to be false by actual voyages, had powerful believers. Not until 1886, when priceless antedating maps were found, was the lie finally laid. On the maps made by Olaus Magnus and Zamoiski, and in the early Florentine and Ulm editions of the Ptolemy manuscript—all published before the Zeno map and long mislaid—Greenland and Iceland and some other places are located as mariners had found them, located as they were to be rediscovered. After centuries of toil and trouble the mischief "concocted by Zeno and his publisher Marcoloni" was stilled.

The publication in about 1462 of a geographical treatise containing Ptolemy's map of the earth was a bombshell that created a tremendous stir in all the universities. The theory, held by the Greeks, of the earth as a sphere was novel, extraordinary, dazzling. It was the thrilling annunciation of a new world to which Columbus was to sail. To Columbus himself, as well as to all others, the land he found was an island, one of those fabulous, mythical spice islands, half paradise, half Eldorado, that dotted the western ocean, bridging the endless Atlantic to the most stupendously enchanted of all—Cathay; Cathay, written of so glowingly by Marco Polo in the middle of the thirteenth century, with its topography of a Christian heaven sparkling profanely under a commercial sun; whose golden pavements could be ripped up and brought home; where the incense of silks and perfumes twitched the senses and the pockets; whose numberless spices whetted greed. Wealth weighted every bush, veined every stone; youth itself was to be repossessed by drinking at its fountains. Those islands were the bright coins and luscious fruits swelling the horn of plenty. The new discovery, the miracle of the magnetic needle, trembled as it pointed.

There is a tradition that in 1480 Columbus appeared in Bristol and there listened to the tall tales told by fishermen of land sighted far to the west, of stories they had heard in Iceland of such land. Always this undercurrent, always land to the west, Wineland the Good.

Five years after Columbus sailed from Spain, another Genoese, also trained at the great school for mariners in Venice, who also had planned to reach the East by sailing due west, carried England's flag to the mainland of North America. Giovanni Caboto, John Cabot, unlike Columbus, found no pleasant isles, and, though the merchants of Bristol were as eagerly hopeful as those of Seville, expecting great results from his reconnoitering expeditions, which covered eighteen hundred miles along the eastern coast of the Americas, Cabot could only tell of a wild land that sprawled between him and Asia. "North America revealed no treasure, no useful commodity but fish. And the activity of Bristol, instead of founding a New England to balance a New Spain, merely discovered a new fishing ground." [2] In the Privy Purse accounts of Henry VII is a note of how that shrewd monarch rewarded Cabot for his work. He gave him ten pounds. The path that Cabot had pointed out was not seriously followed by the English for over fifty years. The sun still stood at high noon for Italian and Portuguese seamen. The haunting hope of the Northwest Passage had not appeared. "Cabot's plan was like an exotic flower springing up in untilled soil." [3]

Columbus's success under the Spanish flag gave an immediate impetus to exploration to the north. His had been a sudden fatal thrust at the established trade that the Portuguese carried on with the East by way of the long, hot sail around Africa. Their supremacy was shaken by this newer, shorter westward path. They made plans to follow. To forestall any friction and avoid possible trouble the Pope set a line, along the meridian that runs from north to south about twelve hundred miles west of the Cape Verde Islands, and decreed that all lands to the west of it belonged to Spain, those to the east to Portugal. This Line of Demarcation was agreed upon by both countries at the Treaty of Tordesillas in 1494 and respected by them, although joined in by no other nation. At one stroke the Portuguese were kept from the west; they could go only north and south along the fence. To the north, land had been reported, and in 1500 the brothers Miguel and Gaspar Cortereal set out to claim it for their King. They landed on Newfoundland and sighted *"terra laboratoris"* —Greenland. They reported on the great fishing-banks of Newfoundland. But Portugal, like England, felt that this was failure—the smell of fish arising from hundreds of Basque boats could never be mistaken for cinnamon. The following year the Cortereals again sailed to the north, never to return. Their venture strikes a simple, sinister chord, the prelude to the tragic theme that is to sound again and again. A prophetic, warning knell.

A host of westward voyages gradually disclosed that Columbus's "spice island" was of continental proportions. It was no longer a find; it had become a barrier blocking the way to Asia. The search became more desperate. Navigators had to find some way to slip through this obstruction. Their desires told them that somewhere in North America a waterway opened on which ships could pass to the East—their desires made them sure. To him who could find that path would come the wealth of Cathay. The three voyages Jacques Cartier made were to that end. The hardy sailors of Saint-Malo had already followed their Basque neighbors to the new fishing-grounds of Newfoundland and hoped that somewhere in that region—thoroughly known to them —would be the Northwest Passage, the sesame to unlock the coffers of India, of China. Cartier did find a mighty waterway that led deep into the interior. He found the St. Lawrence.

When Siegmund von Herberstein's *Rerum Muscoviticarum Comentarii* was published in 1549, it offered two clues to help in this bewildering treasure-hunt. It gave the observations made during the circumnavigation of the North Cape by a sailor, Istoma, and it contained a map that showed Asia just to the east, easily reached by way of the Siberian coast. The path was simple and direct, easy and short. Across the top of Europe to Cathay was the tempting bait offered by the Northeast Passage. It has been truly said that "men will travel far when they can see far, and they will pursue a chimera more eagerly than they will a fact." [4] In these two northern passages men could see as far as the Pole and farther; they could imagine more riches than had ever been seen. The potent legend of Cathay had sprung full-sized from their minds and it grew, as legends will, to godlike measure and immortal life. Like the sun, it was without rival in their skies; it withered all doubts; and they followed it eastward and westward to its rising and setting.

"England has to thank the chimeras in no small degree for the fact that she has become the mightiest sea-faring nation of the world." [5] In England the appeal of the Northeast and Northwest Passages struck with telling effect. To the north lay their only chance of breaking into the lucrative Eastern trade without crossing the dangerous tracks of the more powerful Spanish and Portuguese. England was taking to the sea, not with the native instinct of the Vikings, but as a skill whose whole technique had to be learned. What was to grow into the pride of a nation was acquired at second hand. Their geography came from abroad, their pilots, their system of navigation, and, later, their whalers. It is to their credit that they were to take an alien product and assimilate it into their very blood. When young Edward VI came to the throne, one of his first deeds was to induce Sebastian Cabot, the son of John, to break his long allegiance to the Spanish King. "The climax of the English demand upon European overseas experience" [2] had been reached. The Chief Navigator of Spain became Grand Pilot of England. England, needy and precocious, was to be coached for her great destiny.

Sebastian Cabot was made "Governour of the Mysterie and Companie of the Merchants Adventurers for the Discoverie of Regions, Dominions, Islands, and Places Unknowen." In their initial venture, the launching of the first attempt at the Northeast passage, his duties were threefold. He had as "seaman and geographer [to lay] down the nautical and geographical directions for the voyage. As organizer and leader of expeditions he prescribed rules of discipline and trading methods. As entrepreneur . . . he must have contributed to the organizing of the merchant company of which he was made governor." [2] In the variety and breadth of his instructions to the expedition breathed the accumulated experience of the India House at Seville.

So certain were they of reaching the Indian sea with their three fine ships—the *Bona Esperanza* of 120 tons, the *Edward Bonaventure* of 160 tons, and the little *Bona Confidentia* of 90 tons—"that they caused the ships to be sheathed with lead as a protection against the worms which, they understood, were destructive of wooden sheathing in the Indian climate, and these are probably the first ships that in England were coated with a metallic substance." [6] Sir Hugh Willoughby, "preferred above all others, both by reason of his goodly personage (for he was of tall stature) as also for his singular skill in the services of warre," [7] was made Captain General of the fleet, but both Richard

Chancellor, the chief pilot, and Steven Borough, master of the ship, were experienced navigators trained in the Mediterranean. The occasion of their departure in the spring of 1553 was in the best tradition of both ancients and moderns. "The courtiers came running out and the common people flockt together, standing very thicke upon the shoare; the Privie Consel, they lookt out at the windows of the court, and the rest ranne up to the toppes of the towers." [7] England had stepped into her role; for centuries she was to sail with companies of merchant adventurers.

Of the three ships sent out, only the *Edward Bonaventure*, with Chancellor and Borough, survived. The other two, with officers and crew numbering about seventy, "perished miserably from the effects of cold, or hunger, or both, on a barren and uninhabited part of the eastern coast of Lapland. The ships and bodies were discovered the following year by some Russian fishermen." [6] The wrecked hulls protected against the Indian climate must have mocked the doomed men as they slowly perished in that desolate land, exposed to the undreamed-of horrors of an Arctic winter. They had come to Arctic Russia, not to Cathay.

From the diary of Chancellor, to whom fate was kinder, we know that he left Norway behind and set his course for the unknown, coming at last to where there was "no night at all, but a continual light upon the huge and mighty sea." [7] At Kholmogori, later called Archangel, he met with men from whom he learned that he had come to a land ruled over by Ivan Vasiliovich (Ivan the Terrible). He arranged for his party to make the trip of fifteen hundred miles to Moscow, the capital, where they were received with distinction by the Czar, whose jewels and gold and splendid robes impressed them greatly. To those men who had traveled for months, risking their lives to find the wealth of the East, this rich display was like a friendly, happy smile. The graciousness of the Czar augured well, for he "called them to his table to receive each a cup from his hande to drinke, and took into his hand Master George Killingsworth's beard, which reached over the table, and pleasantlie delivered it to the Metropolitane, who, seeming to blesse it, saide in Russ, 'this is God's gift'; as indeed at that time it was not only thicke, broad, and yellow colored, but in length five foote and two inches of assize." [7] The ensuing lucrative Russian trade was solidly built on mutual esteem.

Even though this first Arctic expedition had fallen short of its mark and cost many lives, still the Merchant Adventurers were enriched by what had been accomplished. The business offshoot of this exploration, known as the Russia Company, was incorporated by a charter in 1555, and through it the Merchant Adventurers lost no time in enjoying the trade that bloomed luxuriantly from the seeds sown by discovery. Though they were not displeased at having stumbled on Muscovy, more than ever they hoped to reach Cathay. They were certain it lay near by, hidden behind Russia. They sent out another expedition.

That very year Chancellor was drowned as he returned from Muscovy escorting the Russian Ambassador, who survived the wreck and was handsomely received in London. By his death Steven Borough became the chief pilot for the Russia Company and commanded the *Searchthrift,* which set out in the spring of 1556 to find lands to the east of Muscovy. Off the Kola Peninsula Borough met with Russian fishermen whose lodias—ungainly river boats—guided him past the White Sea as far as the Pechora River. Here his tiny pinnace was dwarfed by a creature evoked from a gargantuan imagination, an island that rose and sank, that snorted and spouted, that was alive. A whale! "There was a monstrous whale aboord of us, so neere to our side that we might have thrust a sworde in him, which we durst not doe for feare hee should have overthrown our ship . . . all of us shouted, and with the crie that we made hee departed from us." [7] The whale was a little page-boy sent ahead of the terrible banners of the Arctic. In the distance they saw the purple of far-off hills; they came to Vaygach and Novaya Zemlya and, threading the strait between them, looked out over the Kara Sea. There they faced the full intensity of ice and fogs and freezing gales. Their very blood thickened. Past that they could not go.

The utterly discouraging picture that Borough brought home of the impassable Kara Sea was a deterrent to further attempts for twenty-five years. In those years the Russia Company was occupied in extending its trading-field in the interior; it was content to use its energy to create its own school of seamen and navigators, so that when it ventured forth on discovery it did not have to seek assistance or advice abroad.

One more voyage to the northeast, and only one, the English made. In 1580 two tiny ships, the *George* of 40 tons, commanded by Arthur Pet, and the *William* of 20 tons, with Charles Jackman in command, were sent to pierce the ice of the Kara Sea. Neither of these men lacked courage. Pet sailed through Yugor Strait, to the south of Vaygach, which for a time bore his name, only to be turned back by the continued ice and fog of the Kara Sea. Jackman never returned. Exploration to the eastward stopped; the Russia Company gave up all hope of accomplishing the Northeast Passage. Then it was forgotten in the beating of wings that carried hope exultingly to the west.

Martin Frobisher, a gallant man who had spent many years in the Levant trade and there mastered seamanship, had become interested in the Northwest Passage, "the only thing of the world that was left yet undone, whereby a notable mind might be made famous and fortunate." [6] He was convinced that as Magellan had found a navigable path from the Atlantic to the Pacific by sailing to the south of the Americas, so he would find one to the north, "that such a passage was as plausible as the English Channel." [6] He used the Zeno map to prove the existence of such a channel; he enlisted the aid of important men in advocating the superiority of that route over the Northeast Passage. He finally succeeded in having the Russia Company finance an expedition of two small ships. He set out in the spring of 1576 and was honored by having Elizabeth the Queen wave her hand as they sailed down the Thames under her window.

They sighted the southern tip of Greenland, which rose "like pinacles of steeples all covered with snow." [6] They were the first since the Vikings had found and lost it. Confused by the Zeno map, they identified it as Friesland. Terrific gales harried them as they made their way toward the American side, where they observed a "strait" (Frobisher Bay) and where they met with Eskimos in kayaks. These natives, the first they saw, with their Mongoloid features, were a welcome confirmation of their proximity to Cathay. With them they tried to establish friendly relations, but it ended disastrously, for five emissaries sent ashore in their only boat failed to return. All Frobisher could get to console him for his losses was one lone native whom he hauled on board, kayak and all, and brought back to England. This "strange infidele, whose like was never seen, read nor heard of before," [7] died of a cold soon after they landed. Frobisher's chance to try again for the passage to the East was as likely to die of the chilly reception that awaited him at court, but for a lucky accident.

Among the souvenirs brought home from that strange land was a black stone that, to eager, willing eyes, "glistered like a bright marquesset of gold." [7] As if trumpeted by the wind, this rumor spread. Gold, gold, there was gold in that land! The search for a passage was lost in the rush for gold. Even the assayers found what everyone wanted them to find—a considerable quantity of gold. People could hardly wait for the coming spring, when another, larger expedition was to sail. Frobisher, in command, was "specially directed by commission for the searching more of this gold ore than for the searching any further for discovery of the passage." [6] Elizabeth cautiously called the new land Meta Incognita—worth unknown—but gambled by purchasing shares in the Cathay Company, the gold-mining company. Before his three ships left England in the spring of 1577, the Queen allowed Frobisher to kiss her hand.

They finally reached Meta Incognita and the very spot whence the stone had been taken, but could not find another "piece so bigge as a walnut." [7] Their search was not fruitless, however, for in the neighborhood they came to a place where "all the sands and cliffs did so glister and had so bright a marquesite that all seemed to be gold." [7] In their encounter with the natives they were again unfortunate. As they were bartering, "one of the savages, for lack of better merchandise, cut off the tayle of his coate and gave it unto the generall for a present." [7] This ungracious gesture precipitated a fight. Both sides were unarmed, but the agile Eskimos reached their weapons first and, turning on the Englishmen in the most orthodox slapstick manner, "chased them to their boates, and hurt the generall in the buttock with an arrow." [7] The end came when the white men returned to the field of battle and, supported by guns, gained a victory that left five natives dead and took two prisoners. With these and two hundred tons of ore, they sailed for home.

As yet they had not proved the honorable proverb: "All is not gold that glistereth," and plans for further development marched bravely ahead. They were even more ambitious this time. Their plans called for the establishment of a fort and a colony—a handful of men were to be left to take possession of the frozen north of America, to follow the pattern that had been started in England's trade with Russia. Fifteen ships were to carry one hundred settlers, their house, their supplies and provisions. They were to keep three of the ships, while the remainder were to return heavy with gold ore. Of this expedition, in which England put her bravest foot foremost, Frobisher was made both admiral and general, and the Queen, alive to the national sentiment, decorated "her loving friend Martin Frobisher" with a golden chain and allowed his captains to kiss her hand.

The last day of May 1578 saw the start of England's first attempt at colonization in the New World. Like a group of gallant, proud horses the ships danced about, eager to be off.

Their troubles began as soon as they left Greenland. The crossing to the American side was made perilous by gales that set icebergs and the drifting pack in diabolic motion. Frobisher's "strait" was clogged with ice, and, in trying to force its way in, the bark that carried sections of the prefabricated winter house and a large part of the colonists' provisions was nipped by the ice, sinking instantly. For thirteen hours they tasted the combined fury of ice and wind, which drove some of the ships deeper within the "strait" and carried others out to sea. Fog and snow added to their distress, and they were bewildered by the churning tides and currents. When the storm had died down, Frobisher and the remnant of the fleet hurried to get the colony started. They saw how serious had been their loss when they compared the bills of lading with what was left them and found that they had only the east and south sides of the house—both badly damaged at that— and lacked sufficient fuel and drink for the men. Bitterly they understood that they could not establish a colony. They spent the few days left them in loading up with ore. Their bad luck held to the very last, for a gale scattered and hurtled them back across the Atlantic, and upon their arrival at various English ports they were greeted with the news that the worthlessness of the ore had been determined during their absence.

The Cathay Company and all the stockholders were bankrupt. The three voyages made by Frobisher were regarded as total failures. The hope of immediate gain was gone, carrying with it the initial object of his explorations. But Frobisher had set a mark for Englishmen to aim at through the coming centuries; they were to continue his work, carry on the daring, the courage, the perseverance of his spirit.

Despite Frobisher's failures the Northwest Passage remained on every map to spur men to further trials. "America [still] promised both trade-route and treasure-trove." [2] Drake's piratical voyage around the world with its return of ten thousand per cent illustrated handsomely the fabulous sums to be found in all four corners of the globe; but the heart of England turned to the north, as is evidenced by the ample recording of the number of voyages made there. For in the south, supreme and vindictively powerful, lay Spain. At home John Dee, the most eminent of English geographers, and the Hakluyts, the assiduous promoters of discovery, trade, and empire, backed by the men who had risen to influence and importance with England's swift maritime growth—all worked to organize the scattered forces eager for another search for the Northwest Passage. At last in 1584 a patent was granted, and the next year the Northwest Company was chartered. They chose as head navigator John Davis. "John Davis, of the Northwest Passage and all the seven seas, is perhaps the most brilliant example of the new age; for, although he was a sailor and an explorer all his life and died in service, he found time to contribute his own independent treatises to the nautical art and to perfect its instruments of observation." [2] His voyages were a clear light that dispelled confusion and inaccuracy, that established a method and a path for future explorations.

In his two ships, the *Sunshine* and the *Moonshine*, he set out that very year. A fog accompanied him across the North Atlantic, and blindly he heard the ominous roar made by "the rowling together of islands of yce"[7] as he neared the east coast of Greenland. There it cleared and he saw a "land being very high and full of mighty mountains all covered with snowe, no viewe of wood, grasse or earth to be seene, and the shore two leagues into the sea full of yce. The loathesome view of the shore and irksome noyse of the yce was such as to

Eskimos Dancing
A *native woodcut from Rink's* DANISH GREENLAND.

breed strange conceits among us."[7] Properly he named it Land of Desolation. Sailing round its southern tip, he reached the western side, where he found many ice-free spots, until in Gilbert Sound near the present town of Godthaab he anchored. No diplomat could have shown more graceful wisdom than he in his first meeting with the natives. He ordered his musicians to strike up a tune, commanded the sailors to dance, and thus made his first overtures with innocent, merry gestures. Small wonder that he found the Eskimos to be a "very tractable people, void of craft or double dealing, and easy to be broughte to any civilitie or good order."[7] That first season he was content to notice the head of Cumberland Sound, to list the flora and fauna and familiarize himself with local conditions, to appreciate the amount of preparation necessary to the actual negotiating of the Northwest Passage. At the close of the season he sailed home. Davis knew that patience and slow progress were imperative to exploration.

The next year, through the generosity of merchants, two more ships, the *Mermaid* and the tiny *North Star,* were added to his expedition. Hoping to accomplish more by dividing the work, Davis sent two of the boats along the east coast of Greenland, which they were ordered to follow as far as the eightieth parallel, while with the *Moonshine* and the *Mermaid* he traced the western shore. The *Sunshine* and the *North Star* were deflected by heavy ice toward Iceland. Unable to advance northward, they made for Gilbert Sound and, after a wait, sailed for home. Davis, meanwhile, tried to land on the southern tip of Greenland, but could not get through the outflung ice-pack. Hence he called it Cape Farewell. He then made for Gilbert Sound, where he was joyously welcomed by the Eskimos. Unusually heavy ice blocked his passage farther north. He waited for conditions to improve, cruised carefully in and out of the winding fiords, went inland to test the temper of the land, and observed the language, customs, and mode of life of the inhabitants. But his limited time was passing; the ships continued to be enshrouded in ice and blanketed in fog. Disheartened as the cold sapped their strength, the men begged Davis to head for home, "not to leave their widows and fatherless children to give him bitter curses." [7] Sending the *Mermaid* back, Davis set out for the west in the *Moonshine,* manned by volunteers. Through foul weather they sailed to the American side, where it grew warm and they were troubled by the "muskyto, [which] did sting grievously." [7] They traced this coast southward for hundreds of miles, greatly cheered at finding a "strait" (Frobisher's) and the wonderful fishing-grounds off Newfoundland. Davis thought that future exploration might be made to pay for itself by bringing back cargoes of fish, a belief he stated to his patron, Mr. Sanderson, upon his return. In his report he also wrote: "I have now experience of much of the northwest part of the world, and I have brought the passage to that likelihood, as I am assured it must bee in one of foure places, or els not at all." [7]

The *Moonshine* was worn out, but not Davis. In the *Sunshine,* the *Elizabeth,* and the *Ellen,* the last not quite 20 tons, Davis set out the next year on his third voyage. A few days out the *Sunshine* sprang a bad leak. To keep her afloat they had to pump day and night. But Davis kept on. At Gilbert Sound he sent the two larger ships to Newfoundland for their cargo of fish, while he set out in the *Ellen* to explore the north. The sea, as if to atone for its cruel behavior the preceding year, was ice-free; but again trouble beset them when the *Ellen* suddenly began to leak. To go forward was a serious matter, and yet the path lay clear. Davis had to make a decision, and it was worthy of him. He told his men that he would rather push on and die gloriously than turn back and live long years in safety and disgrace. They sailed on, as far as Sanderson his Hope, north of 72°, a high headland, a mark to be proud of, whence he saw "the sea all open to the westward and the northward." [7] A northerly wind forced him to turn westward, to cross the widest part of Baffin Bay. In the crossing they were stopped by large ice-floes; they had met with the famous "middle pack" as it drifted southward, a broken line eight feet thick, extending as much as two hundred miles. They drifted with it, a dangerous matter, past Meta Incognita, which they sighted but did not recognize because, according to the Zeno map, it lay on the east coast of Greenland, not America. To the south they came to "a mighty overfall, with divers circular motions like whirlpools," [7] whose mystery Hudson was to probe. Davis came home (1587) from his third voyage to find England tensely awaiting the Armada. That danger stopped all thought of further exploration. It was his last trip to the northwest.

John Davis had a lasting influence on all future Arctic exploration when he published his two books, which added to the art of navigation and to a more definite knowledge of the Arctic regions and the rewards to be found there; but, above all, it was he who "lighted Hudson into his strait . . . he lighted Baffin into his bay." [8]

5

The Dutch in the Arctic

THE DUTCH began the search for the Northeast Passage a few years after the English, discouraged by Pet's unfavorable report, abandoned the same objective. Like the English they failed, and, as with them, the failure was softened by valuable discoveries. To us, however, the interesting part of their venturing is not that the Dutch discovered Spitsbergen; it is rather that a small Dutch party were the first Europeans to winter on an uninhabited Arctic coast. The record kept by these Dutchmen has preserved the full flavor of their adventure. And though there are more exciting episodes and more significant voyages of discovery in Arctic literature, it is hard to find "a more inspiring record of fortitude, suffering, and high faith than in the pages which Gerrit de Veer so scrupulously wrote down with numbed fingers by the flickering light of an oil lantern in that frozen cabin under the North Pole during the winter of 1596–7." [1] *

This remarkable story has an equally remarkable prologue. It was due to the efforts of one man that the Dutch were aroused to take up the search for the Northeast Passage. The merchants of the growing

---

* The full title of the account written by Gerrit de Veer is: *The True and Perfect Description of Three Voyages, so strange and woonderfull, that the like hath neuer been heard of before: Done and performed three yeares, one after the other, by Ships of Holland and Zeeland, on the North sides of Norway, Muscouia, and Tartaria, towards the Kingdomes of Cathia and China; shewing the discouerie of the Straightes of Weigates, Noua Zembla, and the countrie lying under 80 degrees; which is thought to be Greenland: where neuer any man had bin before: with the cruell Beares, and other Monsters of the Sea, and the unsupportable and extreame cold that is found in those places. And how in that last Voyage, the Shippe was so inclosed by the Ice, that it was left there, whereby the men were forced to build a house in the cold and desart Countrie of Noua Zembla, wherein they continued 10 monthes togeather, and neuer saw nor heard of any man in, most great cold and extreame miserie; and how after that, to saue their liues, they were constrained to sayle aboue 350 Dutch miles, which is aboue 1000 English, in little open Boates, along and ouer the Maine Seas, in most great daunger, and with extreame labour, unspeakable troubles, and great hunger.*

ports of Holland soon heard of the tremendous commercial benefits to be derived from northern exploration, and ten years after the English had begun trading with Russia the Dutch set out to establish a rival trading-post in Archangel (1565). The man entrusted with the delicate negotiations was Oliver Brunel. He was intelligent, enterprising, and adventurous, and, while these qualities brought success to the Dutch White Sea Trading Company from its very start, they also marked him out for an amazing career. He learned the native language in order to deal directly with the hunters, and his drive and initiative soon made him such a formidable rival to the English traders that they decided to get him out of their way. They denounced him to the local authorities as a spy, for which he was thrown into a Russian prison. There he was expected to languish and rot. But not Brunel. Somehow he was paroled and put in the custody of the Stroganov family—the Russian Astors of that day. As their agent he made his famous overland trip to the distant river Ob, the first European to get so far. Still as their agent—but at bottom a determined Dutch patriot—he induced the Stroganovs to trade directly with his countrymen. Both the Russians and the Dutch found this a highly profitable procedure and were eminently satisfied. Years passed. Brunel studied and planned for the day when he would be sent to find the Northeast Passage. He watched as Pet and Jackman sailed to effect that passage; he saw them turned back before they had gone as far as he himself had. He felt that he, more than anyone else, was qualified to achieve what all desired. To that end his whole life had been shaped. By accomplishing it he would place his country first among the nations of Europe.

Balthazar de Moucheron, a wealthy Brussels merchant, financed Brunel's expedition of 1584. Ostensibly he went to trade with the natives of northern Asia, but his real purpose was to find the Northeast Passage. Brunel sailed eastward from Archangel. As he went along he carried on a brisk trade. Soon he appreciated the power and tenacity of the ice. He could not get through Pet Strait. Neither his skill nor his desire availed him. He was forced to admit his defeat. As he retraced his course, his troubles increased. His ship, heavily laden with furs and Muscovy glass, ran on the shoals of the Pechora River and could not be budged. In that treacherous, shifting silt he buried his fondest hopes—he had lost his cargo, he had failed in his search. The Netherlands were too pressed for money to outfit him again. He could not return to his Russian employers. He had to seek out another country wherein to exercise his talents. Brunel subsequently made three voyages for the King of Denmark, searching in vain for the long-lost

Greenland colonies. After that he sailed to the north for the English. Then he vanished. However Brunel had failed, he had not been a failure. It was he who made the White Sea Trading Company of the Dutch a success; he was the first Dutch Arctic navigator. Others were to follow along the path he had blazed.

Moucheron, Brunel's backer, continued to assert the feasibility of the Northeast Passage, and in 1594, ten years after Brunel had taken the first Dutch ship to the north, three ships sailed to make their way through Pet Strait. They were the *Swan*, commanded by Nai, the *Mercury*, piloted by Tetgales, and another *Mercury*, outfitted by the merchants of Amsterdam, commanded by Barents. Willem Barents, the greatest of Dutch Arctic explorers, was an outstanding navigator of his day who became interested in the north. It was for him that Hakluyt, the authority on exploration, had the accounts of Pet and Jackman translated. Three times Barents sailed to the north, and on one of these voyages he discovered Spitsbergen. His quality of leadership is evidenced by the account of that first Arctic wintering, for it was Barents who sustained and encouraged the sailors throughout their long ordeal.

On that first voyage Nai and Tetgales planned to force their way through Pet Strait, while Barents tried to sail round the northern end of Novaya Zemlya. Upon parting from the other two he continued through open water northward along that barren coast until he had passed Cape Nassau. From there to the Orange Islands he had to pick his way through heavy ice. He maneuvered his ship from patch to patch of open water, advancing, retreating, dodging, advancing, putting his ship about eighty-one times. After twenty-five days and more than fifteen hundred miles of sailing, his zigzagging stopped. His ship could go no farther, nor would his men. Returning, he met the other ships, as had been prearranged, and heard from Nai and Tetgales how they had penetrated Pet Strait and even made a little headway into the Kara Sea. This last achievement was the most encouraging of all. Surely now the goal was near at hand. This small advance stimulated the most sanguine hopes. The merchants of the Netherlands needed no further encouragement. The promise of the prize had been given.

The next year seven ships sailed to the north. There were two from Amsterdam, two from Zeeland, two from Enkhuizen, and one from Rotterdam. Enthusiastically those towns furnished men and ships to battle an adversary more puissant than Spain. The state of the ice that year, 1595, killed all hopes. The very entrance to Pet Strait was bristling with ice "most frightful to behold." The high expectations fell with the temperature, and their lively plans froze as they vainly waited at Vaygach for the ice to lift. By October they were back home. The Dutch States General took the lesson to heart. Their interest was bestowed elsewhere. Like a man with a purpose, they turned away from such a provocative wench who continued sullen, obstinate, unyielding.

Barents alone remained hopeful. The failure to penetrate Pet Strait was merely proof to him that the true path to the East lay to the north of Novaya Zemlya, the way he had first tried. Again he found willing

"How We Caught a Bear"
From *Hulsius*: DE VEER NARRATIVE, *Part iii* (*Nuremburg, 1593*).

backers in the Amsterdam merchants. In 1596 they sent out their third expedition. Jan Cornelis Ryp and Jacob van Heemskerck each commanded a ship. Barents was pilot for the latter.

Instead of following the length of the Scandinavian coast they headed north from it and early in June sighted a small, precipitous island. There they landed and killed a large white bear, commemorating this adventure by calling the place Bear Island. They had reached the most southerly outpost of the cluster of islands that compose Spitsbergen. They continued to the north. Hemmed in by fog and drizzle, they did not see land again until they reached the northwesternmost tip of Spitsbergen. There the sun came out and revealed land, which Barents, by taking an observation for latitude, placed at 79° 49′ N. His only error was in thinking that he had touched at Greenland. Going ashore, the men collected thousands of birds' eggs to add to their larder. Though Barents tried to sail still farther to the north, heavy ice blocked the way and he turned back for Bear Island. Unable to agree as to the next step, the ships parted. Ryp returned home, Heemskerck, influenced by Barents, sailed toward Novaya Zemlya. They were eager to have another try at passing to the north of that land.

Again and again large ice-floes stopped the ship. But superb navigation found a way through and Barents rounded Cape Mauritius, the northern tip of Novaya Zemlya. If he had expected to find less ice along the east coast, he was soon disappointed. The ice closed in on the ship; powerfully, relentlessly, it drove tighter together. Frantically the ship twisted and dodged, trying to extricate itself from the crushing embrace of the ice. Toward the latter part of August it took refuge in Ice Haven, on the northeast coast, an inadequate shelter. On the 26th of that month the men had their first intimation that, were the ship to be caught, they would be forced "in great cold, poverty, misery, and grief to stay all that winter."[2] They watched the ice viciously attack the ship, squeezing it, smashing it, a terrible spectacle that "made all the hairs of our heads to rise upright with fear."[2]

Then a few days of fine weather, and the retreat of the ice seemed to promise a reprieve; until the middle of September those luckless men had hopes of getting free. But as days passed without sign of release, they took counsel together, and "after we had debated the matter, to keep and defend ourselves both from the cold and the wild beasts, we determined to build a shed or house upon the land, to keep ourselves therein as well as we could, and so commit ourselves unto the tuition of God."[2] Investigating the possibilities offered by that bleak coast, they found that there was a good supply of driftwood, "for there was none growing upon that land. That wood served us not only to build our house, but also to burn and serve us all the winter long, otherwise without all doubt we had died there miserably with extreme cold."[2] While they were putting up their shelter, the carpenter died. The conditions under which they worked were dishearteningly severe. "It froze so hard that as we put a nail in our mouths, there would ice hang thereon when we took it out again, and made the blood follow."[2] Bears constantly interrupted them while the house was in construction. Over and over again they had to stop what they were doing and run for their lives. Not until a month later were they ready to move in.

To this shelter, thirty-two feet long by twenty feet wide and with a chimney, they transferred all the provisions and valuables from the ship. "We set up our clock, so that it went and struck the hour. And we hung up a lamp to burn in the night time, wherein we used the fat of the bear, which we melted and burnt in the lamp." [2] They made a bathtub out of an empty wine cask. They washed their shirts, "but it was so cold that when we had washed and wrung them, they presently froze so stiff that, although we laid them by a great fire, the side that lay next the fire thawed, but the other side was frozen hard." [2] As

"The Exact Manner of the House Wherein We Wintered"
From Hulsius: DE VEER NARRATIVE.

long as light lasted, they went out daily. Invariably they had terrifying encounters with bears, in whose thick fur their bullets usually lost their potency. "Meantime there came a great bear towards our house, which made us all go in, and we levelled at her with our muskets, and as she came right before our door we shot her into the breast clean through the heart, the bullet passing through her body and went out again at her tail, and was as flat as a copper doit that has been beaten out with a hammer. The bear feeling the blow, leapt backwards, and ran twenty or thirty feet from the house, and there lay down, wherewith we leapt all out of the house and ran to her, and found her still alive. And when she saw us she reared up her head as if she wished to see who had done it to her; but we trusted her not, and therefore we shot her twice into the belly again, and therewith she died. . . . We flayed her and took at least a hundred pounds of fat out of her belly, which we melted and burnt in our lamp. The bearskin was nine feet long and seven feet broad." [2]

Then the long, dark winter days were upon them. It was so dark, so very cold, it seemed as though they would never get warm again. Then one day they tried to make the house weatherproof, stopping up all the leaks, stuffing all the cracks, the doors, the chimney. "And so went into our cots to sleep, well comforted with the heat, and so lay a great while talking together; but at last were taken with a sudden dizziness in our heads . . . and found ourselves to be very ill at ease, so that some of us that were strongest started out of their cots, and first opened the chimney and then the doors, but he that opened the door fell down in a swoon with much groaning upon the snow. . . . And when the doors were opened, we all recovered our health again by reason of the cold air. And so the cold, which before had been so great an enemy unto us, was then the only relief we had; otherwise without doubt we had all died in a swoon. After that the Master, when we were come to ourselves again, gave every one of us a little wine to comfort our hearts." [2] Carbon-monoxide poisoning had barely missed snuffing out the entire party. Throughout the entire narrative runs the refrain of cold. "It was so extremely cold that the fire cast almost no heat; for as we put our feet to the fire, we burnt our hose before we could feel the heat, so that we had constantly enough work to do to patch it. And what is more, if we had not sooner smelt than felt them, we should have burnt them quite away ere we had known it." [2] All through the dark days they were pestered and teased by hundreds of mischievous foxes that scattered their trim woodpiles, inquisitive foxes that ran all over their roof and poked their snouts down the chimney.

The Dutch clock ticked sturdily on, counting out the minutes, the days and weeks, that slowly passed. "With great cold, danger, and disease we had brought this year unto an end, we entered into the year of our Lord 1597." [2] January blustered in foully, keeping them within doors, cooped up without exercise. Sickness appeared, and death, too. They celebrated Twelfth Night by making "pancakes with oil, and we laid to every man a captain's biscuit made of wheaten flour which we sopped with wine. And so fancying ourselves to be in our own country and amongst our friends, it comforted us as well as if we had made a great banquet in our own house. And we also distributed tickets, and our gunner was King of Nova Zembla, which is at least two hundred miles long [eight hundred English miles] and lieth between two seas." [2]

On the 27th of January "one of our men went forth of the door . . . and saw the sun, and called us all out, wherewith we all went forth and saw the sun in his full roundness a little above the horizon . . . and we gave God hearty thanks for his grace showed unto us, that that glorious light appeared unto us again." [2] From that time on, the sun appeared daily and daily increased the length of its stay. But the long period of confinement and darkness had weakened them badly. The return of sunshine encouraged them to walk out of doors, and that helped them both physically and mentally. "We went along by the sea side, and there we saw, in the end of March and the beginning of April, the ice was in such wonderful manner risen and piled up one upon the other that it was as if there had been whole towns made of ice with towers and bulwarks round about them." [2] By May fine weather had come and it was "agreed that all of our men should go out to exercise their bodies with running, walking, playing at golf and other exercises, thereby to stir their joints and make them nimble." [2] The return of sunshine and good health increased their desire to be on their way home again.

Their ship had been so battered and broken by the ice as to be unfit for use. Their one chance of reaching the outposts of civilization lay in making their small boat and yawl seaworthy. "We began to mend it and to heighten the gunwales, so that it might be the fitter to carry us over the sea." [2] Again as they worked they received unpleasant visits from bears. "There came another bear, as if they had smelt that we would be gone, and that therefore they desired first to have a taste of us, for that was the third day, one after the other, that they set so fiercely upon us; so that we were forced to leave our work and go into the house. For if we had lost these three men perhaps we should never have got from thence, because we should have had too few men to draw and lift at our need." [2] By the beginning of June the boats were ready and loaded with what was absolutely necessary. Before they left, Barents wrote three letters relating their experiences and their hopes for the future. One he left in the chimney of the house and one was given to each boat, so that in case of disaster there would be a record of what he and his comrades had achieved and suffered. These letters were painfully written by a dying man. For Barents was carried aboard mortally sick. On June 13 the weather was fine. They started out, carried by an easy breeze over "indifferent open water." [2]

Barents was dying. He knew it and yet he gave no hint of it. Rather he sustained the hopes and courage of his men. To Gerrit de Veer he said as they rounded the extreme tip of Novaya Zemlya: "Gerrit, if we are near Ice Point, just lift me up again. I must see that Point once more." [2] And when Heemskerck asked how he felt, "Quite well, mate. I still hope to be able to run about before we get to Vardö." [2] The easy breeze changed to a gale, setting the floes whirling and crashing. To save themselves and their boats they scrambled on to a large floe, pulled up the boats, and camped there. And there (June 20), on a floe, as the gale broke up the solid ice and opened a way for the returning mariners, Barents died. "The death of Barents put us in no small discomfort, as being the chief guide and only pilot on whom we reposed ourselves next under God." [2]

Hugging the west coast of Novaya Zemlya, the men went southward. They sailed when they could and rowed when they had to, but, rowing or sailing, it was a continuous struggle. Either they had adverse winds to contend with, or they were threatened by inimical ice. Their strength was fast being used up, and they all felt the first painful symptoms of scurvy. At last they reached Vaygach, where they landed. They picked some scurvy grass, which grew there abundantly, and, eating handfuls of that fresh green, were soon rid of the disease. On they went. Slowly, wearily they made their way along the Russian coast to Kola. At Kola they found Jan Cornelis Ryp, master of the other ship, from whom they had parted a year ago. They were safe. Their heroic voyage made in tiny open boats through stormy, ice-filled seas was over. They had negotiated the sixteen hundred miles that had stretched between death and life.

It was on Ryp's ship that they reached Amsterdam, "where many men wondered to see us, as having esteemed as long before that to have been dead and rotten." [2] As long as they lived they were called on by eager listeners to "rehearse our journey, both our voyages and adventures." [2]

Ice Haven, the scene of that first successful wintering within the Arctic Circle, was not entered again until 1871. In that year the Norwegian sealing-captain Elling Carlsen followed Barents's path round the northernmost point of Novaya Zemlya; and there in Ice Haven at the head of the bay stood the house just as it had been left almost three hundred years before. Protected from decay, guarded from prowling destructive foxes and bears by a thick layer of ice that hermetically sealed the house, were the books, instruments, clothes, tools, engravings, utensils, used by Barents's men during their long captivity. There were found the clock, the muskets, a flute, the small shoes of the ship's boy who had died there, and the letter Barents put in the chimney for safekeeping.

The homecoming of Barents's men from the north coincided with the return of the first Dutch fleet from the East Indies, reached by way of Cape Horn. The first group came home minus their ship, thankful to have escaped with their lives; the other party sailed into port laden with rich cargoes. To the Dutch this was an eloquent, a pointed lesson. Primarily a trading nation, they no longer had the need or the desire for further discovery in the north. In 1602 the Dutch East India Company was chartered, with exclusive rights in that country to reach the East by way of either Cape Horn or the Cape of Good Hope. But this meant that all shipowners not in the company were barred from sharing in this lucrative trade. It became imperative for them, if they were to survive, to try to reach the East in the only direction left. The north stood out as the last hope of the free-traders, and they tried to secure a monopoly on the northern passages as the East India Company had on the southern routes. But the latter were out for the same prize: if there was a way to the East through Arctic waters, they wanted it for themselves.

Henry Hudson, an Englishman who had made two voyages to the north for his own countrymen, was hired by the Dutch East India Company to lead an expedition in their ship the *Half-Moon* in 1609. Thus it happened that for the first and only time Hudson sailed under Dutch colors. He was ordered to follow Barents's route to the north of Novaya Zemlya, but, long before he neared that land, his mutinous crew, fearful lest they be caught and forced to winter there, made him turn about for the west. To the west Hudson sailed until he came to Newfoundland and, coasting along the American shore as far south as Chesapeake Bay, looked for a Northwest Passage. His keen eye could find no loophole in the continental barrier. He retraced his course to the north. This time he located the mouth of the Hudson River and sailed up it almost as far as Albany. Then he turned back home and reported that his search had been a failure. As a poor second-best the Dutch East India Company a few years later, in 1613 or 1614, started the trading-post and colony of New Amsterdam—now New York.

Two years after Hudson had tried to find a northern water route to the East, an expedition was sent out with orders to sail due north, neither to the east nor to the west but north, straight across the Pole. It went to test a theory then in vogue that both cold and ice were at their worst at the sixty-sixth parallel—on the line of the Arctic Circle; that to the north of that parallel, as to the south, the cold and ice diminished; that beyond that frozen wall lay an open polar sea; that "the sun at the far north was rather a manufacturer of salt than of ice." This was one theory and one expedition. But in the ensuing years, to prove this theory or that, ship after ship left Dutch ports, hopeful of passing from the Atlantic to the Pacific by some northern passage.

Little by little their efforts abated, their hopes dwindled. They went into northern waters not for discovery, but for fishing, for hunting. Discovery took a new trend: discovery for discovery's sake ceased; it was carried on and kept alive only incidentally by whalers who combined it with their business. It was whalers who were forced to explore that they might have new territory to despoil. Their ventures are the story of Spitsbergen, the land Barents had discovered.

6

Smeerenburg and the Whale-Oil Rush

Next in value to bread is oil.—JEFFERSON.

To THE NORTH and west of Spitsbergen, lacking just ten degrees of the North Pole, is the dot of Amsterdam Island. It offers a flat field and a sheltered sound; it once boasted a boom town. There stood Smeerenburg, Blubbertown, dressed in the brief exaggerated garments worn by all towns where men's fortunes are quickly made. Surrounded by a rocky wilderness, the wooden houses huddled together on the broad plain like a bunch of scared children far from home. At its height its shore was crowded with buildings with not a spare inch, its harbor was solid with boats at anchor. Every available square foot was covered—there were twenty cookeries, some two stories high and a hundred feet long, ample warehouses, more than a dozen huge copper vats and furnaces, three massive cooling-troughs, and large wooden dormitories coated in tile that housed the land workers. But not everything was given over to industry. There were liquor shops, early Dutch versions of frontier saloons, where stocky red-faced men drank beer and schnapps through endless white nights; stores offered home delicacies; there were bakeries, and the baker's horn announcing fresh hot rolls was as irresistible as the Pied Piper's pipe; there were houses where adventurous vrouws summered surreptitiously; there was a church, a fort. For a season of six midsummer weeks it was bustling, noisy, active—it was alive with the rasp of saws, the hollow dry thud of the cooper's hammer; guttural Dutch voices joked, swore, commanded, sang; there was the unceasing tramp of feet. For those six weeks hundreds of ships transported more than fifteen thousand men; all through that time fires burned under full vats, and, like soft drab pennants held rigid by the wind, smoke trailed from tiled chimneys. Men's eyes were turned to the sea, to the water

46

where swam the whales. Out of whalebone and whale blubber this town had been built; the stink and grease of dead whales touched everything. Far within the Arctic Circle, it was the miracle of Blubber and Bone.

This is the story of Blubber and Bone; of tons and tons of train oil and sperm oil needed for lubrication, for light, for soap; of pounds of spermaceti used as a base in ointments, cerates, cosmetics; of pounds of ambergris treasured for perfumes, spiced wines, and aphrodisiacs; of hundredweights of baleen that stiffened parasols and corsets for modish ladies.

Throughout the Middle Ages Europe had a limited supply of oils —olive oil, oil rendered from the fat of domestic animals, and whale oil, the last the principal source of wealth of the French and Spanish fishermen who hunted the whales that swam in the temperate waters off the Biscay coast. From Saint-Jean-de-Luz to Santander, from all those tiny ports, the Basques sailed out to kill the Biscay whale. They were the only men in Europe who knew the art of hunting the great sea mammals; the very language of whaling incorporates Basque words such as *harpoon,* and the laws that governed the Spitsbergen whalers were a codification of ancient Basque customs. Both the Biscay whale and its giant first cousin, the great polar whale, found only in circumpolar waters, are whalebone whales and are popularly called "right whales" because they are the "right" kind of whale to hunt. They both yield quantities of oil—the polar whale having as much as thirty tons—and both have whalebone, or baleen, growing in the place of teeth in the upper jaw. This, formed in a series of thin parallel plates—three hundred and fifty to four hundred on each side—varies in length from a few inches to twelve feet. Baleen acts like a sieve, strains the many barrels of water gulped down by the whale as with open mouth it grazes the surface of the water, and protects it from swallowing anything but the myriads of small molluscs on which it lives. Baleen is unique among animal substances, having a peculiar combination of lightness, toughness, flexibility, elasticity, and durability, and, because of its formation, it can be split for its entire length into strips of any desired thinness. For these many reasons whalebone has been used down to the present day as a sort of structural steelwork in the ever changing style of feminine architecture.

In the parade of the female silhouette there is a dramatic change from the Middle Ages to the Renaissance, when the long, unbroken line girdled loosely at the waist was cut asunder into a bodice and skirt. At that moment there was "gaily ushered into the lady's life one of the most sinister phenomena in her history, the corset." [1] At first the mechanism of confining curves within a tight bodice consisted either of a modified straitjacket of steel or wood or, less rigorously, of an unyielding dam that ran vertically down the front. As the waist tapered in, the skirt was flared out by a farthingale; all graceful and natural contours were crushed beneath this artificiality; the lady of the Renaissance had the beauty of a pinched and blown water-bottle. These ladies who had been imprisoned in wood and weighted by steel breathed easier and lighter and thanked God for whalebone. Baleen became their ally in the defiance of the absolutism of nature. "The corset was an article of faith" [1] clung to throughout the waking hours and abandoned not even in sleep.

Besides the "right whale" there is the spermaceti, or sperm, whale, a toothed whale that, in addition to the blubber thickly padding its great length of sixty feet, has an enormous square head in which is the valuable spermaceti, once thought to be the seed of the whale. The importance of whaling becomes evident when it is understood that it suddenly made available hundreds and thousands of tons of oil to turn wheels and light lamps. The nation that controlled the Spitsbergen waters was, in a sense and in modern terms, at once the leading plant furnishing light, the foremost distributor of lubricating oil, the largest manufacturer of soap, and the source whence derived the vast trade of cosmetics.

For profits far less than these, brothers have fought, friends turned to foes; it is little wonder, therefore, that, as this potential wealth was grasped and exploited, it should have been an acid that drop by drop ate into and destroyed the goodwill that had animated the English and Dutch in their common fight against Spain. Far-off Spitsbergen involved them in bitter, futile disputes that could end only in war. During the period between 1613 and 1644, when whaling was confined to the coastal waters of Spitsbergen, when every inch of shore, every sheltered bay, was as valuable as the land near an oil "gusher," when "rights" and "priority" were argued and acridly reargued— even though the whalers had come to a working-agreement as company fleets stood by to keep matters friendly—both had good cause for the claims advanced. The Dutch insisted that Spitsbergen was theirs, for it was the land touched first by Barents; the English insisted that it was Hudson who had traced the whole western shore, who had observed the number of whales and pointed out their importance. And both were right.

We have seen how in 1596 Barents sighted and landed on Spitsbergen, which was known only as Barents's Newland or the land under 80°. Until Hudson touched there eleven years later, its isolation continued undisturbed. There it was, the land under 80°, a land of stern magnificence, where icebergs rear up almost to the very mountaintops, and mountain rises above mountain; there it was, inviolate, alive to the raucous voice of millions of birds, the continuous staccato bark of foxes, the castanet click as the hoofs of great herds of deer fell in a swinging trot; there it was, surrounded by waters whose surface was slashed and sprayed by schools of walrus and whales that had swum there before ever man was born.

In the first decade of the seventeenth century England had been forced anew into exploration, for both in the northeast, where the Dutch had made inroads in the White Sea trade, and in the northwest, where the Danes were actively seeking to re-establish contact with the lost colonies of Greenland, the lead she had taken was threatened. "The name of Henry Hudson is the symbol of the new enterprise. For it was Hudson who in 1607 scoured the Arctic, from Greenland of Spitsbergen, along the ice-pack and who forecast a profitable whaling trade for the Russia Company. It was Hudson who in 1609 attempted the Northwest Passage for the Dutch and made claims to the New Netherlands in the valley of the Hudson River. And it was Hudson who in 1610 added Hudson Bay to the English dominion and the story of his own desperate end to the heroic English record." [2]

To find a new field where they might trade without competition was the thought uppermost in the minds of the Russia Company when it commissioned Hudson to sail "by way of the northern regions, whether across to Cathay or elsewhere." [3] To Hudson, as to Barents, the path due north, across the Pole itself, was the one that promised most. To that end he set out in the *Hopewell* and, braving the terrible ice off the eastern coast of Greenland, reached as far north as Cape Hold-with-Hope. Confused by the Zeno map, he figured that he had gone too far to the west and turned eastward along the ice-pack until he saw through the mist the outline of Cape Bird, on the Newland of the men of the Netherlands. From there "wee saw more land . . . trending north in our sight . . . stretching farre into 82 degrees," [3] and, though the ice-free sea tempted him, Hudson turned back, certain that the passage to the north was not to be found in that meridian. On land, where the sand and soil were patterned by the footprints of many animals, in the water, darkly shadowed with the large bodies of seals, walrus, and whales, "Hudson had discovered a source of wealth which served to enrich . . . the ensuing centuries." [3] As the season drew to an end, Hudson turned homeward, passed Bear Island, and, continuing, sighted a few days later the high, perfect outline of a mountain, the lofty termination of a submarine volcanic range running

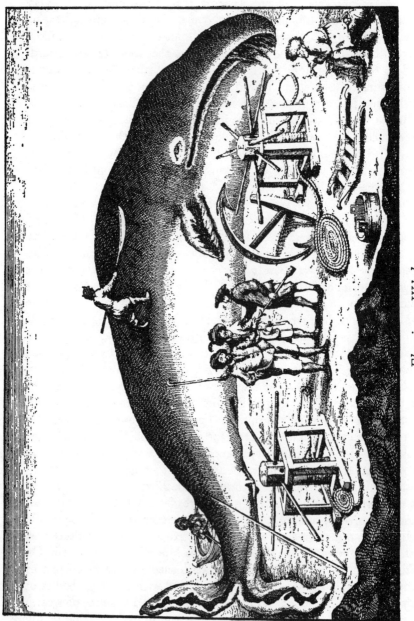

Flensing a Whale
From Hulsius: SCHIFFFAHRT.

out northeast from Iceland, Mount Esk, the most northerly of volcanoes. To the tiny fog-laden island he gave the name of Hudson's Touches; later, though it had been discovered and named by Englishmen, it was, much to their chagrin, occupied by the Dutch and renamed, with lasting effect, Jan Mayen.

Hudson's failure to reach China by way of the Pole in no way affected the important by-product of the voyage: his strong recommendation that the Russia Company exploit the great sea mammals. Two years passed before his advice was followed. They then sent Jonas Poole, an able captain in their service, to reconnoiter and complete the survey of the western coast of Spitsbergen. It was he who named Bell Sound and Ice Sound and brought back still more glowing reports of the abundance of game both on land and on sea. "The great stores of whales" that crowded the coastal waters, and the herds of "tall and nimble deer" that swarmed over the land, were an irresistible lodestone. But Poole was unable to bring home any whales, for neither he nor any of his men had the experience necessary to capture those monsters of the sea. It was one matter to creep up on, surprise, and kill herds of walrus sunning themselves drowsily on the shore; it required much more than brawn to subdue tons and tons of lashing, dodging animal that wanted only to escape. As had happened before, in the days of Sebastian Cabot, England was forced to seek abroad for men who had acquired the technical skill she lacked. And so the English, and, later on, the Dutch, the Danes, and the men of northern France, were forced to learn the art from the Biscayans, who were at the start the directors of this new industry. In 1611 Poole again piloted an expedition sent to Spitsbergen, an experimental one that included six men from Saint-Jean-de-Luz who were "to be used very kindly and friendly during this their voyage"; [3] while the crew were instructed to "observe and diligently put into practise the executing of that businesse of striking the whale as well as they." [3] The ship carried everything that the Biscayans wanted for boiling down the blubber—copper vats and barrels—a modest start to those whaling establishments and cookeries, built by every nation along the coast, that culminated in Blubbertown.

The Englishmen's well-laid plans were blown to bits as though by some lusty comic genius, for they lost some of their boats, they secured only walrus oil, and they were forced to taste the bitter indignity of paying for both their own homeward passage and that of their freight on a ship commanded by Captain Thomas Marmaduke. He was a daring and able sailor, an interloper, an outsider who sailed from Hull to annoy the trade carried on under the monopoly of the Russia

Company. He is said to have reached as far north as 82°, but we know little of him except as he appears suddenly to harass the boats of the company. At the very outset, from 1613, when the Russia Company secured the exclusive English right to pursue the whales off Spitsbergen, it met with competition from the Dutch, from the Danes, the French, the Biscayans, as well as from interlopers from all countries. Exploration ceased; only the roar of men shouting for riches was heard. In that year the ship the Russia Company sent out again carried Biscayans who "killed that yeere seventeen whales . . . of which they made 180 tunnes of oyle with much difficultie; as not being experienced in the businesse." [3] Every nation made plans to share in this; the rank smell of train oil was a perfume their greed could not get enough of, there was no saturation-point to the amount of blubber they could consume; fighting and fishing had become inextricably linked.

Ill feeling between England and Holland had been smoldering since 1609, when the Dutch were forbidden to fish for herring off the British coasts; it came out into the open when the English tried similar tactics with the whaling-fisheries of Spitsbergen. With the arrogance and egotism that characterize all national gestures, each nation claimed a monopoly, and each fought bitterly to maintain it against foreigners. Henceforth they sailed in fleets with the most powerful allotting the sites, with cargoes protected from marauders and privateers, with bad will growing season by season, with treaties solemnly made and constantly broken by interlopers who were in no way bound. Men spoke and wrote of compromise—vainly, since all were possessed by an adamant righteousness. And so we find here that, though discovery went forward, it came under the shadow of a secrecy that covers the whole Spitsbergen Archipelago. Discovery was a trade secret to be guarded jealously from eager followers; discovery was a scout opening up new whaling-grounds; discovery was discreetly kept dark, lest any information prove useful to competing nations. For the first and only time Arctic exploration took on the same color and shape that today is assumed by chemical industries with their secret, guarded formulæ. We know that within the next two decades the outline of the Archipelago was traced, that parts were discovered and then rediscovered, that the combined efforts of many captains sailing farther and farther to the east and north outlined those islands.

As early as 1611 the Dutch had taken possession of Hudson's Touches, calling it Jan Mayen, as the base for their whaling. As long as the whales came into the inland bays, the process was easy and direct. In those days a ship would anchor near a level beach, launch the whaleboats, kill the whales as they came into the bay, and tow the bodies ashore. There the layers of blubber were removed—flensing, it was called—and boiled down. All that it required was a copper caldron for boiling, wooden cooling-troughs, and barrels in which to carry the train oil back to the local Dutch refineries. After a season or two the whalers realized that hauling this simple but bulky equipment to and fro doubled the work and wasted valuable space. The logical course was to establish camps on shore where, from season to season, the necessary paraphernalia could be stored, and where the men whose tasks were all on land could be housed. Permanent cookeries were quickly built all along the coast—quickly and successfully, for within a few years these stations were yielding so much oil that special ships were needed to carry home the thousands of tons. But the Dutch were not content to confine their activities to the tiny island of Jan Mayen; they aimed at the larger, more dazzling hopes held out by the coastal waters of Spitsbergen.

It was here that they clashed with the English, who were pursuing the art of harpooning and the business of extracting oil and whalebone as they had been taught by the Biscayans. For several years the whalers were chaperoned by fighting-ships, the larger and more powerful scaring off all others. One season it might be the turn of the English, as when, backed by a man-of-war, they appropriated a cookery built by the Dutch in Bell Sound; then, as in 1618, the tables were turned and a mighty Dutch fleet worsted their English rivals and dictated the terms. But neither side wanted to continue this hazardous rivalry. They could not afford to. Hostility created a constant tension, a sense of insecurity that made them unwilling to establish the necessary stations as long as there was the risk of losing them. It ate into the short working-season. They were willing to compromise, to divide the territory. Holland and Denmark got the best station on the northern coast, while the western shore from Fair Foreland to the southern tip was given to England and France and the ships sent out by the towns of the Hanseatic League. England was forced to acquiesce by the presence of the superior Dutch fleet. No sooner did the Dutch taste peace and security than they built cookeries on shore. It was at that time that Blubbertown was started; it reached its greatest size within a short time, and for two decades was without equal on that busy coast. The Dutch fisheries were the most profitable in the world, and hundreds of boats would go to Jan Mayen and then, following the eastward path of the whales, continue to Blubbertown.

The English, the Dutch, the Danes, and the French—represented by companies holding monopolies for Spitsbergen whaling—were sub-

Blubbertown

A Cookery Showing the Caldrons for Boiling, the Wooden Troughs for Cooling, and the Barrels Being Filled with Train-Oil. *From Hulsius: Schifffahrt.*

ject to competition and attack from interlopers of all nations; ships commanded by men who not only fished without a royal charter giving them the right, but from time to time raided the stations of all countries. They were not pirates, they were adventurers, freebooters, who pursued the tactics of a Drake against those prosperous settlements in the far north. It was to be made safe from their attacks that the companies hoped to make the stations permanent, hoped for all-year occupancy. Also, if that could be done, the cookeries could accumulate additional oil during the winter for the ships to take back in the summer. This idea appealed most to the English, who considered importing Lapps to stay with their men and teach them the routine of life in the far north. The directors of the Russia Company even secured the reprieve of criminals on condition that they would winter there, well housed and well supplied. But those who had volunteered, hoping to have severe sentences commuted, looked with such horror on their intended abode "that they preferred to return home and be hanged rather than stay on those desolate shores." [4] Man's first wintering on Spitsbergen was accidental.

In the light of what we know today, the fact that the men from London Town who first wintered in 1630 in the high latitude of Bell Sound were left there inadvertently—totally unprepared, obliged to depend on their own efforts and the resources of the country—was the deciding cause of their survival. From the detailed account written by one of the men, we know that they had only a harpoon and two lances and a tinderbox, that they housed themselves tolerably well in a Dutch whaler's hut; we know in fine not only their mode of living but the very thoughts that possessed them during those long months of waiting for the returning fleet. Their despair was such as is now experienced by men in a submarine trapped hundreds of fathoms below the surface; and their deliverance was as miraculous as such a deliverance would be. They killed reindeer, foxes, walrus, and bears; the fat gave them light—for twenty weeks they did not see the sun—the skins protected them from the intense rigors of winter in a land where cold, like a vampire, sucks the very blood from the heart, cracks rocks with the report of thunder; where their breath fell like snow on the floor of the hut and the snow burned like fire; where iron carried off whatever skin it touched; where clothes lifted out of boiling water immediately became as stiff as armor. Exercise kept them healthy, fresh meat saved them from the bloated torment of scurvy. The success of their wintering became known to men of all nations who fished there in the summertime.

When, the following year, one of the largest whaling-stations on

Jan Mayen was plundered and destroyed by Biscayan interlopers, enough Dutchmen, fortified by the experience of the Englishmen, volunteered to winter both on Jan Mayen and at Blubbertown. Their country's heavy investments had to be protected. The stories of the two outposts are very different. The men in Blubbertown had an energetic leader who kept them busy, insisted that they eat fresh food, sustained their morale (they celebrated a Spitsbergen Carnival); whereas those in Jan Mayen neither hunted reindeer nor looked for scurvy grass, did nothing but mope and pray to God—of no avail as a protection against scurvy. They all died. Jan Mayen loomed in dark and evil colors as a place accursed.

Accursed and abandoned. Within two years it was deserted, and, from the stores and equipment left there, it would seem precipitately. It was not that it became more and more difficult to reach Jan Mayen through the ice-covered sea; rather it was less and less worth the labor of trying to reach waters from which the whales were fast disappearing. The history of whaling is the constant killing of the goose that laid the golden egg. From Jan Mayen down to the present phase of whaling in the Antarctic, the whalers have despoiled and exterminated the great sea mammals as they pursued and hunted them from Pole to Pole. As the fear of scurvy frightened away man, so man with his ruthless greed had frightened away the whales. By 1635 Jan Mayen was deserted.

The Dutch then concentrated on Blubbertown, and it suddenly leapt to the peak of its prosperity. Extra ships—some making two trips a season—were needed to carry home the vast amount of oil that was prepared there; but, like an Arctic winter's day, twilight stepped close on high noon's heels. As at Jan Mayen, so at Blubbertown. By 1640 the whales were beginning to be "shy of the Cookeries and the anchorages of the ships shallops, and what pertained to them." [3] The whaleboats were forced to stand out more to sea and less within the bay. The end of coastal whaling was at hand; it was the period of transition to whaling on the open sea. For a few seasons, with much sweat and many curses, they towed the tons and tons of dead whale back into the sound, back to Blubbertown; but it was arduous, inefficient, inconvenient. Quietly they began to fish in the open seas—a practice started by the Biscayans and followed much later by Yankee whalers from Nantucket—boiling down the blubber on the deck. What began quietly was within two years acknowledged, recognized. It was *the* method. The Dutch had their own routine: they flensed the whales where they were killed, either on an ice-floe or on a near-by shore, and brought the unboiled blubber back to the individual home towns, where greater care was used in reducing it, where there was less waste. By the time the inland waters were too forsaken for whaling to be profitable, the new technique had been perfected.

The day of the Dutch bay fishery was over. Blubbertown slid down greased ways with a fatal velocity. Ten years after Jan Mayen had been abandoned, Blubbertown was doomed; it was used merely as a storing-place. Soon it was not even touched at. When Friedrich Martens* visited it in 1671, it was as deserted as a ruin, desolate as a forgotten grave; the copper caldrons had been taken home, the furnaces demolished, the cooling-troughs broken; the houses had fallen in. It was valueless. It sagged and rotted. Through the empty streets a solitary polar bear shuffled, and foxes sniffed at the church, the fort. Only the land animals were left. The whales were gone; Blubbertown remained a ghost. Man had gone.

Close to decaying Blubbertown is Deadman's Island, the cemetery for more than a thousand fishermen. Not even the shallowest grave did that hostile frozen soil offer them. Not to the sea where they had labored nor to the earth they had walked did they return. On bare rock they were laid, covered by rocks; each one "like a dead Prometheus; the vulture, frost, gnawing for ever on his bleaching relics, and yet eternally preserving them." [5]

The period of whaling in the coastal waters had come to an end. Of all the nations, only the English clung to the old way. Each year the number of whales grew smaller and their fisheries starved. They did nothing about it. Yearly their whaling-fleet shrank; more oil was smuggled into England. They were content to lie in wait and occasionally plunder a Dutch or Biscay ship. By 1669 only one whaling-ship went north from England; it was the very last of their feeble, failing efforts. England was too preoccupied with civil war to assert herself on the horizon's rim.

To the Dutch and Biscayans the coastal fishing had been but a prelude to the great catches made on the open sea. No question of monopoly applied there. Anyone and everyone could join. Newer ships were built, larger ships, until more than three hundred sailed annually and for a hundred years brought back cargoes whose value was a handsome balance on the ledger sheets of the Dutch.

When Peter the Great, Czar of all the Russias, visited Holland at the close of the seventeenth century, the people of Zaandam, a city important in the whaling-industry, staged in his honor a mimic whale-hunt. And there he heard tall tales of exciting encounters with bears,

---

* Surgeon aboard the *Jonah-in-the-Whale*, whose description of Spitsbergen, its flora and fauna, was a source-book for a hundred and fifty years.

of the foxes and reindeer that lived on Spitsbergen, of the millions of birds. The pageant impressed Peter; the images evoked by their tales remained with him, for some years later (*ca.* 1715) Spitsbergen was visited by lodias—large cumbersome boats manned by Russian peasants who were ignorant of compass, clock, sounding-line, and the simplest kind of nautical observation. These huge bearded men turned their backs on the sea and the coast and were the first to seek out the valleys hidden behind the mountains. They were disconcerted neither by the two long months spent in reaching Spitsbergen nor by the prospect of being solitary trappers in a region new and unknown. Their thick, clumsy fingers somehow knew the art of setting delicate snares. Their muskets rang out with sudden death. For more than a hundred years they kept coming; for a hundred years they brought home thick piles of pelts—walrus, seal, bear, fox; clouds of soft, warm eiderdown —to add to the stock of the White Sea Trading Company. They killed the reindeer only when they needed food. They wintered in misery and filth. The thousands of huts that dot the valleys show this and speak not so much of the numbers that went there as of the many changes of habitat necessary to secure the animals, which quickly became wary. When they went out, the hunters fortified themselves with glasses of raw vodka, and on their return they again needed vodka to forget. They had to forget the long months when scurvy brooded over their waking and sleeping, their many comrades who had perished there—for more than a third of them died. They told stories of evil witches whose dazzling beauty lured men to their death. Slow and stupid they were, but they were not ineffective, for by the middle of the nineteenth century they had practically killed off the animals they sought. It no longer paid them to go there.

Again there is one of those fascinating Arctic Robinson Crusoe stories—of four men who were stranded with nothing but a musket, twelve rounds of ammunition, an ax, a small kettle, a knife, a tinderbox, about twenty pounds of flour, and a bladder of tobacco. Except for one who died, they used the meager materials at hand to feed and clothe and shelter themselves for six years, returning to their homes with a fortune in skins and a ton of reindeer fat. And there is Starashchin, the most famous hunter of all, who lived through thirtynine Arctic winters—including fifteen consecutive years—and died safely at home.

And so at the turn of the nineteenth century the Russians, who had found their way into all the ice-free sections of the archipelago, sent fewer and fewer lodias. They stopped altogether when they met with rapidly growing competition from Norwegian hunters who came to

Spitsbergen from the town of Hammerfest. Always adventurous sailors from that town had caught a few seals and walruses and whales in the coastal waters; but now they, like the Russians, turned their backs to the shore and sought the more profitable land game. Little was left but the herd of reindeer that the Russians had killed only for food. But it was food for the home market that the Norwegians sought. The great herds that for countless centuries had roamed the valleys of Spitsbergen now became so many carcasses strung up in the holds of Norwegian sloops.

Only now, under the protection of Norway and renamed Svalbard, animal life is being protected there. If one has luck today, one can hear the bark of a fox where once hundreds swarmed; through binoculars one can see, far off, a polar bear, a walrus. The proud and magnificent grandeur that Martens described is again visited and pictured after an interval of two hundred years. A note of sadness pervades the description of the bleak mountains that mourn with the barren valleys. "A kind of baby glacier actually hung suspended half way on the hill side, like a tear in the act of rolling down the furrowed cheek of the mountain." [5]

The land that Barents had touched at, the land whose teeming fauna Hudson had observed, had known successive waves of men. First they had looted its waters for blubber and bone, then they had ravaged its valleys for fine peltry, and lastly they had hunted down the reindeer herds for meat. The wild citizens of the waters, the coast, and the inlands were exterminated. The tragic reign begun by the harpoon was finished by the gun. The rape of Spitsbergen was complete.*

* See Appendix I, pp. 320–2.

7

Hudson and His Strait;
Baffin and His Bay

JOHN DAVIS had pointed out the two likely doors that might open on the waterway to the East. By 1616, the year Shakespeare died, those doors had been opened and the thresholds crossed. Both had been forced by men of proved worth, of experience, of dauntless courage. Henry Hudson sailed past the "furious overfall" of Davis, down a magnificent strait that led to the Mediterranean of North America, the bay forever linked with his tragic death. William Baffin sailed northward past Sanderson's Hope, Davis's farthest, to reach a latitude that in those waters remained unequaled for over two centuries. He reached the inner hallway and marked down and named three mighty channels—each a passage to the polar ocean, Smith Sound, Jones Sound, Lancaster Sound. Yet it was Baffin's fate that for two hundred years the route he had disclosed was ignored and his very work denied. By a curious coincidence Hudson and Baffin made their epochal voyages in the same ship, the small, sturdy fifty-five-ton *Discovery*; both were served by the same mate, Robert Bylot, whose record is a unique mixture of fidelity and treason. He stood by silently while Hudson was sent to his ghastly fate, capably brought the ship back, and was clever enough to clear himself with the authorities at home of any complicity in the crime. He was pilot for the relief ship sent the following year and he served Baffin twice and served him well. Hudson and Baffin (and even Bylot) were the last navigators of the era begun by Frobisher; men ignorant of their destination, with their sailing-orders sealed by fate, who made deep and precious inroads on the unknown territory of the north.

They were commissioned and backed by the group of Merchant Adventurers. These men, motivated by no haphazard dream of empire-building, were convinced that they would attain their goal—

60

the passage to the East—by systematically trying every path. They were at once the cheering-squad, the bankers who subsidized, and the merchants whose pockets would be filled when trade was established where discovery had led. In the process many were bankrupted. Some were explorers in their own right. There was William Sanderson, Davis's patron, who commissioned Molyneux to construct the first English globes; Sir Thomas Smith, the Cecil Rhodes of his day; Richard Hakluyt, a clergyman who became the authority on exploration, the consultant whose advice was sought by all, the collector and collator who in the three volumes of his *Principall Navigations* has preserved for posterity the record of their achievements. From Hakluyt Headland in Spitsbergen to Smith Sound, the bays and sounds and capes are sown with the names of those men; their work and names live on in every notable contour of the land; they persist as landmarks, significant signposts.

It was the Merchant Adventurers who, at the beginning of the seventeenth century, took for England the lead in Arctic exploration. The two vessels they sent out in 1602, under the command of Captain Weymouth, with orders to seek the Northwest Passage, were forced to return when a mutiny, headed by the chaplain, broke out. Four years later Captain Knight sailed with the same objective, and though his ship came safely home, it came without him and three others who went for a walk on the coast of Labrador. They had been seized and killed by natives. Neither the mutiny nor the loss of an able captain could stop the efforts of the Merchant Adventurers. Four years later they secured the services of Henry Hudson, who had done valuable work for them in the Spitsbergen quadrant and who had just made a brilliant voyage in the *Half-Moon* for his Dutch employers. They wanted him to explore the "furious overfall" noted by Davis. His ship, the *Discovery*, was provisioned for six months; his crew, except for a few loyal and honest men, were, as later events proved, rascals and traitors.

Hudson touched at Iceland and then, keeping to the east coast of Greenland, looked—following the Zeno map—for a passageway through. Heavy ice kept him offshore; he passed Cape Farewell and at Cape Desolation turned his ship due west. There he found a strait, ice-free, down which he sailed until he saw before him a great body of water, a sea fully grown. He named an island that lay at the entrance Digges and noted that millions of birds were breeding there. That is the last written word we have of Hudson. His journal ends on the 3rd of August. What follows was written by Habakkuk Prickett, an unscrupulous survivor, and is confused, unsatisfactory, and not above suspicion. The path taken by the *Discovery* we cannot trace, but we know that it followed the eastern shore to James Bay and was there beset by ice.

Caught—they were caught for the long winter and they had only two months' provisions left. Even though Hudson immediately

Map of Hudson Bay and Davis Strait

organized hunting- and fishing-parties, they faced an endless procession of dark days, a constant gnawing hunger teased by short rations, a bitter cold that drove them despairingly closer together on their tiny ship. They could do nothing but wait, and patience demands character. Through those slow empty hours they daydreamed. Cooped up and miserable, they brooded; their privations, their grudges, their thwarted ambitions were the fatal ingredients set to simmer. Ringleaders appeared: Juet, a mate who had sailed twice before with Hudson; Green, a protégé of the master, who served as clerk; Wilson, a boatswain who had been demoted for using vile language. They huddled close together. They talked, each encouraged by the others. They plotted. Soon three sailors had joined them, Thomas, Pierce, and Moter. Six heads close together. They schemed, they planned.

The ship broke out of winter quarters the middle of June. There were barely a fortnight's provisions left. And they had still the passage home to face. They knew of Hudson's plan to restock his larder from the myriads of birds on Digges Island, but they felt that they would never get enough to feed them all. They thought of the sick men and were convinced that those who were well and strong would be sacrificed to pull the weak ones through. And they needed their strength to get safely home. That thought made them desperate. They planned to put the weak and sick adrift in a boat. Hudson and any who would not stand with them in their ruthless scheme for survival would have to be sacrificed. They perfected the details, guarded their secret. The fatal day came.

Hudson, coming on deck, was seized and bound. He struggled, he called for help. King, a mate, Staffe, the carpenter, and a sailor ran to his side. So easily were the loyal men weeded out. Bound and helpless, they had to watch the conspirators take command, watched as a small open boat was brought alongside, into which the sick men, dragged from their berths, were dumped. Hudson was forced in, his young son John, and the three loyal men. Juet passed them a fowling-piece, a little powder and shot, some meal, an iron pot. The mutineers begged Staffe to stay; they needed him. His words came clearly over the side of the ship. He told them he had chosen: he preferred to die rather than live among Judases. Nine men—four strong, four sick, one boy—crowded in an open boat, nine mortals adrift on an inland sea set in an ocean of harsh unknown wilderness. They had no retreat, they could not conquer. They eventually died. The *Discovery*, manned by thirteen guilty men, fled as if from a ghost.

At Cape Digges five of the ringleaders, the unholy five—Juet, Green, Wilson, Thomas, and Pierce—went ashore unarmed. They met a party of natives. While two of them bargained for meat and two picked sorrel, one stood guard at the boat. Suddenly the peaceful scene changed. They were attacked, wounded. Mortally hurt, they stumbled to the boat and pushed off. In a few days they had all died. Retribution, like an ancient Jehovah, struck surely and swiftly.

Bylot, the sole remaining mate, and six survivors brought the ship home to England.

Those three northwestern expeditions were almost like an incantation voiced on a moonless night: a mutiny, a tragic loss, a tragic mutiny and a loss. The Merchant Adventurers heard it not; their ears were filled with the clear voice of their eager desires; and they had set their hearts on the Northwest Passage. In 1612 "the Governor and Company of the Merchants of London, Discoverers of the Northwest Passage," was incorporated. Their first task was to carry on along the way pointed out by Hudson.

What story Bylot told upon his return is not known, nor how convincing it was. What is known is that his employers were so anxious to explore the bay Hudson had found that no charges were pressed against him. He was the one man capable of piloting a ship along the route Hudson had found. They needed him too much not to give credence to the tale he told. And so the *Discovery* was again made ready and sent out that very year in company with another ship— both provisioned for a year and a half—under the command of Sir Thomas Button. Bylot was to navigate him into Hudson's bay. Button was the first to cross the bay to its western coast, wintering at the mouth of Nelson River and tracing as far north as Southhampton Island. He felt that in the northwestern corner was the waterway that would lead to the South Sea. Even though Bylot and Baffin as a result of their duplicate voyage of 1615, in which they confirmed Button's discoveries, advised the directors that, because of the tides, the currents, the flow of ice, and the soundings made for depth, it was extremely improbable that the ocean-to-ocean passage was to be found there, many men sailed to follow up the false clue. There was John Hawkridge in 1619, who never even got past the ice-packed strait. Jens Munk in 1619, who commanded the *Unicorn* and the *Lamprey* for Christian IV, King of Denmark, crossed the bay and wintered disastrously at the spot where the town of Churchill now stands. Of the brave company all except Munk and three others died of scurvy; those four managed to sail the *Lamprey* back home. In 1631 Captain James wintered unhappily and to little purpose in the extreme south-eastern dip of the bay, and the account of his voyage is verily a "book of lamentation and weeping and great mourning." [1] That same year Luke Foxe, the self-styled Northwest Foxe, explored the waters to the west and east of Southampton Island. He poked into Sir Thomas Roe's Welcome, mistook it for a bay, and then sailed a little way up Foxe Channel, pompously calling his turning-point "North-West Foxe his Furthest." A shrewd, gay man, he named a cape Wolstenholme's Ultimum Vale, for the reason " that I do believe Sir John Wolstenholme will not lay out any more monies in search of this bay." [2] He was right. Not until ninety years, later in 1741, did Captain Middleton retrace Foxe's route into Roe's Welcome and explore every opening: the estuary of the Wager River, a bay whose temper invited the name of Repulse Bay, and Frozen Strait, which led back to Foxe Channel. To settle the cruel accusation and bitter arguments made by Arthur Dobbs against Middleton—that the Wager was not a river but *the* strait—Captain Moore sailed in 1746, confirmed Middleton's findings, but suggested that to the south, at Chesterfield Inlet, the passage might be found. This inlet was thoroughly surveyed by Captain Christopher in 1761 and Captain Norton in 1762. Not until we sail with the brilliant Parry do we travel over that route again.

These many ships went into Hudson Bay though Baffin in 1615 had reasoned from his observations that such a route was futile and in his memorable voyage of 1616 had opened up the only route by which the passage could be negotiated. William Baffin was not merely a skillful seaman and dauntless explorer: he was a careful observer, a man of science who in the study and practice of nautical astronomy has been recognized as a genius. He was that rare thing for those days, a self-made man who rose by sheer ability. He had shown the stuff of which he was made on his two voyages in the Spitsbergen quadrant; he added to his fame by the chart he drew of his voyage to Hudson Bay, the report he tendered, the journal he kept, with its tabulated log, his observations for latitude, his notations on the variation of the compass, and, above all, by being the first to take a lunar observation at sea. In his last voyage in Arctic waters he reached a latitude that in those seas was unequaled for two hundred and thirty-six years.

Hudson had followed one of the leads pointed out by John Davis; it was Baffin who sailed to the north of Davis Strait to explore the other route he had opened. In the spring of 1616 the little *Discovery* was made ready for her fifth sailing into the unknown waters of the northwest. Bylot again served as mate. Tracing Davis's course along the west coast of Greenland, on the last day of April Baffin came to Sanderson's Hope, Davis's farthest. He sailed on, but was stopped by heavy floes the next day. Anchoring off a little island, he called it Woman's Island because all the Eskimo men had fled from it, leaving their women behind. It is close to where the Danish station of Upernivik now stands. No sooner had the ice opened up a bit than Baffin left the anchorage and forced a perilous way through the dangerous "middle pack," a feat shunned by the steam whalers of today. Dodging and twisting, they advanced "until we could see no place to put in the ship's head"; they wisely put into the Greenland shore at Horn Sound, where Eskimos in kayaks offered sealskins and narwhal horns in trade. Again Baffin stood out to sea, headed northward, and by the first of July reached the open water, the "North Water" above Melville Bay. He now had clear sailing. He rounded Sir Dudley Digges his Cape, passed Wolstenholme Sound, and, when a severe storm blew, took refuge in the lee of Hakluyt Island, which "lyeth between two great Sounds, the one Whale Sound—'this sound seemeth to be good for the killing of whales, it being the greatest and largest in all the bays'—and the other Sir Thomas Smith's Sound; this last runneth to the north of 78°, and is admirable in one respect, because in it is the greatest variation of the compasse of the world known; for by divers good observations I found it to be above five points, or fifty-six degrees varied to the westward." [3] The *Discovery*, guided by Baffin, stood three hundred miles north of where Davis had turned back.

Turning to the south, he passed and named the Cary Islands and reached the west shore, sighting Sir Francis Jones his Sound. To the south lay another great opening, Sir James Lancaster's Sound. The course southward was marked by the appearance of scurvy. Heavy ice kept the ship offshore so that the men could not pick the necessary greens. Good health was imperative. Baffin crossed the bay to Greenland, and there, at Cockayne Sound, picked a supply of scurvy grass and sorrel. The scurvy grass, boiled in beer and served with sorrel, restored them completely. They reached home at the end of August.

Of this magnificent voyage Purchas, Hakluyt's literary legatee, saw fit to include in his book only Baffin's short narrative, his letter to Sir John Wolstenholme, in which he states that, while it is problematical whether or not Baffin Bay is a passage to the East, it is worthy of attention since profits might be made from whalebone and oil, sealskins, walrus ivory, and narwhal horn. England, two centuries later, was to prove the truth of his words, to fish and hunt for the wealth he had pointed out. But Purchas threw out the "map of the author, with the tables of his journal and sailing," as being "somewhat troublesome and too costly to insert." [4] The verdict of a landlubber! So, thanks to Purchas, this masterly exploration was lost for two hundred years, until the very existence of Baffin Bay was questioned; the serious and honest *Chronological History of Voyages to the Arctic Regions* (1818) written by Sir John Barrow, Secretary of the Admiralty and an enthusiast for Arctic exploration, presents a map with a blank space to the North of Davis Strait.

For two hundred years the wake made by the *Discovery* was lost; no other ship plowed the waters of Baffin Bay; and not until England had gone through her civil wars, settled and lost her colonies in America, and shipped Napoleon safely off to St. Helena did she turn to the north again. There she had to rediscover the bay charted by William Baffin. He was the last of the Elizabethans, coming at the end of that first great thrust for expansion; he closed the English epic that had as its theme the "search and discovery of the most unknown quarters of the world."

8

Russia: the Great Northern Expedition

WHEN, at the end of the seventeenth century, Peter the Great visited the great countries of western Europe—France, Holland, England—he saw bishops blessing thousands of tiny boats that sailed each year to fish in northern waters; he saw whole towns actively engaged in refining whale oil and preparing whalebone; he talked with important merchants who had made fortunes in handling the pelts of northern animals; in universities and learned societies he heard arguments and speculations about the geography of the northern regions.

Peter was interested in the business of fish and oil and baleen and furs; he listened attentively to all that scholarly men said as they explained maps and atlases; he was anxious to learn everything. He alone knew that during the time that Spain and Portugal and France and Holland and England were sailing to the north and south and west, there to find new lands and seas, Russia had been steadily pushing to the east. He alone knew how the Russian Empire had been expanding.

About the time that the English first came to Muscovy, Russian traders had started to push into Siberia. This expansion had been humbly started by pioneering traders, who made peaceful commercial treaties with near-by Samoyed tribes for the highly lucrative trade in furs and mammoth ivory. It became a conquest when the Cossacks,* under their leader Yermak Timofeyev, headed northward. These professional soldiers wandered into the territory controlled by the

---

* *Cossacks*, a Tatar term, was applied to those men who, when serfdom was being firmly fastened on the Russian peasant, fled to the open eastern boundaries along the Don and the Volga and there formed themselves into armed communities of freemen. The social and political ideas of these Russian frontiersmen were expressed in their republics, which recognized neither class distinctions nor private property. It was men of such independence who conquered the vast eastern expanse of Siberia.

Stroganov family—who held a monopoly for the northeast trade—and threatened their security and prosperity. Maxim Stroganov faced the delicate task of gently ridding himself of his unwelcome guests without offending them. He diverted Yermak's attention from himself to Sibir—whence the name Siberia is derived—the fabulously rich settlement of the Tatar Khan Kuchum, and offered to outfit the band if they would conquer it. Just so were the Cossacks led into the wilder-

Samojedian Hartsleds

From Ides: MOSCOW OVERLAND TO CHINA (*London, 1706*).

ness of Siberia and to their great task. Sibir fell (1584), but they continued to the east; the virus of conquest was in their blood; tales of greater riches led them on; and even when Yermak died, the Cossacks did not turn back. Generation after generation kept on, advancing step by step across thousands of hard miles, crossing mountains, plains, and forests, gathering in the gold of fur-yielding animals, until in 1697 they had reached Kamchatka and gazed wearily on the broad ocean, while their envoys headed for Moscow to inform the Czar of this great addition to his Empire, making sure of their welcome with a huge, eloquent tribute of magnificent pelts.*

* This eastward movement, like the later westward one in North America, was of two kinds: penetration and settlement. Long before the settlers—an or-

Peter the Great accepted their offering and questioned them. They told him of their struggles, their hardships, of the vastness of the country; how, as they came to a noble river, some would stay to build forts and drift in flat-bottomed boats northward to an icy sea, while the rest pushed on. They spoke of the terrible cold that bound the land and rivers in ice for nine months of the year; they told of wealth to be obtained. They craved rewards, titles, and grants. Yes, yes, did all the rivers empty into the frozen sea? No, the Anadyr flowed eastward, but between it and the Kolyma, which flowed to the north, lay the land of the unsubdued Chukchi. How far did that stretch? We don't know, Little Father; the natives tell us that their land goes far to the north and east. And Peter the Great, dismissing them, wonders if the land of the Chukchi might not go so far to the north and east as to join with the continent of America, where France and England are each busily carving out chunks of wilderness. Maybe, maybe. He has a vision of an empire embracing half the circumference of the earth.

And not only Peter wonders. Men of science, men of daring, of commerce, scan the map published in Paris (1706) in which its author, Guillaume Delisle, geographer to Louis XV, speculating about the mountains that rise from the jutting northeastern tip of Siberia, the Chukchi Peninsula, wrote: *"On ne sait pas où se termine cette chaîne de montagnes, et si elle ne va pas joindre quelque autre Continent."* ("It is not known where this mountain chain ends, or whether or not it is joined to another continent.") Years will pass before facts current among the Cossacks in Siberia—men who know their country but are ignorant of even reading and writing—are collected and set down in cartological terms. The French map, weighted with authority, posed the problem; it was there for all to see, for all to accept; it was there to set dreams and plans in motion.

Six years before Peter the Great gave official expression to the scientific interests and imperialistic hopes that motivated the Great Northern Expedition, he secretly commissioned two men to sail from Kamchatka to determine whether or not Asia and America were con-

---

ganized, continuous movement with political and territorial implications—went the traders, the trappers, the adventurous solitary groups whose trails are unrecorded and forgotten. By stories handed down by word of mouth, by an occasional discovery of artifacts and skeletons, we are reminded of these earlier efforts. And so we know, for example, that in the 1360's, more than a century before Columbus sailed, enterprising merchants from Novgorod traded with natives in their villages on the banks of the distant Ob; that before 1619 a party of Russians had sailed as far as Cape Chelyuskin—almost three hundred years before Nordenskiöld steamed past the northernmost tip of the Old World (see p. 270).

nectea. Feodor 'Luzhin and Ivan Yevreinov probably reached the Kuril Islands, but since they failed in the main objective and since their confidential report was made to the Czar personally, nothing is certain. All that is certain is that Peter the Great was still hopeful, for when he drew up the concise but inclusive memorandum that launched the Great Northern Expedition, he told Alexei Nartov, who was in constant attendance on him, that it had been "on my mind for many years but other affairs have prevented me from carrying it out. I have reference to the finding of a passage to China and India through the Arctic Sea. . . . In my last travels I discussed the subject with learned men and they were of the opinion that such a passage could be found. Now that the country is in no danger from enemies, we should strive to win for her glory along the lines of the Arts and Sciences." [1] Six months before he died, he outlined the work:

1. To build in Kamchatka or in some other place one or two decked boats.
2. To sail on these boats along the shore that runs to the north and that (since its limits are unknown) seems to be part of the American coast.
3. To determine where it joins with America. To sail to some settlement under European jurisdiction and, if a European ship should be met with, learn from her the name of the coast and take it down in writing, make a landing, obtain detailed information, draw a chart, and bring it here.

He placed in command Vitus Bering, a Dane who for twenty years had been with the Russian Navy and had had experience in sailing eastern waters, and specified that Martin Spanberg, another Dane, and Alexei Chirikov, a Russian, were to be his two assistants.

Peter the Great died in 1725. The work he had outlined went on actively, doggedly, for seventeen years, though in that time five different rulers sat on the imperial throne; went on overcoming almost insurmountable difficulties of cold and ice and scurvy, of inadequate equipment and officials incompetent, jealous, and quarrelsome, of building ships three thousand miles of wilderness distant from the base of supplies, of transporting men, materials, and provisions—all necessary before the voyage of exploration could start. And all to achieve no material gain: the goal was simply to ascertain a fact.

"To build in Kamchatka or some other place"! But first they had to reach Kamchatka or some other place. To begin with, they chose Okhotsk, a tiny settlement on the mainland across the inland sea from the Kamchatkan peninsula. From the time Bering and his twenty-five men left St. Petersburg in January 1725 until they reached Yakutsk in the middle of the following summer, their path had been a strenuous journey from outpost to outpost, an endless procession of waterways, an endless routine of making rafts, loading them, floating, paddling, unloading, and portaging. From Yakutsk, the chief base for men, materials, and supplies, to Okhotsk, it was only seven hundred miles, but seven hundred miles of mountains, torrents, swamps. Bering sent the carpenters on ahead while he followed with two hundred horses, leaving Spanberg to bring up the rear with the main body of men, the important equipment and heavy provisions. A hard and early winter touched their struggles with fatality. Many of the horses died, and Spanberg's boats were frozen in when he was still three hundred miles from the goal. He transferred everything to hand-sleds, and the men, harnessing themselves, started to drag the bulky loads. Cold and hunger slowed them down; half of them gave up the struggle, abandoning their sleds, and the others saved themselves by chewing their leather boot-tops and devouring the half-eaten remains of horses they were lucky enough to find. They straggled in to Okhotsk—to join in the work that had been started.

One ship, the *Fortune,* in the summer of 1727 reconnoitered the sea route to Kamchatka, but it was not until the following summer that the other ship, the *St. Gabriel,* was finished, well provisioned for a year, and started on her way north. More than three years had passed since Bering said adieu to St. Petersburg before he was ready to start his work. He had shown his mettle as an organizer. Was he a little tired, inclined to be a shade more cautious? No one will ever know how much the fine edge of his ability had been blunted by the lengthy and exhausting preparation.

Blown by a gracious wind, the *St. Gabriel* crept northward, following the shore. August came, sickly with fogs and rain and querulous winds. They sailed into the indentation of the Gulf of Anadyr. There they met their first party of natives: a boatload of Chukchi paddled out to observe the foreigners. Bering wanted to question them, but his Koryak interpreters could not make themselves understood across the water. At last one Chukchi braver than the rest swam to the *St. Gabriel* on waterwings made of inflated bladders. From him Bering learned "that their land forms two bays and turns to the mouth of the river Kolyma, that the sea was all about them and large sandbanks, and that the sea into which the Kolyma falls always has ice on it. That they . . . go sometimes to the Kolyma on their deer sleds but never by water. That there was an island in the sea on which live some of our people." [1] Nothing was known of other islands or lands. From then on, Bering was content merely to test the truth of what the Chukchi had told him. He sighted an island, named it St. Lawrence after his patron saint, and, continuing northward, stood abreast of East Cape, whence he could see the land fall sharply away

Both photographs from Sovfoto.

The islands north of Siberia where the soil is a mixture of sand and ice and the ivory of animals long since extinct.

Tower built by the Cossacks during their conquest of Yakutsk, 1650–60.

Barentsburg, Norwegian Island, Spitsbergen. TWO SOVIET COLLIERS TAKING ON COAL AT MINES LEASED BY THE USSR. TRANSPORTED TO MURMANSK IT FEEDS THE SHIPS NAVIGATING THE NORTHERN SEA ROUTE.

Snow-capped mountains look down on the Bering Sea.

to the west. Bering was certain that he had corroborated the Chukchi's statements, that he had accomplished his mission. Chirikov begged him to continue, as long as no ice blocked him, to the mouth of the Kolyma, and so clinch the matter by actual proof; Spanberg warned him to be mindful of the lateness of the season and the risk of being caught for the winter far from their port. The advice of the latter prevailed, and a cautious captain gave the signal to steer to the south. On the homeward voyage they sighted and named the islands of St. Diomede, where the natives wear bone labrets in their lips. It must be said that fate was unkind to Bering, for both times that he passed those islands heavy fogs hid from him the startling and magnificent sight that Captain Cook saw on a flawless day. Had the curtain lifted, he would have seen the continental coasts of both Asia and America.

The expedition returned to Kamchatka, where it passed the winter. Bering listened eagerly to the stories told him by old residents; they all spoke of a great island to the east. That summer Bering headed the *St. Gabriel* eastwards, but when, after two days, the island did not materialize, he turned back. A little farther, and he would have seen the island that was to be his final home.

Instead he turned back to Okhotsk, the first step in his journey home to St. Petersburg, where the results of the expedition were eagerly awaited. Traveling light and fast, he reported to the Empress Anne the next spring. He had been gone more than five years.

And all that he had to show was a chart of Kamchatka. His report was merely a statement that Asia and America were separated by a sea. His authority was his own half-hearted verification of a native's narrative. He did not see that he had failed, that for the leader of a scientific expedition any argument was a bad argument where a scientific demonstration was required, that "it was hardly worth while to send him to Kamchatka to bring back the opinions of the Chukchi and hunters."[1] He had tangible proof of the dissatisfaction of the Empress, the nobles of the Senate, and the members of the Admiralty College when he was neither raised in rank nor paid his back salary until several years had passed. Had he failed because his equipment was insufficient, they would have pardoned him; had he turned back because the forces of the Arctic were too strong, they would have understood; but they could not understand, could not forgive, his timidity in the face of—nothing. And Bering, an honorable man, knew that he had to redeem himself. He had influential friends, he had the goodwill of the group of young, enthusiastic foreign scientists whom Peter the Great had brought into Russia, and they supported his plans for another expedition.

73

His proposal embraced the several geographical problems for whose solution European rulers and savants were waiting: the nature of the lands to the east of Kamchatka—America?—a sea route to and the charting of Japan, and the mapping of the Siberian coast along the Arctic. The vastness of this project failed to daunt its promoters; the instructions were perfected and the program translated into work. It was placed under the supervision of the Admiralty College, which was to have control of the personnel and the necessary funds. In 1733 the gigantic task was officially authorized. Bering, with Chirikov and Spanberg, started east for Okhotsk, the first two to sail to America while the third undertook to carry out the mapping of Japan. But first they had to build and provision their ships. They did not even have the use of the *St. Gabriel*, fashioned for the first expedition; it had sailed the year before on a strange and forgotten mission.

In 1727, the very year that the keel of the *St. Gabriel* was laid, Afanase Shestakov, a Siberian Cossack, had appeared before the Senate in St. Petersburg and there presented a plan whereby the land of the warlike Chukchi, the northeastern part of Siberia, could be subdued. Though his reasons sounded plausible, his principal argument was an arrogant hope. To help him carry out his plan the Senate gave him fifteen hundred men and the necessary war materials and supplies, and since he was to attack from the sea, they sent out a pilot, an assistant pilot, and a geodesist, Gvosdev. They kindly gave him, too, without his asking, Dmitri Pavlutsky, who was to share the command. The two leaders agreed so well that they spoke to each other only to hurl an insult or provoke a quarrel. Finally Shestakov took the two ships that had been built, loaded on most of the men, and sailed to do battle. They were fated not to subdue the Chukchi; to a man they were killed in their first engagement, and Shestakov's dried head was kept as a memento by the victorious natives. For the first time Pavlutsky did not insist on sharing his position with Shestakov, and, to forestall being sent to avenge the defeat, he ordered the pilots and Gvosdev to use the two ships that had been left by Bering to sail to the east, there to find the "large country" told of by all the local inhabitants. So it was that in 1730 the *St. Gabriel* again sailed to the east.

The pilot, too ill to go, remained behind, and the assistant pilot, Fedorov, was carried to the ship on a stretcher. The real command lay in the hands of the geodesist Gvosdev, for his Siberian Cossacks were sailors only under compulsion, knew nothing of navigation, and were incapable of using marine instruments. This unplanned expedition was the very first to touch at the American coast that lies just across the strait named for Bering. Upon their return the assistant pilot died, and Gvosdev sent his log book and report to his commander at Okhotsk. And there it disappeared, was lost, never was forwarded to St. Petersburg. It would never have been known of had it not been casually mentioned five years later at the trial of a sailor who was sent home to Russia from Siberia under criminal charges. So narrowly did the achievement of Fedorov and Gvosdev miss oblivion. St. Petersburg was frantic to get the latter's report (they were already frantic at Bering's slowness), and order after order was issued to locate the missing documents. Nothing was found, and not until ten years after he had sailed did Gvosdev rewrite as best he could the details of his voyage. That long lapse of time must certainly account for his vagueness, but it cannot be the reason that this Russian Columbus was wholly unaware that he had touched on the American coast. The "large country" was to him just another large island, one of the islands that the men of Kamchatka knew of from the Chukchi traditions. Blindly and unknowingly, the inconspicuous Gvosdev accomplished what Bering hoped to do.

Bering, working and struggling in a near-by wilderness (near-by to us who have airplanes and telephones and wireless), knew nothing of what had been done. He knew only that every difficulty and hardship that had presented itself on his previous venture was magnified and intensified out of all proportion in this larger undertaking. There were mountains of unwieldy shipbuilding machinery to be transported, crowds of mechanics, and delicate scientific instruments that demanded tender handling. Only the thousands of poods of food and the necessary lumber could be obtained locally. The Empress had ordered artisans sent to Okhotsk and colonists who were to make a town out of this base in the wilderness. To govern this settlement, to relieve Bering of all secondary problems, she transferred the exile Pizarev to Okhotsk. He was to have everything organized before Bering's arrival. Following his old trail, Bering took much longer than previously to move the stumpy cannon and massive anchors across those same mountains and torrents and swamps. As for Pizarev and the other Siberian officials to whom he showed the imperial ukase that commandeered their assistance, they bowed low before it and remained prostrate. They were so many broken reeds to lean on. In his first expedition Bering had had to contend with Siberia and the Arctic; in this one he had to contend with Siberia, the Arctic, and Pizarev. Of the three, he felt that Pizarev was the worst. While Pizarev was there blocking progress by his inefficiency and troublemaking, Bering was unable to create order out of bedlam. And he who had left St. Petersburg so hopefully in 1733 saw the years drag past. It was the command of the Holy Little Mother who sat on a throne three thousand miles away that kept him from fleeing that purgatory.

Order upon order reached him as the years passed, and he was still unprepared to sail. He was deluged by a constant stream of impressively sealed documents asking for a reckoning of accounts, as the twelve thousand rubles that he had set as the outside cost for the undertaking piled up to the staggering sum of three hundred thousand. At last, seven years after he had left Russia, his two ships, the *St. Peter* and the *St. Paul*, were finished and provisioned. That summer he sailed to Ávacha Bay, on Kamchatka, where in honor of his ships the port was named Petropavlovsk.

Bering, in the *St. Peter*, had Georg Wilhelm Steller, a German naturalist who served as surgeon; Chirikov, commanding the *St. Paul*, had the young French astronomer Louis Delisle de la Croyère.* Each ship carried a crew of seventy-six men. Bering's original plan to winter on the American coast was altered when a large amount of their supplies was lost, and, though he had planned to sail early in May, not until June did the favoring wind they prayed for blow. For a fortnight the two ships bore each other company, and then, in a heavy fog, they parted. Ships and sky and water were welded into an unbroken grayness when they parted, never to meet again.

Chirikov, waiting patiently for the *St. Peter* to reappear, finally resumed his course and after a month came to a shore where great trees looked darkly down on a sparkling beach. A break in the line hinted at a sheltered bay. He sent ashore one of the boats with ten men. Night came and they did not return. Morning showed the forest bland, innocent, inhuman. Days passed and still they did not return. After an anxious week he sent his remaining boat with four well-armed men to look for traces of them, to learn the fate of their fellows. And they too disappeared. Not a shot was heard, not a sign —they passed out of sight round a bend, never to reappear. What had happened? Had they been ambushed by Indians, killed before they could fire, or had they drowned in the treacherous tide of Lituya Bay? Chirikov watched; he waited, agonized at their fate. The horror of the inexplicable frightened his men. They were badly in need of fresh water, but they had neither the boats nor the courage to send ashore for it. Chirikov decided to retreat as quickly as possible to Kamchatka. Like a fugitive, the ship turned and ran. The winds carried it swiftly to the west. Some days later the vessel came close to an island, so close that the men could see not only the mountainous

* Half-brother of Guillaume Delisle, the great geographer.

outline but the very grass. Here they hoped to fill their water casks, already a crying need, but they could secure only a pitifully small amount before a storm drove them away. Every drop of rain was harvested in spread canvas, and they collected enough, just enough, to keep them from going mad with thirst. Days passed, days of foul gales, of hardship that inexorably culminated in sickness. They lacked the water to cook their food properly. They shivered for days as they sailed through fogs, while stiff winds drenched them in icy spray. All were touched by scurvy, and some died. Consumption fed upon the indomitable spirit of Chirikov and chained him to his berth. Tottering men worked in pairs to pool their strength. Even the ship seemed ravaged by weakness and disease: her sails and rigging rotted. Wasted and feeble, like a captive who has escaped from barbarous torturers, the *St. Paul* crawled home to Avacha Bay. Croyère, the astronomer of the expedition, died as they lay in the harbor—he was the twenty-first. Fifty-five men wept bitterly as they tasted the peace and security of homecoming.

A worse fate was in store for those on the *St. Peter*. After they had spent precious days vainly looking for Chirikov and his men, they kept on to the east, eager for the sight of land. For land was promised them as they slipped through tangled seaweed; land could not be far off if sea-otters swam here. Wind and tide at last brought a coastline to their anxious eyes. From a bright beach they looked across a dark, thick forest to a shining mountain. This was the new continent of America that they had sailed to find! They shouted; they almost ran about their tasks; their weather-beaten faces glowed with elation. Success gilded everything; all were possessed by it. All except one, Bering, their leader. For him it had come too late. Already his gums were swollen, his joints stiffened, by scurvy. Fifteen years of heart-rending labor, fifteen years of reverses, had broken his courage, sickened his spirit. He was too old to feel enthusiasm himself, too crushed to reflect theirs. The high sun of his noon had come too late; he was mortally tired. He had struggled so arduously for so long that his one hope was to return. The adventure of wintering on a strange land spelled horror to him; he could respond only to fear; he could not endure the thought of starvation or privation. Fill the water casks and start home, the season is far advanced, lose no time.

The antagonism that had flared between Bering and Steller—the disdain of the man of action for the scientist, matched by the acid disapprobation voiced by the scholar for the commander who had learned in the school of hard knocks—sounded an evil crescendo when Bering disregarded Steller's plea for time to investigate and explore, "to walk the inviolate earth for newness' sake." Before the naturalist's eyes was a paradise untouched, unknown. Had they come all this distance merely to bring American water back to Asia? In vain did he plead and curse; Bering would not linger.* Though twenty casks still remained to be filled, the favoring breeze was not to be denied. They turned back for Avacha Bay.

The favoring breeze died down, and for weeks they knew only winds that were contrary, winds that mounted into gales; and gale after gale battered them as they staggered through uncharted, island-strewn waters. The *St. Peter* was bruised by storms, soaked by rains, smothered in fog. What should have taken them but four days was prolonged ten times—forty days of vermin, cold, hunger, thirst, despondency, and scurvy, forty days with men dying almost daily.

They kept on, slowly eating the miles that separated them from Kamchatka. They were so certain of reaching it that they dodged islands that offered refuge; they even took in sail at night so that they would not run ashore. Adverse winds made it impossible to bridge the short gap. When finally land appeared, they were positive that they had come to the northern part of the peninsula, and half-dead men crawled up to look at it. Unable to reach the shore, they put back to a bay they had passed. November winds shrieked through sails long since cut to ribbons; a heavy surf almost smashed them on a reef. Unable to steer or struggle, they were saved by a huge wave that lifted them over the barrier into the calm beyond. They lay at ease on quiet waters. Whatever the land they had come to, it was their refuge, a last-minute haven before the dark and cold of winter.

Steller, with one helper, went ashore to prepare a shelter. They were cheered by the sight of game on land and in the water; they knew they would not starve. They knew that man had never set foot there before, because the animals did not run from them. Blue foxes gathered in teasing, inquisitive crowds and pestered the two men as they worked to fashion a crude hut of stones and earth. The first day they killed sixty foxes with their axes and pikes. The second day even more were killed, and the men used the bodies to stop up the gaps in

---

* On the one day Steller spent on shore he observed a host of facts: scattered bones near the remains of a fire showed him the animal life of the island, mainland, and near-by waters; shell-heaps and bits of dried fish presented the native customs; from an abandoned dwelling-place he secured utensils, smoked salmon, sweet grass, bows and arrows, fire-drills, and so forth, that by their similarity indicated the proximity of Asia and America. He listed the flora and fauna; nothing escaped him, no clue was too small, no deduction too remote. All this he accomplished in one day.

the hut. The sick and dying sailors were transferred to this miserable shelter, where they lay cold and hungry. The foxes tugged at both the dead and the quick, scattered provisions, spoiled precious food, and carried off clothing and utensils. They were like a visitation, a plague that allowed of no peace. Yes, food was to be had, fuel too—and the men set about providing for themselves. Before the year was out, Bering died. Like Barents, he was a victim to scurvy, falling far from home, in a lonely spot, leaving his men to face a hazardous journey home. He was glad to rest after all his struggles and half-successes; he was tired of seeing man after man of his crew die. He gave his name to that island, midway between Asia and America. There he rests, the "plodder," who faithfully and to the best of his ability performed a piece of work that made him famous; but he lacked the courage and initiative that mark the great discoverer as a man of genius. He remains a pathetic figure because it cannot be forgotten that he was an explorer who made two voyages to find America, that "on the first one he never set eyes on America, and that on the second he did just that and nothing more."

By the first of the year the survivors, under the able care of Steller —bad feelings and feuds forgotten—organized their mode of living. Sickness and misery disappeared. Divided into three groups, they attended to their daily needs and secured food and wood to prepare their meals. As the days lengthened they made reconnoitering trips, ascertaining that they were on an island, that they still had to reach the mainland. High on the beach lay the *St. Peter*. It was impossible to float her. But from her they could salvage enough to make a smaller boat. By August they had finished the tiny new *St. Peter;* they launched her with prayers and hopes. Into this boat, forty-two feet long, forty-six men, their supplies and provisions were jammed. The first night barely missed being fatal, for a leak appeared, and had they not found it quickly, they must all have perished. Fair weather blessed them. Two weeks later they reached the harbor whence they had sailed the year before. Like men risen from the dead, they trembled at their victory over death; they were dazzled by life.

The voyage of the *St. Peter* and the *St. Paul* was only part of a larger, more inclusive program, the Great Northern Expedition. The far-flung front that Siberia turns to the Arctic Sea was to be system· atically explored and charted. Bering's plan, adopted in 1733, in· cluded the mapping of the coast from the mouth of the Ob to that of the Anadyr, the complete delineation of the shoreline of northern Asia. The vast territory had been divided into five sections: (1) from Archangel to the Ob; (2) the Ob to the Yenisei; (3) the Yenisei to

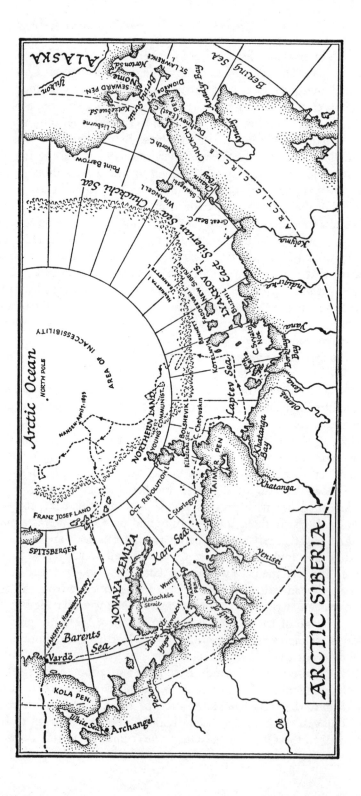

Cape Taimyr; (4) Cape Taimyr to the Lena; (5) the Lena to the Anadyr. A simultaneous advance was to be made in all sectors. Each group was commissioned and supplied for a two-year period, and if by the end of that time the work had not been finished, the officer in charge was to report back to St. Petersburg to await further orders. It was planned at first to have Bering direct the undertaking, but as he became more and more involved in his own problem, the supervision and direction were assumed by the Admiralty College.

Look at the map! Note the high latitude; there is an ominous line of offshore drift ice. Remember that, since sailors first looked on the Kara Sea, it was never mentioned without an adjective denoting dread or terror; it is the "ice-cellar." The men recruited were from river settlements, had never seen the sea or known seasickness or navigated a ship through drift ice, and were ignorant of all the homely arts of the sailor. And the boats they had! Not a *St. Gabriel,* or a *St. Paul* or a *St. Peter,* built under the knowing eye of a seagoing Dane. They dared the Arctic sea in a *koch* (70 feet long, 21 feet wide, and 8 feet deep), a kind of scow, flat-bottomed, secured by wooden pegs and leather straps and protected by twigs, through which the sharp ice easily cut; with wooden masts supporting sails of deerskins sewn together, which became sodden in damp weather; its main motive power the paddles of its crew of fifty; its anchors of stone and wood fastened by cables of leather thongs. Cumbersome, gawky boats, as different from the swift dancing beauty of the Viking ships as a dray horse is from an Arab stallion. And yet the groups made a brave showing, what with pilots and assistant pilots, surgeons and priests, surveyors and mineralogists. They were all there to labor and endure for the glory of the arts and sciences and the Holy Little Mother.

(1) From Archangel to the mouth of the Ob demanded the rounding of the Yalmal Peninsula, sailing far out into the Kara Sea. Under the joint command of Lieutenants Muravyov and Pavlov, two kochi left the Dvina in the summer of 1734 and, passing through Yugor Strait, found the Kara Sea free of ice. Moving eastward, they stopped at the peninsula to take on driftwood and fresh water and then followed the coast northward. Delayed by head winds and pack ice, they did not come near to rounding the tip until the middle of August, and then, with the task almost finished, they turned back because of contrary winds, the lateness of the season, and the astounding assertion that they "were not far from the mouth of the Ob." They returned to a village on the Pechora, where a herd of reindeer had been sent to serve them as food for the winter. The next year the Kara Sea was in a different mood. They could barely advance through the heavy ice.

At the end of the second year the two lieutenants reported back to the Admiralty College and, because of the constant quarreling between them and the charges made against them by the villagers, they were both removed and the work entrusted to Lieutenant Malgin.

In 1736 he started, but he was too early and lost one of his boats in the ice. While waiting for the new ones that were promised, he surveyed White Island. The next summer he set out again. The season of 1737 was a remarkably mild one; it not only favored this expedition but was the factor that determined the success of almost all the groups. The weather was fine, the ice almost negligible. Malgin rounded the peninsula and, hugging the coast, entered the mouth of the river Ob. He hurried back to St. Petersburg to report his work, leaving his officers to sail the boats home. It took them two years.

(2) It seems only a short jump from the mouth of the Ob to that of the Yenisei, but the path lies entirely within the ice-clogged, fog-larded Kara Sea. Lieutenant Ovtzin was in charge of this section; he made his first attempt in 1734. His first two seasons were unsuccessful. He spent his time in preparation and laid down a series of food depots along the channel of the river, charted the channel, and erected lighthouses. When he reported back to the Admiralty College, it extended his command for another two years and unstintingly provided him with additional supplies and equipment. It did everything possible to sustain Ovtzin's zeal. The third year was as fruitless as the two before had been, and he was forced to be content with extending his survey, laying more depots, and building lighthouses, even as far as the Yenisei. The magic summer of 1737—the year of his fourth attempt —saw him slowly advance from one river to another. The supplies that had been cached were used, and slowly, slowly, despite head winds and delays, he crept round the cape into the bay of the Yenisei River. Ovtzin had discharged his duty.*

(3) Between Siberia's two mightiest rivers, the Yenisei and the Lena, is the ominous hump of the Taimyr Peninsula, the northern-most reach of Asia. The offensive laid down by the Admiralty College intended that this fortress be attacked from both sides. The pilot Manin was to lead the forces from the Yenisei and connect his work with the surveying that had been started from the Lena. He did not begin until 1738, unfortunately missing the unusual mildness of the

* Ovtzin, who had worked thoroughly and painstakingly, charting both by land and by sea, had been seen talking with a noble exiled to Siberia. This trivial occurrence so overshadowed his sustained labor that upon his return to St. Peters-burg he was reduced to the rank of sailor and sent to the eastern wilds of Siberia, where he met Bering and sailed with him on the *St. Peter*.

previous season. The two attempts he made were ineffectual; he could find no path through the heavy ice that sealed the waters. He tried the sole remaining way: he sent his assistant Sterlegov out to map the coastline by land. Snow-blindness tortured and incapacitated Sterlegov and forced him to turn back at the cape that has been named after him. When Manin reported to his superiors, at the end of two years, it was not his two failures that moved them to dismiss him: their confidence had been shattered by a host of charges made against him. They did not replace him; they concentrated their hopes and their resources on the expedition that was making inroads on the peninsula from the other direction.

(4) The Lena and Cape Taimyr section had been entrusted to the young and enthusiastic Lieutenant Pronchishev. To him the expedition was part of a honeymoon, though neither he nor his bride came back alive from this strangest of all wedding trips. Starting in 1735, he sailed the first season from Yakutsk to the mouth of the Lena and then to a tiny hunting- and trading-town on the Olenek River. There he wintered, held by the ice until the following August. The next year he pushed on, past the Anabara, dodging and circling through thick ice, past the deep bay, the estuary of the Khatanga, northward, northward, creeping inch by inch to the tip of the peninsula. Then, almost at his goal, he was stopped. He could not advance either by sailing or by twisting and squeezing. The frozen sea had beaten him at the very last. It was as they made good their retreat to the winter quarters on the Olenek that he died. His wife survived but a few days.

Not until 1739, three years later, was the work continued. Khariton Laptev assumed command, and the Admiralty College furnished him with all he asked: storehouses were put up on the Anabara, Khatanga, and Taimyr Rivers; hunters concentrated there to keep them supplied with food; the kochi were overhauled—the struggle went on. But the Arctic was too strong. It wrecked their boats, and had it not been for the courage of the leader it would have overcome them all. But he had been filled with the determination to succeed. A vision claimed him and goaded him on to accomplishment. If he failed by water, he would yet conquer by land.

He divided the work into three parts. His pilot, Chelyuskin, with two soldiers and three sledges, was to chart the coast from the Pyasina to the Taimyr; Chekin, the geodesist, was to follow the coast from the Khatanga to the Taimyr; the commander himself was to go down the Taimyr to establish a large depot at its mouth. Of the three, only Chekin was unable to carry through, and it left the whole enterprise minus that one link in the chain forged around the peninsula. This was supplied in 1741 by Chelyuskin, reaching the extreme point, which was named in his honor, and so achieving the goal that had been set.

(5) Eastward from the Lena stretches the promontory of Svyatoi Nos and beyond that the unknown length of the Chukchi coast. At the same time that Pronchishev sailed down the Lena to work his way westward, Lasinius, who was in charge of the last section, started floating down the river to make his way to the east. Weeks passed while he tried to find his way through the shifting, swampy maze of the delta—and by then it was imperative to seek a spot for wintering. He chose Borkhaya Bay. Only nine men lived to greet the spring. When Bering was informed that Lasinius and forty-one men had died of scurvy, he lost no time in sending provisions, a new personnel, and a new leader. He chose Dmitri Laptev, Khariton's brother. The next season was spent in rescuing the survivors and establishing winter quarters at a place less fatal. The favorable year of 1737 passed with nothing attempted, while Laptev hurried back to St. Petersburg to get his commission renewed and his supplies restocked.

The Admiralty College acceded to all his requests, for it was very eager that Svyatoi Nos be charted, as many stories of land to the north of it had been reported. Laptev resumed operations two years later, dividing the work to be done. His surveyor, Kindyakov, was to chart the coast from the Lena to the Yana, and a sailor, Loshkin, was to continue from there to Svyatoi Nos. Both his assistants were successful. Then he dispatched Kindyakov to trace the course of the Indigirka while he himself attempted to sail round the cape to its mouth. Laptev and his men were able to round the cape, but almost perished before they found the mouth of the Indigirka. Luckily they met the other party there. Worn out and suffering, they followed Kindyakov to a village, where they wintered. The terrific hardships he had sustained made Laptev a ready listener to the stories the local inhabitants had to tell during the winter. They convinced him of the impossibility of circumnavigating the East Cape, of the foolishness of trying to map a coast controlled by the warlike and, hostile Chukchi. And this he reported to the Admiralty College. It ignored his misgivings; it reiterated its demands that the work be pushed to a successful conclusion.

In 1740 he set out again for the east. He mapped as far as Great Bear Cape, east of the mouth of the Kolyma, and there he was stopped. He went no farther along the Arctic coast. He was not replaced; at that point the advance made by land and sea was ended. The Admiralty College had set a goal too far for its straining fingertips. Except for that last pull, it had a comprehensive outline of the northern coast. Though it had fallen short of its mark, it had not really failed. The important question, the core of the whole expedition—whether or not Asia and America are united—was not satisfactorily answered. But men knew for certain now the impracticability of attempting a northeast passage; they knew that the coast of Asia extended eastward farther than they had ever imagined. The Russians had touched the western shore of North America; they had discovered the Aleutian Islands. Though imperfect, the discoveries of the Great Northern Expedition have remained the groundwork, the solid base, on which later expeditions have built and refined. Clearly and boldly the coastline of Siberia on the Arctic Sea shone forth.

Vast progress had been made; a mighty collection was piled on the store of man's knowledge of his world—but at what cost! With what great sacrifice! Hundreds had died, and those who lived were scarred with the agony of achievement. "Even those who lived to return to the scenes of their childhood were so broken in health that the joy of living was nearly gone. The exact spot where the ashes of Bering, the Dane, lie is not known; Steller, the German, died a lonely and pitiful death in the wilds of Siberia; Walton, the Englishman [Spanberg's captain], fell by the wayside unnoticed and forgotten; the rain has long since washed away all traces of the grave where Delisle de la Croyère was laid to rest. Chirikov, the Russian, contracted a disease from which he suffered for three years after his return home, until death came to his relief." [1]

Peter the Great had set in motion a herculean undertaking for the glory of the arts and sciences of Russia. And it was his wish, his spirit, that, persisting in the rulers who followed him, sustained the men of the Admiralty College. Their task had been to find the right men to carry out the work, to defend it against those who cried out at the waste of money and life. It was the wish of the Autocrat of all the Russias that fired the men in the field to face the impossible, to labor, to suffer, to die, to triumph.

9

After the Great Northern Expedition

THE STORY of the Cossack Simon Dezhnev was the challenge and the impulse to further exploration of the Siberian Arctic. From the oblivion of the Yakutsk archives the eminent German historian Müller lifted the report of this Siberian Cossack and, almost a hundred years after the deed, made his name famous. According to his own reports Dezhnev, in 1648, was the first to circumnavigate the forbidding East Cape.

Since the reports were found by Müller in 1736 (his book was not published for another twenty years), Dezhnev's claim has been scrutinized and questioned. The bare, rather indefinite accounts sent by the Cossack to his commander at Yakutsk are notable for the amount of room they allow for doubt. To pick our way understandingly through the elaborate and minute discussion, we must weigh not the specific facts but rather the over-all picture. If it is a precise recital we want, the reports will not satisfy us; if we are skeptical that untutored Cossacks in inadequate kochi succeeded where trained men and good ships failed, then we will say that what Dezhnev wrote was a wish, a dream; or we can see it as just another attempt to malign a superior and claim the Czar's reward. But if we spell our way, as Müller did, past the vagueness to pick up the bright nuggets of fact, then subsequent corroborative evidence clinches the argument in favor of Dezhnev. For Müller found, as Strahlenberg * had before him, that the

* A Swedish officer captured by the Russians at the Battle of Poltava, Strahlenberg spent thirteen years (1709–22) in Siberia. Interested in geography, he was able to travel widely. Everywhere he heard talk—precise, factual talk—of Russian discoveries in northeastern Siberia. His first map, prepared at Tobolsk in 1715, incorporated his travels and the information he had received from the Cossacks. This map, like a second one made three years later, was stolen. He presented his third map to Peter the Great when, after the Peace of Nystad, he was on his way home. His book, published in 1730, included a duplicate map, on which opposite the mouth of the Indigirka was written: "from here, Russians crossing a sea covered with ice, reached under great difficulties and danger the territory of Kamchatka." [4]

people who had made expeditions into the Chukchi Peninsula to try to collect taxes and tribute confirmed what Dezhnev had written—that the ocean surrounded the land of the Chukchi—and that his voyage was referred to when the natives were asked if they had ever seen white men. In a new land where conquest and fur-trapping are the main occupations, geography is an important and never ending topic. And there in Siberia Müller found in addition masses of documents—reports, crudely drawn maps, claims, official investigations—in which the country and its people were described. The contour of the Chukchi Peninsula was an academic question in the scientific circles of Europe; in Yakutsk it was a matter of life and death, of tribute and taxes; it was immediate, it was real, it was known.

Simon Dezhnev was a member of the Cossack band that, under the leadership of Mikhail Staduchin, reached the Kolyma River in 1644. Like everyone else, he was fired with the desire to be the first to reach the East, to garner its wealth and secure for himself fame and distinction. He tells how in 1648 a large party set sail in six miserable, inadequate kochi going eastward from the Kolyma. Without compass, without chart, without knowing if they could go all the way by sea, they started for the Anadyr River, the next landmark to be looked for on the road to Kamchatka. Starting the middle of June, they arrived three months later at a large promontory. Offshore they found two islands, the Diomedes, where the natives had large teeth—labrets used by the Eskimos who inhabited those islands. Here they were attacked by the Chukchi. They escaped. Continuing along the coast they passed the Gulf of Anadyr, where driving ice slashed their kochi and monster gales overwhelmed them. All but Dezhnev's party perished. He and his men were wrecked on the shore. They faced a winter in a region so barren that it was destitute of inhabitants. They could not find wood. Starving, frozen, barefoot, they wandered on an unknown coast for ten weeks until they found the Anadyr. Following its banks, they reached a native village. They attacked it, subdued the natives, razed the houses, and built their own fort, Anadyrsk. When summer came they floated down to the mouth of the river and there, where the river pours into the gulf, their most avaricious dreams came true: they drifted onto a sandbank where lay a fortune in walrus ivory. Years after he had made this heroic odyssey, Dezhnev sent his reports to his commander at Yakutsk. Seventy-five years later Müller found them, proclaimed Dezhnev's achievement, and became his champion.

Müller's book, published in 1758, came at a time when the results of the Great Northern Expedition were occupying the attention of the scholarly world, when men appreciated that the keynote of the expedition, the question that had interested Peter the Great and occupied his successors, was still unanswered. As long as no one had made the passage from the Arctic to the Pacific Ocean, as long as the Chukchi coast was unsurveyed, no one knew for certain whether or not Asia and America were joined. Bering's voyages were double-edged, cutting equally on either side of the controversy. The information of the Chukchi was no more to be relied upon, some people said, than the tales told repeatedly by Siberian hunters of mountains that crouched on the horizon to the north of Svyatoi Nos. To Müller, Dezhnev's reports corroborated Bering's claim. But why, asked those who were unconvinced, could no one else follow Dezhnev's route? And why, we might add, was his voyage not repeated until the great driving power of steam forced ships through the terrible ice? The uniqueness of the Cossack's exploit over so many centuries would seem to be the crux of the argument. And the answer must be that it was not the ice alone that kept from that coast other men eager for riches or knowledge: it was the warlike Chukchi. For a long time after Dezhnev, expeditions were sent to subdue the natives, and again and again bloody encounters took place as the Chukchi fought off all attempts to make them pay tribute.[5] Even as late as 1820 Wrangel took great care to make it clear that he came into their peninsula on a mission of peace.

Dezhnev's voyage became a story, a challenge, and an impulse that spurred men on to secure the exact delineation of that northeastern tip of Siberia. That alone would settle the problem, would conclude the work and fill in the gap left by the Great Northern Expedition.

Just the opposite reaction to the Great Northern Expedition was felt by natives and colonists of northern Siberia. To them exploration was synonymous with misery. To live there demanded a constant and unceasing struggle for a precarious subsistence; life was a narrow, uncertain ledge laboriously cut in a treacherous cliff. During the long years of the expedition the slender resources of the inhabitants had been consumed and not replenished. The colonists were exhausted and impoverished. Unable to understand the end for which their misery was payment, they could feel only a deep hatred. Twenty years had to pass, an embittered, afflicted generation had to die, before it was possible to continue exploration.

The government did not at once renew the task of circumnagivating the northeastern tip of Siberia. The next expedition, in 1760, was a private one, led and financed by a wealthy merchant of Yakutsk, Shalaurov. Only rarely does the world see a Schliemann, a Gauguin, leave the profitable pursuit of business to follow a compelling siren song that sounds for him alone. The fortunes of such men, the peace of their last years, even their lives, are offered gladly to a labor odd and unique. In their company Shalaurov takes his place, for we know that he abandoned his home and his affairs so that he might be free to realize his dearest wish—to sail from the Kolyma to the Anadyr.

No official aid lightened his work. He recruited his crew from among the exiles, and from his own pocket paid for everything. In 1760 he sailed down the Lena and reached the Yana River, spent the first winter there, and next season passed his first real obstacle, Svyatoi Nos, whence he, too, saw the outline of distant hills. Was that land, or was it merely the play of light on ice? He dared not stop or pause; while yet the breeze held he must push on to the Kolyma. Arrived there, he fortified himself against the oncoming winter. His hut, sheathed in water-hardened snow, had small cannon to guard it; he was now in the unexplored land of the warlike Chukchi. An adequate camp, it appeared to the natives and hunters a palace, luxurious and magnificent; it was a magnet that drew them from miles around. Shalaurov had found a spot teeming with reindeer and abounding in fish, and the time passed quickly and in comfort. He spent a second winter there after vainly trying to double Cape Shelagski. By that time he had exhausted his supplies and, what was worse, the willingness of his men to continue. It meant that he had to replenish his stocks and renew his crew, that he had to give up the advance he had made and begin again from the Lena. In this he persevered. Ever hopeful, he headed seaward on his fourth attempt. And so he is stamped in our minds—for neither he nor any of his men came back from the land of the Chukchi. It is said that he penetrated as far as Chaun Bay, but the proof is not conclusive.

Had Shalaurov circumnavigated East Cape, he would surely have been eager to explore those hills to the north of Svyatoi Nos. That was left for another merchant. In March 1770 Lyakhov, while on a business trip to a native village on Svyatoi Nos, witnessed the arrival of a great herd of deer. They came over the ice from the north. Lyakhov was interested. He knew that these animals depend on land for their sustenance; he knew that they instinctively do not venture far from feeding-grounds. Were those outlined hills real, then, not a mirage, and was what had been ridiculed as legend the truth? Lyakhov could not rid his mind of the urge to know whence the herd had come. The clear path of their hoofs fascinated and impelled him. The next month he set out, using a sledge and dog-team. He followed the highway marked by the herd. Always it kept to the north; there was no faltering or hesitation; it led on straight and unerringly. After having gone about fifty miles, he came to an island. Still the trail beckoned. Pushing on fifteen miles farther, he reached a second island. Still the hoofs beat out a trail. He kept on; but though the deer had crossed, he was stopped by huge hummocks of ice that made the path torturous, neck-breaking. He was forced to turn back.

Lyakhov volunteered a report of his findings to the Empress Catherine (not yet known as "the Great") and received from her the exclusive right to hunt animals and dig up mammoth ivory on the land he had discovered. It was her official policy to aid private enterprise by allowing concessions and granting monopolies. In this way she gave the necessary incentive for individuals to seek abroad for new and lucrative territory. She further ordered that the islands be named after Lyakhov. He returned to them three years later, rowing the distance with another man, and wintered there. They found a fourth island—all were fabulous, outlandish islands wrought of sand and ice, richly sown with mammoth remains.* They piled their boat with a valuable cargo and reached home safely.

That policy of Catherine the Great was justified, for daring merchants pushed out into the frozen sea to find many islands, to return with profitable cargoes of ivory and furs. The trader Sannikov discovered the islands of Stolbovoi and Fadeyev; Sirovatsoi found New Siberia; and Byelkov gave his name to the island he located. The last petitioned the government for permission to establish a hunting- and trading-station on his island, in the hope of breaking the Lyakhov monopoly. His petition came before Count Romanozov, who had the power and the desire to push Russia's progress on all frontiers—even into the Arctic—and it resulted in the surveying of many of the islands that constitute the archipelago. The exile Hedenström, a man of education and training, was put in charge of the work.

He had only the merchant Sannikov and a surveyor to help him. While the last two mapped Fadeyev and Little Lyakhov, Hedenström pushed on to New Siberia, the southern coast of which he traced. The next year, 1810, they returned to New Siberia and completely outlined that island. There they found an ivory ax and other relics indicating that those islands had at some far-distant time been inhabited. There he saw the "Hills of Wood," incredible hills composed

---

* The pleasant thought that occurred to Nordenskiöld, when he investigated the islands a hundred years later, that, "if the temperatures were raised, these cliffs might change into liquid porridge and dissolve,"[1] seems more than pure whimsy. The *Soviet News* (September 12, 1946) reported that many of the islands are gradually shrinking. According to Sukhotsky, of the Northern Sea Route Administration, Vassilevsky Island, explored in 1823, could not even be found in 1936.

of alternating horizontal layers of tree-trunks, intact but turned to coal, and sandstone. The hills rise to a height of two hundred feet, and projecting from the summit are rows of stumps, giving to the profile of the northern coast the outline of a saw. From those hills he sighted land still farther to the northeast. That he must reach. Alone, Hedenström started off across the frozen sea. Four days out, he came to open water. His advance was stopped. His food ran low. He turned back, but his progress was slow, for the current was against him. His food was gone, and he needed every ounce of strength to reach land over the drifting ice. He would have died had he not killed some bears. Forty-three days after he set out, he came back to the wooden hills.

The contribution Hedenström made to geological history by his exact and scientific investigation of these incredible islands was as nothing compared to his report of land glimpsed still farther to the northeast. That was pounced on by men eager to believed that it was part of the American coast or, better still, the coastline of a continent that extended across the Arctic to reappear as Greenland on the Western Hemisphere. In those days men took the plastic stuff of unknown lands and seas and molded them to the form of their sanguine theories.

Neither the voyage of Captain James Cook in 1778 nor the Russian expedition under Joseph Billings settled the question conclusively. Cook, in his third circumnavigation of the world, had hoped to sail home from the Pacific by way of either the Northwest or the Northeast Passage. He tried the American side. Heavy ice stopped him at Icy Cape. Then, crossing to the Asiatic shore, he followed it to North Cape, where again he was stopped by the ice. Coming abreast of East Cape, Cook saw what Bering had missed. "The weather becoming clear, we had the opportunity of seeing, at the same moment, the remarkable peaked hill, near Cape Prince of Wales, on the Coast of America, and the East Cape of Asia, with the two connecting islands of Saint Diomede between them." [2] Cook had seen enough to convince him that the continents were separated; he was also impressed with the futility of attempting a passage through the frozen boreal sea. He turned southward. Fatal winds blew him to the Sandwich Isles, to his death at the hands of naked warriors. Captain Cook had made another contribution to polar exploration. It must not be forgotten that Cook had to contend with the ravages of the scurvy that broke out on all lengthy sea voyages. He was the first to note and make use of the antiscorbutic value of fresh limes. Lime juice became a vital factor, a lifesaver to all men who for long periods of time had to go without fresh foods. Cook gave them the health and strength necessary to plunge into the unknown.

Ten years after Cook had sailed, Catherine the Great in 1788 endorsed the plans for a new expedition. All that was specified was that the coastline from Great Bear Cape, where Dmitri Laptev had stopped, to North Cape, the point Cook had reached, should be sailed along and mapped. It meant the rounding of Cape Shelagski—a halfway point—to complete the outline of northern Siberia. Joseph Billings, an Englishman who had served under Cook, was appointed commander, and his officers included distinguished men from all Europe. The Empress knew how to equip and outfit with a lavish hand, and she stinted on nothing that might ensure the success of the undertaking. For months the expedition was the fashionable topic at court. Time passed, and then, and then—the results dribbled in. Between thick slices of apology and explanation lay a lean fact: nothing had been attempted by Billings. His timidity and incompetence rendered him unfit to make the simple forward thrust that had been asked of him. Completely at a loss, he beat about the bush, dissipating his supplies and energy in doing a million little nothings. The Arctic had bluffed him out of a victory.

Cape Shelagski still held itself inviolate. The story of the Cossack Dezhnev was there, more than ever now a challenge to the pleasant conceit that, in the northeast, land met land, undivided by the flow of tide and current. Men could imagine what they pleased. A century had passed since Peter the Great first tried to get a definite outline of the Chukchi Peninsula—a century, and nothing conclusive had been obtained.

In the third attempt made by the government Lieutenant Ferdinand von Wrangel was commissioned to survey the coast from the Kolyma to East Cape. He did not even consider the possibility of sailing the distance. From the first he planned to attack from the land, using dog-teams. Starting in 1820, he made his way from the Kolyma to Cape Shelagski. "The doubling of this cape was a work of great difficulty and danger. We had often to ascend steep icebergs ninety feet high and to descend at great risk to the sledges . . . at other times, we had to wade up to our waists through drift snow, and if we came to smooth ice it was covered with sharp, crystallized salt which destroyed the ice-runners and made the draught so heavy that we were obliged to harness ourselves to the sledges, and it required our utmost efforts to drag them along. . . . Both men and dogs were completely exhausted. We had only three days' provisions left, and it appeared very doubtful whether we might venture further. . . .

However, I decided on going sufficiently far to judge of the general trending of this coast, which was supposed . . . to form an isthmus connecting Asia with America. . . . Luckily we found a narrow strip of ice which enabled us to get on rapidly. . . . To judge by the immense blocks of ice close to the shore, the depth of the water must be very considerable, and the absence of bays must render navigation dangerous as vessels would be exposed to the pressure of the ice without any place of refuge. The want of provisions now obliged us to return; and I was forced to content myself for the present with having ascertained that for forty miles to the east of Cape Shelagski, the coast trended in a southeast direction." [3]

The next two years were spent by Wrangel and his assistant Anjou in making many sorties from the land to the north over the ice. The work was hazardous, and many times the ice cracked at their very feet, threatening to swallow them, dogs, sledges, and all. And though they had pushed out almost two hundred miles at various tangents, they found neither the land nor the ice-bridge that was supposed to join the two continents; they were always stopped by open water. Always they were confronted by the wide, immeasurable ocean. Wrangel was impressed by the ability of the native sledge-drivers to find their way unerringly across the wilderness of hummocky ice, innocent of any distinguishing landmark, with no instrument to guide them. They depended on the *sastrugi*, wavelike ridges of snow set by the prevailing winds, and were never misled by similar ridges superimposed by temporary gusts. They knew which were the true sastrugi, and experience had taught them at what angle to cut across them so as to reach a given spot. This was the technique they had perfected in traversing the endless stretch of tundra when it lay buried deep and unrecognizable under snow.

Wrangel had accomplished a great deal—even though most of it had amounted to not finding land where it was supposed to be—but he was not satisfied. In the fourth year he set out from the Kolyma and, rounding Cape Shelagski, reached the Chukchi village at North Cape. He had now tied his work up with that of Cook, completing the coastal survey. He was able to impress the natives with the peacefulness of his mission, trading beads and tobacco for seal and walrus meat. On the goodwill that he established rested their willingness to have business dealings with the Russians. Before Wrangel returned to his base he decided to strike out once again from the shore to verify the statement of the natives that on clear days land could be seen to the north of Cape Yakan. When he was seventy miles from shore, a violent gale smashed the solid ice under him; lanes of water yawned wider and wider, stretching between him and the land. He had to turn back. That he reached the shore at all was due to the speed of his racing-dogs, to their ability to negotiate the leads of water that veined the ice by swimming across and towing the men and sledges huddled on a pancake of ice. He arrived at his base on the Kolyma after having covered 1,530 miles in seventy-eight days, the greatest sledging-trip of that generation. So ended the attempts made by Russia to determine the geographical relationship of Asia and America.

Baron Admiral Ferdinand von Wrangel became first Governor of Russian America—Alaska—and director of the Russian-American Trading Company. He established the first trading-station on St. Michael's Island in 1831 and had the lower Yukon explored. His traders and hunters pushed steadily to the east until somewhere in Arctic America they stood face to face with Englishmen who had started from the Atlantic and ranged north and west for the Hudson's Bay Company. Both nations had gone almost halfway around the earth to garner the furry wealth that is at its best in high latitudes. Wrangel lived to see his country sell the territory he had governed to the Republic she had only just recognized.

Baron Admiral Ferdinand von Wrangel in subsequent years saw various men poke their way through Bering Strait to the waters beyond: Beechey, in 1826, reached Icy Cape, whence he sent Elson forward in a boat to trace the American coast for one hundred and twenty-six miles to Point Barrow, the second most northerly point of North America; Kellett, as part of the Franklin search in 1849, sighted the "legendary" land to the north of Cape Yakan; in 1867 the American whaling-captain Thomas Long rediscovered Kellett Land and traced its southern coast. Long did not know that it had already been sighted, but he did recognize it as the land Wrangel had tried to reach and so was responsible for renaming it for the latter. In those fifty years whalers of many nations calmly penetrated waters that had once been the frontier of the unknown. The sea Wrangel had charted was frequented more and more by ships, until it became as familiar as a path across village fields. The route that Dezhnev blazed had become a highway along which was borne the treasure of ivory and furs of which all had dreamed.

IO

The British Attack the Arctic

By Sea

IN THE frontispiece map in Sir John Barrow's *Chronological History of Voyages into the Arctic Regions,* published in 1818, the coast of northern Siberia winds its way for thousands of miles, jutting and curving, its main features carefully traced by the persistent men of the Great Northern Expedition. Of the northern coastline of America there is nothing save two widely separated points, points set down by Samuel Hearne and Alexander Mackenzie, where each had explored a river to its junction with the polar sea. These points beckoned out of the encompassing emptiness, summoning men to further exploration. Looking at this map (see p. 96), it was easy to see what long-drawn-out dangers were attendant upon an attempt at the Northeast Passage, whereas neither the heart nor the mind dared imagine a similar situation in the northwest. There it would be different; there, ignorance argued, a short and simple route could be effected. They had only to sail along Arctic America to be able to set its stern shore down in delicate lines and fill in the unpleasant blank. The hope of easy achievement, the need to verify what could only be surmised—these were the forces to which England responded.

England, since Trafalgar, was mistress of the seas and eager to test her power, to extend her sovereignty. The only mortal enemy capable of threatening her security now brooded helplessly at St. Helena. She transformed her lust for conquest into a desire for discovery. Exploration of the north it was to be—the golden north that had given birth to the Russia Company, that had smiled on the Spitsbergen whale-fisheries, that more than ever was being gracious to the Hudson's Bay Company. And the northern waters, according to William Scoresby, Jr., the outstanding whaler of the day, had been so

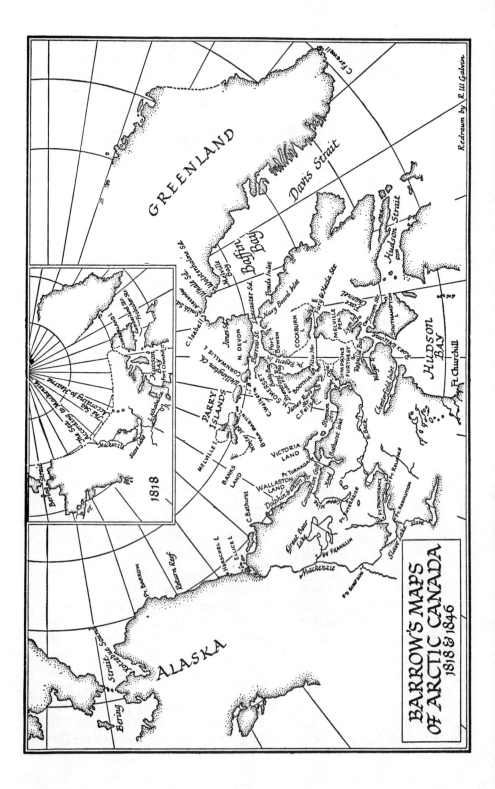

GREENLAND

Davis Strait

Baffin Bay

Hudson Strait

Redrawn by R. W. Galvin

Cumberland St.

C. Farewell

Navy Board Inlet

Pond Inlet

Lancaster St.

Melville Bay

Admiralty St.

Wellington St.

Barrow St.

C. Isabel

N. DEVON

Jones St.

CORNWALLIS I.

Port Bowen

Pr. Regent Inlet

Fox Channel

SOUTHAMPTON

Hudson Bay

COCKBURN I.

MELVILLE PEN.

Fury & Hecla St.

Repulse Bay

SIMPSONS FURTHEST

Fort Churchill

PARRY ISLANDS

SOMERSET

C. Walker

Boothia

James Ross St.

Felix Har.

Chesterfield Inlet

MELVILLE I.

BYAM MARTIN I.

VICTORIA LAND

C. Felix

Rae St.

BANKS LAND

WALLASTON LAND

Pt. Turnagain

Dolphin & Union St.

Coronation Gulf

Bathurst Inlet

Back R.

Pt. Pechell

C. Bathurst

ELLICE I.

HERSCHEL I.

Return Reef

Pt. BARROW

ALASKA

Bering Strait

Strait of Anne

Mackenzie

Great Bear Lake

FT. FRANKLIN

Ft. PROVIDENCE

Slave Lake

Great Slave Lake

Ft. RELIANCE

Ft. SIMPSON

BARROW'S MAPS
OF ARCTIC CANADA
1818 & 1846

1818

Cumberland St.

Frozen St.

Repulse Bay

Fox Channel

HUDSON BAY

Fort Churchill

"The Supposed Territory of Jaartac"

Mackenzie

Slave Lake

Bering Strait

remarkably free from ice during the two preceding seasons as to give the fairest promise for Arctic navigation in 1818. His practical suggestion added its weight to the glory and dividends of the past, and English ships again sailed to the north. Four ships were sent out by the Admiralty, two with orders to sail via Spitsbergen directly across the Pole to Siberia, while the other two, sailing by way of the Northwest Passage, were to meet them on the other side of the earth. So certain were they of reaching that destination that their instructions gave them elaborate and precise rules for their behavior upon their arrival at Bering Strait. There was nothing they knew of to prevent a successful voyage. So lightly were dismissed the labors of Barents and Hudson, of Frobisher, Davis, and Baffin!

This double-headed expedition of 1818 is like the prologue of a play recited before the still closed curtain. It defines the course of action, the motives and resources of the protagonists; the principal characters are introduced; the setting is described. It is important as a help in understanding the ensuing drama, as a beginning to a heroic tragedy. But—nothing happens.

In this expedition two goals were defined: the completion of the Northwest Passage and the attainment of the North Pole, two goals that were to claim the attention of many men in England, France, Germany, the Scandinavian countries, Austria-Hungary, Italy, and the United States for the next century. What began on the single pure note of discovery was extended to include, as a regular part of the work, scientific observations of all kinds. Soon this became as important as exploration per se, then eclipsed it, until it is today the dominating note—so much so that the records of observed facts are the most precious item of an expedition; and to the end that such records might not be lost, men have sacrificed their lives. As the work progressed, the technique and methods became an integral part of the undertaking. The era thus begun came to an end only in 1924, when Rasmussen, having completed his last great sledging-trip, hailed the advent of polar aviation, but blessed "the fate that allowed me to be born at a time when Arctic exploration by dog sledge was not yet a thing of the past." [1]

Among the officers in the expedition of 1818 were Edward Parry, John Franklin, George Back, Edward Sabine, John Ross, and his nephew James Clark Ross—men destined to achieve a lasting fame for exploration in the north, the first of a long list of fearless, tireless men who struggled to chart the unknown Arctic coastline of America. They could find no rest while the northernmost limits of a vast continent were a blank. They enlisted to do battle against a wily adversary that fought to keep its secret by starving them out, freezing them out, rotting them out with scurvy—a powerful adversary that could hold their ships tight in its grasp, could crush and overwhelm them.

Four ships sailed from England in May 1818; four ships parted, hoping to meet again on the other side of the globe: the *Alexander* and the *Isabella* heading for the west, the *Dorothea* and the *Trent* heading due north. Captain Buchan in the *Dorothea*, with Lieutenant Franklin as second in the *Trent*, laid down a course for the waters north of Spitsbergen, following the same path that had been taken forty-five years before by Constantine Phipps in the *Racehorse* and the *Carcass*. This earlier North Polar voyage is memorable mainly because the fourteen-year-old Horatio Nelson served on it as midshipman. Buchan's chief guide was the chart Phipps had made, which "is still the marvel of those who take an interest in Spitsbergen surveying, for its extraordinary badness." [2] But Buchan was stopped "where Baffin, Hudson, and indeed almost all the early voyagers had been stopped," [3] when a screaming gale forced the two ships to take refuge in Magdalena Bay. No sooner had the gale subsided sufficiently to allow them to come out of their shelter than they were beset by the thick ice of the main pack. For thirteen days they were held fast; neither the pull of the sails nor the stoutness of the oak planks served against the puissant ice. It needed a gale to smash the pack and liberate the ships. And when the gale blew, it set the floes madly whirling, hurling massive mountains of ice, like inimical battering-rams, against the ships. Buchan knew that between the implacable tenacity of the pack and the fury of the wind no ship could find a likely path. He abandoned all hope of sailing to the north. He was grateful that Fair Haven harbor offered a safe retreat where the badly battered ships could be repaired. It took a month to make them safe for the homeward voyage, a month that they spent in discarding the worthless Phipps chart and drawing up the first well-surveyed map of northwestern Spitsbergen. They returned to England having failed of their objective, as had Hudson and Phipps before them.

Meanwhile the *Isabella* and the *Alexander*, under the command of Captain John Ross, with Lieutenant Parry as second, headed for the bay Baffin had discovered two centuries before. This bay, forgotten by subsequent generations, was dubiously noted on Daines Barrington's map * as "according to the relation of W. Baffin in 1616, but not now believed." Whatever Ross's shortcomings, it was he who restored that body of water to northern charts and with it the good name and glory of Baffin. Sailing northward along the west coast of Greenland,

* Second edition, 1818.

he reached as far as Melville Bay before his ships were beset. The short time that they were part of the pack was one of constant danger. Ross noted how the pressure of the ice increased until "it became very doubtful whether the ship would be able to sustain it; every support threatened to give way, the beams in the hold began to bend; and the iron tanks settled together. . . . When it seemed impossible for us to bear the accumulated pressure much longer, the hull rose several feet; while the ice, which was more than six feet thick, broke against the sides, curling back on itself." [4] The movement of the pack forced the two ships toward each other, threatening to smash them together, when all at once— "At this eventful instant . . . the force of the ice seemed exhausted; the two fields [of ice] suddenly receded." [4] The danger, for the time being, was over.

Rounding Cape York, they saw the crimson snow * that streaked the cliffs of Cape Dudley Digges like streams of blood. They stopped long enough for a landing-party to examine this spectacular phenomenon and then, continuing northward, spied a party of Eskimos coming toward them over the ice. Again they stopped, this time to exchange greetings with a tribe isolated for centuries, cut off from all contact with the other Greenland peoples, their habitable valleys islanded by impassable seas of ice. To them Ross gave the name of Arctic Highlanders, and he studied their way of living, their manner of dress, their weapons, dog-sledges, and knowledge and use of meteoric iron. This tribe, always helpfully minded, was to play *deus ex machina* to more than one expedition. It was the tribe made famous by Peary as the Etah Eskimos.

But the Admiralty had not sent Ross out to examine the "red snow" or to study the Arctic Highlanders. He was in command of two ships with orders to search for the Northwest Passage and to ascertain whether it was to be found by way of one of the three great waterways Baffin was said to have pointed out: Smith Sound, Jones Sound, and Lancaster Sound. In this he failed. For he passed too far to the south of Smith Sound to make certain if it were a channel, content merely to give the names of his ships to the two cliffs that mark its southern boundary—Capes Isabella and Alexander. Neither did he penetrate Jones Sound. But he did sail down the wide magnificent Lancaster Sound for some fifty miles until he "distinctly saw the land round the bottom of the bay, forming a chain of mountains connected with

* Protococcus—a rapidly multiplying unicellular plant filled with chlorophyll-green cytoplasm, which often changes to red by exposure. *P. nivalis* is the well-known "red snow" that frequently and swiftly covers large tracts of snow in Arctic or alpine regions.

those which extended along the north and south side." [4] An unfortunate fancy, a sad mistake. His second in command, Parry, did not see those mountains and begged him to push on. But Ross turned back—turned back for home when he should have kept on. Had he sailed on, he would not have returned to his country amid a chorus of dissatisfied voices. England felt that he had failed. Everything he had accomplished was forgotten in a general disapproval. His valuable series of magnetic, meteorological, and hydrographic observations (he invented the deep-sea clam to further his study of the flora and fauna), his confirmation of Baffin's discoveries, his extending Lancaster Sound, all counted as nothing before his failure. And England, which had only just sent Napoleon into exile, did not choose to brook a failure. Within a month after the *Alexander* and the *Isabella* had returned, preparations for another expedition were under way. Ross, discredited, stayed at home, watching the brilliant success of the young Parry, who dared, who persevered, who won the laurels that Ross might have worn.

Everyone was certain that the much sought channel leading directly to Bering Strait opened from Lancaster Sound. The two isolated points of Hearne and Mackenzie now seemed very near at hand.

Parry—later Sir Edward Parry—was one of the great Arctic explorers. When he was given the command, he was not thirty, though he had already been in the navy fifteen years. He was more than a good sailor and an accomplished officer with a special interest in hydrography and nautical astronomy: he was a masterly navigator. His was the perfect combination of fearlessness and caution; he knew when to take risks and when to play safe. He was an athlete whose hobby was playing the violin, an actor, a young man easily lionized, who yet remained unspoiled. Above all, he had the knack of organization and administration; he was a genius at leading men. Small wonder that Lady Luck was on his side. The characteristic qualities of youth hover over the expedition of 1819. Parry in the *Hecla* had with him Lieutenant Sabine, "the most persistent and successful magnetic observer of his day," who was of his own age, while the other officers ranged from seventeen to twenty-three. A similarly young group served under Lieutenant Liddon, in charge of the *Griper*.

Both ships were provisioned for three years, stocked, in addition to the regular fare of meats and soups, with lemon juice, vinegar, pickles, sauerkraut, and herbs to serve as antiscorbutics. They sailed from England in May 1819; sailed to advance the knowledge of geography and navigation and kindred sciences—a beckoning goal on a distant horizon, a cause to which youth could respond whole-heartedly.

By the 21st of July Parry had worked his way up the Greenland coast to Sanderson's Hope. There he himself climbed into the crow's-nest and looked westward toward Lancaster Sound. Ahead lay eighty miles of heavy ice, the treacherous "middle pack." Around him he counted eighty-eight towering icebergs. Undaunted, he ventured to risk the crossing. His men cheered his courageous decision. Fortune was with him, and he forced his way through safely. A week later—more than a month sooner than Ross—he was at the entrance to the sound. In front of him lay open water, with never a suspicion of an encircling chain of mountains. The rocky coasts rose out of the water like a gigantic wall. A fresh wind carried the ships westward into the unknown.

Lancaster Sound, the waterway along which he sailed, is like a wide metropolitan boulevard leading to a great square: to the west it becomes Barrow Strait, which terminates in the expanse of Melville Sound. Southward from this highway open three streets: Prince Regent Inlet, Peel Sound, and McClintock Channel. Melville Sound has but two outlets to the west: McClure Strait and Prince of Wales Strait, ice-congested alleyways that connect it with Beaufort Sea, the open polar sea. He named the many islands he passed: those to the north of Lancaster Sound were North Devon, Cornwallis, Bathurst, and Melville; those to the south were Cockburn, North Somerset, Prince of Wales, and Banks. All the islands tied by those waterways constitute the Parry Archipelago. It was this system of thoroughfares that Parry and his successors discovered and explored.

After sailing a hundred and fifty miles due west on Lancaster Sound, Parry saw ice ahead. Hoping to avoid it, he penetrated Prince Regent Inlet until a warning ice blink made him retrace his way. Once again on Lancaster Sound, he found that the ice had opened the path to the west. He noted Wellington Channel to the north, but did not explore it. His way lay to the west, and to the west he sailed through Barrow Strait to Melville Sound. By September he "had the satisfaction of crossing the meridian of 110 degrees west from Greenwich . . . by which His Majesty's ships under my orders became entitled to the sum of 5000 pounds, being the reward offered . . . to such of His Majesty's subjects as might succeed in passing thus far to the westward within the Arctic Circle."[5] From where he was he could see McClure Strait (then called Banks Strait), the last passageway leading to the hoped-for open polar sea. But he could not reach it; heavy ice lay ahead. Behind him his course lay past bleak

THE
NORTH GEORGIA GAZETTE,

PER · FRETA · HACTENUS · NEGATA ·

AND
WINTER CHRONICLE.

N°. XIX—MONDAY, MARCH 6, 1820.

To the EDITOR *of the* Winter Chronicle.

THE cry of Reform having reached even to North Georgia, I shall request of you to exert your interest with Z in my behalf, trusting that the commiseration which my case must excite, will induce him to adopt measures for effecting its speedy amendment. You must know then, that I am very fond of telling a good story, or what is technically called " spinning a yarn ;" have doubled the Cape, been at Pulo Penang, Palambang, Tanjong, Goonting, Mangalore, Cannanore, and most of the pulo's, bangs and ores in the Indian and China seas.

What I have to complain of is this—having finished what I believe to be a very marvellous story, up rises one of these gentlemen, whom I shall distinguish by the appellation of a walking phenomenon, who, not having doubled the Cape, is not a privileged man, and relates something similar, but three times more extraordinary, and immediately robs me of that awe and admiration which we Cape men are alone entitled to.

Now, Mr. Editor, I'll leave it to your impartial judgment, whether my case does not deserve notice. Pray, do all you can for me with Z, and use your editorial influence and authority to lay these unqualified wonder-mongers.

I am, Sir,
Your obedient Servant,
NATHAN LONG-BOW.

To the EDITOR *of the* Winter Chronicle.

MY DEAR SIR—Captivated by the delicacy, the exquisite sentiment, and the tender-

Facsimile of a Page of the North Georgia Gazette
From Parry's JOURNAL OF A VOYAGE FOR THE DISCOVERY OF THE N.W.
PASSAGE IN 1819–20.

islands and barren rocky coasts; before him the land was covered with verdure and alive with game. But the season was late; young ice was fast sealing the water; further progress became impossible. At Melville Island, in the shelter of Winter Harbour, he made ready for the onrushing winter night.

That wintering is remarkable for the great care Parry took to promote good health, high spirits, and comfort among his men. He used wagon-cloth to cover the top decks so that they would have a place to exercise regularly in all sorts of weather. The same oven that daily baked fresh bread heated their quarters. Beer was brewed—except when the cold was so extreme as to prevent fermentation. Every week the men were examined, and every week the bedding was thoroughly aired. Not content with these physical details, Parry made provision for mental relaxation, aiming to eliminate despair as he had scurvy. A school was formed to teach the men to read and write. Captain Sabine edited a weekly, the *North Georgia Gazette and Winter Chronicle*, for the amusement of the officers, and they in turn amused the men. Fortnightly a farce that had had a successful run in London was given. Christmas was celebrated by a special dinner and an operetta, *Northwest Passage*. Pleasantly and quickly the months slipped by. And all the while, like the beat of a metronome through a jolly mazurka, various scientific observations went on.

With the return of warm weather the men were able to saw the ships out of the ice. In June Parry set out with four others on an expedition to explore the interior of Melville Island. In this he was the first to extend a sea quest by a land expedition. He improvised a cart on which they transported provisions and supplies.* They traveled at night and slept during the warmth of the day, reaching the northern shore of the island in a week. On the return they kept to the west, passing through "one of the pleasantest and most habitable spots [we have seen] in the Arctic," [5] where moss covered the earth and dwarf willows, saxifrage, and ranunculus grew. They shot deer, hares, ptarmigan, musk-ox, ducks, and geese to supplement their scant larder. They returned to the ships after having been gone a fortnight. This modest little expedition was "the first naval Arctic travelling of modern times." [6]

By the beginning of August the ships were free to sail out of Winter Harbour. Westward! was the cry. But McClure (Banks) Strait to the west was jammed from shore to shore by a wall of solid ice, ice-floes fifty feet thick, on top of which high hummocks reared. Fearlessly Parry tried to force a way through; again and again he charged

* The tracks of this cart were clearly seen by McClintock thirty years later.

the dangerous pack. His courage and skill did not avail against the implacable ice. And on the other side of McClure Strait lay the open Beaufort Sea and the easy attainment of his goal.

Parry sailed for home.

The nation cheered him for his memorable work. Not only had his ships carried the flag more than halfway round the earth, high within the Arctic Circle, not only had he discovered vast new lands—he sighted nearly every one of the large Arctic islands in the Western Hemisphere—but he had opened Lancaster Sound to the whalers, in itself worth thousands of pounds annually. As exciting as Parry's achievement had been the work of Captain Sabine, who had observed at one place, as the ships sailed westward along the sound, the needle of the compass point due south instead of due north. They had sailed to the north of the North Magnetic Pole!

Active preparations were immediately made to send Parry out on another expedition.

He was convinced that no passageway could be made in the high latitude he had tried, that farther south, along the coast of Arctic America, the ice-pack would not be so heavy, and that there, along the path pointed out by Hudson, in the region of Middleton's Frozen Strait and Repulse Bay, a way might be found. Parry's assumption was based on hope alone, for the maps of North America still showed only the two isolated doubtful points set by Hearne and Mackenzie. (The land expedition commanded by Franklin, which had started at the same time that Parry sailed, had not yet returned.) The *Hecla* was made ready, and in place of the outworn *Griper* the *Fury*, an exact twin of the *Hecla*, was built. Thus Parry applied the basic idea underlying the new industrial methods; he had his two ships built "precisely alike . . . so that any article belonging to either . . . might be transferred from ship to ship, and at once applied to its proper use, without selection, trial, or alteration of any kind." [7] Several improvements were made in the equipment: a tank was built over the galley fire for melting snow for additional water, the rations per man were increased, and so on; and in May 1821 the ships weighed anchor for the northwest.

As Parry sailed down Hudson Strait, he had occasion time and again to appreciate the precision of Baffin's observations. He reached Frozen Strait and by skillful navigation made his way through to Repulse Bay, which he examined thoroughly. He proved conclusively that this was a landlocked bay, not a route to the west. But he spent a valuable fortnight in so doing. Heading northward, Parry meticu-

"The Crews of H.M.S. Hecla & Griper *cutting into Winter Harbour, Septr. 26th 1819."*

"H.M. Ships Hecla & Griper *in Winter Harbour."* THE TOP DECKS WERE COVERED OVER SO THAT THE MEN WOULD HAVE A PLACE TO EXERCISE IN ALL SORTS OF WEATHER.

Both from Parry's JOURNAL OF A VOYAGE . . . 1819–20.

"A Winter View in the Athapuscow Lake, by Saml. Hearne, 1771."

Hearne's JOURNEY TO THE NORTHERN OCEAN.

They towed the boat safely up all the rapids and falls.

Franklin's NARRATIVE OF A SECOND EXPEDITION . . . 1825-7.

lously searched every inlet from which a passage might open, but in vain. Winter set in and he was forced to stop on Melville Peninsula.

This winter was passed much as the previous one had been: the scientific observations were carried on; the school was well attended; the theatricals were more splendid, augmented by magic-lantern shows. And this year the men were further occupied and delighted by the arrival of an Eskimo tribe. A brisk trade was carried on—needles and knives, beads and mirrors exchanged for skins and walrus ivory— and seal and walrus hunts were organized. These simple and kindly natives became their friends. The Eskimos drew crude but effective maps that gave the general lie of Melville Peninsula, picturing the narrow neck of Rae Isthmus to the south, the outline of Committee Bay to the west, and the existence of a strait to the north. As soon as the light began to return, Parry sent out several parties on land trips, and their findings confirmed the essential truth of the natives' topographical information. On these trips, for the first time, explorers adopted Eskimo sledges and snowshoes for hauling and walking. In July the ships were sawed out of the ice, and by August the water was open for sailing. Steering to the north, Parry came to the strait— which he named Fury and Hecla Strait after the ships—and followed it to its western end. There the water was covered with a still unbroken sheet of ice, and there at Igloolik, the Eskimo name, he decided to winter, hoping that another season's work would reveal a second channel leading westward. (Not until a decade later did Ross discover how far into the Arctic the mainland of America stretched in the Peninsula of Boothia.) In the third season Parry turned eastward for home. His men were enfeebled and sick; the doctors were adamant in their counsel, and wisely he listened to them.

The discovery of Fury and Hecla Strait, a waterway to the west, was the silver lining that shone through the dark cloud of failure. England applauded her youthful hero and eagerly made preparations for a third voyage that he was to command. The *Fury* and the *Hecla* were thoroughly overhauled and provisioned; the same corps of officers was assigned to aid him. This time Parry planned to sail from Lancaster Sound down Prince Regent Inlet, sighted on his first expedition. He was certain that thus he could reach the western end of Fury and Hecla Strait and from there continue successfully to the west.

The season of 1824 was an unusually bad one. The ice on Baffin Bay was so tightly packed that it took forty days of poking and pushing, twisting and dodging—desperate thrusts—to reach Lancaster Sound.

"As the crossing of Baffin Bay had of itself unexpectedly occupied nearly the whole of one season," [8] even though Lancaster Sound was found to be entirely free from ice, the season was so far advanced that young ice was already setting on the water. They were forced to winter at Port Bowen, on the eastern shore of Prince Regent Inlet. "This spot was the most barren I ever saw," [8] a perfect sample of that desolate shore. Land trips were made in the early spring to chart the coastline. By the end of July the ice had thawed sufficiently to allow them to cross to the western shore. They sailed southward, groping through heavy fogs. Suddenly a strong wind blew the fog away. But it also drove the ice from the middle of the channel toward them, pinning them against the shore. The *Fury* was nipped, then hurled upon the beach. No sooner had the men worked her off than she was beaten and beached again— again and again, until she was a mass of gaping leaks, and her crew were worn out manning the pumps. Parry decided to land her stores, in the hope of lightening her so that they could heave her over and mend the keel. But she lay broken beyond hope of repair. He gave the order to abandon her and, leaving the supplies he did not need, took all the men on the *Hecla* and sailed for England.

This was Parry's last attempt to search for the Northwest Passage. The start had been blessed with dazzling success, but only the snarling of a malevolent and savage nature was heard at the end—malevolent savagery that had set at naught another English expedition that same year. Captain Lyon, who had commanded the *Hecla* on Parry's second voyage, had been dispatched in the refitted *Griper* to carry out a piece of exploration suggested by Parry. Lyon had been instructed to winter at Repulse Bay, cross the Rae Isthmus by sledge, and examine the body of water that lay to the west (Committee Bay), of which the Eskimos had spoken. But he never reached Repulse Bay, for in trying to push through Roe's Welcome the *Griper* was so tossed and battered by ferocious seas, smashed by fields of ice, overwhelmed by furious gales—the ice jammed the rudder right up into the ship—that he was forced to make for home. It was an achievement in itself that Lyon was able to bring his ship back with all hands safe.

These last two expeditions discouraged the Admiralty from continuing the search. Public curiosity was satiated; the zeal of the government sank into apathy. The initiative now rested on private shoulders, on men who were willing and able to express their interest in the concrete terms of outfitting another expedition. Felix Booth, Sheriff of London, was the patron of the next venture (1829–33), which was to follow the route of Parry's third voyage, sailing down

Prince Regent Inlet, there to seek a passage to the western ocean. John Ross, shelved since his mistake of 1818, was placed in command. He had with him his nephew James Clark Ross, who had served under Parry on his three voyages. Together they made a happy combination, the caution and care of the older man manifesting itself in the way he brought his men through four Arctic winters, while the dash and energy of the younger secured for them the honor of locating the North Magnetic Pole. Their ship was the *Victory*, the first steam-driven ship to be used in northern waters. It was a paddle steamer, and so much valuable space was taken up by the engine that the stores and supplies had to be loaded on a sloop, which was to be towed. The debut of this new locomotive power was a dismal failure. "Even with a pressure of 45 pounds on the inch, we could never obtain more than fifteen strokes in the minute; and as it thence followed that the outer edge of the paddles had no greater velocity than five miles in the hour, that of the vessel could not possibly exceed three. The boilers also continued to leak, though we put dung and potatoes in them . . . the men were so fatigued by the work required at the extra pump" that, before the season was over, "we had ceased to regard her as aught but a sailing-vessel . . . the engine was not merely useless; it was a serious encumbrance; since it occupied, with its fuel, two-thirds of our tonnage." [9] This crude, useless, bulky engine was, with a sigh of relief, discarded. A far cry to the great steam icebreakers, the *Krassin* and *Malygin*!

Ross followed the route Parry had taken, across Lancaster Sound, down Prince Regent Inlet, to Fury Beach. The wrecked *Fury* had disappeared, but the stores Parry had left on the beach were intact and in good condition. Ross helped himself to canned meats, vegetables, powder, flour, sugar, "yet all we could stow away seemed scarcely to diminish the piles of canisters." [9] Southward he sailed, past Parry's farthest, tracing the coast of North Somerset to its southern tip, charting more than two hundred miles of shore. Once again Ross's eyes played tricks on him; once again he surmised when he should have investigated; he passed "Brentford Bay," now known as Bellot Strait. He failed to detect that this was the waterway to the west, dividing the northernmost point of continental America from the Parry Archipelago. He missed this link in the Northwest Passage. The land to the south of "Brentford Bay," whose desolate coast he followed to Felix Harbour, where he wintered, he named Boothia Felix in honor of his patron.

A large party of Eskimos built their winter village near the *Victory*, friendly contact was established with them, and the months passed quickly and pleasantly. To the Englishmen, clad neatly in blue jackets and trousers, wearing Welsh wigs and carpet boots, the superstructure of furs worn by the natives was a source of unending comment. Even so were the precision and celerity with which they erected their circular snow-houses that boasted of windows made of thin, translucent pieces of ice. Like the Eskimos Parry had met, these Boothians knew their country and were able to depict it. Ross learned from them that Boothia Felix was connected with the mainland by a narrow neck of land. A series of land trips undertaken by James Clark Ross, in which the Eskimos aided, proved the truth of their statements. From the magnetic observations made on these sledging-trips James Clark Ross was certain that the North Magnetic Pole was near by.

Spring and summer passed, and still the *Victory* was fast in the ice. The next winter James Clark Ross set out, determined to locate the exact spot of the North Magnetic Pole.* On the low and unimpressive western coast, on the last day of May 1831, he saw his needle dip to 89° 59′ while the horizontal needle was totally inactive. There he erected a cairn. He wished that a "place so important had possessed more of mark or note . . . and I could have pardoned anyone among us who had been so romantic or absurd as to expect that the magnetic pole was an object as conspicuous and mysterious as the fabled mountain of Sindbad, that it was even a mountain of iron, or a magnet as large as Mont Blanc. But Nature had here erected no monument to denote the spot which she had chosen as the centre of one of her great and dark powers." [9] He had to "be content in noting by mathematical numbers and signs, as with things of far more importance in the terrestrial system, what we could but ill distinguish in any other manner." [9]

For two winters the *Victory* lay in Felix Harbour, held imprisoned by the ice, and in those years James Clark Ross covered great stretches by land trips. It was he who first sighted to the west of Boothia Felix the outline of King William Land and explored it beyond its northern tip, Cape Felix, to Victory Point on the west coast. But because of a covering of heavy ice and snow, he failed to note that he had crossed a narrow strait separating these two low-lying shores. This error in observation was to spell tragedy to the last Franklin Expedition. For two years the *Victory* was held in Felix Harbour, and every change of breeze, every shower of rain, every movement of the ice was viewed with the hope of release. Though they were secure from the evils of

---

* Unlike the mathematically determined point known as the North Pole, the North Magnetic Pole, concerned with terrestrial magnetism, is an indefinite, non-fixed area. As of April 1947 the center of this area was at about 76°N, 103°W.

cold and hunger and though they were in sound health and good mind, they were prey to an endless ennui. "We were weary for want of occupation, for want of thought, and (why should I not say it?) for want of society. Today was as yesterday, and as was today, so would be tomorrow." [9]

At last their hope was rewarded: the *Victory* was moved. Slowly they sailed northward, amid much ice. Too slowly, for they were caught by the ice before they could reach Lancaster Sound. During the third winter, spent on board the ship in Victory Harbour, scurvy, dreaded and debilitating, threatened them. Their one chance to escape was to abandon ship and pull their small boats over the ice to Fury Beach, where necessary provisions could be obtained, and then sail on across the inlet until they could be picked up by a whaler. At Fury Beach they found three of the *Fury's* boats, and in these the Rosses, with picked crews, reconnoitered ahead to examine the state of Lancaster Sound. Hope of getting home that season was given up when they caught a view of the channel jammed with ice. They returned to Fury Beach, where a house had been built and where the fourth winter—a miserable one—was passed. When spring came, the ice opened and they pushed forward. In their tiny boats they rowed and sailed northward to the sound. They were weak and despondent. Fair weather lightened their troubles. At last, off Navy Board Inlet, they saw a sail in the offing. A ship! Saved! They burned wet powder to signal her. It was not seen. The sail bellied out in a brisk breeze, and the ship began pulling away from them. And then the wind died down. Hope and despair gave them strength to devour the intervening distance. The ship hove to. A boat was lowered. It came alongside. Ross asked the name of the ship. "The *Isabella* of Hull, once commanded by Captain Ross!" [9]

All England turned out to welcome the men of the *Victory*. Ross had redeemed his good name. His expedition had achieved a unique record in having passed four winters in the Arctic with but three fatalities (two from non-Arctic causes); the northern extremity of continental America had been determined; five hundred miles of adjacent country had been charted, a new land discovered; the series of continuous observations was the most valuable ever made. They had located the North Magnetic Pole.

In the fifteen years since the double-headed expedition of 1818 had sailed from England to conquer the Arctic, the spirit of ignorant bravado had changed to one of persistent research, where each little additional fact was important to the attainment of the final goal. As yet victory lay with the Arctic, but it was a Pyrrhic victory. For, despite the rebuffs and frustrations and retreats that man had suffered at the hands of nature, an increasingly precise knowledge was being gained. More and more black lines were drawn on what had been a blank; new lands and new waters were chartered. Bit by bit the puzzle was being put together. It was clear that before the invasion of the north could be successful, men must prepare the way thoroughly. England had learned the invaluable lesson of patience. At the instance of the Royal Geographical Society, the government commissioned Captain Back, who had proved his fine mettle in various land expeditions,* to attempt what Lyon had tried to do—to sail to Repulse Bay and proceed from thence overland—and by so doing to fill in the last link in the northern coast of America.

Back's ship was the *Terror*. He set out in June 1836, a year marked by unusual ice and intense cold, so that he was beset at the end of August, when Parry in the same latitude had enjoyed "almost the warmth of summer. . . . The rigour of a precocious winter [was] thrust upon us, at a moment when we were almost in sight of our port. . . . It was an omen. . . . To see open water within one hundred yards, and yet be unable to reach it was a type of the torment of poor Tantalus." [10] Every ingenious method, every ounce of strength was tried—but in vain. "Nothing was left but to submit." [10] From September, when they were caught, through the long winter and the long spring, the *Terror* was assaulted and battered and twisted and pressed and strained and heaved up and smashed down as the tides and winds toyed with the great ice-fields that held her. Any moment during those ten months might have been fatal as "moving towers of ice frowned on every side." [10] For four months the ship was stranded, high out of the water, on a huge floe, and when in the following summer it floated again, it was a mass of gaping leaks.

"I had waited for the verification of my apprehensions before I could bring myself to relinquish the object of my mission; but my last hope having now vanished—the ship crazy, broken, and leaky—I no longer had a choice; and, accordingly, assembling the crew on the deck, I told them that they were now going home." [10] That homeward voyage! At times the rudder did not answer to the helm. The maddened ship staggered out of the fields of loose ice to pitch and roll in the high swells of the North Atlantic. The entire stern frame became more and more loosened, the fastenings and bolts rickety and twisted. Daily her speed slackened as she became sodden and heavy; the leaks gained on her; she was sinking; she was waterlogged; she was unmanageable, hysterical, after a year's bullying by Arctic ice.

* See pp. 112 ff.

Only just in time did the *Terror* reach the Irish coast, where she swooned on a sandy beach.

"It is not a little remarkable," wrote Back, "to reflect on the various ineffectual attempts that have been made by different commanders . . . to fill up the small blank on northern charts, between the bottom or south part of Regent's Inlet and Point Turnagain. Parry's and Franklin's achievements are too well known to require . . . eulogium from me; yet the former could not penetrate through Fury and Hecla Strait, and the latter found it impracticable . . . to proceed beyond Point Turnagain. Of Sir John Ross's eventful expedition all have heard. My own, in search of him, is also before the public. Captain Lyon, in trying to reach Repulse Bay by the Welcome, was baffled by a succession of bad weather and heavy gales; and now again, I, acting upon the united experience of most of the distinguished names just mentioned, under circumstances considered favourable, after getting nearly within sight of my port, am stopped by drift ice, at what is generally considered the very best period for navigating Polar Seas—am frozen fast, in Oct. 1836, at the entrance of Frozen Strait—and now, June 16th, am carried into Hudson's Strait, on the very same ice that originally begirt the ship, without having had it once in my power either to advance or retreat. In short, from north, south, east, and west, the attempt has been made, and in all equally without effect; and yet with a tolerably open season, the whole affair is within the accomplishment of six months." [10]

By Land

To John Franklin, commanding the *Trent* in the futile attempt to sail to the north of Spitsbergen in 1818, looking at the map of North America where its northern limits were provokingly blank except for the two widely separated points noted by Hearne and Mackenzie— to him, as to no one else, this was a situation that was unendurable. To know what that blank concealed, to chart in the northern shore of the New World, was to mean more to him than food and shelter, more than advancement and honors, more even than life. The magnitude of such an undertaking, the unflagging zeal with which he pursued it, his eventual success in the face of the most harrowing obstacles—all stamp him as one of the true, one of the most persistent Arctic explorers. His magnificent accomplishments heightened and intensified the tragedy of his death. Living, he was one of the most indefatigable, courageous, and undaunted of men; dead, his name became the battle-cry with which men of many nations attacked the hostile north.

In 1819—when Parry sailed on his first voyage—Franklin left for York Factory on Hudson Bay to commence his land explorations. With him were his friend Dr. Richardson, who was to have sole charge of the natural-history observations, two midshipmen, Back and Hood, and Hepburn, a sailor. Men and supplies were to be furnished in America; the governors of both the Hudson's Bay Company and the Northwest Company had pledged their aid in furthering this task of surveying the coast eastward from the mouth of the Coppermine River. The slender volume—a minor classic in the field of exploration—written by Samuel Hearne fifty years before contained all the available information about their objective; however slim the material, however obscure the facts, the tremendous difficulties in store were made sufficiently plain.

Samuel Hearne had been sent out in 1769 by the Hudson's Bay Company to seek a river that Indian rumors represented as flowing through banks of copper to the northern sea. His traveling-companions were Indian guides, his provisions were scant, his equipment negligible; he intended "living off the country" like a native. This meant "either all feasting or all famine; sometimes we had too much, seldom just enough, frequently too little, and often none at all. It will only be necessary to say that we have fasted many times two whole days and nights, twice upwards of three days, and once near seven days, during which we tasted not a mouthful of anything, except a few cranberries, water, scraps of old leather, and burnt bones." [11] And on this uncertain fare he snowshoed mile upon mile, pulling a little sledge on which he had loaded all his necessaries.

Hearne's first two starts were unsuccessful. The first time, deserting guides forced him to return to Fort Prince of Wales on the Churchill River; he returned the second time—after having been gone nine months—to replace his broken quadrant. A fortnight's rest, and he was off again. That he was to be successful on this third attempt was due largely to the friendship and organizing genius of the Indian chief Manatobie. The chief had plenty of women in his party—he never traveled without from five to eight wives—for, as he said, "one of them can carry, or haul as much as two men can do." Manatobie's plans took into account certain primary facts: their route led from the forest belt across the barrens, and they would face a long winter and a short summer. He timed their northward trek to coincide with that of the migratory caribou; before leaving the forest he provided himself with birch bark and wood to make small, light canoes to use in crossing lakes and streams, with tent-poles and snowshoe frames, with skins prepared to be made into clothes, footgear, or tents, with sinew for sewing, and with pemmican to sustain them on hurried dashes. He and his tribe—braves, squaws, and children—set out with Hearne in December 1770, trekked for seven months across hundreds of miles to the northwest, and reached the Coppermine River, which rose close to the Arctic Circle. There dwelt their traditional enemy, the Eskimo. Here the canoes were assembled and here the women and children were left, while Hearne horrified but powerless, surrounded by braves happy in their war-paint, paddled northward. Stealthily they advanced toward the Eskimos, stole upon them, and massacred the whole tribe. Triumphant chants sounded as they went on. Around them treeless hills cut by marshes supported herds of deer and musk-ox and a varied multitude of birds; salmon flecked the river, and beaver dams made an intricate pattern, linking islands and shoals. At last they came to the Arctic Sea. Hearne looked out across its icy covering to an unbroken horizon. Then he turned back. On his homeward journey he visited a native mine where copper lay gleaming on the surface.

Hearne by his exploration had set at rest the sanguine theory that, to the south of the Arctic Sea and parallel with it, a strait joining the Atlantic and Pacific Oceans cut through the wilderness of North America. Because his scientific instruments were simple and his observations few, his work was either disparaged or discredited. Not until Franklin had retraced his route was Hearne's intrepid pioneering confirmed.* In addition to locating the mouth of the Coppermine— a long journey made mainly within the sub-Arctic—Hearne's importance rests on the fact that he was the first of the Hudson's Bay men to bring their methods into Arctic exploration. Parry, Ross, Back, Franklin, all were British naval officers who approached the Arctic as a challenge, a hazardous sport, who thought in terms of men *against* the Arctic. Hearne, and the other Hudson's Bay men after him— Mackenzie, Simpson, and Rae—had a radically different orientation

* But not without some residue of doubt. E. A. Boadway, geologist and aviator for the Dominion Explorers, Ltd., during 1928–30 covered the territory explored by Hearne and says of the latter's journey: "North of Red Rock Lake there is such a wide discrepancy between Hearne's account and the natural features of the country, especially certain striking topographical phenomena which Hearne does *not* mention, that grave doubts are raised as to his even having gone beyond that lake. His account of the country between that point and the Arctic Ocean may probably have been gained from native reports."

and different methods bred of a different background: to open up new country was their business. They knew that wherever there were people—Indian or Eskimo—they could go if they would live as the aborigines lived, travel as they traveled, copy them faithfully in adapting to new surroundings. Donning the garments bequeathed them by the French voyageurs, the Hudson's Bay men pushed north and west. They went light, relying on game large or small, on fish, on berries, and they ate the same food that sustained the Indians; they could make a canoe or paddle it or break a snowshoe trail as well as their Indian friends; they were as much at home in the great north country as the Cree and Chipewyans whose home it was. This method—men *adapt* to the Arctic—which was to become known as "living off the country," had its inception when the Hudson's Bay fur-traders carried their techniques into the Arctic.

Hearne, at the far-off end of a long trail, had set down a point where the Coppermine River joined the Arctic Sea. What had been his goal was merely the starting-place for Franklin, who hoped to chart a goodly stretch of the Arctic coast. Franklin, arriving at York Factory the end of August 1819, was off for Fort Chipewyan on Lake Athabasca within ten days, though winter was expected daily. It was almost a thousand miles to Fort Chipewyan. At first they paddled and towed the canoes up swift, treacherous rapids and through swamps; later, when winter had covered the land with snow and stilled the streams under ice, and the cold was so intense as to freeze the newly made tea before they could drink it, they advanced on snowshoes, guiding the dog-sledges. "The task of beating a track [with snowshoes] through the deep snow for the dogs was so very fatiguing that each of the men took the lead in turn. . . . Soon after we encamped the snow fell heavily, which was an advantage by its affording us an additional covering to our blankets . . . the suffering [snowshoeing] occasions can be faintly imagined by a person who thinks upon the inconvenience of marching with a weight of between two and three pounds constantly attached to galled feet, and swelled ankles." [12] Before Franklin could explore, he first had literally to learn how to walk.

A thousand miles and then half a thousand miles more, the long trail led from Fort Chipewyan to the northern side of Great Slave Lake—the old Fort Providence—and thence to Fort Enterprise on Winter Lake, drained by the Coppermine River, where Franklin built his winter quarters. It was almost two years before he was ready to descend the river and begin his real work. His party included Canadian voyageurs—among whom were Michel, who was to act as Iroquois interpreter, and three of the men's wives, who were to sew for the expedition—and a tribe of Indians, whose chief, Akaitcho, promised Franklin to hunt and lay in a supply of food against the party's return to Fort Enterprise. On this promise Franklin counted.

The Indians turned back at the place where the Eskimo massacre had been perpetrated before Hearne's eyes. "Several human skulls which bore the marks of violence, and many bones . . . strewn about the ground" [12] earned for the spot the name of Bloody Fall on Franklin's map. A few hours after passing that gruesome spot the explorers came to the Arctic Sea. Behind them lay 334 miles of river, of which a hundred was difficult portage. In his chapter "Navigation of the Polar Sea in Two Canoes as far as Point Turnagain, to the Eastward, a distance exceeding Five Hundred and Fifty Miles," [12] Franklin tells of how for five weeks they pushed to the east, taking observations constantly as they traced every cape and island and bay. In frail birch canoes they paddled those many miles, beating a hazardous trail between the hostility of a rock-bound coast and the menace of waters armed with massive ice-floes; during the entire time they had to exhort and reassure the Canadians, who, never having seen the sea, had but one desire—to get away from it. On they went, on until the 18th of August, when at Point Turnagain Franklin felt it was time to start back for their winter quarters. He decided that he dared not risk returning along that rocky coast at a season when gales prevail, and he put in at Arctic Sound. He planned to paddle as far as possible up the Hood River, then, constructing smaller canoes out of the material of the larger ones—to make the portages lighter and easier—to strike across the Barren Lands for 149 miles to Fort Enterprise. Once there, his troubles would disappear, for Akaitcho had promised to have supplies on hand.

In high spirits the party left the valley of the Hood River to march across the Barren Lands. In the face of oncoming winter it was a stony wilderness where a sturdy lichen, tripe-de-roche, was all that grew; a sterile plain that afforded neither shelter from the stabbing wind nor wood with which to build a comforting fire. Their scant supplies gave out; rarely did the hunters bring in game. Tripe-de-roche became their only food—an unpalatable, noxious weed that produced in many an enfeebling diarrhea. For days they plodded on, twenty starving men, abandoning more and more of their equipment, desperately burning the canoes for a little warmth. The country grew more rugged, stony hills cut by stony ravines—obstacles that delayed them, exhausted them. At last, after a month of starving and stumbling, they reached the Coppermine River. It would have to be crossed before they could get to the fort, and not a canoe was left.

Dr. Richardson offered to "swim across the stream with a line, and haul the raft [made from willows that lined the bank] over . . . when he got a short distance from the bank, his arms became benumbed . . . still he persevered, and turning on his back, had nearly gained the opposite bank when his legs also became powerless. . . . We instantly hauled on the line . . . and [he] was gradually drawn ashore in an almost lifeless state." [12] Wrapped in blankets and warmed before a good fire of willows, he recovered. "I cannot describe what everyone felt at beholding the skeleton which Dr. Richardson's debilitated frame exhibited. When he was stripped the Canadians simultaneously exclaimed, 'Ah, que nous sommes maigres.' " [12] Finally they succeeded in making a tiny canoe in which they reached the other side.

Back meanwhile pushed ahead for the last few miles to find the Indians and prepare things at the fort, for some of the men had come to the end of their strength. They fell at every step; then they were unable to stand; at the end they could not even crawl a few hundred feet to the fire. Hood was among the weakest, and Richardson offered to stay behind with him and Hepburn. The next day Michel and three Canadians turned back for the rest camp, but Franklin and the others kept on, and in four days, to their great joy and relief, reached the fort. They shouted. There was no answer. They entered. It was empty. No provisions. No trace of Indians. Slowly, unwillingly, their hearts drank in the bitterness of this neglect. "The whole party shed tears, not so much for our own fate, as for that of our friends whose lives depended entirely on our sending immediate relief from this place." [12] A note left by Back was their only hope, for he wrote that he had pushed on to find the Indians and, failing that, would walk to Fort Providence for help, his waning energy permitting. Nothing remained but to wait and hope.

Day by day their vitality shrank. They gnawed discarded deerskins and bones found among the ashes. It seemed as if their very blood must freeze as they lay before an ineffectual fire while huge gaps in the walls let in the 20°-below-zero temperature. Noises, voices. Hope gave them the strength to get to their feet. "*Ah, le monde,*" cried the Canadians. It must be the rescuers. The door opened. Richardson and Hepburn stood there alone, and Franklin knew that Hood and the others had perished. They had a ghastly story to tell. Michel, who had left Franklin with three companions, arrived alone at Richardson's camp. He told a plausible tale of how the others had died from exhaustion and starvation, though he seemed to be well fed and

strong. His actions became increasingly suspicious: when he went out
hunting, he carried a hatchet instead of the knife customarily used
for cutting up newly killed game, as though "he took it for the purpose of cutting up something he knew to be frozen" [12]—until Richardson and Hepburn were certain that he had killed his companions
and was waxing strong on this revolting fare. Daily he grew fatter,
and daily they were weaker. The ghastly climax came when they returned to camp one day, after gathering tripe-de-roche, to find that
Hood had been murdered. Wasted and defenseless, he had been shot
through the head, butchered. Plainly, the Canadian felt that the
starving Englishmen were completely in his power, while they knew
that they were too weak to resist an open attack. Their one chance to
survive lay in the death of Michel. Richardson shot him. Then he
and Hepburn set out for Fort Enterprise.

There they all waited—waited and sank slowly into the last stages
of starvation. Two of the Canadians died. More would have if help
had not arrived. Three Indians sent by Back came to their aid and
with infinite tenderness fed and cared for the white men, whose
emaciated bodies, sunken eyes, and sepulchral voices told a pitiable
story that needed no translating. One of them left to report to Akaitcho, while the other two, Crooked Foot and the Rat, "set about with
an amazing speed . . . cleared out the accumulation of dirt . . .
kept up large and attractive fires . . . and prevailed upon us to wash
and shave ourselves." [12] By the middle of November all were able to
travel slowly toward Fort Providence. There they found Back and
Akaitcho. Had Back not chanced on those three Indians, he must
surely have perished, for his strength was fast going and his food
consisted of a pair of leather trousers, a gun-cover, an old shoe, and
a handful of tripe-de-roche!

When they left for England the following spring, Akaitcho bade
them farewell and referred to their inadequate supplies as the source
of all their agonies. "The world goes badly, all are poor, you are
poor, the traders appear to be poor, I and my party are likewise poor;
and since the goods [that had been promised as payment to the Indians for their supplies] have not come in we cannot have them. I do
not regret having supplied you with provisions, for a Copper Indian
can never permit white men to suffer for want of food on his lands,
without flying to their aid. . . . It is the first time that the white
people have been indebted to the Copper Indian." [12] Graciously he
had refrained from telling Franklin what he was to learn, that he and
his men had starved and some died because the two rival trading-

companies—the Hudson's Bay Company and the Northwest Company—had been completely preoccupied with their own murderous feud.

If it is extraordinary and baffling that some men forfeit the pleasures of companionship, exiling themselves to lonely frontiers, it is hard to understand why Franklin, Back, Richardson, and Hepburn, having come out alive from the valley of the shadow of death, should, within three years of their arrival at home, return again to the place of their sufferings. Perhaps it was that their achievement mitigated past pains, or, more simply, that this was their way of life.

When Parry sailed for the third time to try to effect a Northwest Passage by way of Prince Regent Inlet, Franklin set out to co-operate with him by further land explorations. This time he, Back, Richardson, and a Mr. Kendall—replacing the murdered Hood—were to descend the Mackenzie River. The first two were to trace the coast westward as far as Icy Cape, where Beechey waited in the *Blossom* to greet Parry should he find his way to Bering Strait, while the others were to map the coast between the Mackenzie and the Coppermine. Again the faithful Hepburn served his officers. This time they made plans a full year in advance, in order that there should be no repetition of tragedy, and before Franklin left England he had definite news that all the preparatory steps had been meticulously executed. They even had three special boats built, light enough to carry over portages, shallow enough to sail through shoal waters, strong enough to stand up to the ice, and stable enough to bear "the concussions of waves in a rough sea." [13] Franklin intended that the shore of Arctic America should be a continuous known line from Point Turnagain to Cook's farthest, Icy Cape.

On the location and course of the Mackenzie River he had only the slim book written by Alexander Mackenzie to guide him. And in the report of that voyage made in 1789—Mackenzie had hoped to reach the Pacific by following a river that flowed northwestward from the Great Slave Lake—little more was stated than the bare fact that the author had followed it for a thousand miles to its mouth. Mackenzie was the second European to reach the American polar ocean, and the point noted by him on a chart was the second black dot to break the blank covering the American Arctic. This second precious fact beckoned reassuringly to Franklin.

Franklin and his party, arriving at Cumberland House, were greatly encouraged to learn that the necessary provisions and supplies were awaiting them at the designated places. At Fort Chipewyan they were greeted by their friend Akaitcho. A few days' rest, and they pushed on easily and quickly down the Great Slave River to Fort Resolution, across Great Slave Lake, and from there to the head-waters of the Mackenzie. They sailed past Fort Providence, down the river, past Fort Simpson, always northward, to Fort Norman, the furthermost reach of civilization.* Some six or seven weeks of navigating season still remained, time for reconnoitering and preparation. Besides the necessary Canadians, their party was augmented by Peter Dease, chief trader for the company, whose advice and good offices were of inestimable help. Franklin, with Kendall, sailed down the river as far as Ellice Island, where "the sea appeared in all its majesty, entirely free from ice." [13] Richardson crossed Great Bear Lake to determine where it was nearest the Coppermine River, marking the spot so that it would guide him the following year; and Back and Dease built Fort Franklin on Great Bear Lake and stocked it for the coming winter. Back had profited well by the terrible lesson of starvation and built enough fishing-stations to keep fifty Indians busy.

The months passed quickly, and in the small cosmopolis of Fort Franklin Englishmen, Scotchmen, Canadians, Eskimos, and Chipewyans, Dogrib, Hare, and Cree Indians all lived in harmony. June came, and the explorers were eager to be off. Dease remained behind to maintain the supply of food at the fort, lest there be a repetition of the bitter homecoming to barren Fort Enterprise. By July 4 the explorers had come to the mouth of the river and they separated, going their opposite ways. This time they were equipped with excellent boats and three months' provisions, not frail birch canoes and scant supplies. To ensure their cordial reception by both Eskimos and Indians, they had a trader's stock of beads, knives, and assorted trinkets.

Franklin's party was almost stopped at the start when their two boats were surrounded by a swarm of kayaks and umiaks from a large Eskimo village. The natives readily accepted their gifts, and that would have been all, had the receding tide not stranded the boats and left them helpless. When the Eskimos saw this, their desire for more trinkets prompted them to pillage. Franklin's main concern was "to prevent the loss of arms, oars, or masts, or anything on which the continuance of the voyage, or our personal safety depended." [13] Using their guns as clubs, the explorers struck heavily all about them, but with little result; they dared not fire, for they were "beset in such numbers, [that] the first blood we had shed would have been instantly revenged by the sacrifice of all our lives." [13] They had to wait

* All these forts were trading-posts of the Hudson's Bay Company, for the traders had quickly followed the path Mackenzie had blazed.

for the tide to release them. When the boats floated, they set sail. Several Eskimos pursued them—not to kill or harass, but to return items that had been stolen! They had been merely curious, playful. Never again—and they met with many more tribes of Eskimos—did the explorers have any but the most friendly encounters.

Their westward journey was frequently halted by heavy ice that tied the land to the horizon. They kept going whenever they could, through shoal water, dragging their boats over reefs, rowing in and out of drifting ice, lashed by gales and driving rains, tormented by clouds of mosquitoes; and not until a smothering fog imprisoned them did they stop. For six days they sat on the sand of Return Reef and waited. Navigating icy seas in a fog is suicidal, for a drifting piece of ice-floe has the power to wreck, and shoal water is calamitous. Had they not been detained, they must surely have got as far as Point Barrow, where they would have met with the advance party sent out by Beechey; the two parties were within 160 miles of each other. But half of August was gone; Franklin had no choice but to return to Fort Franklin and be content with having carefully charted 374 miles of new coast. They reached the fort at the end of September, having covered 1,980 miles over land and water. Richardson had preceded them.

Richardson and Kendall had a like story to tell. They had met with rapacious Eskimos (of whom Richardson notes that they are expert traders, "cautious not to glut the market by too great display of their stock in trade, producing only one article at a time and not attempting to outbid each other").[13] They had been troubled by shallow waters, gales, rains, fog, and mosquitoes. Attending to the work allotted them, they had rounded the jutting peninsula of Cape Bathurst and proceeded through Dolphin and Union Strait (named after their two boats), calling the land to the north Wollaston Land. They had gone as far as the mouth of the Coppermine. There they had left their boats and superfluous stores and started walking up the river, carrying a small canvas boat, *Walnut-Shell*, to serve as a ferry.

Franklin returned to England in the fall of 1827. In the decade since he had first entered the Arctic Circle, vast areas had been charted by land, and in this work he had played a large and important part. The coastline of Arctic America had been traced—save for those few miles separating Point Barrow and Foggy Island—from Alaska to Point Turnagain; the Coppermine and Mackenzie Rivers had been surveyed; Hearne and Mackenzie were at last recognized for the work they had done; and the great blank that Barrow had pictured in his map was cut and crossed by thousands of miles of intrepid exploring.

England recognized the importance of Franklin's achievements by knighting him; he was subsequently appointed Governor of Tasmania. His wife had died shortly after he left on his second land trip, and he now married again. Sir John and Lady Franklin will reappear in the annals of the Arctic—he as the hero in the most famous of all northern tragedies, she as the unwavering, unstinting heroine of the most far-flung of searches.

Merely to state that Hearne and Mackenzie and Franklin navigated the unknown lengths of the Coppermine and Mackenzie Rivers fails to do justice to their skill and daring. The initial descent of a great river necessitates a never failing wariness and resourcefulness. A quick, sure eye, lightning judgment, perfect control—all are needed to negotiate safely a river that, without warning, tears through canyons, becomes ensnarled in treacherous rapids, lunges down mighty cascades. The story of the next land expedition is an epic in the descent of rivers that cut their way through northern America to empty into the Arctic Sea.

The Rosses had steamed away in the *Victory* in 1829, and when after three years there was still no news of them the worst was feared. It was deemed impossible for Englishmen to survive four successive winters in such high latitudes. A private expedition was made ready to ascertain the fate of the Ross party. Back accepted the command and had with him the surgeon Dr. Richard King, two carpenters, and a shipwright. They set out in February 1833 for Great Slave Lake, to locate the headwaters of the tongue-twisting Thlew-ee-choh-desseth, or Great Fish River, which the Indians said flowed northeastward to the frozen sea, closely approximating the direction in which Ross had set out. The Hudson's Bay Company helped out by furnishing fifteen additional men, supplies, and food. Arriving at the eastern tip of Great Slave Lake, Back left half of the men to establish Fort Reliance for their wintering, while he pushed on to locate the Great Fish River. His preliminary survey was successful, and he returned to Fort Reliance to find it almost completed.

Fort Reliance had not been christened vainly; the Indians of that whole district relied entirely on Back to care for their aged, sick, and burdensome young during the long, hard winter. His modest outfit was swamped under the pitiful pressure of starving dependents; the fishery, while yielding plentifully, was too small to cope with the demands of this unplanned-for mob; and their misery was increased by the unusual severity of the winter. It was so cold that many times when Back washed his face before a fire, it was coated with ice before he could even dry it! The inhabitants of Fort Reliance were saved from starvation when their old friend Akaitcho arrived bringing a large supply of meat.

On May 13 a "single goose, the harbinger of summer, flew past the house." [14] Soon after this welcome sign came other news. A Hudson's Bay Company messenger made his way to their barren and desolate spot to tell Back of Ross's safe arrival in England. This radically altered the purpose of the expedition; but it did not change Back's determination to trace the Thlew-ee-choh-desseth. It would have been stupid to do nothing after having done so much.

Not until July were they ready to begin the actual descent. They soon learned that they had tackled a river whose maniacal ferocity of rapids and waterfalls was only here and there marked by a flash of calm. Often the river ran through deep defiles in whose settled gloom all that lived was the hollow roar of the water. Each yard involved struggle, every moment held a crisis. McKay, the steersman, stuck at his job, unruffled, asserting his mastery. The narrative is a breathtaking recital of continuous adventure, as when they came to a "succession of falls and cascades and whatever else is horrible in such 'confusion worse confounded' and . . . from the western shore issued another serpentine rapid and fall . . . while to the right there was the strife of surge and rock. . . . The space occupying the centre from the first descent to the island was full of sunken rocks of unequal heights, over which the rapid foamed and boiled and rushed with impetuous and deadly fury. At that part it was raised into an arch; while the sides were yawning and cavernous, swallowing huge masses of ice. . . . The portage was over scattered debris of the rocks . . . and afforded a rugged and difficult way to a single rock at the foot of the rapid, about a mile distant." [14] Unable to complete this portage—none of them thought of turning back—the only course left was to try the falls "whatever the consequences. . . . Every precaution that experience could devise was adopted; double lines to the bow and stern were held on shore by the most careful of the men, and McKay with another man took their station at each end of the boat with poles, to keep her from dashing against the rocks. Repeatedly did the strength of the current hurl the boat within an inch of destruction, and as often did these able and intrepid men ward off the threatened danger . . . the gallant fellows succeeded in guiding her down to the last falls." [14] Many times the madcap river threw itself into a paroxysm of falls, rapids, and eddies in the space of a few yards. Once McKay volunteered to ascend a peak to obtain the direction of the river and the nature of its course and saw "from the giddy height [that] the rapids below looked smooth and even as oil; and in that supposition . . . we pushed off and the next minute were in it. I shall never forget the instant of the first descent down . . . a steep hill. There was not a single break in the smoothness of the surface; but with such wild swiftness were we borne along that it required the very tug of life to keep the boat clear of the gigantic waves below, and we succeeded at last, only to be tossed about in the Charybdis of its almost irresistible whirlpools." [14]

Success was theirs when they "arrived at the mouth of the Thlew-ee-choh-desseth, which, after a violent and tortuous course of 530 geographical miles, running through an iron-ribbed country without a single tree on the whole of its banks, expanding into fine, large lakes with clear horizons most embarrassing to the navigator, and broken into falls, cascades and rapids to the number of no less than eighty-three in the whole, pours its waters into the Polar Sea." [14] But Back was not satisfied with only having mapped the river and the barren land it drained; he wanted to push westward along the coast as far as Point Turnagain, to extend Franklin's coastal survey. But it was impossible, for though the men were loaded as lightly as they could be, they sank up to their knees in the boggy soil at every step. Only the estuary and the large island of Montreal were mapped before they started back on the long homeward trail.

The Thlew-ee-choh-desseth is now known as the Back River.

Hudson's Bay Company

The horror and suffering experienced by the first Franklin land expedition had taught the Hudson's Bay Company a terrible lesson. They knew that in exploration half-hearted and inefficient co-opera-tion leads inevitably to disaster, and in subsequent expeditions they gave valuable and effective aid. Also they were not blind to the imme-diate advantages of the fine peltry brought in from the new territory that was being opened in the far north. There still remained to be explored the coastline from Franklin's farthest westward—Foggy Is-land—to Point Barrow, and on the east from Point Turnagain to Re-pulse Bay. The directors of the company undertook to have these unknown portions surveyed. Dease, the company's chief factor, who had smoothed and safeguarded Franklin's second journey, was put in charge of this work. He had as his second a much younger and most remarkable man, Thomas Simpson.

Simpson was an explorer who could translate an overwhelming resolution by amazing personal exertion into magnificent achievement. Back is a man to admire, Simpson one to marvel at. To the west of the Mackenzie he completed the desired survey; to the east he reached as far as King William Land, lying off the mouth of the Back River, and, but for his tragic and untimely death, he would have carried through his proposal to map as far as Fury and Hecla Strait. While Dease wintered at Fort Chipewyan, Simpson went south to the Red River settlement at Fort Garry, now Winnipeg, to brush up on his astronomy, making this side trip of thirteen hundred miles alone, through the dead of winter, covering on snowshoes as much as fifty miles a day, rejoining Dease on the very day he had planned.

Dease had built the two twenty-four-foot boats, the *Castor* and the *Pollux,* in which they were to travel. He planned to go down the Mackenzie and map westward as far as Point Barrow, return to winter quarters, which were to be prepared at Great Bear Lake, and the following spring descend the Coppermine River and map eastward as far as the mouth of the Back River.

They started early in 1837 and by the beginning of July reached the Arctic Sea, saluting it with joyous cheers. During the next two weeks they were following the coast Franklin had explored and, like him, they were bothered by fog, slowed by shoals, blocked by ice. By the end of that month they had arrived at Return Reef near Foggy Island; before them lay the unmapped stretch and the real work. But the going had been hard and slow and precarious. It was so cold that the fog turned to sleet, and most of the men suffered from severe colds and bad sore throats. Simpson would not give up. He determined to walk to Point Barrow, and he set out with five men. "The day was dark and dismal . . . with a fog that hid every object at a distance of a hundred yards. We were, therefore, under the necessity of closely following the coastline, which much increased the distance and fatigue. The land is very low, and is intersected by innumerable salt creeks. In fording these we were constantly wet up to the waist, and the water was dreadfully cold." [15] With no shelter to shield them from a bitter north wind, they lay down cold and wet on the soggy ground and slept. The next day they met a band of Eskimos from whom, after they had established friendly relations, they borrowed an umiak—a large flat-bottomed boat that can float in six inches of water. This solved their difficulties and speeded their progress. In a few days Simpson "saw with indescribable emotions, Point Barrow stretching out to the northward." [15]

The small party rejoined the others and, making for their winter camp, at the end of September reached the "infant establishment," [16] Fort Confidence on Great Bear Lake. On that very day "a solitary Canada goose, the very last straggler of the rear-guard, flew past to the southward." [15] To the Dogrib and Hare Indians Fort Confidence was the same happy winter dumping-ground that Fort Reliance had been, and to provide for them Simpson was forced to make many hunting-trips. A stupendous task, since they were still hungry after a daily ration of from eight to twelve pounds of meat per person! He also explored the surrounding country to discover the easiest way to transport their boats to the Coppermine River. In this he covered more than a thousand miles. The path he chose lay via the Dease River and across the Dismal Lakes.

Ice proved a heavy and adamant foe. As late as the middle of June (1838) the Dismal Lakes were still frozen as solid as in midwinter; so they loaded the boats on iron-shod sledges and sailed over the ice. Franklin had descended the Coppermine when it had subsided to the comparative tameness of its summer level; they swept down with the spring flood. On a swollen tumultuous stream strewn with loose ice between banks piled high with ponderous icy fragments they struggled and miraculously reached the sea alive. And the sea! From the sand to the horizon the ice lay solid, white, unbroken. They sawed and hacked and cut and by the end of the season had reached Point Turnagain. From there Simpson set off with seven men for a ten-day trip on foot. Progress was painful and fatiguing, trekking over soft sands and loose pebbles, sloshing through countless rivulets; but before he turned back he had the immense satisfaction of seeing open water to the east and land to the north. In honor of the young girl who had been crowned Queen of England this new coast was named Victoria Island. Retracing their route, they reached the mouth of the Coppermine. By painstaking labor, though Hearne and Franklin and Richardson had declared it impossible, they towed the boats safely up all the rapids and falls and cached them and their supplies at the point closest to Fort Confidence, for use the following season.

All that summer those who had stayed at the fort had hunted and fished, with the result that the long winter passed pleasantly, without hardships. By the middle of June 1839 Simpson was off to descend the Coppermine again. From both land and water the ice had withdrawn its harsh dominion, and they progressed down the river, over a navigable sea, and were soon sailing past Point Turnagain. Before them was a coast "never yet trodden by civilized man." [15] Fine weather favored them as they unraveled the intricate path—a rare piece of good luck, for as they approached closer and closer to King William Land and the North Magnetic Pole their compasses were rendered useless. On the 10th of August they entered a strait fully ten miles wide that separated the continent from the King William Island discovered by James Ross. On the 13th a sudden turning of a sharp cape revealed the sandy desert described by Back as the site of the mouth of his river. The major part of their task had been accomplished, "and even the most despondent of our people forgot, for the time, the great distance we should have to return to our winter quarters." [15] That connecting strait was named for Simpson.

His identification of Montreal Island was confirmed when he found a cache left by Back. Though he had traveled far and accomplished much, Simpson was eager to push along to the east to determine whether Boothia Felix was joined to the continent. But adverse winds delayed him, the advanced season forbade, and he turned back, naming his farthest point Castor and Pollux, after the boats. On his homeward voyage he traced sixty miles of the southern coast of King William Island and mapped 156 miles of the new-found coast of Victoria Island. The last day of September, "in the teeth of a strong northwest wind, with blinding snow . . . we reached at dusk the friendly shelter of Fort Confidence." [15] Behind him lay a boat journey of 1,408 geographical miles (*ca.* 1,600 land miles)—one of the longest in the records of the Arctic.

In the dead of winter Simpson left for the Red River settlement— a walk of almost two thousand miles. There he hoped to find an answer to a letter he had written the previous spring, asking the directors of the Hudson's Bay Company to allow him to complete the coastal survey as far east as Fury and Hecla Strait. He found no answer. He did not know that their letter of authorization was coming on the next packet; he did not know that his work and his personal attainments were everywhere being acclaimed—he had worked too hard and for too long a period in the far north. His heart was full of bitterness as he turned his back on the north, taking the shortest trail for the nearest port. The red mist of Arctic hysteria clouded his keen mind.

From the sworn testimony of one of the four men who set out with him comes the story of his death. A terrible frenzy possessed him. Without provocation he shot two of the men. Horrified, afraid, the other two ran for their lives. They caught up with him the next day.

A shot rang out. Whether Simpson killed himself or was killed will never be known. He was only thirty-one. On that last day he had walked forty-seven miles in a straight line.

The expedition Simpson had proposed and was to have led was entrusted five years later, in 1845, to another Hudson's Bay official, Dr. John Rae. Where Simpson had wanted to work eastward from Castor and Pollux Bay, along Boothia Felix to Hudson Bay, Rae decided to reverse the direction. He hoped to meet, if possible, with the gallant expedition that Sir John Franklin was leading along the Northwest Passage. Compared to that elaborate venture Rae's was a crude affair. Where the government spared nothing to make the naval effort complete and successful, the Hudson's Bay Company expected Rae to do much on the smallest possible outlay. He was charged to "determine astronomically all remarkable points, make bearings of all intermediate portions of the coast, chart these daily, attend to all the botany and geology, to zoology in all its departments, to the temperature of the air and water, to the atmosphere, ice, winds, currents, soundings, magnetic dips, and inclinations, aurora borealis, refraction ‚of light, ethnographic peculiarities of the Eskimo, and other observations as may suggest themselves to you." [16] In addition to this, since he had supplies for only four months and the work was expected to take from fifteen to twenty-seven months, he would have to spend considerable time hunting. Ten men were to help him; but the all-important part of the expedition was Rae—Rae who could outhunt ten men, Rae who could survey on foot more coastline than his two twenty-two-foot boats could sail along.

Sailing from Churchill, Rae reached the head of Repulse Bay by the end of July 1846 and immediately questioned some Eskimos he found there about the topography. Following their information, he crossed the narrow neck of land now known as Rae Isthmus to Committee Bay, the southernmost part of Prince Regent Inlet. Cloudy weather and heavy fogs made observations impossible, and the ice that completely filled the bay precluded all chance of sailing along its shores. He could do nothing. He returned to Repulse Bay to get ready for the winter, crossing country so stony and rough that his shoes and socks were worn through long before he reached his destination. Some of the men built a house—twenty feet by fourteen, with stone walls two feet thick, padded on the inside with mooseskins and covered with a roof fashioned out of boat sails—naming it Fort Hope; some fished, some collected wood for fuel, and Rae did most of the hunting. They had plenty to eat, but, being short of fuel, they cooked only one meal a day. It was so cold within doors that one of the men "had his knee frozen in bed, and . . . got heartily laughed at for his effeminacy." [16]

At the very first sign of spring Rae resumed his exploratory trips. He used two sledges, drawn by dogs and men, finding shelter in snow igloos, Eskimo style. He intended surveying the western coast of Committee Bay to find, if it was to be found, a strait that would cut through to the west. The going was so arduous that two of the eight dogs died and the others had to be left in a camp to recuperate. With three men Rae pushed on so as to reach Ross's most southerly discoveries, "which could not now be more than two days' journey." [16] Soft snow made the advance exhausting. At last he saw the vast ice-covered expanse of Lord Mayor's Bay, dotted with the many islands that Ross had happily named "the Sons of the Clergy of the Church of Scotland." Rae had reached one goal and had forged an important link in the coastal survey. By walking along that shore he had determined that no strait existed there. The whole party returned to Fort Hope the beginning of May, having been gone less than a month, "all well, but so black and scarred on the face from the effects of oil, smoke, and frost bites, that our friends would not believe but that some serious accident from the explosion of gunpowder had happened to us." [16]

A ten days' rest, and he set out for his second goal, this time to map the eastern shore of Committee Bay to Fury and Hecla Strait. Again their progress was slow and fatiguing; again the spent dogs had to be left behind; again they encountered snow in which they sank to the knee at every step; again in the absence of fuel they had to take a kettle full of snow to bed so that by the warmth of their bodies they could melt enough for drinking. They ran short of food, but on they went, not turning back until their reckonings showed them to be but ten miles south of Fury and Hecla Strait. By the middle of June they were back at Fort Hope, having traced in all more than six hundred miles of new coastline and settled the question of a waterway from Fury and Hecla Strait to Point Turnagain, since it was now certain that Boothia Felix was a peninsula and not an island.

Thirty years had passed since England took up the challenge of the Arctic. The map in Sir John Barrow's second book, on the *Northern Regions,* published in 1846, speaks eloquently of the great progress made in that time (see p. 96). The thousand-mile stretch between Cook's Icy Cape and Parry's Fury and Hecla Strait had been traced by Franklin, Richardson, Back, Simpson, and Rae, and an intricate series of waterways had been charted and sailed over by Parry and the Rosses. Bulky volumes held a vast accumulation of scientific data. During those thirty years England's roving spirit had cut great chunks out of the unknown; in the next decade she was to push her discoveries farther. The adventurous quest on a sudden was to be turned into a tragic search.

Rae, traveling along the eastern coast of Boothia Felix in the summer of 1847, was unaware that not far off the buzzards of doom were gathering over the Franklin Expedition. The most ambitious of expeditions was soon to be the most famous of all Arctic tragedies.

II

Franklin's Last Voyage

Two STOUT VESSELS, the *Erebus* and the *Terror*, rested idly in
Woolwich harbor after having served Sir James Ross faithfully
on his three memorable Antarctic voyages of 1839–43. Like chained
dogs they rode at anchor, awaiting a word of command to be free
and away.

For seven years—since Back had been battered at Repulse Bay—
the British government had steadfastly refused to send another expedition out into Arctic waters; for seven years the Royal Geographic
Society had agitated persistently for such an expedition, and each year
sentiment and interest had grown more favorable as the various succeeding land expeditions brilliantly carried forward the coastal survey. At last it was felt that the groundwork had been laid, the lands
and waters of the American Arctic sufficiently charted to let ships sail
from the Atlantic to the Pacific on known waterways, past known
shores. The time had come to do what many had attempted since
Frobisher first set out to sail the Northwest Passage. At last the
English felt ready to receive the reward won after generations
of stern apprenticeship. And the Admiralty gave the necessary
orders.

The *Erebus* and the *Terror* were made ready for Arctic service.
They were overhauled, strengthened, provisioned, and completely
outfitted for three years. Each was equipped with an auxiliary engine
and screw to be used during calms; they were the first screw steamers
to be used in the Arctic. The official instructions outlined the hopes
and laid down the course. All possible speed was to be made for Lancaster Sound, which had "been four times navigated without any
impediment by Sir Edward Parry. . . . In proceeding to the westward, you will not stop to examine any openings, either to the northward or southward in that strait, but will continue to push to the
westward without loss of time . . . to that portion of the land on

which Cape Walker is situated [the southern landmark at the beginning of Barrow Strait]. . . . From that point, we desire that every effort be used to endeavour to penetrate to the southward and westward, in a course as direct as possible towards Bering Strait as the position and the extent of the ice, or the existence of land at present unknown, may admit.

"We direct you to this particular part of the Polar Sea as affording the best prospect of accomplishing the Passage to the Pacific. . . . But should your progress in the direction be arrested by ice of a permanent appearance, and if when passing the mouth of the strait between Devon and Cornwallis Islands you had observed that it was open and clear of ice . . . you will duly consider . . . whether that channel might not offer a more practical outlet . . . and a more ready access to the open sea."

The commander to whom these instructions were addressed was Sir John Franklin, who twenty years before had traced hundreds of miles of the Arctic coastline of America. He had just returned to England after having been Governor of Tasmania for seven years, the last of which had been made miserable by petty intrigues within the Colonial Office. The Arctic was as far as he might humanly and honorably get from the Colonial Secretary. And though Sir James Ross had declined the command of this expedition on the ground that he was too old, Franklin, fifteen years his senior, made every effort to secure it. Nothing was "dearer to my heart than the completion of the survey of the northern coast of America and the accomplishment of the Northwest Passage." And both of these were combined in this expedition. For such work he was too old; he was fifty-nine. He reminded everyone that in his youth he had served well, but he forgot that in those days he had been superbly served by his youth. The Lords of the Admiralty felt that Franklin had done more than his share of the allotted work, that he could justly rest on his laurels. Lord Haddington, then First Lord, reflecting this universal opinion, said dubiously: "I might find a good excuse for not letting you go, Sir John, in the rumour that tells me you are sixty years of age." "No, no, my lord," exclaimed Franklin eagerly, "I am only fifty-nine." And so he was appointed, an ageing but experienced St. George, happy to do battle with his old adversary the dragon of the north.

The finest officers of the navy were picked to sail with him: Captain Crozier, who had served under Parry; James Fitzjames, who at thirty-three had been made Commander for distinguished work in the China War; Graham Gore, who had sailed with Back; Irving,

Des Voeux, Fairholme, young men who had proved their mettle in Africa and Australia. When the *Erebus* and the *Terror*, with 129 men aboard, sailed down the Thames the 19th of May 1845, the whole nation felt that success must follow, for here seasoned experience was fused with youthful impetuosity. The sought-for-prize must fall.

The *Erebus* and the *Terror* touched at Disko on the west coast of Greenland, whence the men sent letters home, bidding their friends answer them at Petropavlovsk, so confident were they of reaching Bering Strait. In the latter part of July, Dannett, a whaling-captain, saw them moored to an iceberg, awaiting a favorable moment to cross the middle pack and enter Lancaster Sound. The right wind came. The *Erebus* and the *Terror* gallantly sailed away from the whaler. Never more were they seen by civilized man.

But they left a record of the route they subsequently took. They sailed down the open sparkling waters of Lancaster Sound, according to their instructions, as far as Cape Walker. Before them lay Barrow Strait choked with ice. Availing himself of the alternative route, Franklin headed northward along Wellington Channel—it had been noted by Parry on his first voyage, but never investigated—found it ice-free, and went north for a hundred miles to 77° N. But he was anxious to get to the west—not north—and he returned to Lancaster Sound, skirting the west coast of Cornwallis Land and thus establishing its insularity. With the close of the season the two ships found safe anchorage in a snug harbor formed by Beechey Island. These few facts are known. The spirits and hopes of the men must have been high, since few expeditions before had accomplished so much in a first season.

Of the months spent at Beechey Island a little can be reconstructed. Most probably the men and officers worked in the various shops and observatories, went on several sledge journeys and hunting-parties, and amused themselves with theatricals. Summer came, and the ships, sawed out of the ice, were made ready to sail to the west. Three men were left behind in a little cemetery.

Barrow Strait was as ice-choked as it had been the autumn before, but along the western coast of North Somerset an uncharted waterway opened invitingly to the south. They sailed along it to the latitude of Ross's Magnetic Pole. Before them lay King William Land, bordered as far as they could see by blue water. Should they sail to the east of it or to the west? On the east the cartographers had drawn, according to the findings of James Clark Ross, a slender isthmus that connected King William Land with Boothia Felix. For Franklin, therefore, there was really no choice. His only chance—by reason of that mortal flaw in the map—lay in following to the west. To the west he sailed, right into the fatal spiderweb the Arctic had spun to trap the unwary. For to the west he sailed into the polar pack —great masses of ice that, frantically seeking an outlet into warmer waters, impinge on the low-lying northwestern coast of King William Land or are stranded on the shoals of Victoria Strait. The *Erebus* and the *Terror* were beset, the middle of September, in the open sea, twelve miles north of King William Land. Never were they to get free.

Caught fast, they drifted to the west with the pack ice, and that fed their hopeful conceit that soon they would see the Pacific. The second winter passed, neither so happily nor so securely as the first. Not only were they prisoners of the ice in a state of constant jeopardy, but they were also threatened by another, more terrible danger. Of their great stores of tinned goods more than half, when opened, were found to have become putrid and unfit for use. The expedition was like a besieged fortress weakened by internal treachery.

In the spring, sledging-parties were sent out to explore the unknown coast of King William Land from Ross's Cape Felix to Simpson's Cape Herschel—and only one hundred and fifty miles away, on the other side of the Boothia Peninsula, Rae was mapping the last of its uncharted eastern coast. In the cairn that James Clark Ross had built at Cape Felix in 1831, one of the parties commanded by Gore deposited the following memorandum:

28 of May, 1847.   H. M. ships *Erebus* and *Terror*
wintered in the ice in lat.
70°05′ N; long. 98°23′ W.
Having wintered in 1846–7 * at Beechey Island, in lat. 74°43′28″ N. long. 91°39′15″ W., after having ascended Wellington Channel to lat. 77°, and returned by the west side of Cornwallis Island.
Sir John Franklin commanding the expedition.
All well.
Party consisting of 2 officers and 6 men left the ships on Monday 24th May, 1847.
Gm. Gore, Lieut.
Chas. F. Des Voeux, Mate.

The men who sledged along the western coast of Boothia knew what had not been known before, that there was no isthmus cutting across the open waterway that led southward to Simpson Strait, that

* Obviously an error for 1845–6.

London John Murray, Albemarle Street. 1859.

H. M. S. *ships* Erebus and Terra
(Wintered in the Ice in

28 of May 184 7 { Lat. 70° 5′ N. Long. 98° 23′ W

Having wintered in 1846—7 at Beechey Island
in Lat 74° 43′ 28″ N. Long 91° 39′ 15″ W after having
ascended Wellington Channel to Lat 77° and returned
by the West side of Cornwallis Island

Sir John Franklin commanding the Expedition.

Commander.

All well

WHOEVER finds this paper is requested to forward it to the Secretary of
the Admiralty, London, *with a note of the time and place at which it was
found:* or, if more convenient, to deliver it for that purpose to the British
Consul at the nearest Port.

QUINCONQUE trouvera ce papier est prié d'y marquer le tems et lieu ou
il l'aura trouvé, et de le faire parvenir au plutot au Secrétaire de l'Amirauté
Britannique à Londres.

CUALQUIERA que hallare este Papel, se le suplica de enviarlo al Secretario
del Almirantazgo, en Londrés, con una nota del tiempo y del lugar en
donde se halló.

EEN ieder die dit Papier mogt vinden, wordt hiermede verzogt, om het
zelve, ten spoedigste, te willen zenden aan den Heer Minister van de
Marine der Nederlanden n 's Gravenhage, of wel aan den Secretaris der
Britsche Admiraliteit, te London, en daar by te voegen eene Nota,
inhoudende de tyd en de plaats alwaar dit Papier is gevonden geworden

FINDEREN af dette Papiir ombedes, naar Leilighed gives, at sende
samme til Admiralitets Secretairen i London, eller nærmeste Embedsmand
i Danmark, Norge, eller Sverrig. Tiden og Stædet hvor dette er fundet
önskes venskabeligt paategnet.

WER diesen Zettel findet, wird hier-durch ersucht denselben an den
Secretair des Admiralitets in London einzusenden, mit gefälliger angabe
an welchen ort und zu welcher zeit er gefundet worden ist.

Party consisting of 2 Officers and 6 Men
left the Ships on Monday 24th May 1847

Gm Gore Lieut
Chas F Des Voeux mate.

Facsimile of a Record Left by the Franklin Expedition

From McClintock's VOYAGE OF THE FOX IN THE ARCTIC SEAS (*London,*
1855).

had they sailed to the east along that route they would have put King William Land between them and the impassable ice-fields that now beset their ships, and that they might even then have been breasting the swells of the North Pacific. They returned to the ships to find Sir John Franklin dying.

On the 11th of June 1847, having just celebrated his sixty-first birthday, the commander died. To the last he was confident that in a few days the ships would clear the ice and sail freely to the west. He died while there was still hope of release, before the ships had been so badly battered that they would have been sunk had the ice loosened its deathly but sustaining grip; he died unaware of the approaching calamity.

They had drifted within fifteen miles of Ross's Victory Point on King William Island when the third winter in the Arctic closed in on the expedition. The men were weakened by lack of food and slowly poisoned by what little they ate. Gore and seven other officers died, and twelve men. Crozier and Fitzjames, on whom the command fell, made plans to abandon the ships in the spring. By that time their line of retreat lay down King William Land, across Simpson Strait to the mainland, to the mouth of the river Back had traced through its iron-ribbed, barren valley. From there they would still have to ascend that ferocious highway for more than a hundred miles before reaching the farthest outpost of civilization. They had to have boats to ferry them, but that meant dragging those boats where they would be needed. All were weak and sick, and yet each was called on to drag a load of two hundred pounds.

On April 22, 1848, 105 men started on a forlorn march. Starvation forced them, for had they been able to wait, they could have covered much of the distance by boat. Starving, they faced a trek of two hundred and fifty miles. With their vitality sapped by scurvy, they yet hoped to be able to pull at the heavy drag-ropes. They reached Victory Point and found the report Gore had written the year previous. Thawing out some ink, Fitzjames wrote on the wide margins:

In 1848, H. M. Ships Terror and Erebus were deserted on the 22nd April 5 leagues N.N.W. of this, having been beset since 12 Sept. 1846, the officers and crews consisting of 105 souls under the command of Captain F. R. M. Crozier landed here in Lat. 69°37′42″ N. and Long. 98°41′. This paper was found by Lieut. Irving under the cairn supposed to have been built by Sir James Ross in 1831 4 miles to the northward where it had been deposited by the late Commander Gore in June, 1847. Sir James Ross's pillar has not however been found, and the paper has been transferred to this position, which is that in which Sir J.

Ross's pillar was erected—Sir John Franklin died on the 11th June 1847, and the total loss by deaths in the Expedition has been to this date 9 officers and 15 men.

James Fitzjames, Captain
H.M.S. Erebus

F. R. M. Crozier
    Captain and Senior Officer.
And start on to-morrow 26th for Back's Fish River.

And on the morrow they started. They abandoned everything but what was absolutely necessary, casting away cooking-apparatus, clothes, blankets, canvas tents, shovel, pickax, the medicine chest. They struggled along the western shore, and though the loads were lightened, men fell and died every day. By graves and skeletons they marked their line of retreat from Victory Point to Todd Island. Some survived to cross the strait and reach Point Ogle and Montreal Island. A few may have dragged themselves inland for some miles. But one and all they died. One hundred and five souls. Perhaps the gallant Fitzjames was the last to die, that ghastly "last" whom one pictures "after the death of his last remaining companions, all alone in that terrible world, gazing around him in mute despair, the sole living thing in that dark, frozen universe. . . . The setting sun looks back to see the last wretched victim die. He meets her sinister gaze with a steady eye, as though bidding her defiance. For a few minutes they glare at each other, then the curtain is drawn and all is dark." [1]

Franklin's old friend and companion Sir John Richardson pointed out that, "by their wearying and fatal march down the western and southern sides of King William's Land, the party who reached Montreal Island to die there . . . connected Lancaster Strait with the navigable channel that extends along the continent to Bering's Strait" and thereby "forged the last link of the Northwest Passage with their lives."

Many ships were to sail in an effort to trace the course and learn the fate of the *Erebus* and the *Terror*.

12

The Mystery of the Missing Ships: the Franklin Search

T HE OVERWHELMING tragedy that descended on the Franklin
Expedition could not have happened today. At least it is pleasant to think so. By virtue of the wireless and radio the outside world would have been able to follow the daily progress of the *Erebus* and the *Terror* and participate in everything but the actual task. The exact course would have been known, the death of the leader mourned, the purposeless and doomed floating with the ice-pack appreciated for what it meant, and rescue undertaken as soon as starvation and disease enshadowed them. Rescue swift and sure—airplanes soaring and swooping—ice-breakers slowly and irresistibly smashing a path through—men and records saved. This bright fantasy is the reverse of the somber fact. No words winged through the air; there were only uncertainty and the slow, fatal passage of time. There were no sensitive antennæ to catch the desperate cry for help, only a vague presentiment of disaster, which gradually sharpened. Rescue, which was months in getting started, was more months in reaching the scene. And then the rescuers knew not where to go. A gigantic labor it was to comb that immense territory (perversely, so it seemed, taking every path but the right one), to explore the north, south, east, and west, seeking a precious bit of humanity that was perishing miserably somewhere in the dark heart of the unknown.

In the ten years after 1847 forty searching-parties set out to find the missing men. Of these, six went overland to the coast of Arctic America; thirty-four explored the great number of waterways that tie the maze of islands together, enlarging their radii by sledging-trips. Though most of them were under government orders, several were financed by private persons; Lady Jane Franklin, wife of the lost leader, outfitted four different ships. At first it was hoped that the lost expedition would be found.* After years of fruitless search, the expeditions strove only to learn the fate that had overtaken the *Erebus* and the *Terror*. To find some definite proof that those 129 men had not vanished utterly, to salvage some records of the work they must have accomplished—that was the sustaining, the only hope.

Never before had there been such an invasion of the Arctic, such a concerted drive to know the unknown. The search for the missing men extended man's horizon in the high northern latitudes, filled in great blanks on the maps, riveted the attention of Europe and America on the region around the North Pole. And even after the sad search

* "The sad fate of Sir John Franklin and his gallant companions is rendered still more melancholy by the reflection that some at least of them might have been saved. When no news arrived in 1846 [a year after they had sailed on a three-year voyage], prompt measures should have been taken, but the Admiralty asked advice and did nothing.

"Dr. King, who had accompanied Sir George Back down the Great Fish River in 1833, made earnest and repeated appeals to the Admiralty and to the Colonial Office in 1847 to send a relief party down that river, and he pointed out quite correctly the position where the *Erebus* and *Terror* had been beset. His letters were not even answered. For Sir James Ross had told them there was not any reason for anxiety and gave a strongly expressed opinion that the crews of the *Erebus* and *Terror* would never under any circumstances make for the Great Fish River. Other authorities concurred. This sealed their fate. Admiral Beechey alone thought that a boat should be sent down that river.

"The year 1848 arrived, but no news reached England. Sir John Richardson was accordingly sent out to examine the coast between the Mackenzie and Coppermine Rivers, but not to extend his voyage to the mouth of the Fish River, where even then he might have saved a few. Two ships, the *Enterprise* and *Investigator*, were also fitted out to go to the relief of the lost expedition, and Sir James Ross received the command. . . . But Sir James went in the full conviction that he would meet the *Erebus* and *Terror*, or that they would pass him and that he would find them in the Thames on his return." (Markham: *Lands of Silence*, p. 248.)

On the other hand Sir John Richardson himself remarks: "Had it been actually known that Capt. Crozier had left the ships for the mouth of the Great Fish River, and Sir John Richardson gone in that direction to meet him [upon reaching the mouth of the Coppermine in 1848] . . . [he] could not have reached Montreal Island till some months after the last of the party had perished. . . . Matters would not have been mended by dispatching a party in 1847 [a year earlier than the limit of the expedition's equipment] via Canada, to travel in a light canoe. . . . Without a year's previous notice to the Hudson Bay Co., its stores would have been exhausted, and the voyageurs, instead of being in a condition to descend the river, would be under the necessity of establishing fisheries for their subsistence. . . . To have given such a party a fair chance of success, arrangements should have been made in 1846 . . . to have men and boats . . . a sufficiency of provisions . . . thus enabling a detachment to travel to the sea [via the Great Fish River route of Back] . . . early in 1848. All this would appear preposterous without the express knowledge of the course intended to be pursued by the crews of the ships when beset."

was over, the interest remained, the last expedition taking place in 1878. If drama had been lacking in the heroic work of exploring the Arctic regions, that need was now supplied; if men had asked what need there was for such exploration, that question was now answered; if during his lifetime Sir John Franklin had uncovered vast stretches of the Arctic coast; by the mystery of his death even greater areas were traced out.

The relief plans—started in 1847 for the next year—were based on the simplest and most effective military maneuver. The enemy was to be surrounded and its captive freed. With this in view the first expedition was composed of three distinct groups. One was to try to find Franklin by following the course he had been ordered to take. The second, dispatched to Bering Strait, was to stand by him as he completed the Northwest Passage. The third group was to make for the Arctic coast of America, reaching it overland from the south, on the chance that Franklin, having lost his ships, would make his way to land. This last group was commanded by Dr. John Richardson, Franklin's old friend, who was superbly assisted by the indefatigable Dr. Rae. They planned to examine carefully both shores of Dolphin and Union Strait, but heavy ice and terrific gales, in both 1848 and the following season, frustrated their heroic efforts.

Captain Kellett, in command of the *Herald*, assisted by Captain Moore in the *Plover*, was in charge of the second group, who were to aid Franklin upon his arrival at Bering Strait. Failing to meet him, they spent the open season in exploring the unknown waters to the west. They discovered the isolated, bleak island that they named in honor of the *Herald*, which a few years later was to be known in connection with the De Long tragedy.

The leader of the first group was Sir James Ross, whose knighthood had been earned by his brilliant work not only in the Arctic but also in the Antarctic regions, commanding the *Enterprise*. He was seconded by his old assistant Captain Bird, in the *Investigator*. With Ross was a young lieutenant, Leopold McClintock, who was to work out of the technique of Arctic sledging—step by step scientifically approximating Eskimo techniques—the basis for all future land exploration. It was he who eventually unraveled the mystery of the missing ships. Like the overland group, the *Enterprise* and the *Investigator* were stopped by heavy ice. They could not advance beyond Lancaster Sound; both Barrow Strait and Prince Regent Inlet were frozen from shore to shore; and they had to winter in Port Leopold, at the northeastern end of North Somerset.

That spring a sledging-party was sent southward eighty miles to

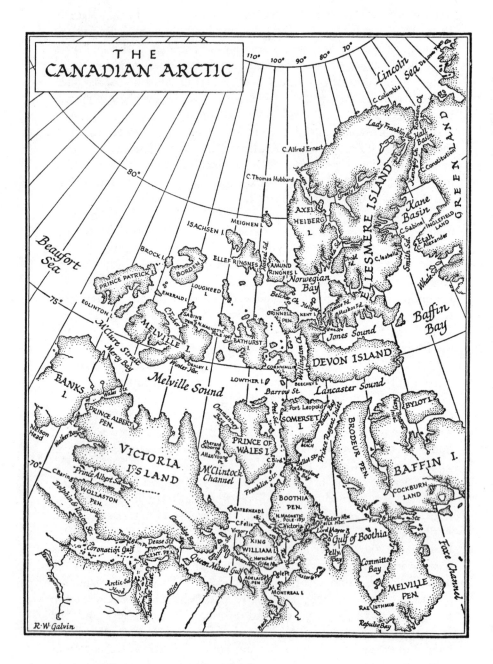

Fury Beach to ascertain whether Franklin had put in there to replenish his stores, while Ross with McClintock undertook a more
extended trip to the west. This was McClintock's first sledging-trip.
They reached Cape Bunny—sighted by Parry—and found it to be
the northwest point of North Somerset. Heading southward, they
faced an unknown coast, which they traced within fifty miles of Cape
Bird, which they sighted. When they turned back, they little knew
that they had turned away from the very spot for which they were
searching. They reached Port Leopold after an absence of thirty-nine
days with all but McClintock exhausted by the terrific exertion and
insufficient food. They had covered five hundred miles—one hundred
and fifty of which had been over a new coastline—dragging sledges
that were too heavily laden. Every circumstance had been carefully
noted by McClintock: the equipment, the food, the weight of the
rations, the clothes, the construction of the sledges—everything to
the very last detail pondered over, worked over, improved.

The whole summer was spent in warding off scurvy—they shot
2,300 birds, their only supply of fresh food—and in sawing a long
lane through the ice to free the ships. When, at the end of August,
the ships were finally clear and headed for Barrow Strait, they were
again beset. Powerless and helpless, they drifted with the pack. Back
along Lancaster Sound into Baffin Bay they drifted for a whole
month. And when at the end of September they were at last released,
the only course left them was to sail home.

The simple, effective military maneuver had failed. The enemy
was too strong, too vast, to be surrounded. The failure was an alarm
that sounded throughout the civilized world, enlisting sympathy and
aid. The rescue assumed larger proportions.

The *Enterprise* and the *Investigator* were overhauled and recom-
missioned and, with Captains Collinson and McClure, were dispatched to aid in the search from the Bering Strait end. Captain
Kellett, in the *Plover,* accompanied them as far as Bering Strait.
Meanwhile, two "bluff-bowed, barque-rigged vessels of 410 and 430
tons, named the *Resolute* and *Assistance,*"[1] were made ready, with
two pointed-bowed screw steamers, the *Pioneer* and the *Intrepid,* for
tenders. These four under the command of Captain Austin, the brigs
Lady Franklin and *Sophia* commanded by William Penny, a famous
whaling-captain, and the schooner *Felix* with its supply ship, outfitted
by Sir Felix Booth for old Sir John Ross to command—these eight
ships headed for Lancaster Sound in 1850. To these were added two
more, the *Advance* and the *Rescue,* sent out at the expense of the
American merchant Henry Grinnell and commanded by Lieutenant

De Haven, U.S.N. Ten ships and one route! For they all aimed to explore Wellington Channel, that northward-leading waterway. Only the eleventh ship, the *Prince Albert*, a schooner equipped by Lady Franklin, under Commander Forsyth, had orders to head southward along Prince Regent Inlet. Always she insisted that the solution lay to the south of Lancaster Sound.

The *Assistance*, Captain Ommanney commanding, was the first of the ships to come within sight of Beechey Island at the entrance to Wellington Channel. A cairn on its summit attracted notice. Traces of a European camping-party were found on shore. The following day the *Rescue* arrived, then Captain Penny's two ships, and soon ten vessels were assembled at that spot. They searched carefully. Everywhere were traces of white men's wintering—plenty of traces, but no written records, nothing to confirm their identity. And when at last definite proof was found, it was in the inscriptions on the graves of three men of the *Erebus* and the *Terror* who had died that first winter. These lonely graves offered the only positive information; they were concise statements of fact offered by death.

The searchers had found something; but they still did not know what route, in which direction, Franklin had sailed after his first wintering. Further progress for that season was stopped by the approach of winter. De Haven's ships, the *Advance* and the *Rescue*, equipped for only one season, were forced to make for home. In Lancaster Sound they were beset and drifted with the pack down to Baffin Bay, through the night of the Arctic winter. They drifted a thousand miles until July, when they were finally released. The *Prince Albert* too returned, bringing news of the discoveries on Beechey Island.

Austin's and Penny's ships wintered at the southern tip of Cornwallis Island. This large group of men were well organized. They kept in perfect health. The ships were dry; the men could bathe, wash their clothes, and exercise in any weather. They were kept amused; there was a theater where plays were given every two weeks, announced by playbills; the *Aurora* and the *Illustrated Arctic News* appeared monthly; and a school was started, with classes for the men. But all this was superimposed on their main task: getting ready for the spring sledging-trips. McClintock, who had been perfecting the technique of sledging, was placed in charge. The autumn months were spent in excursions to lay down food depots along the route to be taken in the spring, when great distances were to be covered; the winter months in assembling their equipment, clothes, and provisions.

Counting Austin's and Penny's crews, McClintock had over two hundred eager, sturdy men to man his sledges. But around them lay millions of square miles of unknown land, and they lacked even the slightest clue to aid them in choosing which direction to take. Penny took the northern route, exploring the length of Wellington Channel. Ommanney led the sledges heading southward, making for the lofty cliff of Cape Walker, a notable landmark off the northeast tip of Prince of Wales Island and the unknown region beyond. He sent one group under Vesey Hamilton to explore Lowther Island, situated in the middle of Barrow Strait; another, under Mecham, farther south to cover Russell Island, from which Cape Walker rises; a third, under Browne, made its way along the eastern coast of the newly discovered land named in honor of the Prince of Wales—in the exact direction of the missing ships; while McClintock himself, with Sherard Osborn, traced the western shore, around the deep indentation of Ommanney Bay, for more than half its length. Osborn noted the tremendous floes of ice that clogged the water to the southwest and precluded the possibility of Franklin's having made his way through it. Not one of them dreamt that the *Erebus* and the *Terror* had been caught and conquered by that very pack.

McClintock turned to the west, toward Melville Island, discovered and wintered in by Parry. For had Franklin, as some insisted, sailed up Wellington Channel and so to the north of Melville Island, he would surely have visited those parts that Parry found abounding in game and wood. McClintock hoped to find traces of such a visit, but the only traces were those left by Parry, the tracks made by his cart, the whitened bones of ptarmigan killed and eaten thirty years before.

This trip, the first of a series under the direction of McClintock, set a new mark in Arctic travel. He had gone 770 miles in eighty days, having put 300 miles between the ship and his farthest. Gales detained him for two and a half days, yet he averaged, as he had planned, ten and a half miles a day. The various units of these three groups explored in eight different directions. They had failed to find the slightest clue to aid them in their search. From Ommanney's and McClintock's reports of what they had found at their "extremes," Captain Austin was convinced of the futility of further exploration to the southward and westward; while Penny's belief that Franklin had gone northward on Wellington Channel toward the open polar sea persuaded him "that the missing men had gone beyond our reach." With this conviction they sailed for home.

Lady Franklin, who had ordered Captain Forsyth to take the *Prince Albert* southward and had been disappointed by his early return, sent that schooner out again. Again she gave orders for it to search to the south of North Somerset, for she was ever mindful of the fact that her husband's favorite theory was that the Northwest Passage would be best secured by hugging the coastline. This time she gave her orders to William Kennedy, of the merchant marine, who was seconded by Lieutenant Bellot, a keen volunteer from the French Navy. They wintered at Batty Bay, not far from the spot where the *Fury* had been abandoned.* During the winter, which was one continuous gale, they prepared for their spring sledging-trip. Not waiting for the spring to come, they set out, using Eskimo sledges and dogs. Going to the south, they reached Ross's Brentford Bay, where "a column of vapour . . . issuing from a space of open water"[2] caused Bellot to investigate farther. "From a high hill in the neighbourhood I could plainly distinguish a sea stretching westward, at an estimated distance of thirty miles with the channel . . . apparently leading to it."[2]

Following this channel (since called Bellot Strait), they found it to be the long-sought, greatly desired western "egress" of Prince Regent Inlet. They reached its western end, making their way slowly through terrific snowstorms that made earth, air, and sky one substance and one color. Before them lay an unknown body of water, beyond that an unknown coast, for they did not know that Ommanney had traced both shores of Prince of Wales Island. Had Kennedy obeyed his instructions and led his party southward, they would have learned the fate of the missing ships. Instead they laboriously traced what Ommanney had already charted, and with the same barren result. They returned to Batty Bay, wearied and dispirited, and set out for home. One by one the searching-parties were to turn away when on the very threshold of success.

Six months before Captain Austin had sailed for Lancaster Sound, the *Enterprise*, the *Investigator*, and the *Plover* were dispatched for Bering Strait to carry on the search from that end. Blown apart by a gale in the Strait of Magellan, they proceeded independently and, as regards the search, unsuccessfully, whereas had they remained together, it is very likely that they might have found the lost expedition. McClure and Kellett reached Bering Strait first. Kellett, ordered to remain there, bade the *Investigator* farewell as she started on her solitary way, a long, perilous path between a shoal coast and a heavy sea of ice.

McClure was of the opinion that Franklin had sailed to the north via Wellington Channel, and he aimed to search those far northern

* Hepburn, Franklin's old attendant, who had been with him in his land explorations, was a member of the expedition.

parts. Cruising eastward along the coast as far as the mouth of the Mackenzie, he sent men ashore frequently to pile up cairns and question the natives. *The one interpreter, intended for both ships, was with him.* From the fact that nothing like the *Investigator* had been seen, McClure deduced that Franklin had not passed that way and that therefore he must head more to the north. Before him were uncharted waters. The ship fairly danced as they found a way past sandbars, through fields of ice. Soon he sighted land. What was it? The western tip of Wollaston Land or the southern reach of Banks? "The south cape, a fine, bold headland . . . Lord Nelson's Head, it was named . . . moss . . . and wild flowers were in abundance . . . numerous traces of rein-deer, hares and wild fowl . . . we made sail to the eastward." [3] Land was seen there—Prince Albert Land it was called. And between these two lands opened a navigable channel—Prince of Wales Strait—to the northeast. It led in a straight line to Barrow Strait. The dangers of navigation, the cold and hunger, were all forgotten. The weather was clear and fair. McClure almost trembled to think that so easily was the Northwest Passage to be accomplished. Barrow Strait was only seventy, then only sixty, miles away.

But the advance was of short duration. The wind shifted; the water became so thickly studded with floes that the ship managed to keep free with difficulty. And then the wind died down, and the ice, "no longer restrained, spread itself abroad with such rapidity that it was observed approaching, its white line clearly defined, running like an unbroken wave, along the dark, smooth water. It encircled the vessel, sweeping her away to the southwest." [3] Winter was upon them. Advance by water for that season was over.

McClure would not retreat to the safety of a harbor. Rather than lose a mile more than he was forced to, he decided to risk wintering in the pack, right where he was in the strait. A sledging-trip was made along the shores of the strait, for McClure was anxious to accomplish in that way what he had been stopped from doing by boat, completing the last step of the Northwest Passage. Making his way northward, he reached Barrow Strait and thus established "the existence of the Northwest Passage." [3]

McClure sent three parties out that spring. One was to search the southeast shore of Prince of Wales Strait, one the northwest shore, and the third to trace the northeast. Though they mapped in great stretches of the coasts of both Banks Island and Prince Albert Land, their search was unrewarded.

Spring came, and McClure's hopes of reaching Barrow Strait were renewed. By the middle of July he was a scant twenty-five miles from his goal. But the faithful guardian of the north was armed and ready, for from shore to shore the strait lay under a thick, unbroken coating of ice. Undaunted, McClure decided to try the other side of Banks Island. The helm of the ship was put about. They passed the southern tip, negotiated the difficult passage up the west coast, rounded the northwestern point, and sailed eastward as far as possible to a spot almost opposite "Parry's farthest west" of 1820. Here, in the harborage of Bay of God's Mercy, with three hundred miles of perilous and hard navigating behind them, McClure and his men took refuge from the annihilating power of the ice. McClure could look back with satisfaction on his achievement: the discovery of Prince of Wales Strait and, save for a few miles, the circumnavigation of Banks Island; but he preferred to look forward—bridging those last few miles —to the accomplishment of the Northwest Passage. He was certain that during the next season the *Investigator* would feel her way eastward to her goal.

The *Investigator* never left the Bay of God's Mercy. From the safety of their harbor the crew witnessed the full power of the ice as it struggled, mass against mass, until its titanic pressure lifted huge floes up the seventy-foot cliff. In the spring McClure set out by sledge for Parry's Winter Harbour on Melville Island, where, under the sandstone rock inscribed by Parry, he found a memorandum left by McClintock, telling of his visit there the previous year. McClure added to that a notice of his visit, giving the position of his ship and a description of Mercy Bay. That note was to be his salvation.

In the meantime Collinson, in the *Enterprise*, more mindful of his orders to proceed in company with the *Investigator*, spent time trying to find McClure, missed Kellett, who was on the lookout for him, and so lost the first season in the Arctic. He wintered in Hong Kong, but with spring was at his post and by the last of July had passed Point Barrow. Unknowingly he followed almost the exact path taken by the *Investigator*, threading his way northward up Prince of Wales Strait. There he found McClure's cache with his note claiming the honor of having completed the Northwest Passage. But McClure omitted to give the course he intended taking. Collinson realized that there was no point in repeating that feat and turned back. Again unknowingly he followed McClure up the west coast of Banks Land, keeping a sharp lookout for a sight or news of him. Finding neither, he reasoned that McClure had not passed that way, and turned back when less than a hundred miles from the Bay of God's Mercy, that refuge and last resting-place of the *Investigator*. He then steered to the south and east and spent the winter in Walker Bay on Prince

Albert Land. Sledging-parties sent out in the spring traced the whole of its western coastline from the head of the deep Prince Albert Sound to Glenig Bay in an effort to find both Franklin and the *Investigator*. In both the search was fruitless.

The *Enterprise* was released in August, and Collinson, not content with the findings of the sledging-party, sailed the whole length of Prince Albert Sound to verify that it was not a strait leading to the east. Then he tried the narrow uncharted waters of Dolphin and Union Strait and threaded his way through the dangerous island-clogged Coronation Gulf into the narrow windings of Dease Strait, where, in Cambridge Harbour, he took refuge for the winter. The Eskimos he met with there had in their possession a steam-engine rod; had the sole interpreter not been on McClure's ship, Collinson would have learned whence it had come, would have had a clue in what direction to search. In that season's work Collinson showed himself a master navigator, feeling his way safely through shoal waters —a task made a hundredfold more hazardous by a dense fog and a compass rendered entirely useless by his proximity to the Magnetic Pole. A second winter passed uneventfully, and with spring a sledging-party was sent out along the southern shore of Victoria Island and up its eastern coast as far as Gateshead Island. A hard, painful path over towering, rugged hummocks—and, at the end of this trail, a note cached by Rae stating that he had already traced that very coastline.* Like Rae they had chosen to trace the western shore of Victoria Strait instead of the eastern; like Rae they missed—and by what a slim, narrow stretch of miles!—finding the lost expedition. If only they had known, as they looked toward King William Land, they might have seen the unburied skeletons, would have seen the grave of the *Erebus* and the *Terror*.

Collinson had planned on staying another year, hoping that in another season he would reach Cape Walker via Victoria Strait. But because his coal, put on in England, was short of the specified amount, he was forced to retrace his course and steer for the west. Thus, with success within his grasp, he was forced to abandon both the search and the attempt at the Northwest Passage. So he started on his way to Point Barrow, a delicate and ticklish piece of navigation, and, after another winter spent in the Arctic, brought the *Enterprise* home to England. She had been gone five and one half years; she had circumnavigated the globe, endured four Arctic winters, and returned sound, with a healthy crew. Collinson's modest work stands out as one of the greatest feats in Arctic navigation. He had maneuvered a

* See p. 154.

sailing-ship of 360 tons forward and backward through 128 degrees of longitude, through narrow straits along the northern shores of continental America—a feat comparable to that of the steamer *Vega*,* to that of the 46-ton *Gjoa*.†

It will be remembered that, upon Austin's return in 1851, the people of England knew nothing but the general whereabouts of the *Enterprise* and the *Investigator*. But they felt strongly that another expedition should sail to Lancaster Sound, both that the search might continue and that assistance might be on hand and available should either McClure or Collinson need it. This next concerted thrust into the Arctic was doomed almost from its inauspicious birth. The Lords of the Admiralty, disregarding the negative findings of Austin and Penny about going northward on Wellington Channel, wrote in their new orders: "We consider no farther exploration . . . to the southward of Cape Walker necessary, and therefore propose that all the energy of the expedition be directed towards the upper portion of Wellington Strait." Likewise, in their choice of commander, they passed over the outstanding available men and, with Gilbertian fatuity, picked "an old officer with bad health, no Arctic experience, and the reputation of being the most unpopular man in the navy, Sir Edward Belcher."[1] In the long list of brilliant, brave men who explored within the Arctic Circle, Belcher stands out as a puffed-up mediocrity, a timorous mule. From his own record it would seem that his main qualification was a gift for prophecy verging on sorcery.‡ Had this been a Gilbert and Sullivan operetta, he would have made his appearance leading the search with a crystal globe and divining-rod.

This expedition, the last of the Franklin search parties sent out by the government, was equipped with every improvement that had been devised. Belcher was in command of five ships: the *Assistance*, the *Pioneer*, the *Resolute*, the *Intrepid*, and the transport *North Star*; he was the superior of the respective commanders: Commander Richards, Sherard Osborn, Captain Kellett, Leopold McClintock, and Lieutenant Pullen. He was ordered to proceed to Beechey Island, where the *North Star* was to remain as a depot ship while the first two proceeded northward up Wellington Channel and the third

* See pp. 270 ff.
† See pp. 274 ff.
‡ "To-day I felt so perfectly satisfied that a sledge was due from Kellett (if he existed) that I fully intended when the master reported noon, to desire him to send a person to look out on the hill. It escaped me, being then engaged on other matters; but my clerk, coming in, reporting, 'A dog sledge, nearly alongside, sir,' my reply, instigated by what was then passing in my mind, was very short and without emotion, 'I know it,' which somewhat astonished him."[6]

and fourth headed westward for Melville Island. As far as the government and the search were concerned, it was a complete fiasco. The five valuable ships were, for no apparent reason, abandoned; not a trace of Franklin was found; and the search was pronounced hopeless on the basis of exploration into what had obviously been the wrong area. But the expedition did bear fruit: Leopold McClintock extended his sledging-experience and, as commander of the *Intrepid*, learned a great deal about ice-navigation; a new generation of explorers received their first taste of the Arctic; and great tracts of new lands and winding waterways were charted.

By the middle of August 1852 the ships had reached Beechey Island and the two divisions gone their ways. Belcher, with Richards and Osborn, sailed north on Wellington Channel almost to its very end, where, on the northwestern part of Grinnell Peninsula, they wintered. During the spring Richards and Osborn covered by sledge the northern coasts of Cornwallis, Bathurst, and Melville Islands.

In the meantime Kellett and McClintock steered for Melville Island. Heavy ice prevented them from reaching it and forced them to be content with the shelter of the near-by Dealy Island. Active preparations were immediately started for autumn and spring sledging, both to be carried out on a larger scale than heretofore. McClintock had able and willing men with him, who rendered invaluable work in carrying through his sledging-program. Outstanding were two young lieutenants, Frederick Mecham and Vesey Hamilton, and George Nares, a mate who later rose by reason of his ability to be Admiral Sir George Nares, commander of the great expedition of 1875. It was on one of the autumn trips that Mecham found, under Parry's sandstone rock, the record left by McClure, giving the position of the *Investigator*, ice-bound in the Bay of God's Mercy. When the spring sledging-parties set out—Mecham striking out due west, McClintock for the northwest, and Hamilton due north—a party under Lieutenant Pim went to find McClure. The first three of these parties performed the routine of exploration in the finest manner, their combined efforts resulting in the mapping of eighteen hundred miles of new coastline, while the fourth party played *deus ex machina* in one of the most famous of Arctic dramas, affording a rescue "just in the nick of time."

Mecham, heading for the west, came to the western limit of Melville Island, crossed over a strait to an island named Eglinton, still kept to the west, crossed another strait, and reached a second island, Prince Patrick, whose southern and western shores he traced within sixteen miles of McClintock's farthest. Along the southern coast of Prince Patrick Island he came upon tree-trunks still covered with bark, standing ninety feet above sea level, and on its eastern coast, where his discoveries again connected with McClintock's, he found reindeer, hares, musk-oxen, ptarmigan, ducks, and geese, which afforded him plenty of fresh food. In all he was gone ninety-one days, covering 1,173 miles.

McClintock, reaching Cape Fisher, the northernmost point of Melville Island seen by Parry, turned southward down the west coast so as to connect his work with Mecham's. He was thrilled by the beauty of the Arctic scenery disclosed; he was excited by the sight of a new and unknown land to the west. To it he gave the name of Prince Patrick Island and, crossing over to it, traced its eastern coast to its northern tip. He continued north to examine the small Polynia Islands. Beyond them in the distance he sighted the jagged outline of towering hummocks, outposts of very heavy pack-ice. Before turning back he made a side trip down the western coast, again to connect his work with Mecham's. On the home journey he discovered the small, moss-covered Emerald Island. Approaching summer made travel agonizingly difficult and dangerous, an exhausting, slow progress through soft, deep snow or a hazardous passage over floes submerged under melted ice. But he regained his ship, having completed "one of the greatest Arctic effort[s] with sledges that has ever been made by men alone," [1] of 1,408 miles.

Hamilton headed for the Sabine Peninsula, the northern extremity of Melville Island, by way of the east coast, making a side trip to Bathurst Island, where he met Osborn, who had traced the northern limits of that island. Returning to Melville Island, Hamilton reached its farthest point, beyond which he discovered two small islands.

The fourth of these sledging-parties had set out to find McClure and the *Investigator*. It will be remembered that McClure had already spent one winter in Prince of Wales Strait (1850–1) and, by March 1853, two winters at the Bay of God's Mercy. He had found, when the time came to draw on his provisions, that a sizable amount had putrefied because of faulty packing and had to be discarded. Scurvy made its dread appearance, and though the crew were able to lay in some fresh meat, destruction by starvation or disease loomed before them. McClure had hoped that he would be free to sail in 1852, but to his dismay he found that in June of that year the ice, far from having melted, had increased its thickness by four inches. The short summer passed. With failing hopes they greeted another winter. McClure's pride made him loath to plan the abandonment of the ship, which was as "sound as the day she entered the ice," [3] because it would be "discreditable to desert her in 1853, when a favourable season would run her through the straits, and admit of reaching England in safety." [3] But he could not ignore the doctor's counsel, he could not jeopardize his men's lives still further; he had to plan for their escape. By proceeding on sledges to Port Leopold they might meet a whaler that would take them home to England. Early in the spring of 1853 orders were given for "thirty of the most weakly hands, divided into two groups of fifteen each," [3] who were to be the first of the traveling-parties, to get ready. When the first death occurred on board the *Investigator*, it ushered in despair for the sick, who knew they would never live to see Port Leopold. They made ready to leave, like doomed men quitting their cells for the last walk to the gallows.

"The sledges were ready, the slender store of provisions was packed, those who were going strove to be sanguine." [3] McClure, depressed and gloomy, paced the ice, discussing with a brother officer how they were to bury in this hard, frozen earth the man who had died the day before. "We perceived a figure walking rapidly towards us . . . from his pace and gestures we both naturally supposed . . . that he was one of our party pursued by a bear. . . . When within about two hundred yards of us this strange figure . . . shouted . . . words which, from the wind and intense excitement of the moment, sounded like a wild screech. . . . The stranger came . . . on, and we saw that his face was as black as ebony . . . and, had the skies fallen upon us, we could hardly have been more astonished than when the dark-faced stranger called, 'I'm Lieutenant Pim of the *Resolute*. Captain Kellett is in her at Dealy Island.'

"The announcement of relief being close at hand when none was supposed to be even within the Arctic Circle, was too sudden, unexpected and joyous for our minds to comprehend at once. The news flew with lightning rapidity . . . the sick, forgetful of their maladies, leapt from their hammocks . . . all rushed . . . to be assured that a stranger was actually amongst them. . . . Despondency fled the ship . . . the rescue . . . had reached them just in time to save their lives." [3] Pim had to tell and re-tell how Kellett, who had waved farewell to the *Investigator* at Bering Strait, was now welcoming them to safety at Dealy Island; how Mecham had, by chance, looked at Parry's sandstone rock carefully and had there found the document left by McClure; how Kellett's anxiety had saved them from the fate that had befallen those they had gone to rescue.

McClure set out at once for the *Resolute* to discuss the solution with

Kellett. He persuaded the latter to relieve him of his sick so that he might have another chance to sail the *Investigator* to Barrow Strait and thence to England. But when the first contingent of sick came aboard the *Resolute* and Kellett saw their pitiable condition and heard that in that short interval two more men had died aboard the *Investigator*, he ordered McClure to abandon the ship with all hands. And so the *Investigator*, cleaned and shipshape, was left in the clutches of the ice; they "hoisted the colours to the mast-head of their dear, gallant bark, and turned their backs upon her as sorrowfully as they would have done on an old, well-tried friend in his extremity."[3] By their retreat to the *Resolute* McClure and his men had again effected a completion of the Northwest Passage.

Subsequently about half the men and officers were dispatched to the *North Star* to be on hand to avail themselves of the first chance to return to England. That opportunity came when the *Phœnix*, under Captain Inglefield, sent by the Admiralty to communicate with Belcher's expedition at Beechey Island, brought them home that same year. To the people of England their news—the splendid voyage of the *Investigator* from Bering Strait, with its thundering climax of rescue and successful completion of the Northwest Passage—was the fitting end to a quest begun when the nation was still young, almost three hundred years before. Almost three hundred years since Queen Elizabeth, standing at a window of her palace at Greenwich, waved farewell to Sir Martin Frobisher as his three tiny ships sailed by; almost three hundred years, and now Queen Victoria was hearing from a young naval officer how he had entered the Arctic at Bering Strait and emerged from it at Baffin Bay, thus going from the Pacific to the Atlantic across the top of the Americas!

In violent contrast to this homecoming was that made the following year when the *Phœnix*, supplemented by the *Talbot*, returned from a second contact voyage to Beechey Island with all the crews of Belcher's four ships. And the story they bore was told not to a gracious sovereign but to stern judges at a court martial. For Belcher had to explain why he had abandoned four of Her Majesty's ships, sound, good ships, whose crews were healthy and well fed; why he had disregarded Kellett's pleading and McClintock's advice and deserted his vessels when he might have brought them home. Belcher explained that the summer of 1853 was slow in coming and short in duration, that he had explored a little, sailing north and east along Exmouth and Belcher Channels, and had been stopped on his return by heavy ice fifty miles from Beechey Island. Then Kellett told the court that, with the rescue of McClure, he had felt his mission done, that he had built and stocked a refuge for Collinson at Dealy Island, and that on his way to Beechey Island he had been caught and held for the winter in Barrow Strait. Not greatly worried, he had sent Hamilton to make the necessary reports to Belcher, and Hamilton had returned bearing orders for all hands to leave the ships and go by sledge to the *North Star*. Unable to believe that this was a command, Kellett sent McClintock to verify it, at the same time allowing Mecham to start on a sledging-trip to Banks Island to ascertain the fate of the *Investigator*. Then McClintock told how he had pointed out to Belcher that the ships would be free to sail and reach England that very season of 1854. But Belcher had been obdurate, would not even hazard a third Arctic wintering, and reiterated explicit orders for the abandoning of the ships. And his shameful order was obeyed; the four fine ships, the *Assistance*, the *Pioneer*, the *Resolute*, and the *Intrepid*, were abandoned and their crews squeezed into the *North Star*. Fortunately for all of them, Inglefield arrived with the two transports, so they were able to reach England in comparative comfort. "The court martial was obliged to acquit Belcher because his instructions gave him such wide discretion, but his sword was returned in a silence more damning than words. Sherard Osborn, whom Belcher had placed under arrest, and Lieutenant May, against whom he had reported, were both immediately promoted." [1]

Two events of the Belcher Expedition need still to be noted. Mecham in his last sledge trip—he died in Honolulu four years later when only twenty-nine—overcame terrific difficulties to reach the Bay of God's Mercy on Banks Island. There he found the *Investigator* keeled over, broken by ice, and ready to sink, absolute justification of Kellett in having ordered McClure to abandon her. Leaving some men to land her provisions and stores, he proceeded down Prince of Wales Strait, where he found the records left by both McClure and Collinson, the latter containing particularly valuable information, and then started back for the *Resolute*. Arriving there he found the gallant ship deserted and a note advising him to make immediately for Beechey Island. This seventy-day trip, covering 1,336 miles, established a sledging-record for both speed and distance—averaging eighteen and a half miles a day going out and twenty-three and a half miles a day coming back—despite the obstacles of heavy fogs, chaotic hummocks, and deep snow.

As though in bitter protest at having been abandoned, Kellett's *Resolute*, now a ghost ship, triumphed over the ice in Barrow Strait and drifted a thousand miles into Davis Strait, where she was picked up the following year by the American whaler Captain Budington.

Brought safely to New London, she was bought by the United States, completely refitted, and sent back to England.

The Belcher Expedition, despite its happier parts, was too bitter a pill for the English to swallow; they turned away from the Arctic. Besides, the national imagination was possessed by a new force. The haunting picture of one hundred and twenty-nine men lying dead in some unknown part of the Arctic was lost in the harrowing news that thousands were dying daily before the walls of Sebastopol. The sustaining interest in the fate of Franklin faded in the red light of the Crimean War, and when in March 1854 Sir John Franklin, Captain Crozier, their officers and crews were officially pronounced dead and their names removed from the Navy Lists, only one voice was raised in protest, Lady Jane Franklin's.

Ten years had passed since the *Erebus* and the *Terror* had sailed, ten years of heroic rescue work carried out on a large scale, and, save for the discovery of Franklin's first wintering at Beechey Island, no clues had been found, no hint of his eventual tragedy. And then, a bare four months after the official pronouncement, came definite news, tangible evidence of where and how the men of the missing ships had met their death.

The same year that Franklin had sailed to advance along the waterways traced by Parry and Ross to realize that great dream, the completion of the Northwest Passage, Dr. John Rae, working for the Hudson's Bay Company, had been dispatched to conclude the survey of the Arctic coast of America. Franklin died not far from where Rae was bringing his labors to a successful conclusion. Rae was called upon by the government to carry on the search from land when Richardson's efforts had been thwarted by bad weather in both 1848 and 1849. Leaving Fort Confidence the last of April 1851, he proceeded on foot to the mouth of the Coppermine and in his preliminary sledge journey crossed Dolphin and Union Strait, headed westward along the southern coast of Victoria Island (Wollaston Land) as far as Cape Baring at the entrance to Prince Albert Sound, returned, recrossed the strait, and hastened to pick up the boats that had been built for him. This sledge journey, a prelude to the serious work he had planned to do by boat, was accomplished in one month. In his boat he steered to the east and passed through Dease Strait to a point not far from Collinson's Cambridge Bay. Here, because adverse winds detained him, the impatient Rae left the boats and proceeded on foot —a hard, exhausting way over limestone debris—to trace the east coast of Victoria Island as far as Gateshead Island. Here he left the note found by Collinson. Had he only been able to see across the fifty miles of Victoria Strait, he would have discovered the *Erebus* and the *Terror* before they sank and have rescued the records that were lost with them. He was to wait four years before finding the solution to the mystery. In this trip he traced for the first time 725 miles of the coast of Victoria Island.

Two years later Rae was sent out again. This time he was in the employ of the Hudson's Bay Company and was to carry out a formidable program. Starting from his old camp at Repulse Bay, he was to cross the Boothia Peninsula from Pelly Bay to Castor and Pollux River, Simpson's farthest point, and from there swing northward along the west coast of the peninsula to Bellot Strait, discovered by Kennedy. And then, when three weeks out on western Boothia, quite by accident he stumbled on the first sign of the missing men. He met an Eskimo. "The man was very communicative, and, putting to him the usual questions as to his having seen white men before, or any ships or boats, he replied in the negative, but said that a party of 'Kabloonans' (whites) had died of starvation a long distance to the west of where we were then, and beyond a large river. He stated that he did not know the exact place, that he had never been there, and that he could not accompany us that far." [4]

Rae immediately questioned and investigated as far as he was able, and obtained the following picture. "In the spring four winters past [1850], whilst some Eskimo families were killing seals near . . . King William Land, forty white men were seen travelling in company southward over the ice, and dragging a boat and sledges with them. . . . None of the party could speak the Eskimo language so well as to be understood; but by signs the natives were led to believe the ship or ships had been crushed by the ice, and they were then going to where they expected to find some deer to shoot. . . . They purchased a small seal from the natives. . . . At a later date the same season, but previous to the disruption of the ice, the corpses of some thirty persons and some graves were discovered on the continent, and five bodies on an island near it, about a long day's journey to the . . . Great Fish River. . . . Some of the bodies were in a tent or tents, others were under the boats which had been turned over to make a shelter, and some lay scattered about in different directions. . . . From the mutilated state of many of the bodies, and the contents of the kettles, it is evident that our wretched countrymen had been driven to the last desperate alternative—cannibalism—as a means of sustaining life. A few of the unfortunate men must have survived until the arrival of the white fowl (say until the end of May), as shots were heard, and fresh bones and feathers of geese were noticed near the scene of the sad event. . . . There appears to have been an abundant store of ammunition . . . a number of telescopes, guns, watches, compasses, etc., all of which seem to have been broken up, as I saw pieces of these different articles with the natives, and I purchased as many as possible, together with some silver spoons and forks, an Order of Merit in the form of a star, and a small plate engraved 'Sir John Franklin, K.C.B.' " [4]

This important side trip in the interests of the Franklin search delayed Rae and he was unable to complete his assigned task. He reached Repulse Bay the end of May, and by the end of July that same year the news of his dramatic findings had been received in England. Because he had found the first definite proof of the fate of Franklin, the government gave him a reward of ten thousand pounds. Public attention was absorbed by the Crimean War, and the Admiralty was content to transfer the responsibility for the corroboration of Rae's information to the Hudson's Bay Company, asking them to investigate the region around the mouth of the Great Fish River, Montreal Island in particular. Neighboring Eskimos were to be questioned, but since the only interpreter was two thousand miles away, he was not included in the party led by James Anderson, one of the chief factors. He was able to converse with the natives only by sign language, but there was no mistaking their expressive pantomime as they portrayed the lost party in the last throes of starvation. For ten days Anderson searched with painstaking care, but found no books, scraps of paper, arms, or a single human bone or grave. Nor would his frail boats allow him to cross to King William Land to continue the search. Like Rae he was able to buy many articles from the Eskimos that they had taken from the dead and was obliged to be content with that. With Anderson's "indefinite information, confirmatory of other indefinite information," the Admiralty was satisfied and declared the official investigation closed.

But Lady Jane Franklin was not satisfied. That all her husband's party were dead brought her no peace. She petitioned the government not to "look on as unconcerned spectators" [5]; she begged that a "careful search be made for any possible survivor, that the bones of the dead be sought for . . . that their buried records be unearthed . . . and that their last written words . . . be saved from destruction. . . . This final and exhausting search is all I seek." [5] Her petition met with a cold refusal. Everything she had—and almost all her fortune had already been spent in outfitting four other independent expeditions—everything she could raise, went toward a final attempt. She directed this last expedition to head for the region south of Bellot

Strait, where she had urged Kennedy to go, where Collinson had had to turn back, where Rae had proof that the solution was to be found. She wanted to garner to the full the grim harvest that was waiting.

Lady Jane Franklin bought and outfitted the steam yacht *Fox*, a tiny vessel of 177 tons. The officers were all volunteers: Leopold McClintock, in command; Captain Allen Young of the merchant marine, youthfully enthusiastic, was master; and Lieutenant Hobson, who had served on the *Plover*, was second in command. Men and officers totaled but twenty-five, of whom more than half had already seen Arctic service. And yet this small group aboard a small vessel was to achieve success. To that godly generation it almost seemed as though the faith and determination of Franklin's widow were the irresistible weapon that helped the *Fox* triumph in its long, unequal struggle with the icy regions, that finally pierced the heart of the Arctic and forced it to yield its dark secret.

The *Fox* left England in July 1857, put in at Greenland, and then headed for Lancaster Sound. The season of 1857 proved to be one of the worst ever recorded. Try as he would, McClintock was unable to force a passage through the middle pack of Baffin Bay; and when in September he had gone 120 of the 170 miles across Melville Bay at a time when scores of ships had crossed successfully, he was beset and faced the "dismal prospect of a winter in the pack."[5] And only twenty-five miles away was a blue-water sky that his experience taught him stretched as far as Lancaster Sound! The tiny *Fox*, in the perilous company of two huge icebergs and a continent of broken-up ice refrozen together, drifted southward. For eight months she was a prisoner of the pack, drifting for the impressive distance of 1,385 miles, almost to the mouth of Cumberland Sound. Her release in April was brutal and appalling, almost fatal. For as the ice approached the open, swelling sea, it was smashed and shattered and whirled about, its huge pieces dashed against one another, miraculously sparing the *Fox*, since "a single thump from any of them would have meant instant destruction."[5]

The *Fox* was free, after a 242-day imprisonment, and the terrific anxiety of that last day made McClintock understand "how men's hair has turned grey in a few hours."[5] And without a moment's hesitation she was headed back for the north. The year 1858 was as kind as the previous year had been villainous. By the middle of August, McClintock was at Beechey Island, where he erected a memorial tablet. From there he steered for Peel Sound, down which he sailed for twenty-five miles until he was stopped by the "sight of unbroken ice extending from shore to shore." [5] Immediately he made up his mind that if that route were barred to him, he would attempt the alternative route via Bellot Strait, and he put about for Prince Regent Inlet. He reached the strait and by "an unsparing use of steam and canvas forced the ship" [5] halfway through. Five or six miles of the ice lay between the *Fox* and the western capes of the strait. But at the turn of the tide she was carried back, eastward, to their starting-point. Five times the *Fox* tried to get through the strait, to be turned back each time. Winter was approaching, and at Port Kennedy, a bay at the eastern end of the strait, McClintock prepared to pass the long Arctic night.

The course of the spring sledging-parties was outlined: there were to be three groups made up of four men with a dog-sledge and driver for each party. McClintock was to go to the Great Fish River, examining the shores of King William Land going and returning; Hobson was to cover the north shore of King William Land and, if possible, cross over to Gateshead Island; Young was to search the southern shore of Prince of Wales Land. But first McClintock wanted to question the Eskimos of western Boothia, for it was they who had given Rae news of the missing expedition. At the same time food depots had to be laid down for the spring journeys. While Hobson and Young undertook this task, McClintock set out in the dead of winter "to communicate with the Boothians in the vicinity of the magnetic pole." [5] The winter trip achieved more than that. He met a tribe of Eskimos who not only were stocked with relics plundered from the *Erebus* and the *Terror* but also gave him the important information that one of those ships had been crushed by the ice out at sea in the vicinity of Cape Felix. In this trip of twenty-five days, during which he covered 420 miles, McClintock completed the discovery of the coastline of North America, thereby adding 120 miles to the charts.

The three-headed, extended spring sledging-trips began on April 2, when Hobson and McClintock, whose paths coincided as far as Cape Victoria, left the *Fox*. Allen Young started out five days later. He crossed the western channel named by McClintock for Franklin, reached Prince of Wales Island, and traced its shore to the south and west. "Fearing that his provisions might run short, he sent back one sledge with four men, and continued his march with only one man and the dogs for forty days! . . . Young completed the exploration of this coast beyond the point marked upon the charts as Osborn's farthest,* up nearly to lat. 73° N., but no cairn was found. Young, however, recognized the remarkably shaped conical hills spoken of by Osborn when he was at his farthest, in 1851, struck off to the west-

* In 1851. See p. 143.

ward. . . . He attempted to cross the channel which he discovered between Prince of Wales Island and Victoria Land; but from the rugged nature of the ice, found it quite impracticable. . . . The coastline throughout was extremely low; and in the thick disagreeable weather which he almost constantly experienced, it was often a matter of great difficulty to prevent straying off the coastline inland. He commenced his return on the 11th May, and reached the ship on 7th June, in wretched health and depressed in spirits.

"Directly his health was partially re-established, he, in spite of the Doctor's remonstrances . . . again set out on the 10th with his party of men and dogs, to complete the exploration of both shores of the continuation of Peel Sound [Franklin Strait]." [5] By tracing the eastern coast of Prince of Wales Island as far as Browne's farthest, and then recrossing the strait and filling in the last gap left on the western shore of North Somerset, Young accomplished his purpose. His trip, while not adding any information to the Franklin search, was rich in geographical results.

On the way to Cape Victoria, Hobson and McClintock again met the same tribe of Eskimos. From them they learned what had been concealed before, that the second of the missing ships had been forced on shore by the ice in a badly shattered state. When the two men parted at Cape Victoria—Hobson heading west for Cape Felix, McClintock to the south for Montreal Island—Hobson was already suffering from scurvy. He noted, as he made his way toward Cape Felix, how the smooth year-old ice of Ross Strait changed to "many very heavy masses of ice, evidently of foreign formation," [5] which choked the waterway of Victoria Strait, and that Franklin had been doomed as soon as he charged into that pack.

It was Hobson who found "the record so ardently sought for, of the Franklin Expedition—at Point Victory, on the N.W. coast of King William's Land." [5] Lying about the cairn were quantities of clothing, a huge heap four feet high, and all kinds of articles, "as if these men, aware that they were retreating for their lives, had there abandoned everything which they considered superfluous." [5] He spent the whole month of May examining that desolate island. Stricken by scurvy, he had to be content with delegating the work to two of his men, who went on toward Cape Herschel. A large ship's boat was their only other discovery. After leaving notes with his complete findings for McClintock, Hobson started back for the *Fox*. He was so ill that he was carried on a sledge the last part of the trip.

But it was McClintock's efforts that brought out the full tragedy of the end of the Franklin Expedition. Continuing southward along the eastern coast of King William Island, he met some natives from whom he bought many more relics—silver spoons and plate—and learned that though there had been many books in the wreck, they had all been destroyed by the weather; that the survivors had made for the Great Fish River, falling and dying as they went along. He reached Montreal Island and, though he searched carefully, found nothing. The heavy seas had probably washed everything away. Recrossing the frozen strait to King William Island, he turned northward along its western shore, along the very route taken by the retreating crews. Soon he came upon a skeleton, eloquent proof that the men of the *Erebus* and the *Terror*, as the Eskimos had said, "fell down and died as they walked along." [5] McClintock hoped to find some record at Cape Herschel, whose slope is crowned by Simpson's conspicuous cairn, past which the retreating men *must* have filed; but there was nothing. Twelve miles beyond he found the note left by Hobson's men. Soon he came upon a boat in which were two skeletons, an amazing number of relics, but only forty pounds of chocolate and a little tea—nothing to keep alive on. At the beginning of June, McClintock reached the cairn at Victory Point and, standing there, reflected that when in 1830 Sir James Ross discovered Victory Point he had named two points of land then in sight Cape Jane Franklin and Cape Franklin, and that eighteen years afterward Franklin's ships had perished within sight of those headlands.

McClintock finished his remarkable trip when he reached the *Fox* on June 19. Not only had he ascertained the fate of Franklin—a task to which for a decade he had devoted his intelligence and energy—but he had made the circuit of King William Island and, by his trek down Rae Strait to Montreal Island, found the only feasible passage to the west. It was this route, blazed by McClintock, that Amundsen followed fifty years later when he sailed the Northwest Passage for the first time.

Their work done, the men rested and recovered. Fine weather increased their desire to be on their way home. Since both the engineer and his assistant, the only men who knew the workings of the engine, had died (both from non-Arctic causes), it devolved on McClintock to get the engines working. By the middle of August the *Fox* was free to leave Port Kennedy, and with McClintock at the engines she steamed slowly toward open waters. There she was, put under sail. By the end of September she had arrived home. The public honors bestowed on the great leader—he was knighted—the praise of the whole nation, were slight rewards compared with the satisfaction and gratitude shown him by Lady Jane Franklin.

13

The Route to the North

WHEN William Baffin in his voyage of 1616 gloriously brought to a close the first great thrust into the north, he pointed the way for future exploration along the three noble waterways he had noted: Lancaster, Jones, and Smith Sounds. From Parry to McClintock, the achievement of the Northwest Passage had been bound up with the penetration of Lancaster Sound. Two hundred and thirty-six years passed after Baffin had named Smith Sound, the most northerly of the three, before it was explored. Sir John Ross, it is true, had reached it in 1818, but he did no more than name after his ships, the two cliffs that mark its southern limit. Cape Alexander and Cape Isabella, the "Northern Pillars of Hercules," after that lapse of centuries, were to see ship after ship sail past, aiming to reach farther and farther into the north. Beginning with Captain Inglefield, the successive penetrations of Smith Sound are bound up with the route to the north, to the polar sea—the route to the North Pole.

Here, too, the search for Franklin was the spur that reopened that northern route. It will be remembered that when Belcher sailed in 1852 there was a strong sentiment that directed the search to the north of Wellington Channel. With this in mind Lady Jane Franklin sent Inglefield in the *Isabel* to look around to the north of Baffin Bay. In a brief summer voyage he steamed past Capes Alexander and Isabella, through open water as far as Kane Basin, bettering Baffin's farthest by forty-three miles. He named Cape Sabine—where Greely was later to suffer—and called the land on the west side of Smith Sound, facing Greenland, Ellesmere Island. Inglefield returned home with no word of Franklin but with the news that Smith Sound was really a channel leading to more northern waters.

The opening of this route attracted the attention and labors of two extraordinary Americans, Dr. Elisha Kent Kane and Charles Francis Hall. If the word *explorer* conjures up a picture of a Viking-like Nansen, then it is well to remember that there were many of slight, almost frail physique. Despite the fact that Kane had "chronic rheumatism, and cardiac disturbance" [1] by the time he was thirty, he had made vast sweeps of the globe, visiting Madeira, Brazil, Ceylon, Luzon, China and its islands, Borneo, Sumatra, Persia, Nubia, Sennaar, Greece, Mexico, the West Indies, Nova Scotia, Newfoundland, and west Greenland. He had tasted the charms of civilized Europe and had dived into an unexplored crater in Luzon; in Egypt he had been sick with the plague; in Africa he had been wasted by coast-fever; he had been wounded by a lance in Mexico and almost succumbed to lockjaw; he was at sea when he suffered a stroke from which he died in his thirty-seventh year. A cheerful, enthusiastic man, a charming personality, he was gifted with many talents, and is to be remembered as much for his brilliant writing as for the achievements he recorded.

As physician with De Haven's expedition in 1850,* Kane had had his first taste of the Arctic. The next two years he spent in making his plans and soliciting funds, combining a search for Franklin with an avowed desire to attain the Pole. In his tiny ship, the *Advance,* with a crew that totaled but seventeen, Kane followed the wake of the *Isabel* until ice stopped him. He was forced to winter but nine miles beyond the point Inglefield had reached, at Rensselaer Harbor on the Greenland coast. He had hoped to trace that coast as far as its northern extremity and had brought along Eskimo and Newfoundland dogs to facilitate the work. But the dogs developed "nerves— barked frantically at nothing, and walked in straight and curved lines with anxious and unwearying perseverance . . . and perished with symptoms resembling lockjaw in thirty-six hours after the first attack." [2] The plans had to be radically altered.

That spring several trips were made. Of an advance party sent out in March to lay down depots, four were badly frozen and were saved from death only by Kane's heroic efforts. Two of the men died later, and the others, who had gone without sleep for eighty-one hours, were crazed for a while. In May, Hayes, the surgeon, with one other man crossed over to the American side, the first to touch at Grinnell Land, a part of Ellesmere Island named for their patron. Meanwhile another party traced the Greenland coast, sighting for the first time the great Humboldt Glacier, sixty miles long, "rising in a solid glassy wall three hundred feet above the water level, with an unknown unfathomable depth below it—a long ever-shining line. . . . Here was a plastic, moving, semi-solid mass, obliterating life, swallowing rocks

* See pp. 141–2.

and islands, and ploughing its way with irresistible march through the crust of an investing sea." [2] In June a fourth party, consisting of Morton, the steward, and Hans Hendrik, an Eskimo, explored to the north of the great glacier. They reached a channel opening northward from Kane Basin, to which they gave the name of Kennedy Channel, and followed it as far as Cape Constitution at its northern extremity. "Beyond the Cape all is surmise. The high ridges to the northwest dwindled off into low, blue knobs, which blend finely with the air." [2] Kane thought they had seen in the distance the open polar sea.

Summer passed, and the *Advance* had not been free to move. Kane dreaded lest a second winter without fresh food or additional fuel spell disease and possibly death. Half of the men under Hayes tried to reach a Danish settlement to the south, only to return after having passed four terrible winter months frozen up three hundred miles from the ship. Kane and the remaining men, ravaged by scurvy, would have perished but for the aid rendered them by the Etah Eskimos, who generously shared their food with them, even when in desperate need themselves. Lack of fuel forced them to burn the upper half of the ship, and when spring came they prepared to abandon her. They began their retreat in three small boats, preserving intact all the records they had kept, and after eighty-three days of hardship and suffering reached Upernivik, a Danish settlement, in August 1855.

Any story of the exploration of the route to the north via Smith Sound must include mention of Hans Hendrik, the Eskimo, who played a vital role, participating in many expeditions. An expert with kayak and javelin, he makes his first appearance as a fat, good-natured lad of nineteen, spearing a bird on the wing. He was first engaged by Kane (for whom he speared the bird as proof of his ability), exchanging his services for a couple of barrels of bread and fifty-two pounds of pork. It was largely due to Han's efforts that Kane had been able to trace as far as Cape Constitution, and more than once because of his prowess the party was saved from starvation. After Kane had gone, Hans married a girl named Markut; together, for the next twenty-five years, they helped Hayes, Hall, and Nares and by their knowledge and skill many times staved off disaster. Hans later wrote his memoirs, which were translated from the Eskimo by Dr. Rink, the Danish Inspector of Greenland.

Isaac Israel Hayes, who had served as surgeon on the *Advance*, undeterred by the hardships he had endured, made plans to follow in Kane's steps. In 1860 he took his tiny schooner, the *United States*, to the north. With him went August Sonntag, a brilliant young astronomer. Three times the ship was blown out of Smith Sound, and Hayes finally took refuge for the winter at Port Foulke, near Cape Alexander. Hayes and Sonntag made many trips into the interior to examine the great Ice-Cap and determined by measurements that one of its discharging glaciers moved at the incredible rate of twelve feet a month. Like Kane, Hayes saw his dogs, on whom his plans for spring exploration depended, sicken and die. Out of thirty-six, but nine were left. In order to purchase additional dogs Sonntag, accompanied by Hans, set out in midwinter to visit the natives of Whale Sound. On their way Sonntag fell through the ice into the water. Hans pulled him out, stripped off his wet, icy clothes, wrapped him in a sleeping-bag, and, loading him on a sledge, dragged him to where they had camped the previous night. "Our road being very rough I cried from despair for want of help; but I reached the snow hut and brought him inside. I was, however, unable to kindle a fire, and was myself overpowered with cold . . . on account of now standing still, after having perspired with exertion. During the whole night, my friend still breathed, but he drew his breath at long intervals, and towards morning only very rarely. . . ." So Hans, in his memoirs, records the death of young Sonntag.

This tragic death clouded Hayes's entire expedition. He had depended on Sonntag to make the correct observations, so vital a part of exploration; and though Hayes proceeded with his spring sledging-trip—crossing Smith Sound and tracing a good way up the coast of Ellesmere Land—his calculations were so inaccurate as to be of little value. Exploration must be precise and accurate, else its primary object is defeated.

When the *United States* returned to Boston in 1860, it passed the *Rescue* (the same that had been part of De Haven's expedition), which was bearing northward for the first time a strange type of explorer. Charles Francis Hall in his forty years had done nothing to qualify as one. He had had only a grammar-school education, had worked at various jobs, including blacksmithing and engraving, knew little of science and less about a ship; and yet by virtue of being "fertile in resources, indefatigable in exertions, sparing no personal effort or exposure, faithful in record and conservative in action," he takes a high place among Arctic explorers. The force that had sufficient power to alter so radically the whole course of his life was the appeal of the Franklin mystery. He hoped that by a prolonged stay among the natives of King William Island he would learn the whole story of that tragedy—not the meager outline McClintock had deduced from scant evidence. To do this he resolved to live with the Eskimos as one of them. This episode he tells shows the true temper of this unorthodox explorer (the italics are his): "My opinion is, that the Esquimaux practice of eating their food *raw* is a good one—at least for the better preservation of *their* health. To one *educated* otherwise, as we whites are . . . feasting on uncooked meats is highly repulsive; but *eating meats raw or cooked is entirely a matter of education.* . . . I saw the natives *actually feasting on the raw flesh of the whale* . . . .

An Eskimo Shaman Singing
A native woodcut from Rink's Danish Greenland.

slicing and eating thin pieces of ligament that looked *white and delicious* as the breast of a Thanksgiving turkey. At once I made up my mind to join in partaking of the inviting (?) viands actually smoking in my sight. . . . I peeled off a piece . . . closed my eyes, and cried out 'Turkey'! But it would not go down so easy . . . because *it was tougher than any bull beef of Christendom.* For half an hour I tried to masticate it, and then found it even tougher than when I began. At length I discovered I had been making a mistake in the way to eat it. The Esquimaux practice is to get as vast a piece into their distended mouths as they can cram, and then, boa constrictor-like, first lubricate it over, and so *swallow it quite whole!*" [3]

In his first stay among the Eskimos of Baffin Island in 1860–2, though he failed in his main purpose of finding Franklin relics, he found many of Frobisher's expedition to Meta Incognita. His firm friendship with the Eskimo couple Tookoolito and Ebierlung, called by him Hannah and Joe, which was then formed, lasted till his death. They accompanied him back to the United States and were with him on his second venture, when he spent five consecutive winters (1864–9) in the Arctic and was successful in finding many objects of the Franklin Expedition. These two remarkable sojourns in territory already charted were magnificent training for his third venture of "discovery to the northern axis of the great globe if possible, or the absolute proof of its inaccessibility." [4]

He realized this ambition and sailed northward again in 1871. The Navy Department had given him a staunch tug, which Hall had re-built for Arctic work and which he named the *Polaris*. Commanding her was Captain Buddington (not the man who had salvaged the *Resolute*) an experienced whaler, with Captain Tyson as chief mate; Dr. Emil Bessels, who served with the German expedition of 1869,[*] was in charge of the scientific work; Hannah, Joe, their small daughter, Hans Hendrik, his wife and child, made up the Eskimo contingent. The season was favorable, and the *Polaris* steamed north-ward through the whole series of waterways leading from Smith Sound to the Arctic Sea—to the unequaled northing, for those waters, of 82° 11′. He was over two hundred miles north of where Kane had been stopped; he had extended the known coastline of Ellesmere Land almost to its northern limits and had reached a part of the Greenland coast where, free from the great inland ice, the land was covered with vegetation and frequented by game. Hall had taken a giant's step toward the North Pole. But the *Polaris* was forced back by the wind and ice, and Hall was grateful for the shelter offered by Thank God Harbor. It was no real harbor, "being an open roadstead on the coast of Greenland," [4] whose only protection was an enormous iceberg—450 feet long by 300 wide and 65 high—devoutly called Providence Berg.

Hall immediately went for a short autumm sledging-trip to Cape Brevoort on Newman Bay and wondered all the while why "he was not able to run before the sledge and encourage the dogs, as on former expeditions, but had been compelled to keep on the sledge."
He did not know that he was ill, and mortally so. Upon his return to the ship he suffered a stroke and, after lingering a few days, died. With his death the heart of the expedition stopped beating, and with him, at Hall's Rest, were buried his great hopes. His chief mourners were his Eskimo friends, Hannah and Joe.

Captain Buddington decided to return home without attempting any further exploratory trips. In August of the following year the *Polaris* was free from the ice, but was soon caught again in the heavy pack of Robeson Channel and, anchored to a large floe, drifted south

* See pp. 225 ff.

ward toward Baffin Bay. When it was almost out of Smith Sound, a gale lashed the pack into a maniacal frenzy. Again and again it struck the *Polaris*, threatening to break in her sides. Suddenly a piece of ice thrust a long arm through the ship and, to be prepared lest she sink, the men, with despair to lend them strength, transferred boxes, barrels, cans, beds, coal, clothes, records to the floe. On one side the ice climbed over the sides of the ship; on the other, two boats were lowered. A crack rent the ice and rapidly widened. Some of the landed supplies were in danger of falling into the sea. Tyson, with some helpers, began lugging them to a safer place. More and more dark cracks streaked through the ice, dividing the floe. With no warning the *Polaris* was swept away. Through the darkness of the Arctic twilight those on board could just see the floe, with its precious freight, disappear. They saw it break into smaller pieces, separating the piles of provisions and stores and, most terrible of all, the men. They saw Hans rush to pick up a bundle—his three-months-old baby. They saw several men try to reach the ship, while they in turn launched boats to pick up the marooned ones. In vain. Faintly they heard those on the ice call out: "Good-by, *Polaris*!"

It was the 15th of October, the beginning of the long Arctic night. The *Polaris*, blown northward, was brought to land at Life-Boat Cove, near Port Foulke. Landing all their stores and provisions, the men used the ship to build the Polaris house, in which they passed their second winter. The near-by Etah Eskimos were faithful friends; in fact, Polaris house became the center of a community of about a hundred and fifty persons who were lively, willing, eager, and helpful. In the spring they built two boats and in June started southward. After three weeks they hailed the whaler *Ravenscraig*. From the whalers the men of the *Polaris* heard the amazing account of the party that had been torn from them that stormy October night and stranded on the ice.

On the floe with Tyson were the steward, the cook, six sailors, and the two Eskimo families—nineteen in all. They had only some scant provisions, two whaleboats, two kayaks, a canvas tent, a boat-compass, and a chronometer. They were unable to reach either the *Polaris*, which they spied the next morning far off on the horizon, or the shore. And on their floe, which measured a hundred and fifty yards each way, they prepared to spend the long winter. Hans and Joe built three snow-houses and went out hunting in their kayaks. Without the Eskimos they must all have died of starvation. It was a hard task feeding eighteen persons—Han's little son was still nursing—and at times all were hungry, so hungry that Tyson tells that their first seal they ate uncooked, skin, hair, and all. Another time: "I have dined today on two feet of frozen entrail and a little blubber. I only wish we had plenty even of that." [4] The most important event was catching a seal, for it meant not only food, but light and heat as well. But after a while food ceased being their chief preoccupation. With the welcome reappearance of the sun, after eighty-three days, they were threatened with the breaking up of the pack. "The cracking up of the floe was so alarming that the people remained up and dressed, and kept themselves and all their necessaries of life ready in case of a sudden disaster. . . . Fortunately the place originally selected for the snow-houses proved to be the thickest and most solid part of the floe." [4] Two comforts they had despite the terrors that toyed with them: they were all in good health, and day by day they were being carried at the rate of twenty-three miles a day nearer and nearer southern waters, closer and closer to the haunts of men.

Their floe gradually became smaller. Then it separated from the pack and sought the open ocean. On April 1 "it was necessary to abandon the floe, which was now wasted to such an extent that it was no longer safe." [4] The party took to the one boat they had left. Constructed to hold from six to eight men, it now had to carry twelve men, two women, and five children—nineteen souls. To keep the boat afloat they had to throw away a hundred pounds of meat and all superfluous clothes. They kept the tent, a few skins for protection, and a little meat, bread, and pemmican. And so they went, driven from floe to floe—and the returned sun melted the ice, and the warmer water thawed it, making the pieces thinner and smaller. Sleet and rain came to plague them. Still they drifted southward.

On the 28th of April they saw their first ship. Joy possessed them. They congratulated one another on their miraculous deliverance. But the steamer did not see them, and it disappeared during the night. The next day another ship appeared and likewise disappeared. On the 30th a fog blotted out the horizon. Suddenly through the fog sailed the barquentine *Tigress*, Captain Bartlett of Conception Bay, Newfoundland. In a few minutes she was alongside the floe and had taken the whole party aboard. And none too soon. "From May 2nd to 4th a storm of extreme severity raged incessantly. The floe party had been rescued in good time; it could hardly have survived this gale." [4] They had been picked up off Grady Harbour on the Labrador coast, having drifted a distance of 1,300 miles!

Hall's work and the interest aroused by the subsequent adventures of the men of the *Polaris* determined the English to have a try at reaching the North Pole. It had taken them twenty years to forget

Smith Sound, October 15, 1872: WITH NO WARNING THE *Polaris* WAS SWEPT AWAY LEAVING NINETEEN PEOPLE MAROONED ON THE ICE.

Hall's NARRATIVE OF THE NORTH POLAR EXPEDITION.

Approaching the western end of Lancaster Sound.   THE
ROCKY COASTS ROSE OUT OF THE WATER LIKE A GIGANTIC WALL—BUT
BEFORE HIM LAY OPEN WATER.

Parry's JOURNAL OF A VOYAGE . . . 1819–20.

*In the great Canadian forest near Fort Chipewyan,
March 15th, 1820.*   "MANNER OF MAKING A RESTING PLACE ON
A WINTER'S NIGHT."

Franklin's NARRATIVE OF A JOURNEY . . . IN 1819–22.

the Belcher fiasco, but in the meantime English whalers had gone more and more into those northern waters, following hard in the wake of the explorers into newer and richer whaling-territory. Business as well as science was eager to learn about the region around the Pole. So in 1874 plans were made.

Captain Nares, one of the ablest navigators of the fleet, was given command of two fine ships, the *Alert* and the *Discovery*. He had with him a group of young officers, each of whom was to display heroic qualities: Commander Albert Markham, Lieutenants Beaumont, Parr, Aldrich, Rawson, Egerton, and Conybeare; he had the advice of the Arctic authorities of the previous generation—McClintock, Sherard Osborn, Clements Markham—in the matter of equipment, provisions, and routine. Little wonder, then, that the Nares Expedition of 1875–6 was to be in line with the great English naval tradition of Arctic discovery, accomplishing a sizable amount of accurate exploration by acts of stubborn pluck and valor and presenting the sphere and problems for future work. And yet as one reads the account of this expedition, one is transported back to the days before the Franklin search, before the Hudson's Bay men and Hall had, with enormous success, covered vast stretches, spent many years, and maintained good health far within the Arctic. It would almost seem as though the British naval mind were incapable of learning the lessons that the Arctic had been, over generations, expounding.

Nares had a foretaste of nature's hostility when he encountered terrific gales in crossing the North Atlantic to Greenland. There, at Godhavn Harbor, he took on additional stores and provisions and Eskimo dogs. He secured the services of a Dane named Petersen and the Eskimo Hans Hendrik. His northward passage, in sharp contrast to Hall's clear sailing, was savagely contested by heavy ice and achieved only by consummate navigation. He ordered caches of supplies placed at various strategic points, and, though not used by him, they were to play an important part in a later expedition. He also had to correct Hayes's faulty and inaccurate charting as he advanced up the western coast. At Lady Franklin Bay, high on the Ellesmere coast, the *Discovery* found winter quarters, while he pushed the *Alert* fifty miles farther through Robeson Channel to Floeberg Beach, facing the great polar sea. "The protected space available for shelter was so contracted, the entrance to it so small, and the united force of the wind and flood-tide so powerful, that it was with much labour . . . that the ship was hauled in stern foremost. It was a close race whether the ice or the ship would be in first." [5] A very close race, for in two days they could walk ashore over the thick ice that surrounded them. Before him stretched the polar sea, not the open polar sea men had hoped for, but the dread sanctum of the formidable polar pack. Here was the birthplace of the ice that "had defeated Collinson and McClure off the coast of America, that Parry vainly fought against off Melville Island, that, passing down McClintock Channel, fatally beset the *Erebus* and *Terror,* that clogs the east coast of Greenland." [5] Nares had only to look northward over that ice, worse than the most tortured of glaciers, to know that "unless we discovered land tending to the north, neither our ship nor our sledges would be able to advance far"; [5] and, modifying the too ambitious goal, he "trusted that we might advance such a distance from the land as would enable us to ascertain the nature of the pack-ice in the offing, and learn whether it could ever be travelled over for a reasonable distance on a future occasion." [5] These, then, were the two aims of their spring sledging-trips: to trace as much as possible of the coasts of both Ellesmere Island and Greenland so as to know how far north land existed, and to test the possibility of attaining the Pole over the ice of the polar sea.

"In other successful expeditions we have had to deal with the work of strong and healthy men. Now we have to contemplate the heroic, indeed almost miraculous efforts of men who attained great results in spite of the ravages of a terrible and deadly disease. The seeds of scurvy had taken root throughout the winter, and no one knew it. The travelling parties had started before the calamity became known, and of 121 men in the two ships there were 56 cases of scurvy, 42 in the *Alert,* but only 14 in the *Discovery,* in which ship a larger supply of fresh meat was obtained from musk-oxen." [6]

Food depots had been laid down in the autumn and complete preparations made when the main sledging-parties started on April 3. From the *Alert* two groups went out: one, under Markham and Parr, aimed for a new record for "farthest north" across the frozen sea; the other, led by Aldrich, was to trace the northern coast of Ellesmere Land. The equipment of the first group was complicated by the presence of two boats, to be used in case they met with open water; hauling these boats over the rough ice accounted for the extraordinary fact that, while their farthest was only a short 73 miles from the ship, they actually covered 521 miles. For instead of the sledges advancing together at a steady rate, all the men were required to move one load—traveling four miles to gain one. Their path lay over never ending ridges of high hummocks, over which the boats were dragged a few feet at a time to the accompaniment of "One, two, three, haul!" And for all their effort they could make no more than one to two miles a day.

They had left the ship hale, strong, hearty, fit. Sixty days on the ice, and they barely escaped alive. They abandonêd one boat. Still their progress was slow. It was a nightmare. "Men getting tired . . . everything frozen hard, our sleeping-bags resembled sheet-iron, whilst our currie-paste was exactly like a piece of brass. . . . Sleepless nights . . . 41 temperature persists in remaining low. . . . Glare from the sun oppressive. . . . Suffering from snow-blindness . . . another mass of hummocks . . . only made half a mile during the afternoon . . . another long fringe of large and troublesome hummocks . . . through this we resolved to cut a passage. . . ." [5] And then scurvy. First one man and then another. Fewer men to haul and more to be hauled. On May 11, at 83° 20′ 26″ N., Markham knew that his men could not go farther. They turned back for the ship. They abandoned the second boat. They reached land the 5th of June, only thirty miles from the *Alert.* "We are now reduced to only six men [for hauling], and they anything but strong or healthy, and two officers. Five men are carried on the sledges and four can just manage to crawl after." [5] Parr, going on alone, covered the thirty miles in twenty-four hours and sent back aid. They reached the ship sick and exhausted, but happy in the knowledge that by their efforts the British flag had been planted nearest the North Pole.

When Nares saw the pitiful condition of those men, he feared for Aldrich's party, who had not as yet returned. A rescue party was sent to look for them, and it was due to this prompt relief that the second group came back at all. Of the robust band that had left the *Alert* in April, only Aldrich and one other remained strong enough to haul the sledges. Scurvy had touched them all, and their homeward trip became more and more of a struggle. "Little by little we crept on, but every moment made our inability to go on for the ship without assistance the more apparent." [5] Those who were well would not abandon the sick, and with a fatal certainty the sick would have dragged all the men to death. The timely arrival of the rescue party saved them. And they had accomplished a splendid piece of work. They had traced the northern coast of Ellesmere Land, with its eruption of heavy pack, for 220 miles, rounding Cape Columbia, the northern tip, as far as Cape Alfred Ernest, where the land dips to the southwest. Nares had every reason to be proud of his men, but he was thankful to have them all back on shipboard again. He was anxious to know what had been happening aboard the *Discovery.*

The *Discovery* had also sent out two sledging-parties. One, under Archer and Conybeare, outlined the deep fiord that lies to the south of Lady Franklin Bay—Archer Fiord. In their sledging-operations they discovered a fine vein of coal close to where the ship had wintered. It was the other party, under Lieutenant Beaumont, that, mapping northward along the Greenland coast, achieved splendid results in the face of ghastly odds. A pioneering party under Rawson left early in April to find the best route across Robeson Channel to Greenland. A few days later Beaumont, with Dr. Coppinger, set out for the *Alert* with two eight-man sledges. There they met Rawson, who led them over to the Greenland coast, where Dr. Coppinger, after establishing a depot for Beaumont, turned back. A few days later one of the men showed signs of scurvy, and Rawson was sent back to the ship with him. Beaumont continued northward, mapping and laying down depots to secure his retreat. But more and more of his men fell victims to scurvy, and he soon realized that he would not be able to go forward much longer. And the season was far advanced. The snow became softer, travel more exhausting; advance was a slow, painful process. Progress meant "literally having to climb out of the holes made by each foot in succession, the hard crust on top, which would only just *not* bear you, as well as the depth of the snow preventing you from pushing through it." [5] Beaumont tried to reach a high mountain on the north side of Sherard Osborn Fiord so as to take bearings. He went on alone through the deep snow. "I covered about one and a half miles in three hours and then gave it up. My strength was nearly exhausted, and I hailed the men and told them to have lunch, but I myself would rather forego three meals than walk all the way back." [5]

On the 19th of May, the day they turned back, Beaumont writes: "No one will ever be able to understand what hard work we had during those days, but the following may give some idea of it: When we halted for lunch, two of the men crept on all fours for 200 yards, rather than walk through this terrible snow." [5] They faced their homeward journey suffering the intolerable pains of scurvy, with stiff legs, their feet skinned raw, and open sores on their shoulders where the traces of the sledges lay. Only Beaumont and one other man were sound when at last they reached a large depot, just across the channel from the *Alert*. They had plenty of provisions, but they were unable to reach the *Alert*: black water holes warned them that the intervening ice was rotten and unsafe. Beaumont decided to go on toward Hall's grave—near Thank God Harbor, forty miles away— on a line with the *Discovery*. Rather than continue along the soft snow, they traveled close along the rocky shore. Rasmussen, who traversed the same path forty years later, writes: "How they managed to pull the sledges up Gap Valley, with all this illness and exhaustion, is a perfect riddle to us who have looked at the stony pass. The English will, which often stiffens into obstinacy, manifested itself here; there is nothing to say but this, that as there was no other way they went up through Valley Pass." [7] At the rate of a mile a day they advanced towards Thank God Harbor, the two able men making three trips to haul all the sick. It was due to the foresight of Rawson, Coppinger, and Hans Hendrik, who went out to find Beaumont's party, that they were saved. For a long time they rested and regained their strength and, thanks to Hans, who kept them plentifully supplied with fresh seal meat, they were greatly restored in health. In a fifteen-foot boat they crossed Robeson Channel—a week of strenuous and dangerous maneuvering over the drifting ice—and reached the haven where lay the *Discovery*.

Although all the men had done valiant work, their results still fell short of what they had proposed to do. But Nares, unwilling to risk another year in the Arctic with his scurvy-ridden men, decided to return to England. A terrific gale at the end of August smashed the pack ice so effectively that he was able to extricate the *Alert* from Floeberg Beach. Joined by the *Discovery*, he picked his way southward, and by the beginning of November they were back home. They had with them an important collection of scientific observations and, though they had come nowhere near attaining the North Pole, had accomplished a valuable amount of work. Henceforth the English were not in the race to see which nation would first reach the northern axis of the globe; wisely they were interested in pursuing scientific investigations, in collecting additional data on Arctic phenomena.

The door to the north, pointed out by Inglefield, was within twenty-five years forced wide open. Nares had wintered on the edge of the polar sea, and his men had struggled for some miles over it. Cape Columbia had been determined as the northernmost tip of Ellesmere Land. It was from that point that Peary was to make his dash to the Pole.

14

Franz Josef Land: the Amazing Drift of the Tegetthoff

THE DISCOVERY of Franz Josef Land is unique. For while discovery always has the quality of finding something concealed within the unknown—of suddenly coming upon a new land, a mighty river, a lofty mountain range, a deep-cut canyon—it has usually been accomplished by men who were free to search and range abroad. But the men of the *Tegetthoff* were not free. For almost a year they were prisoners of the pack. And their discovery presents the picture of a bewildered little boy, held firmly by the scruff of the neck and dragged relentlessly down a long, dark, and strange corridor, gazing at last upon a shining Christmas tree.

The eminent German geographer Petermann dusted off a theory that had not been used since the days of Barents and, in Lieutenant Karl Weyprecht of the Austrian Navy and Lieutenant Julius Payer of the Austrian Army, found two men who were eager to test its validity. Petermann insisted that by following one of the branches of the Gulf Stream after it bifurcates at North Cape an ice-free passage might be found to the north of Novaya Zemlya that would facilitate either the successful accomplishment of the Northeast Passage or the attainment of the North Pole. Barents, it is true, on a similar mission had sailed through open water and found Spitsbergen; Payer and Weyprecht found no open water and achieved neither of their two goals, but, thanks to the ice that they tried vainly to avoid, they did discover Franz Josef Land. This is the story of those two men and their ship, the *Tegetthoff*.

Through the generosity of their patron, Count Wilczek, they made a preliminary voyage in the summer of 1871 northward along Novaya Zemlya. This cruise confirmed their brightest hopes, and the following year they set out in the *Tegetthoff*, equipped for two and a half years. It was the first and last voyage of discovery the ship was to make. Accompanied by Count Wilczek in his yacht, the *Isbjörn*, they reached Cape Nassau, on Novaya Zemlya, where a cache was placed —the first place of refuge in the event the *Tegetthoff* was lost. As far south as that they had to use steam to make their way past a "solemn and continuous procession of icebergs floating like huge white biers toward the south." [1] On August 18 the *Isbjörn* sailed for home and the *Tegetthoff* pointed northward.

The future looked dark. The amount of navigable water had decreased daily, while the ice rapidly assumed greater solidity. Within a few hours, while still in sight of Novaya Zemlya, they were beset. "No water was to be seen around us, and never again were we destined to see our vessel in water. . . . We were, in fact, no longer discoverers, but passengers against our will on the ice. From day to day we hoped for the hour of our deliverance! At first we expected it hourly, then daily, then from week to week; then at the seasons of the year and changes of the weather, then in the chances of the new year. But that hour never came." [1] Fixed firmly on the floe, they drifted northward until the outline of the land they had left was no longer on their horizon and around them was nothing but an icy waste. Like all those who have spent winters at the mercy of the pack, they tasted its capricious and malevolent power. Payer writes: "As we sat at our breakfast, our floe burst across immediately under our ship. Rushing on deck we discovered that we were surrounded and squeezed by the ice; the after part of the ship was already nipped and pressed, and the rudder, which was the first to encounter its assault, shook and groaned. We next sprang on the ice. . . . But just as in the risings of a people, the wave of revolt spreads on every side, so now the ice uprose against us. . . . Noise and destruction reigned supreme, and step by step destruction drew nigh in the crashing together of the fields of ice. Our floe was now crushed, and its blocks, piled up into mountains, drove hither and thither. Here, they towered fathoms high above the ship, and forced the protesting timbers of the massive oak, as if in mockery of their purpose, against the hull of the vessel; there masses of ice fell down as into an abyss under the ship, to be engulfed in the rushing waters, so that the quanity of ice beneath the ship was constantly increased, and at last began to raise her quite above the level of the sea. . . . The pressure reached a frightful height . . . the *Tegetthoff* had heeled over on her side, and huge piles of ice threatened to precipitate themselves on her . . . but the pressure abated." [1] They stood, each with a little bundle containing the minimum of necessaries, ready to abandon the ship, "whither, no one pre-

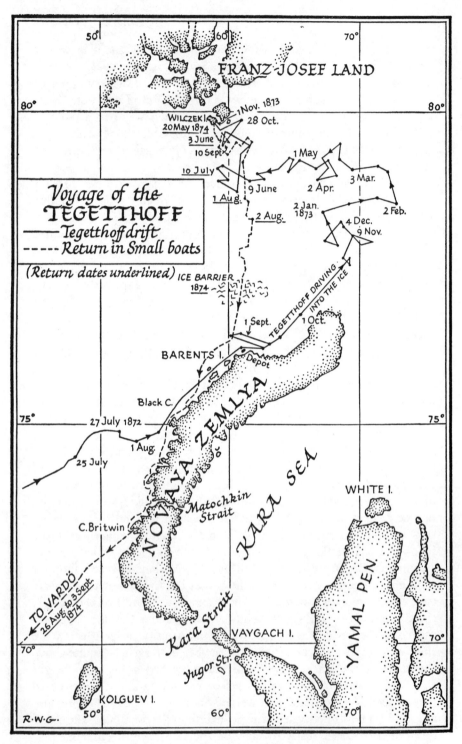

Map of the Drift of the Tegetthoff

tended to know. For not a fragment of the ice had remained whole [there was no vast floe, such as served the men of the *Polaris*]. A sledge would have been swallowed up, and in this circumstance lay the horror of our situation. For, if the ship should sink, whither should we go . . . amid this confusion how reach the land?"[1]

A thousand such moments beset them as they drifted throughout the winter. "All spring, all summer they [the crew] dug and sawed to get the *Tegetthoff* free—to no avail. They bored through the ice to see how deeply they were caught. After going to a depth of 27 feet, they still struck ice."[1] There was nothing left for them to do but wait, wait inactively, deprived of initiative, like "mere insects, who dwell on the leaf of a tree and care not to know its edges."[1] The second summer was gone, and they faced another winter imprisoned on the floe. "Not a man among us believed in the possibility of discoveries, though discoveries beyond our utmost hopes lay immediately before us."[1] On the 30th of August 1873 the miraculous occurred.

"About mid-day, as we were leaning on the bulwarks of the ship and scanning the gliding mists, through which the rays of the sun broke ever and anon, a wall of the mist, lifting itself up suddenly, revealed to us afar off in the north-west, the outlines of bold rocks, which in a few moments seemed to grow into a radiant Alpine land! At first we all stood transfixed, hardly believing what we saw. Then carried away by the reality of our good fortune we burst into shouts of joy: 'Land, Land, Land at last!'[*] . . . There before us lay the prize that could not be snatched from us. Yet not by our action, but through the happy caprice of the floe, and as in a dream we had won it. . . . We beheld from a ridge of ice the mountains and glaciers of the mysterious land. Its valleys seemed to our fond imagination clothed with green pastures over which herds of reindeer roamed in undisturbed enjoyment of their liberty, and far from all foes. For thousands of years this land had lain buried from the knowledge of man, and now its discovery had fallen into the lap of a small band, themselves almost lost to the world."[1] They called it Franz Josef Land and with loud hurrahs drank to the health of their Emperor.

But between the *Tegetthoff* and the land stretched the impassable, fissure-cut ice-field. The ship suddenly drifted southward—then stopped—then northward again, bringing back the tormenting sight of the unattainable land. At last, in October, they reached it. "Snow and rock and broken ice surrounded us on every side, a land more desolate could not have been found on earth than the island we walked on; all this we saw not. To us it was a paradise, and this paradise we

[*] 79°43′ N., 59°33′ E.

called Wilczek Island. The vegetation was indescribably meagre and miserable, consisting of a few lichens. The drift-wood we expected to find was nowhere to be seen. We looked for traces of the reindeer and fox, but our search was utterly fruitless. The land appeared to be without a single living creature." [1]

The second winter spent on shipboard passed quickly. Extensive preparations were made to explore by sledges as much of their newly discovered land as they could in the brief spring. For by the summer they would have to be on their way back to their deposit on Novaya Zemlya. Payer was in charge of land operations, while Weyprecht took command of those on sea. Payer followed McClintock's methods in all his sledging-trips.

The first trip was made to Hall Island near by, a plateau two thousand feet high, where after five days the intense cold of −59° frosted the men severely and forced them to return. "Cold is depressing in its influence and soon enfeebles the powers of the will. At first it stimulates to action, but this vigour is quickly followed by torpidity; exertion is soon succeeded by the desire to rest. Persons exposed to these alternations of increased action and torpor feel as if they were intoxicated. . . . Most of the circumpolar animals escape, as much as they can, the horrors of the frost: some migrate; others, burying themselves in holes, sleep throughout the winter. The fish, which are found in the small pools of sweet water on the land, are frozen in when these pools freeze, and awake to life and movement again only when the pools are thawed." [1] They were experiencing the calm weather, clear atmosphere, and inhuman cold characteristic of the interior of Arctic countries. "The eye-lids freeze, even in calm weather . . . great cold as well as great heat generates the great evil—thirst. . . . Snow of a temperature that low feels like hot iron in the mouth and does not quench but increases the thirst. Snow-eaters during the march were regarded . . . in much the same way as opium-eaters are." [1]

The main party, in which there were ten men and three dogs, left the *Tegetthoff* at the end of March. For a week they fought their way through violent blizzards, were discouraged by rough ice and intense cold, but continued until they saw before them the wide sweep of Austria Sound. At Hohenlohe Island two of the men, who were too exhausted to go on, were left in a camp with another to tend them. Shortly after leaving them Payer had an exciting and almost fatal accident. While the party was crossing a glacier, an ice bridge suddenly gave way. Into the bottomless crevasse fell one of the men and the dogs. The sledge, fortunately, was wedged, and Payer, jerked backward, was stopped at the very brink. He freed himself from the traces and looked down. The dogs dangled in their harness; the man lay on an ice shelf. Payer's Alpine experience stood him in good stead. He could effect a rescue, but he needed the help of the men and ropes he had just left behind. It was six miles to the camp. If only the man on the ledge did not freeze! Throwing off his bulky outer clothing, he raced through the deep snow and was back with help in four and a half hours. And everything—man, dogs, and sledge—was saved.

Undeterred, he pushed northward and by April 12 reached Cape Fligely (81° 51′ N.) on Crown Prince Rudolf Land, the most northerly tip of land in the Old World hemisphere. Standing on this promontory, a thousand feet high, Payer looked to the north and saw, across open water, the outlines of distant lands—King Oscar Land and Petermann Land. Later explorers, hoping to find those lands, discovered that they had been mirages. Payer himself was deterred from trying to reach them because of the prevalence of water holes and rotten ice. Rotten ice and water holes lay also between him and the ship. He was 165 miles from the *Tegetthoff*, and the pack was breaking up. He reached Hohenlohe Island, picked up the men, who were somewhat rested, and, lightening the sledges as much as possible, hurried toward the ship. Suddenly they heard a dull noise coming from the direction in which they were headed. A turn in the path and they understood. Across their homeward path lay the sea! "The spray of its surf dashed for a distance of thirty yards over the icy shore. . . . The icebergs, under which we had passed a month before, were now floating. That on which lay our depot of provisions was floating in the midst of them; and here we were, without a boat, almost without provisions, fifty-five miles from the ship. What were we to do, what direction were we to follow? . . . In what direction did the ice still lie unbroken?" [1] Hungry, battered by furious gales, Payer picked his way forward. Luck was with him when he found his last depot intact, close to the shore. Meanwhile the storms had driven the ice together again. Refreshed, with hope restored, he went on, over a stony plateau, and saw across the endless white waste of the frozen sea the three slender masts of the *Tegetthoff*. They were home.

"We could now return with honour." [1] They had discovered new lands and had sledged over five hundred miles of it—they could now think of retreat, of abandoning the ship. The plan was simple. They would head due south, in three twenty-foot boats, to their depot on Novaya Zemlya, where, their provisions replenished, they would coast along the shore, hoping to meet with a fishing-ship. Everyone worked hard to get ready. They plundered the ship of everything that could be carried off; they packed, they sewed. Speed was essential, for their time was limited. On the 20th of May they left the *Tegetthoff*.

To reach open water they first had to struggle through soft, knee-deep snow, dragging their boats mounted on sledges. After eight days they had gone only five miles. Payer and Weyprecht decided that such strenuous labor was not justified by the meager results. They would wait for the ice to open. They waited, waited, detained there for weeks, eating precious food. At last small leads appeared, offering partial aid. They sailed down the length of one of them, then dragged their loads to the next one. So for weeks it went—sailing, stopping, waiting, dragging, sailing again. "It was a strange life, this abode in boats covered over with a low tent roof. Oars by way of furniture, and three pairs of stockings for each man's mattress and pillow. A time of ennui. Happy the man who has any tobacco, happy he who, after smoking, does not fall into a faint; happy too the man who finds a fragment of a newspaper in some corner or other. . . . Enviable is he who discovers a hole in his fur coat which he can mend; but happiest of all are those who can sleep day and night. . . . There were no events, no sudden occurrence either to excite or alarm us, but the time flowed on, and our constantly diminishing stock of provisions, like the steady movements of the hands of a clock, spoke with a plainness of speech, that could not be resisted, of the doom impending over us. . . . A steady south wind destroyed the little progress we made. After the lapse of two months of indescribable efforts, the distance between us and the ship was not more than two German [eight English] miles."[1]

August came, and slowly but surely the rain and sunshine cleared their path. The leads became larger until far off they saw a fluctuation in the sea level. The swell of the ice-free ocean was within sight, but ice, strong enough to stop them and yet too thin to hold their weight, lay between. They waited again, with every moment important. "Dreadful was the solemn lapse of time."[1] Not until the middle of the month did "a large ice-hole open before us . . . we sailed into it—it was the last one. The last line of ice lay ahead of us, and beyond it the boundless sea!"[1] Rowing and sailing day and night, they covered the two hundred miles to Novaya Zemlya. It was three months since they had left the *Tegetthoff*, and already late in the season. They had to sail almost to the southern tip before they found a Russian fishing-ship on August 24, 1874. "It is with a certain kind of awe and reverence that a shipwrecked man approaches a ship, whose

slender build is to deliver him from the power of the elements." [1]
Before the power of the elements the *Tegetthoff* had been forced to
submit, and she had eventually been abandoned; but that the wind
and currents and ice had not been altogether unkind was evidenced
by the new lands they had revealed to the explorers.

From his limited explorations Payer thought that Franz Josef
Land, consisting of two great islands, Wilczek and Zichy, separated
by Austria Sound, was of continental dimensions. Later more leisurely
explorations were to map it quite thoroughly and reveal that it was
really a cluster of small islands.

The next man to concern himself with this new-found land was
Leigh Smith, an intrepid and enthusiastic yachtsman. In the *Eira*, a
steam yacht especially built for Arctic navigation, he set out in 1880
to ascertain whether there was an ice-free route from Spitsbergen
across the Barents Sea to Franz Josef Land. Excellent seamanship on
his part forced the yacht through the heavy pack, and by the middle
of August he sighted land, a little to the westward of where the
Tegetthoff had drifted. By "sound judgment and great energy" he
traced its whole southwestern coast, from Cape Neale, the western-
most point seen by Payer, to McClintock Island, adjacent to Hall
Island. His survey included not only the large islands, but also the
fringe of outlying ones, and covered 110 miles of new coastline. He
found no trace of the *Tegetthoff*—open water had freed her so that
she sank to her rest. He named and noted the northward trend of
Alexandra Land and observed that near Cape Flora on Northbrook
Island there was a snug harbor. In sharp contrast to Payer's land of
desolation, he found an abundance of walrus and seals. His short
summer survey netted a wealth of scientific data.

The next summer Leigh Smith returned, but off Cape Flora the
Eira was badly nipped and she sank with only two hours' grace.
Smith and his men hustled to such good purpose that they were able
to save a considerable quantity of supplies. Even as the *Eira* settled,
her steam winch worked, and half a dozen barrels of flour and three
hundred pounds of bread were set out on the ice. Ammunition, clothing, boats were salvaged; the sails were cut away, spars and planking
fished out of the water—and they prepared to stay the winter. Unable
to reach the camp they had built on Bell Island, twelve miles away,
they fashioned a hut of stones and earth, collected driftwood, laid in
a supply of fresh meat—34 bears, 24 walrus, 2,500 loons, were killed
and eaten—and the first wintering on Franz Josef Land passed with
all in perfect health. Like the crew of the *Tegetthoff*, the men of the
Eira beat a retreat to Novaya Zemlya in their small boats and after

forty-two days were picked up by a ship that had been sent out to look for them. Aside from the extensive geographical discoveries made by Smith, his voyages were important for the large collections he made of the archipelago's flora and fauna. But most of all Franz Josef Land was to be sought out as the ideal base for future trips to the north, to those lands Payer had seen from Cape Fligely.

Because of the great discrepancies between the findings of Payer and Weyprecht and Leigh Smith, but especially in the hope that from there the North Pole might be reached, further exploration of the archipelago was strongly advocated. Not until 1894 was this undertaken. In that year Frederick Jackson, a sportsman, financed by the newspaper proprietor Alfred Harmsworth (Lord Northcliffe), undertook the double mission of exploration and—it was hoped—of finding a likely route to the Pole. The *Windward* was hired to take Jackson and his party, his Eskimo dogs and Lapp ponies, a sectional log cabin, Elmwood, that was to house them, and three years' provisions to Cape Flora. The ship was to return and make contact trips each of the succeeding summers. That summer the *Windward* encountered heavy ice, and during the long homeward voyage scurvy broke out and two men died from it. The next year it was unable to get through to Cape Flora, but in 1896 and 1897 successful contacts were made.

Jackson settled down and made preparations for the charting of Franz Josef Land. Using the dogs for hunting only, he relied on the ponies to pull the sledges. He followed McClintock's methods, meticulously weighing every bit of his equipment, likening himself to the "distinguished Arctic explorer who is said to have been found in his cabin weighing a pocket-handkerchief and debating whether he should take it or not." [2] In the spring of 1895 he started on his first extended trip. In twenty-six days he added 270 miles to his charts and "entirely altered the map of Franz Josef Land, discovering islands and seas where *terra firma* had been laid down," [2] noting and naming the British Channel, which, separating Alexandra Land from Zichy Land, leads to the most northerly sea in the eastern polar area—Queen Victoria Sea. An open-boat voyage that summer proved that Cape Mary Harmsworth was the western tip of the archipelago. His second sledging-trip, in the spring of 1896, extended from Cape Mary Harmsworth northward as far as Cape Richthofen, where he saw open water. "Thus our explorations entirely upset existing maps and our route towards the North Pole as planned by land has been frustrated by the non-existence of it." [2] He had hoped to explore once again to the north when, that very summer, Jackson had his dramatic encounter with Nansen and Johansen as they were retreating from their attempt to reach the Pole from the *Fram*.* Their information about the northern limits of Franz Josef Land and the condition of travel over the polar ice caused Jackson to give up his plans. When he finally left for home in 1897, the *Windward* brought him the news that Andrée had set out to float over the North Pole in a balloon. It was concern for the latter that made Jackson leave Elmwood stocked with the necessaries of life and sealed up against the elements "for possible use by Andrée." [2]

Others were eager to explore Franz Josef Land and start from there on a dash to the North Pole. For the existence of the lands Payer had seen along the northern horizon from Cape Fligely had not been disproved; they still beckoned to those trying for the Pole. Walter Wellman in 1898–9, the Duke of the Abruzzi in 1899–1900, the Baldwin-Ziegler Expedition in 1901–2, the Fiala-Ziegler Expedition in 1903–6—all imbued with the same idea—fell short of their goal, but added to the more complete and exact delineation of the various islands of the archipelago.

Prince Luigi Amedeo of Savoy, Duke of the Abruzzi, inspired by Nansen's attempt to reach the North Pole over the ice, decided to have a try at it himself. In the *Stella Polare,* a rechristened Norwegian sealer, he sailed for Franz Josef Land. Ice conditions were favorable, and he reached as far north as Cape Fligely before his ship was beset. He wintered in Teplitz Bay. The Duke had intended leading the northward party, but a severe frostbite that necessitated the amputation of a finger prevented him. He relegated the command to Lieutenant Cagni of the Italian Navy. Nothing had been spared to make the attempt a success. Cagni was accompanied by two supporting parties. The first, consisting of Lieutenant Querini and two sailors, left the main party for the ship and were never seen again; the second, led by Lieutenant Cavalli, arrived safely at Teplitz Bay. For forty-five days Cagni headed to the north, experiencing the same difficulties of travel over hummocky ice that had forced Nansen to desist. Before he turned back he had bettered Nansen's record by twenty-two miles and could record jubilantly: "We have conquered! We have surpassed the greatest explorer of the century." [3]

If his outward journey had been hard, his homeward one was harder, longer, and infinitely more hazardous. He had to contend with the steady westward drift of the pack, a drift so steady and strong that it nullified his desperate efforts to overcome it. An incredible struggle, a heartbreaking race over the floes, a fight against

* See pp. 210 ff.

fatigue, hunger, and thirst—and Cagni just barely managed to reach Harley Island, the most westerly land on a line with Teplitz Bay. Cagni's efforts had shown that the lands Payer had sighted to the north were mirages. By his courage and energy he had placed the Italian flag nearest the Pole. When the *Stella Polare* got free of the ice that summer, the Duke ordered her to sail for home. "Should we give up all hope of reaching the North Pole? It would be useless to repeat the attempt of following the same plan. What I should recommend would be to the north of Kennedy Sound." [3] Time was to reveal the truth of his observations.

Various scientific expeditions have stayed at Franz Josef Land and done valuable and important work. The U.S.S.R. has taken over the archipelago and renamed it Fridtjof Nansen Land. From the exploratory point of view the most interesting expedition to these regions was the one that effected its circumnavigation, a feat hitherto regarded as impossible. Professor N. N. Subkov, in August 1932, set out in a small auxiliary sailing-vessel to find a way through the icy seas that lie to the north and east. He was convinced that conditions were unusually favorable to navigation because a heat-wave that had started in Florida in 1928, after creeping along with the Gulf Stream for four years, had reached the polar sea, there to have a marked effect on the ice. His deductions were correct, and though his tiny vessel was many times in danger of being caught and frozen in, he was able to push on and carry through his program. The whole voyage occupied only thirty-four days.

It was in August 1931 that Fridtjof Nansen Land was the scene of another dramatic encounter—and how different from the Jackson-Nansen meeting!—when by prearrangement the Russian ice-breaker *Malygin*, with General Umberto Nobile aboard, awaited the appearance of the *Graf Zeppelin*, on which were Professor Samoilovich, Lincoln Ellsworth, and Dr. Eckener. Radio messages were exchanged; the first sent to Nobile said: "A thousand wireless greetings. Dr. Eckener wants you to come aboard the *Graf* for a cup of tea."

And the *Graf Zeppelin* must have flown over the spot where, sixty years before, the *Tegetthoff* had sunk after her long, helpless, but amazing drift.

15

The International Circumpolar Stations: the Greely Expedition

> *Our torments may in length of time*
> *Become our elements.*—MILTON

A RADICAL CHANGE in the scope and a fundamental shift in the emphasis of polar exploration was proposed by Lieutenant Karl Weyprecht when he returned with Lieutenant Julius Payer from the discovery of Franz Josef Land. Addressing the German Scientific and Medical Association at Graz in 1875, he enunciated a new principle for polar exploration. He pointed out that geographical discoveries in the Arctic were important only as they enlarged the field of scientific inquiry and insisted that scientific investigation rather than geographical discovery should be the primary purpose. Such data would have tremendous importance far outside the Arctic Circle, for they would aid in the understanding of the laws of nature and so affect all mankind. Instead of sporadic, unrelated expeditions obtaining limited and inconclusive results, Weyprecht suggested the establishment of a number of stations where for one year a series of identical observations, employing identical instruments, could be carried out simultaneously and continuously.

At a time when Arctic exploration subsisted on the hope of finding new lands and the emotional appeal of reaching the North Pole, Weyprecht stressed the significance of scientific research, and it is because scientific research has become paramount that Arctic exploration has continued and is today stronger than ever, although no extensive new lands have been found and the Pole has already been attained.

Weyprecht's views were well received. Prince Bismarck appointed a commission to investigate the plan more carefully; the International Meteorological Congress endorsed it unreservedly; and it was submitted to all interested nations. The result was the meeting of an International Polar Conference at Hamburg in 1879, at which eleven nations pledged their support. Several additional conferences were held to outline the work and choose the sites. Weyprecht died in 1881, at the early age of forty-three, too young to see the magnificent flowering of the seed he had planted.

The year 1882–3 was designated for this far-flung experiment, and the various parties set out in plenty of time to establish their stations. There were to be fifteen—eleven in the Arctic and four in the Antarctic—while thirty-four permanent observatories adopted a uniform schedule. To set up or relieve these forty-nine stations some seven hundred men participated—a tremendous gesture of international co-operation for strictly scientific purposes.

The Austro-Hungarian expedition, under Lieutenant von Wohlegemuth, occupied Jan Mayen Island. In addition to the obligatory meteorological observations they charted the whole island. The regular Danish station at Godthaab, Greenland, was under the supervision of Professor Paulsen. The Danes also sent out the ship *Dijmphna,* under Lieutenant Hovgaard,* which, though caught fast in the ice of the Kara Sea, carried on all its work and took supplementary observations. Finland co-operated at her station at Sodankyla where the work was started by Professor Lemström and continued by Dr. Biese. France took over two stations in the Antarctic. Germany had one station in the Antarctic and one under Dr. Giese at Cumberland Sound at Baffin Land, while Dr. Koch, aided by the Moravian mission, did supplementary work in Labrador. Lieutenant Dawson carried on the work at Fort Rae, on Great Slave Lake, for Great Britain. Holland had planned to maintain a station at Dickson Harbor, at the mouth of the Yenisei, Dr. Snellen in charge. His ship, the *Varna,* was beset and sunk in the Kara Sea, and he and his men were forced to transfer to the Danish ship *Dijmphna.* But despite all their dangers they made their regular daily observations. The Norwegian observatory, under A. S. Steen, was at Bossekop near North Cape. The Russians had two stations: one under Lieutenant Jurgens at the Lena delta, the other on the west coast of Novaya Zemlya. Sweden had a station at Ice Fiord, Spitsbergen, under Professor Ekholm. The United States had two stations: one at Point Barrow, Alaska, under Lieutenant Ray, the

---

* Lieutenant Hovgaard had previously served with Nordenskiöld in the *Vega's* circumnavigation of Europe and Asia. See Chapter xviii.

other at Lady Franklin Bay, high on Ellesmere Land, under Lieutenant Greely.

The collected data, filling thirty-one quarto volumes, include a
wealth of scientific material. But it is only the Lady Franklin Bay expedition, occupying the most northerly station, that by combining
discovery with the prescribed observations comes into the story of
Arctic exploration. It is the only one that fell into the ruthless clutches
of starvation.

The Greely Expedition, as it was called after its commander, Lieutenant Adolphus W. Greely, was under the supervision of the United
States Army. Greely had with him Lieutenants Kislingbury and Lockwood, Dr. Pavy, ten sergeants, one corporal, nine privates, and two
Greenland Eskimo hunters, Jens and Frederik. They were transported
in the *Proteus* in the summer of 1881 to the spot where Nares's ship
Discovery had wintered. After a few weeks' stay the ship sailed for
home. Arrangements for contact with the party had been made, and
it was hoped thus to preclude any tragic consequences. As early as
1882 a ship was to be sent northward and, in case it was prevented
from reaching them because of heavy ice, was to land a depot as near
them as possible. Another ship was to visit them in 1883, and, should
that also fail to reach them, it was to leave a party fully equipped to
establish contact over the ice during the winter. The horrible fate that
overtook the Greely party was due to the indifference, the lukewarm
spirit, that governed those in charge of the relief. Everything might
have been different had the leader of the rescue ships been less easily
discouraged, less fearful.

The expedition began its stay under the most auspicious conditions. The house they erected, Fort Conger, was very comfortable
and was set in a delightful spot. Grasses and flowers covered the countryside, brooks sang merrily, game was plentiful, and there was even
a seam of excellent coal near by. Meteorological, magnetic, tidal, and
pendulum observations were started. But unfortunately dissension
began. Greely had somehow managed to alienate his men. Kislingbury resigned his appointment, but reached the ship too late to go
back and was forced to remain. One of the privates, too, stayed on as
a "tolerated volunteer." Dr. Pavy was frequently insubordinate, and
one of the sergeants was finally rebellious. It is Lockwood who stands
out as the most interesting and important man in the expedition,
hunting for the party during the autumn, writing and illustrating the
Arctic Moon, issued during the winter, and carrying on sledging-
trips. For Greely had been instructed to try to reach the North Pole

or, failing in that, to better the English record made by Nares's men.

Lockwood had followed the customary routine of laying down depots during the autumn, and in the beginning of April he left Fort Conger to head northward along the Greenland coast, following the same Arctic highway Beaumont had taken. At the end of that month he sent back ten of the men with the supporting sledges and continued on with only Sergeant Brainard and the Eskimo Frederik. At Cape Bryant he saw the land Beaumont had risked so much to explore; at Cape May he encountered the same soft snow that had exhausted the Englishmen and forced their retreat, and, rather than court the same obstacle, he decided to strike out along the ice and avoid it. On May 1 he stood at Cape Britannia, the distant point seen by Beaumont. He could then have turned back with honor, but he had plenty of caches behind him, his dogs were in excellent condition, and the ice-foot along the shore was smooth. Cape after cape—high, sheer cliffs—they passed, separated by mighty fiords. In the distance loomed Cape Washington, but they were beginning to tire. To get on as fast as possible they stopped for only one meal a day. At the north end of Lockwood Island they reached their farthest. They had gone 150 miles beyond Beaumont and had bettered the record Markham had made over the ice by four miles. Sixty days after they had left Fort Conger they were back, tired but well, and exultant at their results.

Soon after Lockwood had left the fort to head northward, Greely set out on a short trip to explore the unknown hinterland. As contrasted with the great inland ice-cap of Greenland, he found that Grinnell Land, as the northern part of Ellesmere Land is called, was a "broken, rugged country intersected by a system of fiords and lakes, which readily drains, during the short Arctic summer, the inconsiderable snow-fall. The valleys, bare of snow, gave birth to vegetation, luxuriant for the latitude, which serves as pasturage for considerable game." [1]

Spring came early. "One of the most surprising peculiarities of Grinnell Land was the unusually early date on which flowers came into blossom. June 1st the purple saxifrage was in bloom, and three days later the catkins of the willow, followed the next day by the sorrel . . . and ten days later the Arctic poppy." [1] Late in June, when the weather was warm and delightful, the days soft and long, Greely set out again for an inland trip. Butterflies and bumblebees flew about them as the party roamed through valleys covered with luxuriant vegetation. From his tours of the hinterland, in which he explored some five thousand square miles, Greely was convinced that a similar countryside would be found on the north of Greenland, where the Ice-Cap did not exist. Later explorers were to find this deduction true.

Summer passed; autumn came and brought no word from the world. The promised relief ship did not appear. The first ominous note of the impending tragedy sounded. The second winter passed. In April 1883 Lockwood again took the northward path. In a surprisingly short time he reached Black Horn Cliffs, and there he found his way forward stopped by the presence of open water. The road was blocked and he turned back. But he immediately set off to explore the western coast of Grinnell Land, finding and tracing the deep indentation of Greely Fiord. Again summer came and passed and there appeared no ship. That was bad, but even worse was the lack of unity in the expedition. If ever there are conditions in life where comradely co-operation under a firm leader is essential, they are to be found in Arctic exploration, where the few people who live together are absolutely dependent upon one another. A whole series of disagreements came to an unfortunate climax when Greely ordered Dr. Pavy arrested for insubordination. Torn by inner conflicts, they faced a fight with their stern environment. Even choice of the route to be taken in retreating to the south, where rescue was to be expected, caused violent differences of opinion: should they aim for Littleton Island off the Greenland coast, where a depot had been promised, or for the cache at Cape Sabine on the Ellesmere side? The latter was finally chosen.

All was made ready for the southward trip. Their records, weighing about fifty pounds, were all made in duplicate and soldered into waterproof tins to be carried in separate boats, the steam launch and a whaleboat. Their standard instruments were similarly protected and distributed. Coal was loaded for their launch and sufficient food to last them until they met the relief ship. On August 9, 1883 the bay ice opened and they left Fort Conger, where for two years they had done valuable work. They left behind them a mild and fertile Arctic land. They were fated, before a relief ship found them, to undergo "the hardships and horrors of an Arctic winter, with scant food, shelter, and clothing, with neither fire, light, nor warmth, and to face undauntedly intense cold and bitter frost, disaster and slow starvation, insanity and death." [1]

A gull would have flown the two hundred miles to Cape Sabine in a straight line, untroubled by winds and blizzards, indifferent to violent waters churning heavy ice-floes, eating and resting wherever it pleased. Far otherwise Greely's boats: their path was a tortuous zigzag, more than twice the straight distance; they were battered by high winds and threatened continuously by great icebergs; they stopped to examine every cairn, to avail themselves of every food cache. To add to their troubles, Cross, the only man qualified to handle the steam launch, took advantage of his importance to get drunk. Despite all these hardships, they progressed so well that in sixteen days they reached Cape Hawks, with Cape Sabine in sight. But then the gales disappeared, and the ice, no longer kept in motion, expanded and solidified. Winter had come; they were caught, their boats held immovable. They had provisions left for only sixty days. Whither should they go? Across the ice to Cape Sabine, or across the ice to the Greenland coast? They waited, drifting with the ice, undecided. At last they had drifted within thirteen miles of the Ellesmere coast. They would abandon their boats and reach the land by sledge. Only thirteen miles—but a sudden blizzard set the pack in motion, whirled them forward and jerked them back, so that it took nineteen days of exhausting work before they touched land. The last of September they were near Cape Sabine, tired but well, their records and equipment intact. They had covered five hundred miles.

"A bold, high rocky island is the land we seek, hemmed in by glaciers and snow-covered land. . . . With the aid of Providence we had made shore; and all concurred in avoiding a second *Polaris* drift, which could hardly have resulted in the arrival of a second *Tigress* at an opportune moment." [1] They had food for thirty-five days, which was stretched to last fifty. Greely sent two men to Cape Sabine to look for both news and a food depot, and after eight days they returned with the following record:

United States Relief Expedition.
Cape Sabine, July 24, 1883.

The steamer Proteus was nipped midway between this point and Cape Albert, on the afternoon of the 23rd instant, while attempting to reach Lady Franklin Bay. . . . A depot was landed from the floe. . . . There were five hundred rations of bread, sleeping-bags, tea, and a lot of canned goods; no time to classify. . . . A cache of two hundred and fifty rations in same vicinity, left by the expedition of 1881; visited by me and found in good condition. . . . The English depot on the small island near Brevoort Island in damaged condition; not visited by me. Cache on Littleton Island; boat at Cape Isabella. All saved from the Proteus. The U.S. steamer Yantic is on her way to Littleton Island, with orders not to enter the ice. A Swedish steamer will try to reach Cape York during this month. I will endeavor to communicate with these vessels at once, and everything within the power of man will be done to rescue the brave men at Fort Conger from their perilous position. . . .

E. A. GARLINGTON,
1st Lieut. 7th Cavalry A.S.O. Commanding

From this report Greely and his men knew that they would suffer privations and hunger, but they never suspected that they had been abandoned to their fate. They did not know "that there was no boat at Isabella, that Garlington's order to replace damaged caches was disobeyed, that he had no knowledge of the safety of the cache at Littleton Island; that he took every pound of food he could carry, though advised that Greely was provisioned only to August, 1883; that when he reached the *Yantic* safely he did not even ask Wilde [the naval commander] to go north and lay down food for Greely, otherwise doomed to starvation." [2] The net result of these relief expeditions was that, from July 1882 to August 1883, fifty thousand rations were taken north through Smith Sound and that of these only a bare one thousand were cached in various places. The remainder were either brought back intact or were lost when the *Proteus* sank. Ignorant of this, Greely and his men prepared for winter.

Camp Clay on Bedford Pym Island off Cape Sabine was a wretched hut, consisting almost entirely of a boat with the keel turned up. "The rock walls of the house were about two feet thick, outside of which there was an embankment of snow, at first four feet in height, but eventually the winter gales buried the house in snow. The whale-boat just caught on the end wall, and under that boat was the only place in which a man could even get on his knees and hold himself erect. . . . The scarcity of rocks prevented our building higher walls. . . . The only space left free, after twenty-five men with sleeping-bags had packed themselves in, was that in the centre where cooking was done, barrels sawed up, and exercise taken on very bad days. . . . We are so huddled and crowded together that the confinement is almost intolerable." [1] There they stayed for eight dreadful months.

The first step was to collect the clothing, tea, and bread left by Garlington at near-by Cape Sabine. They opened it, only to find that its contents were criminally meager. From newspaper wrappings they got bits of news: they learned that President Garfield was dead, that, on the other side of the Arctic, De Long's polar attempt had been crushed by disaster. Forty days' rations were all they had, and they faced a long winter. It was imperative that they get the food cached by Nares at Cape Isabella, forty miles away. Four men—Rice, Frederick (a soldier, not the Eskimo), Elison, and Lynn—set out to bring back the 144 pounds of English meat. For five days they traveled through bright moonlight, reached the cache, took up the meat, and started back. It was bitterly cold, and the way was hard over the rough ice-foot. On the sixth day Frederick says: "Elison had frozen both his hands and feet, and our sleeping-bag [a four-man sleeping-bag] was no more nor less than a sheet of ice. I placed one of Elison's hands between my thighs and Rice took the other, and in this way we drew the frost from his poor frozen limbs. The poor fellow cried all night from the pain." [1] The next day he frosted again and became so stiff he could not move his legs. To save him they had to abandon the meat, the object of all their struggle. On they toiled. That night they again had to thaw Elison out, but the next day, while marching, the low temperature again froze his limbs and face and glued his eyelids together, striking deeper into his flesh minute by minute. Suddenly a gale struck. If he was to be saved, only one way remained. Frederick and Lynn got into the sleeping-bag on either side of Elison, while Rice, fortified by a small piece of frozen beef, started alone for help, twenty-five miles away. Miraculously he reached Camp Clay in sixteen hours and sent Brainard and the Eskimo Frederik to the rescue. Meanwhile the three men lay in the bag. "We tried to keep him [Elison] warm, but as we laid helpless and shivering with the cold, and poor Elison groaning with hunger [his frozen lips did not permit him to gnaw the frozen meat] and pain, you can imagine how we felt. Lynn was a strong able-bodied man, but the mental strain caused by Elison's suffering made him weak and helpless. In fact I was afraid that his mind would be impaired at one time. We were but a few hours in the bag when it became frozen so hard that we could not turn over, and we had to lay in the same position eighteen hours; until to our great relief, we heard Brainard's cheering voice at our side." [1] They were saved.

At Camp Clay the autumn was passed tolerably well. The hunters brought in foxes and seal to supplement their slim larder. To help pass the endless hours, Greely lectured on the "physical geography of the United States in general; followed later by similar talks on each State." [1] Their rations were cut to the very minimum—four ounces of meat daily and six ounces of bread. On Sundays they celebrated with a " 'sun-of-a-gun' for breakfast. This dish consists of a mixture of hard bread, raisins, milk, and as much seal-blubber as can be properly spared." [1] But with the start of the New Year even that minimum was reduced, and Camp Clay became Starvation Camp, whose daily record is one long tragic recital of human need and misery, relieved only by the men's grit. "Mouldy hard bread and two cans of soup make a dinner for twelve. At Fort Conger ten cans of soup were needed to *begin* a meal. . . . To supplement our scanty fuel we are burning rope, which creates a dense smoke, very irritating to our eyes and throats. . . . After the Eskimo lamp is put out, someone has been in the habit of scraping the rancid seal-oil out and eating it. . . . Lockwood [who had shown his strength and courage on the northward dash] is so weak that I was obliged to assist him in turning over in the bag; as well as sitting up for his breakfast. We are burning bootsoles at present." [1] For a while they had a daily ration of six ounces of food!·

In February two men tried to cross Smith Sound to obtain help from the Etah Eskimos, but open water turned them back. The sun, after an absence of one hundred and fifteen days, appeared low on the horizon. Winter was behind them, but could they hold out until game returned or rescue came? When their supplies finally dwindled to nothing, they ate everything possible: seal thongs, seaweed, lichen, sand fleas, and shrimp, for which they set nets. In April they lost their two professional Eskimo hunters, on whose faithful and tireless efforts they had counted: Frederik died from overexertion, and Jens was drowned when his kayak was cut in half by thin ice as he tried to shoot a seal. It was the beginning of the end. A desperate but unsuccessful attempt was made to bring in the cache that had been abandoned to save Elison. Though Brainard worked the shrimp-nets, gathering more than 450 pounds during May, with the end of that month they had reached the end of their rations. One by one, and day by day, they died. Lockwood, the gallant and energetic hero of the northward dash, was the first officer to go. By the first week in June all of the officers except Greely, all of the noncommissioned officers except Brainard, and six of the privates had died. "To sleep was perchance to die . . . and this constant expectancy of death . . . was a terrible mental strain to the end." [1] Private Henry, who persisted in stealing a large quantity from the general store of food, so that his strength was a danger to the survivors, was ordered shot. At last, of the whole expedition, only seven were left.

"The sleeping-bag cover roasted and boiled to suit each one. . . . The last of the skin divided today [June 15]." [1] On the 21st a gale blew. On the following day some water and a few square inches of soaked sealskin were all the nutriment that passed their lips for forty-two hours; it was then that Greely and his men heard the deathly silence that surrounded them pierced by the shrill whistle of a steamer. They had not been utterly forgotten. Help had come. "Suddenly strange voices were heard calling me; and in a frenzy of feeling as vehement as our enfeebled condition would permit, we realized . . . that the long agony was over." [1]

Captain W. S. Schley and Commander Emory, in the *Thetis* and the *Bear*, had been sent to find Greely. Despite the still early season they had pushed northward. They knew that lives were at stake.

They found a cairn in which was a record giving the results of the expedition's work, their plans, their plight. "Rounding the next point, the cutter opened out the cove beyond. There on the top of a little ridge . . . was plainly outlined the figure of a man. . . . He was seen slowly coming down the steep slope. Twice he fell.

" 'Who all are there left?'

" 'Seven left.'

"He was a ghastly sight. His cheeks were hollow, his eyes wild, his hair and beard long and matted.

" 'Where are they?'

" 'In the tent,' said the man, pointing over his shoulder over the hill. 'The tent is down.'

" 'Is Mr. Greely alive?'

" 'Yes, Greely's alive.'

" 'Any other officers?'

" 'No.' Then he repeated, 'The tent's down.' " [1]

The rescuers ran up the hill. They cut open the flap of the tent and looked in—into the fixed and glassy stare of a dead man. "Directly opposite, on his hands and knees was a dark man with a long matted beard, in a dirty and tattered dressing-gown with a little red skull cap on his head, and brilliant staring eyes. . . . He raised himself a little, and put on a pair of eyeglasses.

" 'Who are you?' The man made no answer, staring vacantly. 'Who are you?' again.

"One of the men spoke up. 'That's the Major—Major Greely.'

"Colwell crawled in and took him by the hand, saying to him, 'Greely, is this you?'

" 'Yes,' said Greely in a faint broken voice, hesitating and shuffling with his words, 'Yes—seven of us left—here we are—dying—like men. Did what I came to do—beat the best record.' Then he fell back exhausted." [3]

And so those pitiful survivors were saved. The horrible suffering and tragedy undergone by that expedition can be laid directly at the door of Robert T. Lincoln, who, as Secretary of War, could not make up his mind to a definite course of action when speed and singleness of purpose were essential to effect a rescue, and of Garlington, who failed in the actual relief because he was stupid, arrogant, and cowardly. Had not Schley, intent on saving, understood the importance of an hour's delay and forced the search at his own peril, there might not have been a man left alive.

Despite all their torments and agony, Greely and his men preserved the most important part of the mass of observations they had made. They had collected valuable meteorological, tidal, and magnetic data, carrying out faithfully their share of the work outlined by the International Circumpolar Congress.

More than a half-century has passed since then. For fifty years the data collected by the various members of that Congress have been the source-book for students interested in magnetism and meteorology. Today not only navigators, but telephone, telegraph, and cable engineers, geophysical prospectors who rely on magnetic instruments to locate oil, nickel, and other minerals lying under the earth's surface, and lastly radio and aeronautical engineers are directly affected by those natural forces. In 1929 in Copenhagen at a meeting of the International Meteorological Organization it was voted to mark suitably the fiftieth anniversary of the first Polar Year.

The Second International Circumpolar Year, 1932–3, had, in addition to fifty-five permanent stations, an equal number of special stations—forty-three in the Arctic, five in the Antarctic, and seven in the Tropical and Temperate Zones—thirty-four nations participating. The observations included continuous photographic registration of the magnetism of the earth, of the electrical currents flowing in the earth, of atmospheric electrical pressure and conductivity, measurement of the height of the Kennelly-Heaviside layer, the radio "roof," study of the relationship of the *aurora borealis* to radio transmission, and complete weather reporting. Both the radio and the airplane were used, not only in research but in bringing the outside world closer to the isolated stations where the work was carried on. They precluded the possibility of another Greely tragedy.

16

Laying a Ghost: the Jeannette
and the Fram

THE GREAT VOYAGE of the *Fram* was based upon the evidence implicit in a few pitiful relics of the wrecked *Jeannette*, which, after floating for three years, were picked up on the other side of the earth, off the coast of Greenland. To appreciate fully the genius, stamina, and courage of Fridtjof Nansen it is first necessary to know the tragic fate of that brave American explorer, Lieutenant George Washington De Long.

De Long, of the United States Navy, since his first taste of the Arctic, when he participated in the search for the *Polaris*, had hoped and planned and worked to one end: to lead an expedition to the Pole. He was convinced that the most favorable approach was by way of Bering Strait, and in this he had the support of two theories then current and both fallacious. "On the supposition that Wrangel Land, now known to be a small island, was a vast continental tract, it was expected that the *Jeannette*, in accordance with the settled principles of Polar exploration, would follow its coastline to the north. When the vessel could work no further, sledge expeditions were to start out along the ice-foot to make a still higher latitude." [1] The existence of the warm Japanese Current flowing northward through the strait was to help in opening a way through the obstructing pack ice, "though it would, for the same reason, increase the difficulties of return. . . . Added to these considerations was the comparative novelty of the course, which would render the expedition fruitful in observation and discovery, even if it failed of its main object." [1] It is interesting that both De Long and his financial backer, James Gordon Bennett of the *New York Herald*, seriously considered using balloons, almost twenty years before Andrée soared away in his *Eagle*. But instead Bennett bought Sir Allen Young's yacht, the *Pandora* (in which the latter had attempted to sail the Northwest Passage in 1875–6), re-named it the *Jeannette,* and turned it over to the navy to be outfitted and manned. With De Long were Lieutenants Danenhower and Chipp; Melville, a naval engineer; Dunbar, an ice-pilot; Dr. Ambler, the surgeon; a meteorologist, a naturalist, and twenty-four men.

The *Jeannette* sailed from San Francisco at the beginning of July 1879, stopped at St. Michaels to take on sledges, dogs, and fur cloth-ing, and then headed northward through Bering Strait for Wrangel Land and the Pole. Relying on the assistance of the Japanese Cur-rent, De Long pushed boldly into the ice-pack near Herald Island. There the ship was caught by the ice and held fast, and with it drifted helplessly to the northwest. Daily De Long expected the pack to loosen and set them free, but this never happened. They drifted past Wrangel Land. Too late they discovered that it was a tiny island, in-nocent of continental vastness. Like Payer on the *Tegetthoff,* De Long understood that "this is a glorious country to learn patience in." [1] Being at the mercy of the ice was like "living over a powder-mill waiting for an explosion," [1] and yet De Long was able to record with lightness and humor: "Occasionally I go out on the ice on these beautiful evenings, and try to make words express my feelings suit-ably; but a lot of dogs wrangling over an empty meat can, trying to find a meal in it, surround me and drag me down to plain matter-of-fact. So I take my half frozen nose tenderly in my hand, and lead myself back to the ship." [1]

Two winters passed, and they were still prisoners of the ice. "Peo-ple beset in the pack before always drifted somewhere to some land; but we are drifting about like a modern Flying Dutchman, never get-ting anywhere, but always restless and on the move. Coals are burn-ing up, food is being consumed, the pumps are still going, and thirty-three people are wearing out their lives and souls like men doomed to imprisonment for life." [1] Slowly but certainly the ship was being carried to its doom.

De Long proved himself a fine commander, keeping his men healthy, cheerful, and on happy terms. A monotonous twenty months had dragged their weary length and the ship was only 320 miles from where it had been beset, still drifting over the comparatively shallow water of the continental shelf. On May 16, 1881 came the electric cry: "Land!" But it was a tiny island—Jeannette—not a majestic Franz Josef Land. "What a poor desolate island, standing among icy wastes, may have to do in the economy of nature I do not know. . . . It is solid land . . . and will stand still long enough to let a man realize where he is." [1] Beyond it lay another, Henriette

Island—another barren speck of rock that supported a spreading ice-cap. They were outposts of the Lyakhov group and were examined by Melville, who reached them by dog-sledge.

But the *Jeannette* was doomed. She was leaking badly. On June 11 the water was shallower, the ice more turbulent. The next day the bruised and broken ship received her death-blow. Food, supplies, clothing, everything that could be saved was dumped out on the ice, and there they camped while the stricken, faithful ship slowly filled and sank. "Towards four o'clock in the morning the watch called out, 'Turn out, if you want to see the last of the *Jeannette*. There she goes, there she goes.' " [1]

The next morning they started for land, the nearest land, the New Siberian Islands. They had a whaleboat and two cutters, boat sledges, six tents, food for a little over two months, twenty-three dogs, and ammunition. Lieutenants Danenhower and Chipp and three men were on the sick list. They were thirty-two men, heavily laden, struggling to reach land to the southwest over a treacherous pack. Each of the three boats was mounted on a sledge, the provisions were divided evenly among them, and ten men were assigned to each. De Long and Ambler were in the first cutter, Melville and Danenhower in the whaleboat, and Chipp and Dunbar in the second cutter. Their loads were heavy because they transported everything, so that each mile had to be traversed seven times. Their path was hard, rough, and circuitous, varied by smooth ice lying under two feet of slush and water that kept them wet up to their knees. Dangerous leads opening suddenly delayed them. Clinging fogs chilled and bewildered them. The sharp ice cut their shoes to pieces. But little by little they advanced nearer their goal. On July 29 they at last stood on land; Bennett Island they called it, the most northerly of the New Siberian group. Here they rested for ten days, detained "by a westerly gale, fog, sleet and snow." [1] All were well, and they still had food for thirty days. Their goal was the mainland, the estuary of the great Lena River. Once there, they would seek out the nearest settlement.

They hoped to cross over to the Siberian coast in their boats, for by sledge they "could not make a mile in a month." [1] For days they rowed and sailed past several islands through ice-laden waters, while far off a water-sky glowed like an invitation; for days they kept together. So a month passed. Their provisions ran low. And still the ice held. Only a gale could disperse it. And when the gale struck, the boats were separated, never to meet again. The second cutter, with Chipp and Dunbar, was lost; no trace of it or them was ever found. Melville and Danenhower made their way to the east coast of Lena delta. Heading inland, they soon came to a village, where, luckily, there was a Russian exile who understood their need for food and shelter. De Long and Ambler reached the very northern tip of the delta, where the heavy silt had built up large shoals through which they tried to find a passage to the shore. "Grounded again. . . . Decided to unload and wade ashore . . . water knee-deep; land one and one half miles off. . . . Snow, hail, and sleet, and a strong wind."[1] Their obsolete maps indicated a village ninety-five miles away. They had only a week's supply of food. It was the end of September, in the heart of a region dreaded for its ghastly cold, unequaled anywhere. "So weak were they after their terrible exposure in the boat open to the cold and wet of the gale, that they could not raise their legs to break through the young ice when wading to the shore, but were compelled to push through it as they moved feebly along. The land on which they landed was a vast morass, that offered no sure foothold. When the weather was mild, the surface was spongy and wet; when frost lay on the ground, or snow fell, the walking was equally hard. They slipped and fell at every step."[1] On October 6, the one hundred and sixteenth day since leaving the ship, the first death occurred, and the next day they had finished the last of their scanty provisions. "One does not like to feel he is caught in a trap."[1] They were. Sick, cold, hungry, bewildered, they had not the strength to continue. Three days later, in a last desperate attempt to find help, De Long sent two men on to a village supposedly twelve miles off, while he and Ambler stayed by the others, who could not move. He lived long enough to see his men die one by one. The last entry in his diary is for October 30, 1881.

The two men who had been sent on ahead, though tormented by hunger, weakened by dysentery, and with no shelter to rest in but holes dug in a snowbank, struggled on until they found a native. Brought to his miserable village, they pleaded frantically by signs for help to be sent to De Long. Had they been understood, there would still have been time to save some lives. But their signs were misinterpreted, and they were hurried southward to where Melville was resting. The latter set off immediately to rescue De Long, but the winter was already too far advanced. The following spring, after covering hundreds of miles, his search ended when he found the sad remains of his lost commander.

The De Long Expedition, "which had set out in such high hope, and returned broken and covered with disaster," had not been utterly in vain. The vast and complex territory of the Lena delta had been charted, some tiny islands discovered, Wrangel Land found to be a small island (confirmed by Lieutenant Berry, U.S.N., who in the *Rodgers* surveyed it completely in 1881, when sent to look for De Long), and, most important of all, the great ocean currents off the Siberian Arctic correctly noted.

The Arctic had murdered the *Jeannette* and her gallant commander. But the ghost of his ship sailed abroad, flying bright signal flags. It took the genius and courage of that mighty Viking Nansen to see them and understand.

Today Nansen is remembered for the part he played in Norway's separation from Sweden; for his work during the war of 1914–18 as High Commissioner in control of the prisoners of war; for his just humanitarianism when after the war, as High Commissioner for refugees, he saved millions of destitute Russians and Greeks and Armenians. And because "his splendid integrity shone across the face of the world, and all mankind trusted him," he received the Nobel Peace Prize in 1923. If in this century his activities singled him out as a new kind of world patriot, his interests and achievements in the last century, though of a narrower, less humane nature, were much more adventurous and exciting. But always there was the man himself: a six-foot, blond, blue-eyed Norseman of magnificent physique, who combined simplicity and kindliness with tremendous will-power and organizing ability. His writings have a poetic, mystical flavor, and yet he was above all a distinguished scientist. Truly it has been said of him that he "should have been born in the Renaissance, before the specialists became civilization's heroes." [5] His life is a succession of great plans and greater achievements.

Born in 1861 of good family, he was only twenty-one when he sailed the east Greenland seas in a sealer to collect zoological specimens. Greenland and zoology, adventurous solving of one of the important Arctic problems and quiet academic research—those dual interests of the young Nansen make their appearance in an incident that occurred when he met a man in the Greenland Service at the first point of civilization reached after his pioneer crossing of the great Greenland Ice-Cap in 1888:

"He asked, 'May I ask your name?'

" 'My name is Nansen, and we have just come from the interior.'

" 'Oh, allow me to congratulate you on the taking of your Doctor's degree.' To put it mildly, it struck me as comical that I should cross Greenland to receive congratulations upon my Doctor's degree, which I happened to have taken just before I left home." [2] Such was the man who became the chief protagonist in one of the most daring of Arctic episodes, who forced the Arctic to labor for him, and who by

Interior of a Greenland winter house. ALONG THE BACK RUNS
THE WOODEN PLATFORM THAT SERVES AS A WORKROOM FOR THE WOMEN
BY DAY AND AS THE BED BY NIGHT. EACH WOMAN DOES HER OWN COOKING.
THE MAN IS SINGING AND DANCING TO THE ACCOMPANIMENT OF AN
ESKIMO DRUM.

Graah's REISE TIL ÖSTKYSTEN AF GRÖNLAND.

The whalers in their struggles with ice and sea form our
outposts of investigation up in the north.

Zordrager's GROENLANDSCHE VISSCHERY.

sheer physical stamina emerged alive, if not entirely victorious, from its inner sanctum. He was still fresh from the completion of his first thrilling adventure * when he perfected plans for a second—the voyage of the *Fram*.

"It was in the autumn of 1884 [he was only twenty-three!] that I happened to see an article by Professor Mohn . . . in which it was stated that sundry articles which must have come from the *Jeannette* had been found on the southwest coast of Greenland. He conjectured that they must have drifted on a floe right across the Polar Sea. It immediately occurred to me that here lay the route ready to hand. If a floe could drift right across the unknown region, that drift might be enlisted in the service of exploration—and my plan was laid." [3] The simplicity and revolutionary daring of this plan—to build a ship that would drift with the current rather than fight against it! Years passed, Nansen proved his mettle by crossing Greenland, and then he started to translate his polar-drift theory into active preparation. Many problems would be solved by such a voyage: whether in the north there existed a polar continent or a polar sea; where there was water, what were its depths, its temperatures, its currents, what kind of ice covered it; what were the prevailing winds; what animal life was found there? All these questions, and many more, Nansen hoped to be able to answer by observations carried out during his long drift. For he deduced from the relics of the *Jeannette* that it would take not less than three years; he was prepared for five. All his plans were based on two factors: the northwest drift and the proper ship. The ship he envisioned was to be "as small and as strong as possible—just big enough to contain supplies of coals and provisions for twelve men for five years. . . . Its engine should be powerful enough to give it a speed of 6 knots; but in addition it must be rigged for sailing. The main point in this vessel is that it must be built on such principles as to enable it to withstand the pressure of the ice. The sides must slope sufficiently to prevent the ice, when it presses together, from getting a firm hold of the hull, as was the case with the *Jeannette* and other vessels. Instead of nipping the ship, the ice must raise it out of the water. . . . The ship ought to be a small one, for besides being easier to manœuvre in the ice, it will be more readily lifted by the pressure of the ice. . . . It must, of course, be built of picked materials. . . . It it true that it would have to travel a long distance over the open sea before it would get so far, but it would not be so bad a sea boat as to be unable to get along, even though the sea-sick passengers might have to offer sacrifices to the gods of the sea." [3]

* See Chapter xvii.

The Jeannette *and the* Fram

In Colin Archer, the son of a Scotch boat-builder who had settled in Norway, Nansen found an experienced craftsman who expended all his skill, foresight, and thoroughness in creating such a ship. Archer embodied in stout seasoned oak and strong iron the qualities Nansen had demanded. The success of the expedition was in large measure Archer's success in building the *Fram* so that she would slip "like an eel out of the embraces of the ice." [3] All the twelve men picked to sail were brave, strong, cheerful, and expert in some line. Otto Sverdrup, captain, had been Nansen's companion in Greenland and in this and subsequent exploration proved his worth. Lieutenant Frederik Hjalmar Johansen was "so eager to take part in the expedition that, as no other post could be found for him, he accepted that of stoker." [3] It was he who was Nansen's sole companion in his dash for the Pole.

Nine years after Nansen had first read the article that had inspired this venture—years of planning, of training, of perfecting every tiny detail—on June 24, 1893, the *Fram* steamed out of Christiania harbor. Before the real work could begin she had to make her way past the north coast of Europe to Yugor Strait, where dogs that had been purchased were taken on board; she had to pierce through the ice of the dread Kara Sea and round Cape Chelyuskin. Only when this last had been safely passed—to Nansen it was the most hazardous part of the whole voyage—did Sverdrup point the *Fram* to the north of the New Siberian Islands. Deep into the pack that had smashed the *Jeannette*, as far as he could get, he steered. By the end of that September the ship was frozen in not far from Bennett Island. The magnificent and novel adventure had begun. Not only was the *Fram* to be subjected to every whim of the pressed-up ice-fields, but thirteen men were to face the test of three—or five—years of monotonous life, surrounded by monotonous icy wastes, severed entirely from all outside contacts.

"It really looked as if we were now frozen in for good . . . by degrees we converted our ship into comfortable winter quarters. . . . The rudder was hauled up, so as it might not be destroyed by the pressure of the ice . . . we had a great deal of work with the engine, each part was taken out, oiled, and put away for the winter. . . . We cleared up the hold to make room for a joiner's workshop down there; our mechanical workshop we had in the engine room. The smithy was at first on the deck and afterwards on the ice; tinsmith's work was done chiefly in the chartroom; shoemaker's and sailmaker's and various odd sorts of work in the saloon. . . . There was nothing, from the most delicate instrument down to wooden shoes and axe-handles that could not be made on board the *Fram*. . . . We began putting up the windmill which was to drive the dynamo and produce electric lights. . . . There was always something to occupy us; and it was not difficult to find work for each man that gave him sufficient exercise, and so much distraction that the time did not seem to him unbearably long." [3]

The *Framsjaa,* a newspaper, was issued under the inventive and amusing editorship of the doctor, with illustrated supplements on special days. No birthday, saint's day, or national holiday passed without fitting celebration in the form of a special dinner, for "food was the chief thing we had to hold festival with." [3] Astronomical observations were taken every other day; magnetic observations and deep-sea soundings with temperatures recorded at various depths were made periodically. Sport was not lacking, for there were sudden, exciting visits from polar bears. In Nansen's journal a bright picture is painted by the recital of stupendous feasts, of a happy, carefree routine, of good fellowship. But there was another side to life in the Arctic. "Oh, how tired I am of thy cold beauty! I long to return to life. Let me go home again, as conqueror or as beggar; what does that matter? But let me get home to begin life anew. The years are passing here, and what do they bring? Nothing but dust, dry dust, which the first wind blows away; new dust comes in its place, and the next wind takes it too. Truth? Why should we always make so much of truth? Life is more than cold truth, and we live but once." [3]

Nansen's two principles, on which the whole edifice of this voyage had been erected, were still to be tested. Would the *Fram* withstand the deadly thrusts of the ice-pack? The first joust was eagerly awaited. "All at once in the afternoon, as we were sitting idly chattering, a deafening noise began and the whole ship shook. This was the first ice-pressure. Everyone rushed on deck to look. The *Fram* behaved beautifully. On pushed the ice, but down under us it had to go, and we were slowly lifted up." [3] Soon "the men have grown so indifferent to the pressure that they do not even get up to look, let it thunder ever so hard. They feel that the ship can stand it, and so long as that is the case, there is nothing to get hurt except the ice itself." [3] But what of the drift—was it carrying them where they had expected it would? At first the *Fram* went so contrarily that Nansen was puzzled. "She went backward towards her goal in the north, while her nose ever turned to the south. It is as though she were longing for southern shores, while some invisible power is drawing her on towards the unknown. Can it be an ill-omen, this backward advance towards the interior of the Polar Sea? I cannot think it; even the crab ultimately reaches its goal." [3] The winter passed, and by spring he knew that the *Fram* was drifting to the northwest, spasmodically, reluctantly, but more and more in the desired direction. He had been right, the *Fram* must succeed.

Only Nansen seemed to be bitten by ennui. Only to him did the routine of good living, free from every care, bring with it a growing desire for a single day of struggle—for even a moment of danger. He could not be content to journey thus, safely immured. Summer passed, a second winter had come, and Nansen was convinced that the *Fram* would not reach the high latitude of the Pole itself. He was consumed by the need to leave the safety of his ship and strike out across the ice for the Pole. He knew that such a trip meant burning bridges behind him, relying on his own efforts to find his way back to Europe, somehow.

No retreat, no retreat, they must conquer or die, who have no retreat.

He planned to leave with one companion when the *Fram* was approximately in a line with Franz Josef Land. "The distance from this proposed starting-point to Cape Fligely, which is the nearest known land, I set at 370 miles . . . and that would be easy enough over the ice, even if it did become somewhat bad towards the land. If once a coast is reached, any reasonable being can surely manage to subsist by hunting. . . . A 'line of retreat' is therefore secured . . . and we can choose whichever route we please: either along the northeast coast of Franz Josef Land, by Gillis Land towards Northeast Island and Spitsbergen (and, should circumstance prove favourable, this would be my choice), or we can go to the south . . . to Novaya Zemlya or Spitsbergen. . . . We may, of course, find Englishmen on Franz Josef Land; but that we must not reckon on." [3] Johansen was chosen to be his companion. They took with them twenty-eight dogs, three sledges, two kayaks to be used in crossing open water, a tent, and provisions for one hundred days. They expected to reach the Pole in fifty days. Sverdrup was left in command, to carry on the scientific observations and see the *Fram* through her great test. On March 14, 1895 Nansen and Johansen bade farewell to the *Fram*, in which were united all the comforts of civilization and the only human ties in that frozen desert. Those two set out to journey farther through that immense waste, into greater solitudes and deeper stillness.

"We found large expanses of flat ice, and covered the ground quickly, farther and farther away from our comrades, into the unknown, where we two alone and the dogs were to wander for months." [3] But this easy traveling did not last. After a week they reached hummocky ice, great pressure-ridges. Over these they went slowly. Their sledges capsized constantly, requiring herculean strength to right them; their kayaks were pierced by jagged edges; they had to detour for miles to get past open water, being loath to use their kayaks, which would be made so much heavier by the coating of ice. The farther they went, the worse it was. The harder they labored, the more they sweated, until the body moisture "condensed in our outer garments, which were now a mass of ice and transformed into complete suits of ice-armour. . . . These clothes were so stiff that the arm of my coat actually rubbed deep sores in my wrists during our marches. . . . When we got into our sleeping-bags in the evening our clothes began to thaw slowly. . . . At last they became wet and pliant, only to freeze again a few minutes after we had turned out of our bag in the morning." [3] And the terrain over which they moved grew still worse. Soon Nansen was forced to admit to himself that "the ice was moving southward, and that in its capricious drift, at the mercy of wind and current, we had our worst enemy to combat." [3] Despair crept into the marrow of their bones. Harder grew the way. "Ridge after ridge, and nothing but rubble to travel over. . . . I went on a good way ahead on snow-shoes . . . and from the highest hummock only the same kind of ice was to be seen. It was a veritable chaos of ice-blocks, stretching as far as the horizon. . . . I therefore determined to stop, and shape our course for Cape Fligely." [3] That was on April 8. In twenty-six days they had reached the high northing of 86° 13′ 6″ N.

Spring was near; the way back to land was long and arduous. At first it seemed as if the return was to be easy, and, in their eagerness to push on while favorable conditions held, they went for thirty-six hours without pitching a tent. Thus it happened that they both forgot to wind their watches and so for the remainder of their adventure were never certain as to their exact whereabouts. (Subsequent checking showed that their watches were wrong by but twenty-six minutes!) To add to their bewilderment, they constantly expected to reach Petermann Land—the land Payer had supposed he saw across the sea to the north. Foul weather came and harder going. Though their loads were constantly being diminished, their dogs were too, since they killed off the weakest to feed the rest, with the result that the men still had the same weight to haul. They dragged the heavy sledges for miles through soft snow, knee-deep. Violent gales detained them. April and May and June passed, and still the same laborious struggle over a curdled sea. But the days were getting warmer, rain fell increasingly; both were welcome for the magic they wrought in opening up the pack.

"July 24th. At last the marvel has come to pass—land, land! . . . We are leaving [the ice], and leaving no trace behind us. A new life is beginning for us; for the ice it will ever be the same." [3] Only two dogs were left—but in a day or two they expected to be on land. They had no fear of hunger, for the water and floes were alive with seal, walrus, and bear, and hunting was a glorious sport. But between them and the tantalizing land lay thirteen days of inconceivable toil, of slow progress, with Nansen crippled for two days by a severe lumbago. Numerous channels filled with brash made their kayaks useless and their advance one of desperate toil. It was a horrible hop-skip-and-jump from floe to floe, dragging their loaded sledges behind them, a constant flirtation with disaster.

One day, while they were working hard to ferry themselves over a lead, Nansen, busied in trying to keep his sledge from slipping off the ice, heard a scuffle behind him. Then came Johansen's voice: "Take the gun!" Looking around, he saw an enormous bear standing over his companion, who had been knocked flat on his back. Nansen grabbed for his gun, the sledge slipped—the sledge that held his gun and everything else that meant life to them. He tried to pull it up as quickly as possible. "I had no time to look around and see what was going on behind me, when I heard Johansen quietly say, 'You must look sharp if you want to be in time!' Look sharp? I should think so. At last I got hold of the butt-end, dragged the gun out, turned round in a sitting position . . . and gave [the bear] a charge of shot behind the ear, and it fell down dead between us. The bear must have followed our track like a cat, and, covered by the ice-blocks, have slunk up while we were clearing the ice from the lane. . . . It was just as the bear was about to bite Johansen in the head that he uttered those memorable words, 'Look sharp!' . . .

"At last, at last, I stood by the edge of the ice. Before me lay the dark surface of the sea. . . . Behind us lay all our troubles, before us the waterway home." [3] For greater safety and speed they decided to lash the two kayaks together, placing the sledges athwart them. "We were ready to set off. It was a real pleasure to let the kayaks dance over the water and hear the little waves plashing against the sides . . . we found that the wind was so good that we ought to make use of it, and so we rigged up a sail on our fleet. We glided easily before the wind in towards the land we had so longed for all these many months. What a change, after having forced one's way inch by inch by foot on ice." [3] After five months of struggle and peril on the ice they had come at last to land. This precious bit of solid earth Nansen named Eva Island in honor of his wife.

On they went, aiming for the southern part of Franz Josef Land, where Leigh Smith had wintered. Past Liv, Adelaide, and Freeden Islands, constituting the Hvidtenland group, they alternately sailed and hauled. They skirted many islands of Zichy Land, and finally on the southern coast of Frederick Jackson Island (so named later), with more than 138 miles between them and Leigh Smith's camp, they decided that they had better prepare to spend the winter. It was the 28th of August, and time was getting short.

Using a spade made of the shoulder-blade of a walrus tied to a piece of broken ski staff, they dug a hole. Around this they erected the walls of their hut, stones plastered with moss and earth. A large drift log held up some walrus hides to form the roof.* It was small and wretched, but to them it was a palace. Walrus blubber furnished them with light and heat. "By the aid of lamps we succeeded in keeping the temperature at about the freezing-point in the middle of the hut, while it was, of course, colder at the walls." [3] Game came to their door, almost too many polar bears for their peace of mind. The long, long night lay on the land. Christmas was celebrated by turning their shirts inside out and bathing in a quarter of a cup of hot water. They were filthy from the smoke of the train oil, from handling the blubber. "If it was difficult to get our bodies clean, it was a sheer impossibility as regards our clothes. We tried in all possible ways. We boiled our shirts in the pot hour after hour, but took them out to find them just as full of grease as when we put them in. Then we took to wringing the train-oil out of them. This was a little better; but the only thing that produced any real effect was to boil them, and then scrape them with a knife while they were still warm. . . . The fat which we scraped off was, of course, a welcome addition to our fuel. . . . I have never before understood what a magnificent invention soap really is. . . . In the meantime our hair and beards grew entirely wild. It is true we had scissors and could have cut them; but as our supply of clothes was by no means too lavish, we thought it kept us a little warmer to have all this hair, which began to flow down over our shoulders. . . . Thus did our time pass. We did our

* In the spring of 1902 the Baldwin-Ziegler Polar Expedition to Franz Josef Land found this wintering-place. Of it Anthony Fiala, a member, said: "The great drift-wood log . . . looked as if only a pair of giants could have moved it."

best to sleep away as much of it as possible. We carried this art to a high pitch of perfection, and could sometimes put in as much as 20 hours' sleep in the 24." [3]

In March they began to prepare for their departure. Out of the next-to-nothing they possessed they outfitted themselves. They were tailors, shoemakers, everything, anything. "I have discovered that it is possible to get 12 threads out of a bit of twine, and am as happy as a king. We have thread enough now, and our wind clothes shall be whole once more." [3] They went over their whole equipment, repairing and altering so that those things essential to travel, shelter, and food would all be in order. They found that they had enough ammunition left to last them several more winters. On May 19, after almost nine months spent in their miserable winter hut, they headed again for the south. Though they were never certain where they were —for the region they traversed did not tally with Payer's map— though they were never able to ascertain exactly their position, they knew that they must head for the south. When bad weather did not keep them from traveling they made good progress. The ice was smooth enough so that they could hoist sail and rush merrily before the wind. When the ice ended, the water was open enough for them to sail over it in their kayaks. Alternating by sledge and kayak, they advanced quickly to the south. Almost a month passed thus when an incident occurred that narrowly missed being a fatal disaster.

"In the evening we put in to the edge of the ice, so as to stretch our legs a little; they were stiff with sitting in the kayak all day, and we wanted to get a little view over the water to the west by ascending a hummock. As we went ashore the question arose how we should moor our precious vessel. 'Oh, well, it doesn't require much to hold these light kayaks,' said I. . . . We went up on a hummock. . . . As we stood there, Johansen suddenly cried, 'I say! the kayaks are adrift.' We ran down as hard as we could. They were already a little way out, and were drifting quickly off; the painter had given way. 'Here, take my watch,' I said to Johansen, giving it to him; and as quickly as possible I threw off some clothing, so as to be able to swim more easily. I did not dare to take everything off, as I might so easily get a cramp. I sprang into the water but the wind was off the ice, and the light kayaks, with their high rigging, gave it a good hold. They were already well out, and were drifting rapidly. The water was icy cold; it was hard work swimming with clothes on; and the kayaks drifted farther and farther, often quicker than I could swim. It seemed more than doubtful whether I could manage it. But all our hope was drifting there; all we possessed was on board—we had not even a knife with us; and whether I got cramp and sank here, or turned back without the kayaks, it would come to pretty much the same thing; so I exerted myself to the utmost. When I got tired, I turned over and swam on my back and then I could see Johansen walking restlessly up and down on the ice. Poor lad! He could not stand still, and thought it dreadful not to be able to do anything. . . . He said afterwards that those were the worst moments he had ever lived through. But when I turned over again and saw that I was nearer the kayaks, my courage rose, and I redoubled my exertions. I felt, however, that my limbs were gradually stiffening and losing all feeling, and I knew that in a short time I should not be able to move them. But there was not far to go now; if I could only hold out a little longer we should be saved—and I went on. The strokes became more and more feeble, but the distance became shorter and shorter, and I began to think I should reach the kayaks. At last I was able to stretch out my hand to the snow-shoe which lay across the sterns. I grasped it, pulled myself in to the edge of the kayak—and we were saved! I tried to pull myself up, but the whole of my body was so stiff with cold that this was an impossibility. For a moment I thought that, after all, it was too late; I was to get so far, but not be able to get in. After a little, however, I managed to swing one leg up on to the edge of the sledge which lay on the deck, and in this way managed to tumble up. There I sat, but so stiff with cold that I had difficulty in paddling. Nor was it easy to paddle in the double vessel. . . . I shivered, my teeth chattered, and I was numb all over." [3] But despite all this he was collected enough to shoot two auks that were lying close to the kayaks as he paddled them back to shore. "The thought of having auk for supper was too tempting; we were in want of food now." [3] Johansen stripped the wet clothes off him and put him, exhausted and trembling, in the sleeping-bag. It took him hours to thaw out. He dozed while Johansen hurriedly pitched their tent and prepared supper. "Auk and hot soup soon effaced the last traces of my swim. During the night my clothes were hung out to dry, and the next day they were nearly dry again." [3] Late the following day they went on.

It was almost as though the Arctic understood at last that it could not vanquish a man whose spirit and stamina could carry him safely through months of arduous travel over a heavy pack, who could survive the long monotony of a precarious and wretched winter, and who could successfully meet a moment of terrible and acute danger;

and it bowed before him. It vouchsafed a sudden ending to all Nansen's worries and problems; he had his fortuitous, his miraculous meeting with Jackson.

Less than a week had passed since that icy bath, and the two men were encamped on a "land which I believed to be unseen by any human eye and untrodden by any human foot, reposing in Arctic majesty behind its mantle of mist," [3] when "a sound suddenly reached my ear so like the barking of a dog that I started. It was only a couple of barks, but it could not be anything else. I strained my ears, but heard no more, only the same bubbling noise of thousands of birds. I must have been mistaken after all. . . . Then the barking came again . . . there was no longer any room for doubt. . . . I now shouted to Johansen that I heard dogs farther inland. He started up from the bag where he lay sleeping and tumbled out of the tent. . . . I meant to set off as quickly as possible, and was impatient to get breakfast started. . . . As we were eating we discussed who it could be, whether our countrymen or Englishmen. If it was the English expedition to Franz Josef Land which had been in contemplation when we started, what should we do? 'Oh, we'll just have to remain with them a day or two,' said Johansen, 'and then we'll have to go on to Spitsbergen, else it will be too long before we get home.' We were quite agreed on this point. . . . I set off in doubt. . . . Was all our toil, were all our troubles, privations, and sufferings to end here? It seemed incredible, and yet— . . . It was with a strange mixture of feelings that I made my way in towards the land among the numerous hummocks and inequalities. Suddenly I thought I heard a shout from a human voice, a strange voice, the first for three years. How my heart beat and the blood rushed to my brain as I ran up on to a hummock and hallooed with all the strength of my lungs! Behind that one human voice in the midst of the icy desert—this one message from life—stood home and she who was waiting there. . . . Soon I heard another shout, and saw, from an ice-ridge, a dark form moving among the hummocks farther in. . . . We approached one another quickly, I waved my hat; he did the same. I heard him speak to the dog and I listened. It was English, and as I drew nearer I thought I recognized Mr. Jackson whom I remembered once to have seen.

"I raised my hat; we extended a hand to one another with a hearty 'How do you do?' . . . On one side the civilized European in an English check suit and high rubber boots, well shaved, well groomed, bringing with him a perfume of scented soap, perceptible to the wild man's sharpened senses; on the other side the wild man clad in dirty rags, black with oil and soot, with long uncombed hair and shaggy

beard, black with smoke, with a face in which the natural fair com-
plexion could not possibly be discerned through the thick layer of fat
and soot which a winter's endeavours with warm water, moss, rags,
and at last a knife had sought in vain to remove. No one suspected
who he was or whence he came.

"Jackson: 'I'm immensely glad to see you.'

" 'Thank you: I also.'

" 'Have you a ship here?'

" 'No, my ship is not here.'

" 'How many are there of you?'

" 'I have one companion at the ice-edge.' As we talked we had begun to go in towards the land. I took it for granted that he had recognized me, or at any rate understood who it was that was hidden behind
the savage exterior, not thinking that a total stranger would be received so heartily. Suddenly he stopped, looked me full in the face,
and said quickly:

" 'Aren't you Nansen?'

" 'Yes, I am.'

" 'By Jove! I am glad to see you!' And he seized my hand and
shook it again, while his whole face became one smile of welcome, and
delight, at the unexpected meeting, beamed from his dark eyes.
'Where have you come from now?' he asked.

" 'I left the *Fram* in 84° north latitude, after having drifted for
two years, and I reached the 86° 15′ parallel, where we had to turn
and make for Franz Josef Land. We were, however, obliged to stop
for the winter somewhere north here, and are now on our way to
Spitsbergen.'

" 'I congratulate you most heartily. You have made a good trip of
it, and I'm most awfully glad to be the first person to congratulate you
on your return.' " [3]

From Jackson's diary we know that he "fancied by what [Nansen]
said that the *Fram* was at the bottom, and that he and Lieutenant
Johansen were the sole survivors. I consequently abstained from asking any further questions about the ship. . . . It was not till nearly
an hour had elapsed that from some remark he made I gathered that
the *Fram* was all right, and that he expected her to be on her way to
Norway. . . . Nansen looks pale and anæmic and is very fat. . . .
Johansen was, if possible, in a dirtier condition than his leader . . . he
is a short, sturdy, muscular little chap, and looks as fit and well as he
might have done had he just come off a yachting trip. . . . They had
a lump or two of evil-looking walrus meat and two or three draggled-
looking loons in their kayaks, which was all the food they had with

them, poor chaps. On the night of Nansen's arrival we sat up talking till 8 A.M. of the following day, and then turned into our blankets, but we soon turned out again and renewed our conversation for hours. . . . A more remarkable meeting than ours was never heard of. Nansen did not know that I was in Franz Josef Land, as I did not leave England until a year after he had started, and I had not the slightest idea he was within hundreds of miles of me; in addition to that, Nansen was very uncertain as to what part of the world he was in. . . . Had he missed meeting with us, he could not have left Franz Josef Land . . . a stretch of practically open sea of more than 160 miles in extent [lies] between Cape Mary Harmsworth and the nearest known land—and cannot be crossed in leaky canvas canoes. . . . Nansen repeatedly remarks that nothing will ever induce him to undertake such a trip again." [4]

Nansen and Johansen were safe. Clean, comfortable, relaxed, surrounded by friends, with letters from the dear ones at home to be read and re-read—"a delightful feeling of peace settled on my soul." [3] Six weeks passed before Jackson's contact ship appeared on the horizon, weeks devoted to long talks, to dovetailing their geographical findings, to scientific observations, to hunting and easy living. On July 26 the *Windward* reached Cape Flora, and on August 7 she started back for home, bearing Nansen and Johansen. A fortnight later she was at Vardö. The telegraph and cable wires burned, sending their story over the whole world. "Only the arrival of the *Fram* was wanting to complete things; but we were quite at ease about her; she would soon turn up." [3] But a few days passed, summer was almost at an end, and still no news of the *Fram*. Doubts arose. Nansen began to feel "that if the autumn should pass without word of her, the coming winter and spring would be anything but pleasant." [3] And then a week later, with trembling hands, he tore open a telegram: "Fridtjof Nansen: *Fram* arrived in good condition. All well on board. Shall start at once for Tromsö. Welcome home! Otto Sverdrup." [3]

The next day Nansen and Johansen boarded the *Fram*. "The meeting which followed I shall not attempt to describe. I don't think any of us knew anything clearly, except that we were all together again—we were in Norway—and the expedition had fulfilled its task. . . . In my heart I sobbed and wept for joy and thankfulness." [3]

Sverdrup had brought the *Fram* home. Steadily she had drifted with the ice to the west until she was north of Spitsbergen. It was May 1896. The pack around her had opened, but she still clung to her floe. Sverdrup decided to force a path to open water. Everything was made ready. In June he blasted the ship free and, with steam raised, butted his way through 180 miles of close-packed ice to navigable water. By the middle of August the last floe was passed. After thirty-five months the *Fram* was again sailing. In Spitsbergen, at Dane Island, Andrée boarded her—and so for a moment their lines crossed: the one at the triumphant end of a daring drift with the ice over the polar sea, the other hoping to start on an equally novel and courageous drift over the ice of the polar sea in a balloon. And with home in sight the ghost of the *Jeannette*, which had summoned the *Fram* to her long odyssey and stayed by her throughout it, could at last sink to rest, her duty done.

Nansen and the *Fram* had both been tested; theirs is a modern saga conceived and executed in the old-time spirit of the Vikings. "The ice and the long moon-lit polar nights, with all their yearning, seemed like a far-off dream from another world—a dream that has come and passed away. But what would life be worth without its dreams?" [8]

The drift of the *Fram* across the polar regions stands out as one of the most important contributions to oceanography. In six folio volumes are contained the scientific results of the expedition. The important conclusions based on the various observations carried on continuously for three years paralleled the high adventure of the voyage itself. They were the vital pieces that integrated what had previously been so many fantastic parts of a giant jigsaw puzzle.

Nansen's interest in the problems of the Arctic did not stop with the voyage of the *Fram*. In 1914 he accompanied a Russian expedition that sailed through the Kara Sea as far as the Yenisei River. In his account, *Through Siberia,* he lists all the expeditions that sailed the Kara Sea, from Borough's voyage in 1556 down to his own. He gathered together every bit of information recorded about that sea's ice conditions and navigability. His work was of inestimable value in opening it up to regular mercantile traffic. In *In Northern Mists—Arctic Exploration in Early Times,* published in 1911, Nansen the erudite and careful scholar spoke out. It is hard to believe that the man who could write this fascinating book—the result of years of painstaking and laborious research—could also have been a man of action. The hero of the *Fram* was a man of many parts.

17

Greenland

MORE IS KNOWN about Greenland at the present day than about any other Arctic land. This is because hundreds of expeditions have explored and studied it, and because it is the only large area where such work has been systematically carried on under intelligent direction for more than half a century. Greenland, a colony of Denmark, is the rare, bright exception in the register of European colonies. Its native Eskimos are among the few primitive people who have not been disastrously submerged under the tide of foreign domination, who have not been brought to ruin and misery by collision with foreign traders. Instead, their mode of life, their culture, their health, have been safeguarded. And this, *mirabile dictu*, has been done even though Greenland *costs* Denmark about $50,000 annually. Its only important mineral wealth is the large cryolite deposit at Ivigtut—the largest in the world; otherwise its main articles of export are seal oil, whalebone, seal-, fox-, bird-, and bear-skins, fish products, and eiderdown. For these products a fair return is assured the natives, because trade is a government monopoly. Under the Royal Trade monopoly the "system of collecting the products along the shore commenced. There are 176 inhabited places scattered over 1000 miles of coast, and 60 trading stations where the products are collected and sent to the chief station." [1] That Greenland has not been exploited cannot be entirely explained by the fact that it has not the purchasing population of India, nor the gold of Peru, nor the continental riches of Africa or America; for this unusual treatment of a centuries-old, strictly maintained benevolent paternalism on the part of Denmark a large debt is due Hans Egede.

The history of modern Danish Greenland begins with Egede's arrival there a little over two hundred years ago, although Greenland had been rediscovered by Davis as long ago as 1585. In the seaport town of Bergen, in Norway, the almost legendary memory of communication between Norway and Greenland had never quite faded out. It was recorded in the sagas; it was remembered there that Scandinavian settlements had existed. And when, in the course of time, the news of Davis's rediscovery reached Christian IV, King of Denmark and Norway, he immediately planned to have Greenland explored. His kingly conscience was bothered by the mysterious fate of the old Norse colony. As the father of his people he wanted to rescue his long-lost children or, if they had perished, to ascertain their end. In 1603 he dispatched two ships under the command of three Englishmen hired for the purpose, James Cunningham, John Knight, and James Hall, the last-named because he was supposed already to have visited Greenland. Landing near the modern settlement of Holsteinsborg, the expedition assembled a collection of furs and narwhal tusks. But their greatest trophies were two live Eskimos, whom they kidnapped, lifting them out of the water, kayaks and all. As with Frobisher, their wildest hopes were aroused by the glitter of silver, and to secure it they returned there the next year, loading their ships with a precious cargo. Like him they were profoundly disillusioned when an assay proved that the ore had been taken from a mountain of lead. After that bitter disappointment the King was content to confine his interest to efforts made to locate the lost colonies. The captive Eskimos did not long survive; only a little longer did the King's enthusiasm. The last Arctic expedition he sent out was the disastrous one led by Jens Munk to Hudson Bay.*

For the next hundred years the dangerous route to Greenland became increasingly well known as the Danes and Dutch vied for the whaling and fishing supremacy of Davis Strait. To further the search for better fishing- and whaling-grounds in Greenland waters, Danish merchants were subsidized; but no one was financed to look for the ancient colonies. Both their countrymen and their church were content to neglect them, content to relegate their very existence to the realm of legend. Only one man read the sagas as statements of fact, gloried in the achievements of those Christian colonists, and brooded over their subsequent silence. He was a young pastor, Hans Povelsen Egede. The more he read and thought, the more clearly he saw that he was the humble tool designated by God to find the lost, abandoned flock. He asked his brother-in-law, who had served as mate on a whaler, about Greenland and its inhabitants. The mate knew nothing of either, though he was well acquainted with its harbors and its waters. Egede would have to search for himself. Neither his parochial duties nor his family ties could still the urgency of the voice within

* See p. 64.

Map of Greenland

him. He was only twenty-four when in 1710 he petitioned his bishop for help in furthering his cause. The reply was friendly and favorable, but stressed the overwhelming difficulties to be overcome. Egede had already reckoned with those difficulties; they were part of the task. There are few obstacles that will not yield to the unswerving purpose of a meek and quiet man. Soon he had inspired his wife to share his hope. In 1718 he sought out his King in Copenhagen. Frederick IV appreciated the goodness of the man and the fervor with which he pressed his unselfish cause. Eventually the necessary financial support was given, and he was ready for his great venture.

May 2, 1721 was a memorable day. It was then that Egede with his wife and their four little children, accompanied by forty men and women, sailed out of Bergen harbor. Aboard their tiny vessel, the *Hope*, were a portable house and food staples. They were setting out to recolonize Greenland, to find their lost countrymen.

After a long and dangerous voyage, during which sea and wind and ice sought to keep the *Hope* from making Greenland, the pioneers reached Gilbert Sound. On a small wind-swept island they erected their house, preparing for the winter. Meanwhile Egede roamed the coast, looking for Scandinavian farms, Christian churches, white settlers. He met only natives in their Eskimo villages. As he searched in vain, he tasted the bitterness of a fruitless errand; but as he mingled more and more with the Eskimos he was charmed with their simplicity and friendliness. He busied himself in learning their language and was too occupied to notice that his settlers were both ill and unhappy. They were not adept at hunting and fishing; only occasionally could the Eskimos spare them food; they were obliged to live on the staples they had brought with them; and soon most of them were touched by scurvy. Weakened, in pain, they counted the days until summer's return, when they would be free to sail back to the safety of their homes. And so the majority went back with the *Hope;* only Egede and his family and a few other hardy spirits stayed on. The next year those few welcomed two ships that arrived bringing provisions. The King had levied a special tax to ensure the maintenance of this colony. That left them free to devote themselves to their main task: searching for the lost colonies. That very year Egede set out on a long boat voyage.

It will be remembered that the ancient colonies were divided into West Bygd and East Bygd, *both situated on the west coast,* the former comprising the northern settlements, the latter the southern. In Egede's time, and for many years to come, it was naturally assumed that East Bygd was to be found on the east coast. Having failed to find descendants of the Norse settlers along the west coast, Egede decided to look on the opposite side. According to the Zeno map, by which he was guided, a strait existed that cut across the island from coast to coast. Locate that strait, sail down it to its eastern limit, and there would be East Bygd, there would be the lost colonies. On such faulty premises did the good pastor build his plans.

In his southern trip of 1723 Egede traced the coastline from Gilbert Sound to Cape Farewell, hoping at each deep indentation to find the Zeno strait. But the strait never appeared. He was in a region of beautiful winding fiords, along whose banks he did find ruins of churches and homesteads, memorials of the past. These were the settlements of East Bygd, but that he did not know and supposed that they were those of West Bygd. He was forced ,to turn back without having reached the east coast. That winter, in the coldest season of the year, he made a trip to the north. He went as far as the Eskimo settlement of Nipisat, where he found the natives actively engaged in hunting the large whalebone whales. There the Danes established a whaling-station. Only these two trips did Egede make. After that he was content to spend his time and efforts in instructing and converting the natives, in perfecting himself in their language.

Meanwhile the Danish King had high hopes for the new colony. Not only did he levy a tax to maintain it, he took steps to acquire the east coast as well as the west. Escorted by four ships carrying materials and men with which to erect and man a fort, a man-of-war brought to Greenland in 1728 Major Claus Paarss, its first and last titular Governor. He moved the colonists over to the mainland, built his fort there, gave it the name of Godthaab, and prepared to pass the winter. This second attempt to create a small colony ended like the first—in scurvy and retreat. Forty men died; the survivors were sent home; and not only did the Danes abandon the fort, but the vicinity was deserted by the Eskimos, who had become frightened at the great number of deaths. Again Egede, firm, though in despair at the turn of events, remained. But his troubles were only just beginning. In 1730 his patron and supporter, Frederick IV, died, and his successor, Christian VI, saw no point in supporting a colony. He felt that colonies were maintained to enrich the mother country, and Greenland, after ten years, was costing instead of producing money. The colony was ordered abandoned, and Egede was offered the choice of leaving with the rest or of remaining and subsisting by his own efforts. For him there was no choice; he stayed. Ten sailors threw in their lot with his. In that dark hour it was the unswerving faith of his loyal wife that sustained him.

Faced by such steadfast adherence to a cause, the King withdrew his decree. In 1733 a ship arrived at Godthaab, bringing the good news that the King had granted Egede two thousand dollars annually to maintain his mission. Three Moravian missionaries had likewise come to erect their station and aid in Egede's work. The same ship also brought an Eskimo boy back to his native land. And here was calamity. For the lad was ill with smallpox; the disease spread with the wildness and speed of a grass fire. The well fled from the dying and infected distant settlements. At one time it looked as though the whole population would be wiped out. About 2,500 souls died. Egede nursed the sick and prayed for the dead. With the approach of winter the epidemic abated. Again Egede took heart.

Then, a bare two years after this terrible catastrophe, Egede's wife died. Without her he was without his inner strength. Of a sudden he knew that he was a tired, spent old man. He longed for rest. He bade farewell to Greenland and sailed for Copenhagen, carrying with him the body of his devoted wife. And she, who had labored and created in an alien land a home, knew rest at last in the land of her youth.

Fortunately for Egede, his work continued. He was summoned to an audience with his King. He spoke of the strange, mighty land where he had lived for fifteen years, of the Greenlanders, a kind, a simple, a good people; he said his son Paul was eager and well prepared to carry on the work. The King was interested; he would continue his support. Egede was appointed Superintendent of the Greenland Missions, and as such was able to keep his watch over his spiritual child. This he did until his death, in 1758. In the subsequent policy of Denmark's rule in Greenland it is impossible to overlook the effect of Egede's gentle, unselfish spirit. The good Hans Egede, the "Apostle of Greenland," whom two kings could neither disregard nor deny, still watches over his flock.

The East Coast

In the six decades from Ross's voyage of 1819 to Lockwood's "farthest north" the west coast was charted almost up to its northern limit. Sailing the waters north of Davis Strait had become by that time comparatively commonplace. It was, and is, a far different matter on the east coast. What had been happening along the dread east coast, past which constantly files the terrible procession of monstrous pack ice and icebergs? This burdened current the Icelandic fishermen knew

and avoided. Only the more experienced, the braver of the Spitsbergen whalers, dared it. It had an insidious and effective ally in the
heavy fogs that bewildered the unwary intruder. This region was invested with the horror common to all inaccessible places.

From Egede's time on, the exploration of that coast may be divided
into two phases, the early and the modern. In both, extensive and
valuable work was done. But whereas in the former the discoveries
made by men of various nationalities were sporadic and disconnected,
in the latter the work was carried on systematically and continuously.
The second period began in 1876, when the Danish Committee for
the Geographical and Geological Investigation of Greenland was
formed. Under its auspices almost a hundred expeditions have been
sent out, and their results, covering all the branches of natural history,
are published in their periodical, *Meddelelser om Gronland.* If a
Scoresby, a Nansen, a Peary are written of at greater length, it is well
to remember that that does not imply that their achievements were
greater. Brilliant as their work was, it is of less importance than the
persistent labors steadily carried on by a large group of Danish explorers and scientists.

The eastern coast was first sighted by Henry Hudson in his memorable voyage of 1607, and, as he sailed parallel with it, he named
three high landmarks: Cape Young, with the lofty Mount of God's
Mercy towering behind it, and then Cape Hold-with-Hope. Subsequently he reached Spitsbergen and Hudson's Touches (Jan Mayen).
In the ensuing century adventurous Dutch whalers, wandering to the
west of Spitsbergen, sighted that forbidding coast across the intervening ice. Old maps preserve their names: Land van Lambert, Land
van Edam, Gael Hamke's Bay; there were Joris Carolus, who first
noted the westerly current that carried the *Fram* many years later, and
David Danell, who beheld the bluish glaciers of Angmagssalik. With
the passing of years and with whaling carried on more and more in
the open seas, whaling-ships in increasing numbers sailed the waters of
East Greenland. In this industry the Dutch were pre-eminent until
in 1733 the British government, at the suggestion of Sir Robert Wal-
pole, stimulated the moribund trade by offering a bonus to British
whalers. By the end of that century more than two hundred and fifty
British ships were engaged in whaling, and the control had passed
into their hands. But though the East Greenland Sea was annually
visited by a goodly number of ships, there still remained the old
danger, the old dread. It is recorded that in 1777 disaster struck the
whaling-fleet. Twelve ships belonging to various countries were caught
in the ice-pack, about forty miles from land. All through the autumn

they drifted southward. One by one the imprisoned ships were crushed and sunk; one by one their number was tragically reduced. Soon all the survivors were jammed on the last remaining ship. And that too crumpled under them Only a few of the crews, huddled together on an ice-floe, managed to live as it carried them southward to Cape Farewell, where they were rescued. In all, 320 men perished off that fatal stretch of coast marked on the maps as the Liverpool Coast.

This tragedy off the Liverpool Coast did not deter men from the hazardous pursuit of whales, from whose mammoth bodies was derived great wealth. During the long decades before the resurgence of interest in Arctic exploration, "the whalers . . . in their persistent struggles with ice and sea, form[ed] our outposts of investigation up in the north." [2] The most successful of the British whaling-captains who hunted in the Greenland seas were the Scoresbys, father and son. They were never content to be mere whalers: they were experimenters, students, leaders. William Scoresby senior was a farmer's son who went to sea, improved himself and his chances by using his spare time to learn the theory and practice of navigation, and entered the whaling-trade, in which he soon rose to be captain of a ship. Before long he was at the head of his profession, acquiring respect and riches; he was a God-fearing man who piously but realistically concluded the log of a prosperous voyage: "Also give me the grace and health peaceably to enjoy the fruits of my labour, to Thy glory and my comfort." [3] Of his thirty trips, in which he never lost a ship or seriously damaged one, fourteen were made in Greenland and Spitsbergen waters, giving him undisputed claim to being the outstanding ice-navigator. It was he who invented and first used the "crow's-nest"—that invaluable aid—to observe better both the ice and the whales, the ice-drill, and the practice of *sallying,* in which the entire crew runs from one side of the ship to the other to make it roll and thus free it from the adhering young ice; and it was he who first suggested using sledges drawn by dogs or reindeer to reach the Pole. The achievements of this remarkable father are overshadowed by those of his distinguished son, William Scoresby junior. Not only did the latter have the advantage of formal education, but he also had a thorough training aboard his father's ship. "Father and son together spent hours at the mast-head, where the boy, half frozen at times, received some of the practical instruction that finally made him at twenty-one the best navigator of the polar seas." [3] In 1806, when only seventeen, he was his father's chief officer when they set a new record for "farthest north" ever reached by a whaling-ship to the north of Spitsbergen. Five years later he was captain of his own ship, bound for the northern whale-fisheries, and each succeeding year he made a highly remunerative voyage. But he was not merely a first-rate whaling-captain; he was devoted to scientific research; he was a keen and careful observer, a questioning student. These various qualities were so happily mingled in him that it has been said that "he never neglected business in the cause of science, but was always mindful of science when business permitted." [4] Where other expeditions were financed either by the government or by private patrons, Scoresby's discoveries were made as he was accumulating a tidy fortune for himself and others.

It was the younger Scoresby who, after Wellington had crushed Napoleon, redirected England's attention to the Arctic and so heralded in a bright era of northern exploration; it was he who, in his book *An Account of the Arctic Regions with a History and Description of the Northern Whale Fisheries* (1820), aroused his countrymen's enthusiasm for completing the Northwest Passage and proposed the study of the many natural phenomena that became an integral part of such exploration. And he was an explorer himself, not merely a promoter. In 1822 in his specially built ship, the *Baffin*, accompanied by his father in the *Fame* and another whaler, he traced the east coast of Greenland from the seventy-second parallel to the sixty-ninth. While his father explored the deep indentation of Scoresby Sound, which he erroneously identified as the mythical waterway bisecting Greenland, the son surveyed the rocky coast with precision. He mapped in more than eight hundred miles, correcting the contour, trend, and extent of that shore. He sketched the rugged barren coast with its cliffs that rear straight up for more than a mile; he landed at several places, noting the flocks of birds, swarms of mosquitoes, the grasses and flowers, butterflies and bees; he found traces of human habitations —ashes of dead fires, spent arrows, discarded household implements; he gave a picture of East Greenland's lands and waters, observing everything with the meticulous eye of an inspired scientist. And all the while he was harvesting a fortune in blubber and bone.

The results of his labors he published the following year in *Journal of a Voyage to the Northern Whale Fisheries* (1823). Except for Nordenskiöld's extensive work, Scoresby's two books were the most important contributions made to a scientific knowledge of the Arctic regions. It is to his "profound faculty of observation that we owe the most significant hints on the nature of the Polar Sea." [5] *

* Scoresby retired from the sea after this voyage, matriculated at Queen's College, Cambridge, and in 1825 was ordained. He became a Doctor of Divinity in 1839. He continued his scientific interests, publishing several papers on terrestrial magnetism, and was elected a Fellow of the Royal Society.

The path that Scoresby had forced through the ice-stream to the east coast of Greenland in his voyage of 1822 was followed the next year by Captains Sabine and Clavering. The latter, in command of the *Griper*, Parry's ship of 1820, was ordered to reach some spot on that coast where Sabine could complete the series of pendulum observations he had begun in Norway and Spitsbergen.* Clavering tried to reach land as far north as possible, but twice he was stopped by a solid ice-field. At last he broke through at the seventy-fourth parallel, where, on Pendulum Island, Sabine set up his observatory. While Sabine carried out his tests, Clavering explored. He sailed warily along the coast as far north as Shannon Island; he made a fortnight's excursion in a small boat into Gael Hamke's Bay, which he identified from the old Dutch whaler's description. He found at the head of the bay a great ice-fiord that calved stupendous bergs, but, more exciting still, in that country as remote as the mountains of the moon he found a community of Eskimos. The whole group, men, women, and children, numbered only twelve. This little lost bit of humanity was hundreds of arduous miles from its nearest fellow men; whether they were the last few survivors of those who had come down the east coast from the north or adventurous pioneers from more southerly settlements will never be known. For when that region was next visited, fifty years later, the little group had perished, leaving many relics and vestiges behind. This is the only case of Eskimos found on the east coast of Greenland north of 66°.

The next expedition to reach the east coast came, not through the dangerous ice-belt from the sea, but from the western side, skirting the coast. They came not to make geographical discoveries, but to locate the ancient East Bygd settlements, although learned scholars had already placed them correctly elsewhere. In 1829 Lieutenant V. A. Graah of the Danish Navy made an interesting and fruitful journey. He wanted to take the route Egede had tried via Cape Farewell. He employed the method used by two previous explorers in their coastwise cruising. Pedar Wallöe, the first European to reach the southeast coast (1751), had made use of the Eskimo women's umiak to skirt the shore around Cape Farewell; the same transport had been similarly used in 1806 by the next European, Ludwig Giesecke, a German mineralogist. Giesecke was a most interesting person. In his youth an actor and author, he is reputed to have written the libretto for *The Magic Flute*. Later he turned to mineralogy, and, as a mining expert of repute, he sailed for Greenland to pass two years in studying

* The pendulum is used to determine the relative and absolute acceleration of gravity at different places, and in this way the configuration of the earth.

Dog Sledges in Front of Winter Houses

A Summer Encampment

WOMEN ROWING AN UMIAK, WITH A MAN IN A KAYAK ALONGSIDE. *Native woodcuts from Rink's* DANISH GREENLAND.

its ores. That was in 1806. War between Denmark and England prolonged his stay until 1813. Using an umiak, he covered all of the known coastline. He got on well with the natives. He was frugal and spent his time "hewing and cleaving stones from morning till nightfall." His mineralogical and ethnological notes were shipped home on board a Danish vessel, which was captured, and his notes were first published without his name in Edinburgh. Later his authorship was acknowledged. He is the man who discovered the presence of cryolite, one of the staples of the Greenland trade.

Graah set out with two kayaks and two umiaks, the latter manned by Eskimo women rowers. He decided to use the umiak for many reasons. "The *umiak*, or women's boats, are made of a light wooden frame with seal skin covering. They are flat-bottomed, easy to haul upon the ice, to carry, or to repair, and at the same time capable of taking a fairly good load." By the first of April his party reached the east coast, where the prevalent brash ice with its sharp edges made their progress in the skin-covered boats particularly dangerous. They waited a month before they could proceed. They then continued northward, past a stern and rocky shore, where every grassy, flowery spot glowed like a jewel in a metallic setting. None of the Eskimos they met had any knowledge or tradition of ancient white settlers. They passed 65° N., north of Vendom or Return Island, before they were stopped by heavy, impenetrable ice. They turned southward and in the Eskimo village of Imarsivik spent the winter. An attempt made the next spring to get farther north was unsuccessful, and Graah returned. His information about the southeastern coast was valuable and voluminous; but most important of all was the fact that he established a pleasant contact between the Eskimos of the west coast and the six hundred Eskimos he had found living on the east coast.

Forty years passed before the east coast was again visited by explorers. Dr. Petermann, the German geographer, had been urging his countrymen to emulate the inspiring example of the English and contribute their share to the exploration of the Arctic regions. At his own risk and expense he outfitted a small ship in 1868, gave command of it to Captain Karl Koldewey, and instructed him to try for a high northing in the waters between East Greenland and Spitsbergen. Koldewey, unable to get near the Greenland coast, devoted his time to the coastal waters of Spitsbergen. But this voyage had the desired effect of arousing the Germans to make another, better, polar venture. The *Germania*, a steam vessel especially built for Koldeway's second attempt, accompanied by the *Hansa*, a schooner, Captain Hegemann in command, was to try to reach the Pole via the east coast of Greenland. With Koldewey went Julius Payer, who was in charge of the sledging-operations. It was here that he received the training so valuable for his subsequent work in Franz Josef Land. The two ships left Bremerhaven the middle of June 1869.

A few days after they had passed Jan Mayen, hidden from them by a dense fog, they ran into heavy ice. The *Germania*, by the aid of steam, pushed through, but the *Hansa*, its sails fluttering in the wind, was beset and caught. A misunderstanding of signals—and the ships parted, never to meet again. Those on board the schooner saw the ice advance toward them, running over the water with incredible speed, saw the *Germania* steam away. They knew what the future held. They were caught off the Liverpool Coast. They could only look back with dread upon that tragedy of a century before; the *Polaris* drift had not yet occurred to hearten them. But they had little time for brooding. The *Hansa* was brutally assaulted by the pressing ice, and they had to be prepared to abandon it. They built a hut of coal blocks on the ice and provisioned it. "The house of coal on the southward drifting ice-fields was destined to be through the long Arctic night our only place of refuge—perhaps too, our grave." [6] The *Hansa* sank slowly. "Round about the ship lay a chaotic mass of heterogeneous articles, and groups of feeble rats struggling with death and trembling with the cold." [6] In their fairly comfortable asylum they floated southward—but not in safety. January came accompanied by foul weather that disturbed the pack. "We thought we heard a peculiar rustling noise as if someone were shuffling his feet on the floor . . . a scraping, blustering, crackling, sawing, grating and jarring sound, as if some unhappy ghost were wandering under the floe. . . . There could be no doubt but that our floe stood in great danger of being smashed to pieces, either from drifting over sunken rocks and bursting up, or breaking against the ice-border; perhaps both at once. . . . Our position, if the floe should be destroyed, seemed hopeless." [6] In the storm more than half of their floe was eaten away. And worse was in store. "The floe surrounding us split up; a heavy sea arose. . . . Between our house and the piled-up store of wood there suddenly opened a huge gap. Washed by the powerful waves it seemed as if the piece just broken off was about to fall on us; and at the same time we felt the rising and falling of our reduced floe. All seemed lost." [6] They camped in their boats, and when it seemed safe they built another, smaller hut. Miraculously they had come out alive from the narrow channel between Greenland and Iceland where the mighty pack jams and smashes its way through. But they had lost most of their supplies, they were reduced to the direst extremity; living on the shortest of short rations, they drifted southward. In May open water invited them to make for land in their boats. Over water, over ice, dragging, sailing, rowing, pushing, they reached land near the Moravian mission of Frederiksdal. They had triumphed in their struggle of 237 days. They arrived home in Germany the very day their victorious brothers saluted the dawn at Sedan.

When the *Hansa* disappeared, so quickly that the *Germania* had no time to follow her, Koldewey knew that he must give up the hope of trying to reach the Pole. He decided to concentrate his efforts on the unknown East Greenland coast north of Pendulum Island, where he established his winter quarters. The men had had no previous experience in Arctic sledging and did not lay down food depots during the autumn, with the result that they could not make extended spring trips. Despite this handicap and the adverse traveling-conditions of bad ice and terrific gales, the party led by Koldewey and Payer did good work. Leaving their vessel the 24th of March, they headed north. For eight days storms confined them to their tent; during this time they tried to eat as little as possible so as to keep their provisions for active work. "Scarcely ever was the fast of Passion week more strictly observed than it was by us." [6] The middle of April they reached 77° N. They had passed a towering headland—Cape Bismarck—had traced a hundred and fifty miles of that forbidding coast, but a diminishing food supply made them turn back. Upon their return to the ship and before it was free to sail, they made four other short sledging-trips.

On their homeward way they steamed southward, skirting the shore. Thus it was that they found and explored the mighty and beautiful Franz Josef Fiord, which stretches "into the very heart of Greenland. We had entered a basin, the shores of which were formed by rocks, which for glorious form and colour I had never seen equalled. Here were congregated huge walls, deep erosion-fissures, wild peaks, mighty crevassed glaciers, raging torrents, and waterfalls; which in Europe, as a rule come but singly." [6] Soon the splendors of this fiord, so unexpectedly met with, were behind them. The *Germania* was headed for home.

The discoveries of the Scoresbys, Clavering, Graah, and Koldewey had been important and illuminating but, when marked off on the great stretch of the eastern coast that extends from Cape Farewell to where the northern coast begins at 83° 20', very limited. To connect these isolated known bits, to reduce that vast unknown shoreline to thousands of charted points of longitude and latitude—this was the task undertaken by the Danes and by them carried through with undiminished zeal.

A modest, careful beginning was made when Commander Mourier and Lieutenant Wandel, of the Royal Danish Navy, made a short voyage in 1879. Theirs was a preliminary examination of the temper and extent of the offshore ice from 65° to 69°, where the Greenland Sea narrows into Denmark Strait, the channel between Iceland and

Greenland. Four years later Lieutenants Holm and Garde, also of the Royal Danish Navy, set out to extend Graah's discoveries beyond his farthest point; like Graah they intended working their way up the coast in umiaks. At Nanortalik, just west of Cape Farewell, they established their headquarters. At the same time Holm stocked a large depot farther south, explored many winding fiords, and made friends with the east-coast Eskimos. At the beginning of May 1884 the expedition—a curious procession of four umiaks and seven kayaks—left Nanortalik. Through the ice-strewn waters they advanced warily, slowly; gales detained them, but also opened the way so that they could progress. At the end of July the expedition divided: Garde with a young scientist, Eberlin, and two umiaks started back for headquarters, making careful observations en route; Holm, with Knudsen, another scientist, and Johan Petersen, their intelligent interpreter, with the kayaks and the remaining umiaks and a year's provisions, continued northward. After a month they reached Graah's Return Island. Before them lay unknown territory. Soon they were abreast of Sermilik Fiord, then of Tasuisarslik, a region of intricate inland waterways dotted with islands called by the natives Angmagssalik. Here Holm decided to winter.

He had penetrated to the very heart of an important new area. He had discovered an unknown tribe of Eskimos, never before visited by white men, and made valuable studies of their traditions and culture. He had explored for its greater part the beautiful and vast Sermilik Fiord; he had investigated the geological formation of the surrounding countryside; he had taken measurements of water levels, observed the movements of the ice. From the last he concluded that for certain reasons the offshore ice is quite open during July and August and that therefore this region can be visited annually by ships. This was confirmed by Nordenskiöld, who penetrated the ice-belt and landed there in 1883. After almost a year's residence Holm started for the west coast in July of 1885; he met Garde, who had carefully examined the numerous southern fiords, and together they took ship for Copenhagen, where they arrived the beginning of October. In 1894, ten years after he had first discovered Angmagssalik, Holm, now Captain Holm, was honored by being chosen to locate and establish the Danish settlement on that coast. He picked for its site a gentle slope on the east side of a large island at the mouth of the Tasuisarslik Fiord, and for the first colonial manager his old interpreter, Johan Petersen. Today, except for the introduction of a wireless station, the settlement of Angmagssalik is the same. It is the center from which Denmark administers and cares for the east-coast

Eskimos—some 550 souls—and it is the nucleus around which the natives have concentrated their villages.

But to continue with the geographical discoveries. The coast between Holm's farthest north and Scoresby's farthest south still remained to be charted. With this in view the *Hecla*, a sealing-ship, was hired and outfitted and, commanded by Lieutenant C. Ryder of the Royal Danish Navy, sent to East Greenland in 1891. The beginning of August, just two months after leaving Copenhagen, he sighted Scoresby Sound, down which he steamed for a hundred miles. There he wintered, exploring and mapping the many long fiords that branched out from it. The next summer he tried to skirt the shore to the south, but menacing masses of ice blocked the way, driving him out to sea. Before heading for home he touched the coast near Angmagssalik. Ryder had done excellent work, carrying out a series of scientific observations and leaving only a small portion of shore south from Scoresby Sound to be surveyed.

To do this, and by so doing complete the charting of that coast from Cape Farewell to Koldewey's Cape Bismarck in 76° 47′, was the goal of the next expedition, in 1900. It was financed by the Carlsberg Foundation, hence its name of Carlsbergfondet Expedition. The Carlsberg Foundation was instituted by a brewer of that name who left his brewery to a trust with instructions that all profits deriving from it be used toward scientific work. Since the brewery has been a highly lucrative business, it has been the important source of much of the funds needed to carry out Arctic exploration. The leader of the expedition was Lieutenant G. Amdrup, who had in 1884–5 done valuable research near Angmagssalik and so had both training and experience to recommend him. Hartz, a botanist, who had been with Ryder, was second in command; the botanist Kruuse, Lieutenant J. P. Koch, surveyor, two zoologists, and a geologist completed his staff. Their ship, the *Antarctic*, had the previous year carried the Swedish professor Nathorst to that selfsame coast in his search for the balloonist Andrée. Failing to find his lost countryman, he had turned his attention to mapping the involved unknown series of interior fiords connecting Davy Sound with Franz Josef Fiord. In the *Antarctic*, then, Amdrup and his party sailed. He planned to trace from Scoresby Sound to Angmagssalik by sailing along the coast in a small boat, while Hartz, commanding the ship, surveyed the intricate outline of that great inland body of water. They pierced through the ice-stream to Cape Dalton, and there the two groups separated. Amdrup with Mikkelsen, then a very young man, and two sailors started southward and after a voyage of forty-four days reached their goal. There they were picked up by the main party, who had completed their share of the work from Cape Dalton to Scoresby Sound. The objective they had set for themselves had been attained, the last gap to Cape Bismarck spanned, and with happy minds they sped homeward.

While the Danes had been systematically making their way up the east coast, an American explorer had penetrated beyond Lockwood's "farthest north" on the west coast, rounded the northern shore, and got as far as Clarence Wyckoff Island—82° 37′ N.—on the east side. Robert E. Peary, an engineer in the United States Navy, was possessed by the desire to reach the North Pole. He was in the tropics surveying the route for the proposed Nicaraguan canal when he read Nordenskiöld's *Greenland*. The book fired his imagination and settled for him his life's interest and work. From his first Arctic trip in 1886 until his eighth in 1908, he labored uninterruptedly toward the solving of some of the important Arctic geographical problems, especially that of the North Pole. Among Arctic explorers his is a unique nature, a paradoxical combination of forethought and prudence with dash and recklessness, of organizing ability with tremendous physical endurance and patience. Above all, patience, the patience to labor and plan for years, lose everything in a few weeks, and then start in from the beginning again, the richer only for that intangible residue, experience. Like no man before him, except Charles Francis Hall, he emulated the life and methods of the Eskimos and used Eskimos whenever possible. His courage and stamina were of the same high quality as Nansen's; he set out in the spring of 1892 on one of his most daring journeys after having sustained a broken leg the previous autumn, and his sledging-trip around the northernmost part of Greenland was carried through even though the previous year he had lost eight of his toes from frost-bite. But it also remains to be said that no other great Arctic explorer was guilty of such inaccuracies as Peary. In the magnitude of his enterprises and the magnificence of his achievements this flaw is likely to be overlooked, but in any study of the Arctic it must be reckoned with. He was not inaccurate on purpose; it is rather that he failed to distinguish between ice-covered water and ice-covered land, rather that he misjudged what he saw. Looking across a frozen sea, it is hard to tell whether distant ridges are mountains or pressed-up ice-floes; looking down on a snow-covered expanse, it is difficult to say whether level land or water lies under the snowy mantle. That Peary saw "Crocker Land" to the northwest of Ellesmere Island was a mistake, a mistake similar to other "lands" seen across other seas; but his inaccuracy about Greenland's northeastern coast became a far more serious error, since inadvertently it led to the tragedy of the Danmark Expedition.

In 1892 and again in 1895 Peary went from his base in Whale Sound across the inland Ice-Cap to Navy Cliff, whence he saw Independence Bay and what he thought was the Greenland Sea.* To the north he glimpsed an ice-free land dotted with mountains, separated from the mainland by a channel. The outlining of that northern land—Peary Land—was done in his expedition of 1898–1902.

Captain John Bartlett, uncle of the famous Bob Bartlett, was in command of the *Windward,* the contact ship of the Jackson-Harmsworth Expedition, use of which was graciously offered by Alfred Harmsworth. In her Peary hoped to sail as far north as possible up the Smith Sound route and then strike out for the North Pole from the northernmost part of either Ellesmere Land or Greenland. Stopped by heavy ice under Cape d'Urville, on the east coast of Ellesmere Land, Peary was forced to establish his winter quarters at Dobbin Bay. In several trips made that autumn he proved that Bache "Island" was a peninsula and that Grant Land and Ellesmere Land were contiguous, extending from Jones Sound to Cape Columbia.

Next he began reconnoitering northward, building igloos and laying down food depots as far as Lady Franklin Bay. Fort Conger, Greely's old headquarters, was to be his base for his polar drive. The way had been sufficiently prepared when in the middle of December he started for that northern base. But the going was bad; the ice-foot along which they sledged grew steadily worse until it was impassable for even the lightest load. Their provisions ran low; biting winds numbed even the Eskimos; and most of the time even moonlight was wanting. "In complete darkness and over a chaos of broken and heaved-up ice, we stumbled and fell and groped for eighteen hours, till we climbed upon the ice-foot of the north side [Lady Franklin Bay]." [7] For two weeks they rested at Fort Conger, obtaining food, light, and heat from the stores left behind fifteen years before. But they could not stay there; they had to alter all their plans and turn back for their ship because Peary had a "wooden" feeling in his feet. His toes were frost-bitten, and, as they thawed out, the dead parts fell away, leaving open sores. "My toes were unhealed, the bones were protruding through the raw stumps on both feet, and I could barely stand for a moment." [7] The Eskimos dragged him all the way back. All work was delayed until his feet were healed. The spring of 1899 passed.

* See pp. 257 ff.

Greenland

In August the *Windward* was free to sail and, after carrying Peary and his party over to Etah on the Greenland side, steered for home. At the beginning of March 1900 Peary left Etah, and by making use of the continuous line of caches he had established from Cape Sabine to Fort Conger—containing fourteen tons of supplies!—he reached the latter place. From there he intended following the route Beaumont and Lockwood had charted before him, up the west coast of Greenland. This zigzagging between Greenland and Ellesmere Land he found a surer and simpler way than trying to traverse the extended mouth of Humboldt Glacier. He had made up his mind to make the dash for the North Pole from the tip of Greenland rather than from the tip of Ellesmere Land, as the Nares Expedition had done. By doing this he was prepared, if his efforts were blocked, to spend his time charting the northern limits of Greenland, an equally important task. He started from Lady Franklin Bay on the 11th of April. For a long distance he had literally to cut a path through the rough ice. On the Greenland side he found the Black Horn Cliffs lashed by open water. He tried to hew a road over the ice-foot. No good. He tried waiting. New ice formed. He waited no more, but raced over this sagging, frail bridge. On, on he went, though his toeless feet hurt. In less than a month he had reached Lockwood's extreme point; one march farther and he was abreast of Cape Washington, which had been sighted in the distance. The mouth of a fiord was crossed, then a glacier, "and when we came within view of the next point ahead I felt that my eyes rested at last upon the Arctic Ultima Thule." [7] He called it Cape Morris K. Jesup, in honor of his chief patron; it is the northernmost point of Greenland, 83° 39′ N.

From there he started out across the ice. North, always north, through thick fog, "groping our way northward over broken ice and across gigantic wave-like drifts of hard snow." [7] The difficult going and the ominous promise of a water-sky ahead caused him to turn back for land. Arriving at the shore, he continued exploring. The next promontory was Cape Bridgman, "at which the northern face of the land trends away to the southeast. This cape is in the same latitude as Cape Washington." [7] He had turned the corner. Another two marches to the east and he was at Clarence Wyckoff Island,* from where, "in a fleeting glimpse through the fog, I saw a magnificent mountain of peculiar contour which I recognized as the peak seen by me in 1895 from the summit of the interior ice-cap south of Independence Bay, rising proudly above the land to the north." [7] He

---

* This was not an island, as later explorations disclosed. See detail map of northeast Greenland on opposite page.

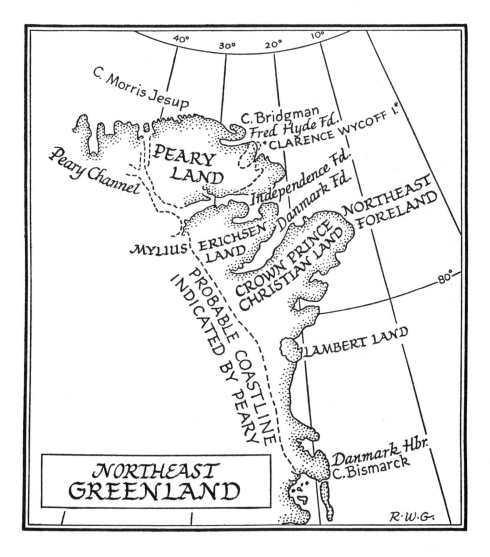

NORTHEAST
GREENLAND

wanted to continue, but a fog held him there for two days; food and time were running low. And there, in 82° 37′ N. and 23° 9′ W., Peary erected a cairn in which he deposited a note giving his route and his findings. His return trip, except for a perilous rounding of Black Horn Cliffs, was made in good time, and he arrived back at Fort Conger on June 10. "In this journey I had determined conclusively the northern limit of the Greenland Archipelago, or land group, and had practically connected the coast southward to Independence Bay, leaving only that comparatively short portion of the periphery of Greenland lying between Independence Bay and Cape Bismarck indeterminate." [7]

The charting of "that comparatively short portion," marked on the maps by a simple oblique dotted line as "probable coast-line, indicated by Peary," was all that remained to complete the known contour of Greenland. To trace from Cape Bismarck (76° 47′) to Peary's cairn (82° 37′), to put the keystone in the great arch of Greenland exploration, was the task to which a young Dane, Mylius-Erichsen, dedicated himself. He had already had some Arctic experience and was imbued with the desire to explore the last stretch of unknown coastline. It was a long stretch, more than four hundred miles, unknown except for a dot to the north of Cape Bismarck where in 1905 H.R.H. Philippe Duc d'Orléans had landed in his yacht *Belgica*. Because the Duc d'Orléans had been able to reach the land so far north, Erichsen was encouraged to steer his ship to the same spot, so as to be at the very threshold of the proposed exploration.

Both the Danish government and the Carlsberg Foundation contributed the funds necessary to buy and outfit a sealing-steamer, the *Danmark*. The Danmark Expedition, as it is called, was also equipped with two motor boats, Eskimo-type sledges, a hundred dogs, and ample provisions and supplies. Erichsen was in charge of the expedition; Lieutenant Trolle, R.N., commanded the ship. The cartographer, Lieutenant Höeg Hagen, and the surveyor, Lieutenant J. P. Koch, who had worked with Amdrup, were both army men; Wegener was meteorologist and physicist; there were a geologist, a marine zoologist, a botanist, an ornithologist, two artists, an ice-pilot, two students who signed up as stokers so as to be able to go, one of whom was Peter Freuchen, and three Eskimo dog-drivers, one of them Brönlund—the whole group numbering twenty-seven men. The *Danmark* sailed from Copenhagen June 24, 1906, and all its members reflected the high hopes, the unbounded enthusiasm, of its thirty-four-year-old leader. "Two years later, in August of 1908, a message from the Danmark Expedition was flashed across the world: Object attained, coast surveyed, the outline of Greenland now known throughout its extent, important scientific results obtained in various fields, but the leader, Mylius-Erichsen, with Lieutenant Höeg Hagen and the Eskimo Brönlund, perished after a heroic struggle against the difficulties of the country." [8]

What had happened? Why had success been attended by such a tragedy? Everything had begun so well. The *Danmark*, after a lengthy fight, had prevailed against the ice and landed a large food depot at Cape Marie Valdemar and then turned south to winter at Danmark Havn, near Cape Bismarck. In the two years that the expedition stayed there, and while the sledging-parties were in the field, the various scientific members of the group thoroughly investigated the surrounding countryside. Soon after they had landed, numerous sledging-parties went out to lay down depots, and during the winter careful and exact preparations were made to ensure the safety and success of the great spring journeys. At the end of March 1907 they were off to the north. There were four sledges, two for extended exploration, two to establish distant food depots. Each sledge had a team of eight or nine dogs, each had provisions for two months for the men and half as much for the dogs. In the first were Erichsen, Hagen, and Brönlund; in the second, Koch, Bertelsen, an artist, and the Eskimo Tobias. The auxiliary sledges were commanded by Wegener and Trostrup. On the 22nd of April Trostrup started back, after establishing a depot, and four days later Wegener did likewise. Erichsen and Koch continued together for a little while. The going was bad and always, despite what they had hoped to find, leading farther and farther eastward until the estimated distance had been increased by almost two hundred miles. At Lambert Land (the Land van Lambert of the old Dutch maps) a depot was laid down containing sufficient stores to bring both parties safely home. At Northeast Foreland, the first of May, they parted: Erichsen heading west to look for Peary Channel, Koch continuing north for the cairn Peary had erected at his extreme point.

Northward of Northeast Foreland Koch found himself traveling over water, out of sight of land. The going was so rough over hummocks or through deep soft snow that he was forced to change his course and head in toward land. Following the shore, he reached his goal after twelve days and thus had the joy and honor of completing the last link in the chain of coastal survey. Though a thick fog bothered him, as it had Peary, he continued as far as Cape Bridgman, exploring Frederick Hyde Fiord en route, and stopped to kill some musk-oxen to add to his provisions. On his return journey, at Cape

Rigsdagen on the 27th of May, he suddenly met Erichsen. The latter told him that he had followed the coastline, expecting thus to reach Peary Channel, but after wandering for a long time he had wearily worked his way in and out of a fiord 125 miles long, Danmark Fiord. Towering, precipitous cliffs surrounded this inlet, mighty dikes that held in check the frozen waves of the inland ice-sea. And though Koch told his chief that he had sighted Independence Bay as far as its head at Academy Glacier, Erichsen decided that he still should explore it and Peary Channel. He reckoned that it could be done in a few days. And so they parted for a second time, Koch for the south and Danmark Havn, Erichsen into the unknown west.

Koch took the home trail, making sure that all the depots were in order, and reached the ship June 23. He had been gone eighty-eight days and had covered 1,200 miles—a trip that for extent, duration, and accomplishment ranks with the very greatest. And, resting on shipboard, he waited. Daily he expected Erichsen to make his appearance. Summer came and went. September, and winter swooped down. Anxiously they all waited. They were uneasy, worried, fearful, and the wind that swept wildly down from the north chilled them with the hint of distant tragedy.

Relief parties could not set out until the ice was sufficiently frozen. In October they tried to locate the missing men and, failing, laid down additional depots at frequent intervals to aid them. Early in March Koch and Tobias started north to search for the lost commander. As they neared the depot on Lambert Land, a strong head wind wrapped a blinding fog about them and piled up huge snowdrifts through which they floundered. It was as though the Arctic struggled to prevent their reaching it. But they located the small cave where the food had been cached, cleared away the snow that choked its entrance, and then dimly made out a stiff huddled human figure. It was Brönlund, the Eskimo. At his feet were his diary and Hagen's maps safely enclosed in a bottle. The diary, written in Eskimo, had this last page written in Danish:

Perished 79 Fiord after attempt to return over inland ice in November. I arrive here in waning moonlight, and could not go farther for frozen feet and darkness. Bodies of the others are in middle of Fiord off glacier (about 2½ leagues). Hagen died 15th of November, Mylius about ten days later.

Jörgen Brönlund.

From the rest of his diary the achievements and tragic sequence of events that befell Erichsen and Hagen and Brönlund were made clear. They had explored a second fiord (like the Danmark Fiord, which Erichsen had first thought to be Peary's Independence Bay) that also ran southwest for 150 miles, ending in a spot near where Peary had placed his "Navy Cliff." Melting ice made travel over land or ice difficult and slow, consuming precious time and exhausting them and their underfed dogs. The return journey, begun the end of August, was a mounting struggle against hunger, a desperate abandoning of everything that was not vitally important. They had not time, strength, or peace of mind to write in their diaries from September to the middle of October. Then came one brief notation to the effect that, blocked by open water at Antarctic Bay, they had ascended the inland ice, that the last dog was dead.

It is due to Brönlund's superb heroism that the work he and his comrades had done at the cost of their lives had not perished with them, that he had triumphed over frozen feet and darkness to die where living men would be certain to find him.

Koch could find neither the bodies nor the diaries of the other two; that was to be done by Mikkelsen in 1909–12. The Danmark Expedition had achieved its main objective—its work was finished. And in addition to the coastal survey made by Koch and Erichsen the expedition had done an enormous amount of valuable work. Besides the large, varied, and important collection of data made continuously over the whole period of their stay in Danmark Havn, exciting inland discoveries had been made. At the same time as the searching-party had gone out, Bertelsen, Wegener, and two others had started to explore inland over the Ice-Cap. After two weeks they reached a nunatak, or snow-free land. Here was a remarkable sight: the ice dropped away, sheer, like a canyon wall, for ninety feet, enclosing below a land free from ice—Dronning Luisa's Land, they called it. Down the vertical ice wall they went and examined its rocks, plants, and fossils.

The Danmark Expedition returned to Copenhagen at the end of August 1908. By virtue of its extensive discoveries and the wealth and range of its scientific observations it is one of the great Arctic expeditions, but there was no elation at the thought of a task well done —it was buried under the sorrow of having lost a gallant leader and two brave comrades. Almost immediately plans were made for a new expedition, the main purpose of which was to find the bodies and diaries of the two missing men. It is due to the Alabama Expedition of 1909–12 under the leadership of Ejnar Mikkelsen that the full story and importance of Erichsen's work and his manner of death have been rescued from oblivion. Mikkelsen also confirmed Erichsen's geographical findings.

Mikkelsen, encouraged by his former commander Amdrup, was

provided with the tiny *Alabama,* of only forty tons, which was over-hauled and equipped and provisioned for an eighteen-month voyage. The entire personnel consisted of seven men—Lieutenant Laub, R.N., Lieutenant Jorgensen of the Danish Army, the engineer Iversen, two mates, and a carpenter. Late in June 1909 the *Alabama* left Copenhagen and, though delayed and hindered and pursued by small mishaps and dangerous tilts with the ice-stream, reached the east coast a little south of Cape Bismarck, where Clavering had landed—Shannon Island. None of them dreamed that "the *Alabama* had made her last voyage . . . that the old ship had met her death-blow out there in the ice-pack." [8] That autumn Mikkelsen made a ninety-five-day trip to the Lambert Land depot where Brönlund had been found. It was a dangerous trip. Delayed by open water and then chancing it over thin ice, Mikkelsen hurried northward, racing against the approaching darkness. He reached the spot where "Brön-lund fought his last heroic fight with the dark and cold, and sank at last, unable to go further with his frozen feet. It is a place of ill-omen . . . awful indeed must his last days have been in this desolate spot, unprotected against the cold and storm. . . . What must he not have gone through? . . . First the summer with his companions at Danmarks Fiord, a time of hunger and misery, then the long journey back, with little or no hope of reaching safety, his comrades dying or dead, and to crown it all, his last lonely journey to the depot, that his comrades' lives should not be sacrificed to no purpose." [8] Mikkelsen found nothing other than Koch had reported. He erected a cairn over the Eskimo's body.

The rest of the winter passed in preparations for the spring trip. In order to reach as quickly as possible the head of Danmark Fiord, where the search was to be focused, Mikkelsen proposed to strike out for it in a straight line, as the crow flies, over the interior ice—a new and perilous route. At the beginning of March five men left the *Alabama.* Mikkelsen and Iversen, each with a dog-drawn sledge, made up one party headed for Danmark Fiord and thence by Peary Channel to the nearest settlement on the west coast. Lacking Erichsen's diary, they did not know that Peary Channel *did not exist.* Laub with the two mates was to explore the circumference of the nunatak, Queen Louisa Land, discovered by Wegener, and then return to the ship. The two parties climbed onto the inland ice together, but they soon parted, Mikkelsen going north, Laub to the west. Instead of completing the circuit of the nunatak, Laub's party was forced by foul weather, incredibly hard going, and a threatened shortage of supplies to return as they had come, without exploring the western side. They arrived back at the ship the end of May to find to their horror that the *Alabama* was submerged and Jorgensen and the carpenter living in a tent. All together they labored to salvage some planks and supplies. On both Shannon Island and Bass Rock they erected cairns and deposited in them full reports of what had happened. Luckily a sealer found their cairn at Bass Rock, learned of their predicament, and came to their rescue. A house was built and stocked, in case Mikkelsen should return there. And the men, realizing that they had done all that could be done and that their staying would only mean consuming needed supplies, left for home on board the sealer.

Meanwhile Mikkelsen and Iversen, ignorant of what had happened, pushed on. Northward along the Ice-Cap they went. "We can see far and wide over this desolate land, so imposing in its utter lifelessness, a great white surface, hard as glass and yet plastic and ever slowly moving, which only the highest mountain can pierce. . . . It is a beautiful and imposing sight, but so impressively silent that one feels an impulse to cry aloud, to strike the dogs until they howl, only to break the silence." [8] By the middle of May, after having experienced for a little the treacherous ice that had exhausted their precursors, they reached the high cliffs that drop straight down to Danmark Fiord. "We lie up there on the mountain-side looking over Danmarks Fiord . . . our thoughts go back to that sad autumn when those three men [Erichsen and his companions] came in with their sledges, wretchedly clad, dangerously short of provisions, and with exhausted teams, but still confident of reaching their ship at Cape Bismarck. What must their feelings have been as they moved about the desolate land, inhospitable in the cold light of the fading year? . . . It is difficult to understand how they managed to get up on the inland ice, and where. . . . What must they have felt, when, after sledging all those tiresome miles out of their way they reached the inland ice at last, only to find a sheer wall of ice a hundred feet in height? But their lives were at stake, and under such conditions the impossible often becomes the possible. Up they must and up no doubt they came . . . but where or how we shall never know." [8]

At last Mikkelsen and Iversen reached the shores of the fiord. "It is impossible to describe the intoxicating delight of this feeling of safety with which one steps out over firm, solid earth—the lurking horror of those hidden cracks now nothing but a nightmare passed." [8] The going was execrable, but they were off the Ice-Cap. They came across many signs of Erichsen's party and finally a cache. There they found a note, and then finally another cairn containing a second report. After telling of his unexpected meeting with Koch on May 27,

Erichsen writes: "We drove westward with twenty-three dogs, until the first of June, reaching Peary's Cape Glacier, and discovered that the Peary Channel *does not exist*, Navy Cliff being connected by land with Heilprin Land [the south central part of Peary Land]. We re-christened Independence Bay, calling it Independence Fiord, and built a cache on a low spit near Cape Glacier. On the way out through the fjord we discovered and explored two smaller fjords, Brönlund's to the north and Hagen's to the south-east, building a cache near the last named. Found also some old Eskimo tent-rugs [rings?].

"Suddenly the weather turned milder; deep snow and melting ice, lack of big game, and sickness and fatigue among the dogs hindered and delayed us on the way out, so we did not reach here until the 12th of June. Further progress over the ice was then impossible. We had only fifteen dogs left alive, of which one has since died. We have lived since then entirely upon what we can shoot. . . . Called the land Kronprins Christian Land.

"Being without further means of sustenance for ourselves and the dogs, not having got big game since the 16th of July, we must today —after having ferried ourselves across to the solid ice on a berg— leave here with fourteen dogs, two sledges and all our belongings, in search of some stretch of coast more rich in game, away from this region where absolutely no game is to be found, and which we have searched in all directions within a radius of five miles. Are all three in perfect health. We are trying to penetrate some miles farther down the fjord lying to the south-west of here, Danmarks Fjord, which we travelled over in May, and where we shot numbers of hare and musk-ox. If we succeed in obtaining a sufficient supply of meat we intend to drive the 125 Danish miles [500 statute miles] or there-abouts back to the ship as soon as the ice is passable, which should be about the end of this month, and hope to reach there before the end of September with or without dogs.

"The caches built in the neighbourhood of this one were set up by Hagen for the purposes of triangulation, and contain no messages.

"We will deposit messages as to our further fate in one or more caches farther down the fjord. 8th August, 1907 (*signed*) L. Mylius-Erichsen, Leader of the Danmarks Expedition to the N-E coast of Greenland 1906–08." [8]

In his second report Erichsen wrote that the going was still bad and tiring, that the dogs were failing and dying, that they were short of fuel, that they had secured enough game to last them fifteen days, and that they were headed for the coast, where they hoped to kill bears. Thus they expected to work their way down to the Lambert

Land depot. Those two messages Mikkelsen found; the rest, save for Brönlund's diary, was as blank and dead as the Ice-Cap itself.

Mikkelsen had found what he had come for; he was also to experience the struggle and despair involved in the homeward trip. He had to revise his plans and return to his ship instead of cutting across to the west coast. He, too, faced the soft snow and surface water of summer sledging; he, too, saw his dogs drop with exhaustion; and he, too, was short of food in a country scarce in game. At Lambert Land their last starved dog died, and Mikkelsen was so crippled with scurvy that for a while he could not walk. Had he and Iversen not had the depots Koch had laid down for Erichsen, they too would have perished. They needed all their strength to advance in the teeth of fierce storms and so could not burden themselves carrying much food. At last, less than twenty miles from the Danmark house, they had to abandon everything so as to be able to reach that haven alive. After they had recuperated there, they tried to retrace their steps to recover their precious diaries. But though they fought against gales and blizzards for a whole week, they could not advance. They decided to make for the *Alabama* and to let some of the other men, not so completely played out, retrieve their records. They did not know that their ship had sunk. They reached the *Alabama* hut paralyzed with exhaustion. All was silent, the hut was sagging; it was empty save for piled-up snow and a note. They were alone.

If Mikkelsen had shown himself to be a hardy and intrepid leader, then Iversen stands out as the perfect companion. He had an indomitable spirit; he was a master at driving a dog-sledge, he was a fine cook, and there was nothing he could not do or make with his hands. When the winter had passed and they had fully regained their strength and health, they went back to recover their papers. They found everything except Mikkelsen's diary, which had been eaten by a bear. Spring passed and summer, and they faced another winter on that desolate shore in that lonely hut. The next summer these two brave men were picked up by a vessel sent to find them and by September 1912 were back at Copenhagen. The Alabama Expedition is one of the most thrilling on record. It is immensely important as well. By its recovery of Erichsen's papers and its own sledging-trip the true outline of northeast Greenland was disclosed.

Erichsen's serious corrections of the knowledge of northeastern Greenland were soon confirmed by the work of a third man. Knud Rasmussen—a Dane born and raised in Greenland, familiar with the Eskimos, their language, their customs, a student of their culture, their traditions, and their history—was not only one of the great explorers of his time but also a most distinguished anthropologist. It was he who in 1910 established the most northerly of the Danish settlements to protect the isolated tribe of "Arctic Highlanders," natives of the Cape York district, from harmful foreign contacts; and his imagination and dreams were invoked when he called his station Thule. It has since become famous as the place from which Rasmussen carried out a series of Thule expeditions, seven in all, covering the immense terrain where Eskimos are found along the Arctic coast from the Bering Sea to the Greenland Sea. The First Thule Expedition, in 1912, had as its primary purpose the finding of Mikkelsen, who had not been heard from and who, it was feared, might have shared Erichsen's fate. Exploration was a secondary motive. On the chance that Mikkelsen had found his way, as planned, across Peary Channel to the west coast and was unable to get past Humboldt Glacier, sledges were sent north to Peabody Bay. Meanwhile Rasmussen, with Peter Freuchen, who had been a member of the Danmark Expedition, and two Eskimos, started in the middle of April 1912 to search for him in the vicinity of Danmark Fiord. Striking out for it in a straight line across the inland ice, they covered the five hundred intervening miles in the remarkably quick time of seventeen days. An anxious period was spent in negotiating the steep rocky walls that drop thousands of feet to the coastal strip, and, though some of the dogs missed their footing and were lost, the men arrived safely at the head of the fiord. They then sledged seventy-two miles to the sea and, skirting along the shore past Cape Rigsdagen, unknowingly retraced Erichsen's route into Independence Fiord. They traveled down the length of this second fiord to where Academy Glacier led back up to the inland ice. To the north of this glacier was a smiling ice-free land—Valmuedalen, Valley of Poppies, Rasmussen called it. Here he rested awhile, here game abounded, and here on the most northerly land in the world, remote and isolated from even the rest of Greenland, he was excited to find traces of Eskimo habitation. On August 8 he commenced the return trip. Like Erichsen before him, he found no channel along which he might pass to the west coast; he had to return by the inland ice, climbing up to it by the difficult and arduous steps of Academy Glacier. Then he reached Navy Cliff, where Freuchen found Peary's cairn with his report of June 5, 1892. They were back at Thule the middle of September—a few days after Mikkelsen had reached Copenhagen—four months after they had set out. They had surveyed and charted accurately the 1,200 miles they had sledged.

Erichsen, Koch, Mikkelsen, and Rasmussen had proved conclusively that Peary's outline of the east coast of Greenland from Cape Bridgman south to Lambert Land was entirely wrong. Where Peary on his map had shown Navy Cliff washed by the waves of the Greenland Sea, they had discovered Northeast Foreland jutting out to the east through twenty degrees of longitude, extending nearly half the distance between Navy Cliff and Spitsbergen; where Peary had placed his "channel," they had found solid land connecting Greenland with Peary Land. The true periphery of northeastern Greenland had been disclosed by their explorations.

Before taking leave of northern Greenland and Knud Rasmussen, it would be well to accompany him on his Second Thule Expedition, in which he sought to trace in detail the great fiord-indented west coast from St. George Fiord to De Long Fiord and to investigate the inland country where Peary had placed his "channel." At the same time he intended carrying on anthropological research in connection with ancient Eskimo migrations across northern Greenland. "The outlines of our work were drawn up by our predecessors, and we therefore knew beforehand that we could not expect any great geographical surprises; it was only the crumbs from the table of the rich expeditions we were to gather, and the role we were to play would be comparable to that of the little Polar fox, which everywhere on the Arctic coast follows the footsteps of the big ice-bear, hoping that something good may be left for it." Where those who had blazed that northward trail had "always preferred to follow the route along the Polar-ice proper, some distance from land, where the going was firm," [9] he intended surveying the inner reaches of those great fiords, where the sledging is arduous and treacherous over the bottomless snow.

After having spent the summer of 1916 in the Melville Bay region, intent on ethnological studies, he wintered at Thule. On April 6, 1917, with Lauge Koch, the nephew of J. P. Koch, the Swedish botanist Wulff, and four Eskimos, he headed north for St. George Fiord. Before they arrived there, where the real work was to commence, they had to travel more than six hundred miles. The coast they passed along was historic; it was a country rich in Arctic landmarks: they ate provisions originally laid down for the men of the Nares Expedition, who explored that route before any of the Thule members were born; they camped one night at the foot of the cliff whereon Hall was buried. "The ground on which we stand is dearly paid for; its exploration has cost the life of many a brave man of iron

243

will. But for each one who fell there were others who offered to take his place; thus our knowledge of the northernmost regions of the earth moves farther and farther north." [0] A month after they had started they reached St. George Fiord. They had only two months' provisions left, half of which they cached in a cairn at Dragoon Point. To find and shoot some game became absolutely imperative, and this need was with them during the next month while they mapped Sherard Osborn Fiord, Victoria Fiord, Nordenskiöld Inlet, and another deep fiord, one new to the charts—J. P. Koch Fiord they called it, in honor of Erichsen's comrade. Not only were they constantly tormented by lack of food—many times they were forced to eat a poor half-starved, exhausted dog—they were detained by snow and gales. But on they pushed until they had reached and mapped De Long Fiord, the last of the great indentations on the northwest coast, and there on a hill they "built a final beacon, the Thule Beacon, near the large mountain that gave us the terminating view of the last regions of Greenland." [9]

It was the end of June when they turned back for home. "We suffered from the heat and went about half-naked; the temperature swung between 3° and 6° C. [between 37° and 43° F.] of warmth. . . . The snow was quickly melting along the coast; great pools lay below the ice-foot . . . heavy snow with water beneath. . . . The warmth had converted the rough Polar ice into a hopeless system of channels and pools, wherefrom occasional blocks push up as islands in a huge swamp of ice. . . . All through the day we wade up to our knees in the ice-water. . . . We have crawled in this way for three days, a three-day long bath in cold water. . . . The cold water takes it out of those dogs who have not yet recovered from their period of starvation." [9] Then, as they suddenly sight a herd of musk-oxen, the picture becomes rosy. "We embraced each other and behaved like lunatics. For what we saw meant not merely food in plenty . . . but also implied rest and drying our clothes for some days. . . . With great difficulty we covered the last piece of the way, under favourable conditions it would have been done in an hour, now it took seven. I arrived an hour after the others, as the sledge for the second time had fallen to pieces and had to be lashed together. I was hoarse with shouting to the dogs [trying to get through the water to the beach whereon the others were sunning and drying themselves] and Dr. Wulff came towards me and told me that during the hour whilst he had been waiting for me, he had experienced the word of the holy Augustine: 'That the joy of the blessed consists in not merely knowing oneself to be on the right side, but also, and that not least, in the constant listening to the despairing cries of the damned!' " [9]

But this was a short, joyous respite. It was a hard fight to reach their depot at Dragoon Point; they had counted on augmenting their supplies by catching seals, but those they shot were so lean that they sank immediately. And between them and home lay the long, precipitous face of the Humboldt Glacier. Taking stock, they figured that by going on short rations and killing some of the dogs they would be able to get to the south of the glacier, where they would be within the hunting-grounds of the Etah Eskimos. But to do this they had to go toward the interior around the back of the glacier, over the Ice-Cap. The way inland was hard, rough, and tiring. At their first camp after leaving Dragoon Point, one of their faithful Eskimos, who had been a valuable member of the Danmark Expedition, never returned from hunting. For three days they stayed there looking for him. "In vain we stared, in vain we stared our eyes tired across mountain and cloughs. . . . Hendrik was destined never to return. . . . The Polar Eskimo has a proverb which says that no man will settle down and take up new land for good until death overtakes him and ties his body to a stone mound; only then is it possible to attach a man to a country. I therefore propose that we hold to this idea, born of the enormous spirit of Liberty of primitive man, and to this island, where Hendrik found his grave, give his name." [9] Saddened, they continued. It was now a matter of life and death for all. They were in a piteous state, their clothes and footgear soaked by ice-water and rain. Slowly they ascended Daniel Bruun Glacier onto the inland ice. It was ten days before they reached the head of that glacier, which hung out over "the ravines like waves stiffened in horror over the mute uncanniness which rests over this eerie landscape in the midst of eternal winter." [9]

They still had to journey along the Ice-Cap. Deep snow, adverse gales, long detours to pass bottomless crevasses, storms and fogs necessitated long halts. Wulff and Koch were tormented by boils that covered their bodies. By the middle of August they had only nine dogs left. Two days later they had drunk their last cup of coffee and were reduced to five dogs. But in the distance they saw land. To reach it they had first to cross rivers that flowed swiftly over the ice. "August 23rd. . . . In the midst of fog and hopelessness, we see the first sign of life from land—a small fly buzzes past us right up on the ice." [9] The next day they had actually escaped from the terrible embrace of the inland ice; the expedition with all its findings was on a stony, barren land. They were 170 miles from the nearest habitation, Etah; Koch and Wulff were ill from exhaustion; their last dog was gone; they were short of ammunition; and all they had between them and starvation was a few skin straps, a cupful of tea, and a tube of glycerin. Only one thing could save them and their work—speedy relief. To effect this, Rasmussen with one Eskimo pushed on for Etah, while the remaining four followed by slow marches.

Rasmussen and his companion traversed a land covered with sharp stones through which frothy rivers tumbled into large lakes. Game was scarce. They made forced marches, stopping for short naps. Mile after mile they walked for four days—and then they met an Eskimo, one who had strayed far from his hunting-party. He had not enough food to send back to Wulff and Koch, so, borrowing his sledge and dogs, the two men sped on toward Etah. They reached it on August 30, so exhausted they could not accompany the relief party that left the next day to find the others. Ten days later they all returned. As Rasmussen hurried to meet them, Koch sat down on a stone, pale and without a word, and the tears that rolled down his cheeks told that Wulff had not lived to return. A catastrophe had overtaken the expedition; Wulff was dead, fallen in the last fight for life. He had been completely worn out, too tired even to eat; and still he tried to crawl on with the others. He knew he was dying and he wanted terribly to live. To the very last he jotted down notes on the surrounding flora. Soon even his will could last him no farther. It was rest he wanted, rest, sleep, death. "This walk was worse than death," Lauge Koch said. "I noticed that peace had settled on Wulff's thoughts. I was therefore highly surprised when, after three hours, he suddenly stopped and said, 'Now I can go no further because of my heart. Will you find a place for me where I can lie down?—preferably near to a lake where I can get something to drink, and where you will be able to find me if you get game in the immediate future.' " [9] Koch tried to dissuade him, but Wulff had come to the last of his strength. And there, so desperate was the situation, Koch bade him farewell. Too weak to write, Wulff dictated a summary on the vegetation of Inglefield Land and a message to Rasmussen. He himself wrote a last note to his parents and to his daughter. A wave of the hand, a last view, and the three men stumbled on. Hungry and weak, they were fortunate enough to kill a hare now and then to sustain themselves. When they met the relief party they returned to bury Wulff and fetch his diaries and notes.

They stayed at Etah for several weeks, resting and regaining their health, and then pushed on for Thule. With their arrival there, the

end of October, the Second Thule Expedition came to an end.*
"Ajako [the Eskimo who had been Rasmussen's companion] bends
down, filling his hollow hands with fiord water, which he raised to his
face to feel and inhale its salt freshness. In these drops he smells the
meat of walrus, narwhal, and seals—flesh of all the blubbery marine
animals which shall now make our days good. Beautiful ocean! I
recognize you, now I am home!" [9]

The Danish Bicentenary Jubilee Expedition of 1920–3, under the
leadership of Lauge Koch, was part of the program commemorating
the two hundredth anniversary of Hans Egede's landing and the
beginning of modern Danish Greenland. The expedition was to head
for the north of Greenland, there to make a topographical and geological map that would connect the Danish mapping of the west coast
with that of the northeast coast made by the Danmark Expedition.
Leaving their base in Inglefield Gulf on March 18, 1921, they traveled along the well-known route via Fort Conger to the north of
Greenland. The party, after the various supporting groups had
turned back, consisted of the leader, three Eskimos, three sledges,
and thirty-two dogs. By the beginning of May they had reached De
Long Fiord, Rasmussen's farthest, where the detailed charting was to
start. By the 21st of that month they were at Cape Bridgman, at J. P.
Koch's camp, and they hoisted their flag to mark the completion of
the whole circuit of Greenland's coasts by Danish explorers.

Then their troubles began. A fog blotted out the land, a two weeks'
snowstorm tired them, and they failed to find musk-oxen. "Our last
pemmican had been eaten; one after another the dogs collapsed. We
were utterly exhausted when suddenly the sun appeared and at some
distance we caught sight of a herd of musk-oxen. But before we could
get within range, the fog came rolling in and it was not until thirty-
six hours later that we found the animals and secured all nine of
them. The youngest of the Eskimos here cast aside all his stoicism
and standing amidst the steaming carcasses, half naked and smeared
with blood, with two musk-ox horns as a drum he sang the ancient
magic incantations of his tribe, while white and heavy flakes of snow
continued to melt on his brown chest and shoulders. Half-forgotten
recollections of exciting bear-hunts in fantastic moonlight, and of

* The Third Thule Expedition of 1919, commanded by Lieutenant Hansen,
R.N., went to Cape Columbia to lay down a food depot for Amundsen. The
Fourth Thule Expedition of 1920–1, led by Rasmussen, went to the east coast of
Greenland to collect popular legends and other ethnological data. The Fifth
Thule Expedition traversed Arctic America (see pp. 278–9). The Sixth and
Seventh Thule Expeditions, 1931 and 1932, went to southeast Greenland for
ethnological and archæological data.

midsummer nights spent under the huge fowling cliff in the company of women and children he conjured up to us, and the song ended in a wild and jubilant impromptu to the very joy of life as one may experience it when the wild and furious struggle for existence in the cold arctic night is over and the land lies warm and radiant before you." [10] For a while their prospects were brighter as, with half their original number of dogs left, they skirted the barren level plains of southern Peary Land, where Mylius-Erichsen and his men fought their last hopeless fight for life. Exploring the length of Brönlund Fiord, they found a cairn of the dead leader containing his report. Soon they were in an entirely unknown region and, climbing a near-by mountain, obtained a wonderful panoramic view. "All Peary Land was laid bare before us like a map. To the north high towering mountains with numerous glaciers, the highest peaks hidden in the clouds; to the south big, inviting valleys; and to the west the big lake in an enormous cañon surrounded by ragged hills. Far into the country the cañon turned northwards and vanished from sight. Like a flash it struck me: this is the Peary Channel. It is a big valley, from sea to sea, partly filled up by a big lake, the surface of which is 200 metres above sea-level. On Midsummer Eve we stood on Academy Glacier and the ascent [onto the Ice-Cap] began." [10]

Koch intended following the route he had taken with Rasmussen to the west coast and relied on striking a food depot that the Eskimos were to lay down for him. He did not know that an influenza epidemic prevented them from doing so. It was the end of June. Sloshing through lagoons of melted snow, after a desperate climb they reached the Ice-Cap. Again game was threateningly scarce. With very limited rations they started for the west, placing all their hopes on the depot. They shot a few hares, but because of their failing supply of gasoline they could do no more than thaw them out and eat them raw. "It grew harder and harder to get up in the mornings. We were suffering from attacks of dizziness and unconsciousness, signs I knew too well from the fatal journey . . . which in 1917 cost my companion, Dr. Wulff, his life." [10] Arriving at Cape Heiberg Jorgensen, where their cache was to have been placed, they found nothing; and in a similar condition they faced the same itinerary as the expedition of 1917. Their one chance to survive demanded that the four men cover the intervening two hundred miles over the inland ice. Ten exhausted dogs were their only provisions. Dragging their sledges themselves, they had gone all but thirty miles, with two dogs still left, when they sighted the high coastal peaks. Next day a stiff wind blew suddenly. But it was a welcome wind, since it came from the ice, not from the sea as was to be expected. They improvised a sail out of their tent and transformed the sledge into a sail-sledge. "Soon the gale was so strong that we ourselves could enter the sledge, and from this moment we lost all control of our bearings. With increasing speed the storm swept us forward. Several times we were blown across ice-covered lakes, and a few times the ice burst beneath our sledge, but the speed was great enough to insure our safety. And thus we sat there without moving a muscle and in a few hours we had covered the last thirty miles, the last two days' travel. In the evening we landed close to our depot," [10] a second depot on Washington Land, which had been stocked. They had succeeded, and were alive.

The Inland Ice-Cap

Greenland is like a soup plate filled with ice. Its most notable feature is the inland Ice-Cap, which covers nine tenths of its total area, an area as large as the whole of Mexico. From the coasts the ice rises steeply at first and then mounts gently in a long series of steps to an almost level central plateau. It is now a stationary glacier, its great size fixed by the balanced forces of accumulation and ablation. It is a relic of the diluvial ice waves that stretched over northeastern America. This appalling tract of ice is the backbone of the country, and to cross it demands both daring and fortitude. Yet from Egede's time to the present, men have tried—at first because it was assumed to be the easiest way to reach the east coast, to reach East Bygd; then to locate the ice-free Arctic Eden it was supposed to enclose; then it challenged men as climbing Mount Everest does today; and most recently it has been attempted for purposes of scientific research. Until it was finally crossed in 1888 no one knew what that region of 750,000 square miles contained; the Eskimos who peopled it with their most powerful demons were no more naïve than the European theorists who placed there rolling valleys, virgin woods, and fabulous mines.

In 1728, when Major Claus Paarss was sent to Greenland, he was ordered "to spare no labour or pains and to allow himself to be deterred by no danger or difficulty, but to endeavour by all possible means and by one way or another to cross the country for the purpose of learning whether there still exist descendants of the old Norwegians." [11] He was instructed to observe the "true nature of the country; whether there are horses, cattle, or other animals suited to the service of man; and whether there is pasturage, coal, minerals, or other things of the kind." [11] He was given horses for this transinsular ride. Horses and men were stopped, when only two hours out, by an immense chasm. Undeterred, he set out again the next year, this time on foot. For three days he climbed higher and higher, only to see the icy expanse lead ever on and ever up. To walk across it must have seemed as impossible as trying to swim the Pacific Ocean. He reported: "Furthermore the ice on which we walked was sharp-edged like white sugar candy—so much so that were any advance possible one must have soles of iron beneath one's shoes, so bad was the ice to walk upon." [11] And so Paarss fired a Danish salvo of nine shots, drank to his gracious King's health, and turned back. The next man to attempt this dangerous and laborious task, in 1751, was a merchant of Frederikshaab, Lars Dalager, whose curiosity was fired by a Greenlander's tale of having seen the mountains of East Bygd far away across the Ice-Cap. "This moved me with a desire to see the land, like Moses of old, and I took with me the aforesaid man and his daughter, together with two young Greenlanders. We committed ourselves to the ice . . . so far the ground was as flat and smooth as the streets of Copenhagen, and all the difference I could see here was that it was more slippery." [11] But soon, like Paarss, he found his footgear cut to pieces by the sharp ice and was moved to laughter by the sight of his toes peeping out from the boots—laughter in the face of the intense cold which prevails on the Ice-Cap and which, he said, is so piercing that it shrivels the body, protected and toughened though it is. Before he turned back he saw distant snow-free mountain peaks and believed that he had glimpsed the east coast. They have since been reached and found to be nunataks, or ice-free mountain peaks rising out of the frozen sea. His whole trip lasted less than a week.

Except for an attempt made by Giesecke, the fact that the Ice-Cap guarded no natural treasures was sufficient to rob men of any incentive to scale it. It was enough for them to know that it was inhumanly cold there, that it was visited by sudden and terrific gales—and for a hundred years after Dalager had been tempted out on its surface the frozen giant slept on undisturbed.

In the middle of the nineteenth century Rae tried to cross it to determine its possibilities as a telegraph cable route. Then a famous Alpinist, Whymper, sought to conquer it, but was twice turned back when a series of unavoidable events conspired against him. The sprawling giant still slept.

Interest in the Greenland Ice-Cap was focused by the work of two men, A. E. Nordenskiöld and Dr. Henry Rink. The latter lived in Godhavn for fifteen years, 1853–68, as Inspector for Southern Greenland. He wrote about the Ice-Cap in such a way as to capture the imagination of scientists. He showed that it was not devoid of interest, but was an immensely important subject for research; he pointed out its enormous thickness and magnitude, emphasizing its role as the source of most of the great icebergs that lumber into the North Atlantic ship lanes; he calculated that by way of its mighty fiords from eight to ten million cubic feet of ice are launched annually. It was he who enunciated the theory of the Glacial Epoch, contending that, as Greenland is today, so once was most of Europe and North America, that it was similar ice-caps that long ago molded those continents into their present contours. What the Rosetta stone was to hieroglyphics, offering the clue that led to the deciphering of the ancient Egyptian writings, the inland Ice-Cap of Greenland would be to the glacial era.

Nordenskiöld, who made the first of his two trips to the Ice-Cap in 1870, went there to obtain a first-hand impression of one of the intriguing wonders of the earth and, if possible, to traverse it at its narrow end near Godthaab. Together with the botanist Professor Berggren and two Eskimos, he started out the middle of July. They dragged a minimum of provisions and supplies for one month loaded on two sledges. Reaching the marginal strip, a region of impassable broken-up ice, they were forced to abandon their sledges and pack as much as they could carry into knapsacks. One day of this was enough for the natives. They deserted, and the two Swedes went on alone until they came to where the snow, wind-pounded into ice, was a smooth incline leading up to a high plateau. They had penetrated some thirty-five miles and were at an elevation of two thousand feet. All around them the ice was dazzling. They found deep, broad crevasses and a majestic river that flowed along the surface until it disappeared into the dark blue depths of the ice in roaring cascades; they skirted small lakes fed by numerous rivulets with no visible outlet. Over the ice lay a deathly stillness, but when they put their ears to the ground they "heard from all sides a peculiar subterranean murmur from the streams enclosed below, while now and again a single, loud cannon-report announced the formation of some new crevasse." [11] But the strangest and most exciting discovery was cryoconite—"cosmic dust"—a fine gray powder, traces of which were everywhere. It had absorbed the warmth of the sun, sunk into the ice, and left a maze of perpendicular cylindrical holes, filled with water. The whole surface was made to resemble a huge sponge.*

Thirteen years elapsed between Nordenskiöld's first trip and his

---

* This dust is now thought to be not of cosmic origin from the surrounding universe, since it is not found deep in the interior, but rather bits of stone blown from the coastal mountains.

second. In that interval other expeditions were made to the inland ice. In 1875 Amund Helland, a Norwegian geologist, measured the rate of movement of various Greenland glaciers. Comparing them with those of Europe, he found that, whereas the largest Alpine glacier, the Aletsch, moved two feet a day, some of the Greenland glaciers moved more than thirty times as fast. The following two seasons the learned Danish Professor Steenstrup made like observations, confirming Helland's figures. In 1878 Lieutenant Jensen of the Danish Army was sent out by the Danish Commission to investigate the Ice-Cap. Tracing Dalager's route from Frederikshaab with two other men, each dragging a small sledge loaded with three weeks' provisions, he hoped to reach the peaks Dalager had sighted. They managed to haul their loads over the bad marginal ice and, though agonized by snow-blindness, kept on until, at an elevation of 4,700 feet, they arrived at their goal. They called these ice-free peaks Dalager's Nunataks. Climbing a summit, Jensen sighted other peaks still farther east. On a second trip made that same season he passed the first group of nunataks and twenty miles beyond reached what he had fondly believed to be the east coast, only to discover that he had found a second group of nunataks. Jensen's Nunataks, as they have been called, are forty-five miles inland. Because of the tremendous hardships sustained by the party the authorities were reluctant to send out another expedition.

Nordenskiöld's second trip came after a lapse of years, during which he had been busy investigating other Arctic problems.* This time he was resolved, if he could not cross the Ice-Cap, at least to penetrate deeply into that stronghold. From the discovery of the nunataks he was convinced that far in the interior he would find rich pasturelands. His party of ten included two Lapps, experts on skis, and was financed by Baron Dickson. The whole party advanced for eighteen days, in which they covered seventy-three miles, and were five thousand feet high. Then they were stopped by soft, wet snow, into which both men and sledges sank. Unable to continue, Nordenskiöld sent on the two Lapps, who on skis could make good time and distance over the snow and ice; he hoped that if they persevered they would reach the inner valley. He ordered them to collect specimens of all the plants they found there, but though they went on for another 145 miles, they found nothing but the same endless tract of ice. After a month Nordenskiöld returned. He had made a start, he had attracted men's interest, but he could not complete the profile of the mysterious interior.

* See Chapter xviii.

One day not long after his return an unknown and untried young man sat in Nordenskiöld's study outlining his plans for crossing the inland ice. The veteran listened as the young man talked—he seemed so young, so sure—and then, after warning him of what he must expect to find, encouraged him. The youthful enthusiast was Fridtjof Nansen, his *Fram* adventure still in the future. In explaining his expedition Nansen showed his genius for arranging and testing everything down to the smallest detail: the skis, the snowshoes, the sledges, the clothing, food, tents, sleeping-bags, footgear, cooking-stove, and so on. He persevered in his intention though the whole world laughed at him. He planned to go with five companions, striking across the island from east to west, knowing that, once his party had been landed, there would be no turning back, nothing to retreat to. To cross would be imperative. His battle-cry was "Death or the west coast!" As has been said of another explorer starting on another fantastic trip, "So bold, so amazing, so marvellous was this determination, that even success in carrying it out seems a minor matter. Success, doubtless, crowns a resolve and gives it a firm standing in history; but it has no bearing upon the significance of the resolve as a heroic deed." [12]

All six of the men were young, all were expert skiers, all were both husky and intelligent. Nansen's comrades were Otto Sverdrup, the surgeon Olaf Dietrichsen, Kristian Trana, and two Lapps. They started out in May 1888 aboard the Norwegian sealer *Jason*, which was to transport them and their equipment to the east coast of Greenland. Their arrangement with the captain called for passage on condition that it would not interfere with sealing, and the party were forced to be patient for months as the captain hunted in Greenland waters. At last in the middle of July, impatient to start, they pushed off from the ship in their little boats to the coast, only two miles away. Only two miles away! But their way lay through storms, through drift ice and currents. When the pack ice, driven by a gale, suddenly coalesced, they had to pull their boats onto the solid pack. So they drifted for days, farther and farther from where they had planned to start. Time, food, strength, fuel—all were consumed as they drifted six sea miles an hour, twenty-four hours a day, for fourteen days. Several times they were almost lost, but finally they reached land and made their way back, two hundred miles to the north. Not until August 16—late enough!—did they start for the west.

The ascent was hard. The snow was so soft that they had to sleep by day and travel by night, for with night the temperature fell to minus 40° F. and the snow hardened; it was wrinkled into irregularities and cut by crevasses. All their strength was needed to pull and push the sledges over it. Execrable weather kept them cooped up for days in their tiny tent. It was unbelievably cold. Still they climbed. Snowstorms piled up huge drifts in which they floundered. They were tortured by unquenchable thirst. "We had already passed the limit of drinking water, and were destined to find no more till we reached the west side. All we get is what we can melt by the warmth of our bodies in the tin flasks which we carry at the breast inside our clothes and sometimes next the very skin." [13] Three thousand feet high, up, up, six thousand feet. The going became smoother. They lashed the sledges together, rigged up a sail, and rode before the wind. Then heavier snow again, harder going, and snow-blindness. Up, up. Nansen knew that, because of their delay in starting, they would not be able to reach Christianshaab, the goal they had hoped for, and he altered the course for Godthaab, the nearest settlement. At 7,930 feet of altitude they came to "a huge flat plain with an almost imperceptible rise to the westwards. For days—I might almost say weeks—we toiled across an interminable flat desert of snow. Flatness and whiteness were the two features of this ocean of snow. We looked like a diminutive black line feebly traced upon an infinite expanse of white. There was no break to the horizon." [13] Progress was made easier when, on September 2, they changed from snowshoes to skis. But they were always hungry, for their pemmican did not contain enough fat.*

The middle of that month they had climbed to the summit, 8,250 feet, and instead of a rise they saw the plain slope downward gently but continuously. "The next day or two the slope became more distinct, but the incline was not regular, as the ground fell in great undulations, like those we had to climb in our ascent." [13] A breeze sprang up, and, lashing their sledges together, they took advantage of its aid. "Our ship flew over the waves and drifts of snow with a speed that almost took one's breath away. They were swirled over the rough surface, and often they simply jumped from the crest of one wave on to another." [13] On the 19th they sighted the ice-free peaks of the west-coast mountains. "As soon as Nansen heard this ['I can see land!'] he stopped and gave us two pieces of chocolate each. It was always our custom, when we reached a spot which we had long wished to reach, to treat ourselves to the best food we had." [13] But that exciting day almost witnessed their destruction. "It was already growing dark, when I suddenly saw in the general obscurity something dark

* Captain Lemon of the British Arctic Air Route Expedition characterized pemmican as keeping the body twitching but not the soul.

lying right across our path. I took it for some ordinary irregularity in the snow, and unconcernedly steered straight ahead. The next moment, when I was within no more than a few yards, I found it to be something very different, and in an instant swung sharply around and brought the vessel [the lashed sledges] up to the wind. It was high time, too, for we were on the very edge of a chasm broad enough to swallow comfortably sledges, steersmen, and passengers. This was the first crevasse, but was not likely to be the only one, and we must now go warily. I creep cautiously to its edge on the slippery ice, and look down into the deep, dark chasm. Beyond it I can see crevasse after crevasse, running parallel with one another and showing dark blue in the moonlight. We must halt for the night." [18]

Cautiously then, very carefully, they crossed this last barricade of "the roughest ice I had ever seen. Absolutely impassable it was not, but ridge upon ridge, each sharper and more impracticable than its neighbour, lay in all directions, while between them were deep clefts, often half filled with water, which was covered with a thin skin of ice not strong enough to bear." [13] But to the men, who had for a month suffered incessant thirst that was never assuaged by their limited rations, this water was the choicest of sights, and they sucked it up like horses. Advancing steadily, they arrived at the outer edge of the chaotic barrier and by the 25th walked once again upon earth and stones. Just to tread the elastic heather and smell the fragrant grass and moss, to be surrounded by a genial patterned landscape—it was heavenly after their passage over an icy inferno. They had crossed Greenland, they had crossed the inland ice; but they still had to travel sixty miles down the length of Ameralik Fiord to reach Godthaab.

Nansen and Sverdrup decided to strike out for Godthaab by the shortest, quickest route, over the water, while the rest of the party, walking leisurely along the winding shore, approached it by land. In a crazy little boat that did not even boast watertightness—"the water ran in increasing streams through her bottom" [13]—built out of willows covered with sailcloth, they paddled down the beautiful fiord. The account of that trip is an idyll of rediscovering the simple joys of living: feeling the warmth of the sun, skimming over blue waters, sleeping on the good earth, watching birds, butterflies, and bees, and feasting on cranberries. Delivered from their weeks of struggle and arid monotony, they recaptured the pure sensations of happy childhood.

By reason of the lateness of the season the whole party were obliged to winter at Godthaab, returning to Norway in the spring. Nansen's homecoming was that befitting a conqueror. And the results of his observations were of great importance, presenting, as they did, for the first time a true picture of that great area. The highest elevation was 8,970 feet, reached 125 miles from the east coast and 226 miles from the west. The great depth of the ice—estimated at 7,000 feet— he was certain remained more or less the same. For as it was being constantly diminished by discharging glaciers and rivers of melted snow, it was continually being replenished by excessive precipitation. Nansen found the moisture there to be almost at the saturation-point; of the forty days spent on the inland ice, it rained or snowed during half. It was in his meteorological results that the most important and far-reaching data were obtained. Today meteorological studies made on the Greenland Ice-Cap are reckoned of prime importance in explaining world-wide weather conditions.

Two years before Nansen successfully crossed the Ice-Cap near its southern end, Peary, with only one companion, Maigaard, a Dane, made a reconnaissance along the Ice-Cap near Disko Bay. He, too, was inspired by Nordenskiöld's lead, and though he had hoped to be the first to conquer the frozen sea and in this had to yield to Nansen, he was determined to attempt the solution of other Greenland problems. He decided to explore the interior ice far to the north near Whale Sound. By 1891, five years after his maiden effort, he had raised sufficient funds and was back in Greenland. With him were Astrup, a young Norwegian who was on this and subsequent expeditions a magnificent assistant, Frederick Cook, doctor and ethnologist, Gibson, a hunter, Vershoef, a meteorologist, Matthew Henson, a Negro, Peary's loyal and indispensable companion on all his polar trips after 1887, whom the Eskimos themselves considered to be a dog-sledge-driver and hunter equal to their own best, and Mrs. Peary, the ideal explorer's wife. It was well that she was with him, for on the voyage out Peary broke his leg, and during the strenuous and important weeks when everyone hustled to get the winter quarters established she was on hand to nurse the helpless leader. Their portable house, Red Cliff House, was set up at McCormick Bay, in the region frequented by the Arctic Highlanders. Early in the new year Peary was well enough to make a preliminary excursion to Inglefield Gulf.

In attempting to cross the Ice-Cap at that high latitude Peary was daringly striking out for an unknown goal set at an unknown distance; for at that time, it must be remembered, the northern and northeastern part of Greenland was a blank on the map. Starting in April 1892, he was accompanied by Astrup, Cook, and Gibson. Each man had a sledge drawn by four dogs. With great difficulty they made their way up the icy path to the great inland ice, not reaching it until the latter part of May. Here he sent back two of the men and continued alone with Astrup. North, north they went, and then east into the interior back of Petermann and St. George Fiords. Ice, always ice, until a month after they parted from the supporting division they saw on the horizon, instead of the endless ice, the sea. This sight made them fairly fly over rocky ridges that lay between them and the east coast. At last, on July 4, the very summit was reached. "A few steps more, and the rocky plateau on which we stood dropped in a giant iron wall, that would grace the Inferno, 3800 feet to the level of the Bay below us. We stood upon the northeast coast of Greenland." [14] And Peary tries to translate into prose the great surge he felt as he and Astrup first beheld for man that sweep of isolated grimness. "I could now understand the feelings of Balboa as he climbed the last jealous summit which hid from his eager eyes the blue waves of the mighty Pacific." [14] Looking northward, he saw an ice-free land "rising in hills and mountains beyond the channel that marks the northern edge of the mainland." [14] He called the cliff on which he stood Navy Cliff. He thought he had established the insularity of Greenland, he thought he looked upon the East Greenland Sea; having accomplished a daring, a magnificent trip, he let his eyes trick him into wrong, fatally wrong, conclusions.

How glorious it was, after those long weeks of laboring over the desolate ice, to rest a few days in a region where bumblebees droned and butterflies floated lazily from poppy to poppy! A musk-ox provided them with a welcome feast. Refreshed by their three-day rest, they started back for Red Cliff House, five hundred miles away. Only a third of the dogs were left, and the climb up to the inland ice was staggeringly hard. For two days they were imprisoned in their shelter while a furious gale raged outside; for two weeks they groped along, blinded by a dense, clinging fog. But at the end of a month they were back at Red Cliff House. In eighty days Peary had covered 1,400 miles.

Acclaimed upon his return to the United States, Peary immediately made plans to continue and extend his discoveries. The next year he was back at Whale Sound, where his portable house was again erected, and there on September 12 Mrs. Peary gave birth to a daughter. The first week in March 1894 Peary was off for the inland ice, with eight men, twelve sledges, and ninety-two dogs. This time the ice showed both its hostility and its strength. Within a week they were smothered by a violent blizzard. Some of the dogs died. Astrup, gallant and strong, and another man broke down and had to be sent home. Peary and the rest kept on. Again foul weather swooped down on them. More dogs died, some of the Eskimos were badly frost-bitten, and more exhausted men had to be sent back. Undaunted and untired, Peary with three chosen men kept on. But though they fought on for two more weeks, they gained little headway. Men and dogs were completely paralyzed with fatigue. In retreat lay their only hope, and that a slim one. To save themselves they were forced to abandon all their equipment and race for home. They reached their winter quarters the middle of April, with only twenty-six dogs left.

A second winter passed, and on the 2nd of April 1895 Peary was out again on the old trail. His party consisted of Lee, Henson, four Eskimos, six sledges, and sixty-three dogs. Again bad weather enveloped them and made the traveling so hard that on the third march an Eskimo deserted with his team. Deep snow exhausted them. Peary was unable to locate the provisions he had cached on the previous trip, on which he was relying; when he was only 134 miles inland he was forced to divide the party. The three Eskimos were sent back, and with Lee and Henson and forty-one dogs he pushed on. It was a rash step for which he almost paid with his life. Lee was soon crippled by frost-bite, many of the half-starved dogs died, and there was very little food left for the men. They must find food if they were to survive. In a frenzy they pushed on for Independence Bay and the ice-free region where Peary had previously found musk-oxen. By the middle of May they were only sixteen miles from the eastern margin of the ice. But Lee was unable to take another step, their last sledge was broken, their eleven remaining dogs were too hungry and exhausted to move. Here Peary made a rest camp, and from there he and Henson headed for the region that had abounded in game. Luckily they found a herd of musk-oxen, but, being without dogs, could kill only two. For a while this staved off disaster. They hoped to obtain more game. In vain they hunted and searched—they found no more. And they still faced the homeward trip. Two more dogs died. It was now a race against hunger, against time, against death. Would they reach home alive? With nine dying dogs and rations for only fourteen days they started back, abandoning everything. They drove themselves in twenty-five forced marches to cover the intervening distance, and the three men, sick with fatigue, arrived at Whale Sound on June 25. They had only four biscuits left.

This trip stands out as one of the rashest gestures man ever made against the frozen north and pulled out of alive. But, for all its

magnificent bravery, its results were as barren as those of the preceding abortive attempt.*

The only other man to follow the perilous trail blazed by Peary
from the Kane Sea to the northeast coast, across the inland ice, was
Rasmussen in his First Thule Expedition. That same year—1912—
two other expeditions undertook to traverse the frozen interior. The
first, led by a Swiss, Quervain, went from Jakobshavn on Disko Bay
to Angmagssalik, on the east coast, crossing near the southern tip of
the island but at a higher latitude than Nansen. He reached an elevation of 9,500 feet and reported sighting a distant peak, Mount Forel,
which, he estimated, rose for another 2,500 feet. The second expedition is in many respects most unusual. Not only was the chosen route
laid on a long diagonal, spanning the island at one of its widest parts;
not only were horses used for the first time since Paarss tried to ride
across the interior; it was the first time that any party wintered within
the margin of the ice.

The leader, J. P. Koch, was the man who had achieved such
splendid results in the Danmark Expedition under the ill-fated
Mylius-Erichsen. With him was Alfred Wegener, who had also
served in the former expedition and had discovered the nunatak
Queen Louisa Land. Two other Danes, Larsen and Vigfus, made up
the rest of the party. Their objective was to winter on Queen Louisa
Land so as to investigate the atmospheric and glaciological conditions
in the marginal zone of the inland ice and then in the spring to cross
to Pröven, near Upernivik. In preparation for their crossing a depot
was laid down for them at Pingut, on the margin of the inland ice on
the west coast. For several reasons Koch chose to use horses for
draught animals instead of dogs, transporting sixteen of them to the
starting-point, Danmarks Havn. A stampede at the landing reduced
the number to ten, for six were never recaptured. Many unforeseen
circumstances conspired to delay them, so that they did not land until
the middle of September 1912. Transferring all their supplies and
equipment up to the inland plateau proved so long and arduous a
task that at the end of two months they were forced to establish their
winter quarters just on the marginal ice. And there the leader had
the misfortune to fall fifty feet down a crevasse and break his leg—
a serious, almost fatal accident. The three others worked busily assembling the materials brought with them, erecting a station and

---

* Peary's trips to Greenland in 1896 and again in 1897 were for the purpose
of bringing back to the United States the famous Cape York meteorites. One of
them, the largest known meteor in the world, weighs close to one hundred tons.

stables. The winter was passed comfortably, though at times the temperature registered as low as minus 72° F. Some of the ponies died and some were killed for food. By spring Koch's leg was healed and everything was ready for the march to the west coast.

On April 19, 1913 they left their winter quarters with five sledges, each drawn by a pony, facing a trek of 700 miles. (Nansen's trail was 350 miles long, Peary's and Rasmussen's 500 miles.) Violent contrary winds trebled their work as they forced their way up the eastern slope; gales and roaring blizzards delayed them, occasioning frequent halts and an unforeseen consumption of food, and the ponies suffered from snow-blindness. From the beginning of May to the beginning of June—for one long month—they saw nothing but ice, ice, ice. One by one, as the ponies became too exhausted to haul, they were killed and eaten. The last one survived till the margin of ice on the west coast was reached on July 4. Two days later they were at their depot at Pingut. Three days they rested there, and then, caching everything not absolutely necessary, they set off again with lightened loads. They carried provisions for five days. Descending the western slope, on the 11th they came to Laxefjord (Salmon Fiord), which they crossed, improvising a ferry out of a sledge and poles. Two days later they had used up the last of their pemmican. Many miles still lay between them and the nearest settlement. A terrific storm broke over them, confining them for thirty-six hours. Fierce hunger, aggravated by a period of short rations, weakened them so that, in order to get the strength to continue, they had to sacrifice their faithful dog Cloë. Just as they were about to eat their sad meal they sighted a boat. Frantically they signaled; they were seen and taken aboard. They came to their destination, Pröven. Thence they sailed for home.

Gradually the work of many men had revealed the profile of the Ice-Cap. Now the emphasis changed and different groups took up the idea originally proposed by J. P. Koch: to winter within the margin of the ice. Independently but simultaneously the British Arctic Air Route Expedition (1930–1), the German Greenland Expedition (1929 and 1930–1), and the Greenland University of Michigan Expeditions under the direction of Professor William H. Hobbs (1926–31) maintained stations on the inland ice to investigate weather conditions. During the time the groups were in Greenland the world was thrilled by the daring of their ventures even while it was mildly amused at the extremes to which men would go in their scientific zeal. And yet only a decade later, when the blitzkreig and bombings were shattering Europe, the importance of their studies was revealed. Then everyone was made aware that storms originating over Greenland's

Ice-Cap cast their long shadows over northwestern Europe; that to have detailed knowledge of the first was to have foreknowledge of the second—an invaluable help in aerial warfare.

Professor Alfred Wegener, who organized and directed the German expedition, had been an important member of Danish expeditions led by Mylius-Erichsen and J. P. Koch. His expedition, it is worth noting, was financed by the Weimar Republic even though the important and voluminous reports were published by a Nazi Germany. Of the expeditions that worked on the Greenland Ice-Cap, Wegener's results are the most impressive.

In 1929 he made a reconnaissance expedition to seek out the best route onto the Ice-Cap and to test new equipment—he planned to use motor-propelled sledges on the smooth interior plateau, and to experiment with an improved method * for measuring the thickness of the Ice-Cap. The easiest road from the west coast to the interior was found at Kamarujuk Bay, near Disko.

The next year the expedition, consisting of twenty members, established three camps along the seventy-first parallel. The main group operated at Kamarujuk Bay, three men carried on studies from a camp on Scoresby Sound, on the east coast, and Johannes Georgi, a meteorologist, and Ernst Sorge, a glaciologist, were to man the Ice-Cap station that had been located midway between the two coasts at an elevation of 9,700 feet. Most appropriately this station was called Eismitte—"Middle of the Ice."

Difficulties hounded them from the very beginning. It took four months of obstinate work to move 125 tons of equipment into their main station, which was not ready for use until October 1. Meanwhile they were also setting up the Eismitte Station, which was 240 miles from the coast. Three separate trips the ten loaded sledges made hauling supplies and equipment to Eismitte, and even then Georgi and Sorge were afraid they lacked sufficient provisions to last them the whole winter. Calculating their needs, they set October 20 as the last day they could hold the Ice-Cap station, and they sent this message to

* In the echo-sounding method a sizable explosion is detonated on the ice to create vibratory disturbances, to imitate the waves set in motion by an earthquake. At a measured distance from the explosion a seismograph records the wave traveling toward it horizontally over the ice as well as the wave which is reflected vertically from the rocks below the ice. Knowing the distance from the explosion and the elapsed time of both waves, it is easy to calculate the distance the vertical wave has traveled—the depth of the Ice-Cap at that particular spot. The results of many such tests indicate that Greenland is like an ice-filled bowl, the coastal rim being 1,000 feet higher than the central portion. At the Eismitte Station, where the elevation was 9,700 feet, the Ice-Cap was 8,775 feet thick; at the coast at an elevation of 5,850 feet, the Ice-Cap measured only 2,600 feet.

Wegener by the last returning dog-team. Abandoning the Eismitte Station would have meant abandoning the very heart of the project; also Wegener feared that were the men to try to return at the end of October, the chances were against their reaching the coast alive. Unlike him, the men at Eismitte were not accustomed to travel on the inland ice. To forestall either of these desperate possibilities, Wegener started out with another party at the end of August. The motor-driven sledge that he had relied on to carry the greatest load bogged down in soft snow when halfway to the station. In this emergency Wegener with his assistant, Fritz Loewe, and an Eskimo, Rasmus Willemsen, pushed on ahead.

He reached Eismitte on October 27. Winter had already started. At −58° F. the petroleum was reluctant to burn. Loewe's feet were so badly frozen that his toes had to be amputated. Wegener had planned to stay with Loewe and let Sorge and Georgi return with Willemsen to the base; but suddenly all was changed. Loewe had to stay; Sorge and Georgi wanted to remain and do their work; there was food for three, but not for five—and so Wegener decided that he would return with Willemsen to the coast. The two men left Eismitte in clear weather on November 1. The Eismitte had no radio and the men at the base knew nothing of what had happened. Not until the first relief party reached the three men at Eismitte on May 6, 1931 was anyone aware that Wegener was dead. Searching-parties immediately retraced the route, and at 113 miles from the coast they saw one of Wegener's skis standing upright. Here the trail ended. For here, deep under the snow, carefully wrapped in blankets and dressed in his furs, lay Wegener's body.

It would seem that the fifty-one-year-old leader, exhausted by a hard forty-day trip to Eismitte, and with only a few days' rest before starting back, had died of exhaustion. Carefully burying his companion and setting the ski as a marker, Willemsen took Wegener's precious notebook and tried to reach the main station. Since no trace has ever been found of the Eskimo or the dogs and sledge, it is assumed that he fell into a crevasse as he sledged on alone. To ensure the maintenance of the Eismitte Station, Wegener had given his life.

The British Arctic Air Route Expedition also experienced difficulties and sudden changes of plans in the manning of their Ice-Cap station; they resolved their problems in an unexpected and unorthodox way: alone, one member of the expedition, Augustine Courtauld, held the station from September until May.

The purpose of the expedition was to investigate the possibilities of an air route between England and Canada via the Faroes, Iceland,

Greenland, Baffin Island, and Hudson Bay—this being the shortest distance. The parts least known were the east coast of Greenland, where a flying-base was needed, and the central Ice-Cap. To study both fully, it was planned to keep continuous meteorological records from stations on the coast and on the Ice-Cap. The British Ministry and the Courtauld family joined in financing the expedition; it was entrusted to the command of Henry George (Gino) Watkins, who, though only twenty-three, had planned the undertaking.

The expedition was equipped with two Puss Moth airplanes adapted for alighting on ice or water, fifty sledge dogs, as well as the necessary instruments, supplies, provisions, materials for building their house, and so on. There were fourteen men in all: four surveyors, two air-pilots, a geologist, a meteorologist, an ornithologist, an aerial photographer, a wireless expert, a man for the sledge dogs, and a medical officer. Except for Watkins and two of the others, none of the men had had any Arctic experience whatsoever, but, as Watkins insisted, and rightly, it was more important for him to know each man and what he was capable of and how he would act in a given situation than for each one to have known the Arctic. They left England July 6, 1930, aboard Shackleton's old ship *Quest,* arriving at Angmagssalik a fortnight later. Forty miles away from the Eskimo settlement they found an ideal spot for their base, and from there they set out to establish their Ice-Cap station, 140 miles inland, at an elevation of 8,000 feet, the highest point in that vicinity between the two coasts.

Besides investigating the possibility of an aerial base on that coast, a large amount of fruitful exploring was done. The same region that Amdrup had outlined in his boat journey of 1901, a distance of 300 miles to the north of Angmagssalik, was surveyed in great detail and further elaborated by a series of aerial photographs. The 600 miles of coastline to the south of their base was traced in a small boat by surveyors who refined the pioneering work done by Holm. The interior, between the base and Mount Forel, sighted by Quervain, was mapped, and a brilliant attempt, which just barely failed, was made to scale the peak. Two long sledge trips were made across the Ice-Cap to the west coast: one heading for Ivigtut, a settlement near the southwest point of Cape Desolation; the other almost following the line of the Arctic Circle to Holsteinsborg. The former headed south along the Ice-Cap, keeping parallel with the east coast as far as Umivik, so as to map the coastal mountains. The other expedition carried kayaks with them so as to be better able to negotiate the long waterways between the Ice-Cap and the settlement. It was the first time kayaks were transported across the island. "They had a narrow escape on one of these rivers, when both their kayaks were overturned by the swift current and Rymill was swept under the ice upside down in his kayak; there was an open stretch of water a little farther on, and he was fortunately able to cling on to the ice and save both himself and his kayak!" [15] But the greatest adventure was connected with manning the Ice-Cap station continuously from September to May. It is as if a winter had been passed in the very heart of winter's stronghold.

The "station house consisted of a dome-shaped tent of canvas stretched over a wooden frame. It was of double thickness with an air space between the two layers of canvas. In the roof there was a small ventilating shaft. There was no entrance through the sides of the tent, but a tunnel was dug so that the entrance was underground. Since the entrance was below floor-level none of the warm air could escape except through the ventilating shaft, and ventilation could be altered as desired." [15]

The trail to the Ice-Cap station was well marked with red flags at each half-mile. It was intended when the station was established, at the end of August, that its occupants should be relieved every month; but the trail, which was hard under the best of conditions, became impossible during storms; and from the middle of October blizzards blew regularly once or twice a week. "The first of these blizzards reached a speed of 129 m.p.h. before it broke the wind gauge; after that it blew even harder. Before leaving England, the Air Ministry told us that there was an average of about one gale every ten years at Angmagssalik. . . . As a consequence of the first blizzards we saw that repeated journeys to the Ice-Cap station during the winter would be impossible." [15] But that did not mean that the station would not be manned throughout the winter. It was with the departure of the second relief party, at the end of October, that the trouble began. Loaded down with wireless equipment and heavy supplies, they ran into foul weather. "The first night on the glacier they had to pitch their tents on hard ice free from snow. A blizzard sprang up and blew away one tent. After that they had a blizzard every few days and had to remain in their tents two or three days at a time." [15] It took fifteen days to do the first fifteen miles, and thirty-nine days to reach the station, four times what it should have. They had been forced to use some of the food and paraffin intended for the station's supplies, and that meant that they must alter their plans. Three courses were open to them: two men could stay at the station, but they would have to relieved in March, a necessity not at all feasible; or one man could stay with enough provisions to last him into May, when relief would

Greenland: THE ICE-CAP SPILLING THROUGH THE COASTAL RANGE
NORTH OF UMANAK. THE PICTURE WAS TAKEN BY FADING AUTUMNAL
LIGHT.

Both photographs by David Potter: Hobbes Expedition, 1928.

Greenland: THE WATSON GLACIER FEEDS THE LUSTY WATSON RIVER.
TAKEN IN THE SUNDERSTROM FJORD, 150 MILES INLAND FROM HOLSTEIN-
BORG. THE ICE WALL IS ABOUT 200 FEET HIGH AND THE RIVER ABOUT
50 FEET WIDE.

Sovfoto.

The tent that housed the Papanin group as they drifted on the ice from the North Pole to the East Greenland Sea.

THE TENT WAS MADE OF BLACK MATERIAL TO ABSORB HEAT FROM THE SUN.

be possible; or the station could be abandoned. Courtauld volunteered to stay on alone. After much argument he had his way, and the four other men started back for the base. It was the 6th of December when he started his solitary vigil on the Ice-Cap; it was understood that he was to be relieved by the 1st of May.

How did Courtauld spend his time? The first week or two he was busied drying his clothes, digging the snow out of the tunnel, and getting his stores into the tent. "Six times a day I dressed up in full kit and sallied forth to read the instruments and inspect the weather. This was an absorbing interest in itself. . . . About Christmas I discovered that some four gallons of paraffin had leaked away, so I had to do without the primus stove except for cooking . . . the small snowhouses gradually caved inwards from the weight of the snow on top of them, but they never actually collapsed, which was a good thing as they were my only means of getting out." [15] Lying in the shelter of the tent, through the shaft he could hear blizzards roaring outside, and these frequent storms carried such an amount of snow that at last they closed up all exits. From March 22 he was confined within doors. For a while three fears bothered him. He was afraid that the air would become vitiated; that the accumulating snow would crush the tent in, now that he could no longer clear it away; and that, since he was no longer able to keep a lookout, the relief party might miss him. The first anxiety was soon dispelled as the air continued perfectly fresh, and with passing time the second likewise passed. "For the third I trusted to the Union Jack on its pole, and the navigation of the relief party. It was clearly futile to get anxious, when by no possible endeavour on my part could I make any difference to the course of events. . . . A more unsatisfactory matter was the cessation of the weather record. A man dislikes changing his habits, and this business of the weather had become a very absorbing habit." [15] His attitude toward his provisions is illuminating. He could have figured out the last possible date to which his food might carry him if rationed carefully, with the possibility of having a surplus left if rescued before that time; but that he would not do. "In the first place I did not like rationing. I prefer, in fact, to eat my cake rather than have it." [15] Fixing arbitrarily on the early date of March 15 as the time of release, he notes: "It was, therefore, all according to plan when stores began to run out. The paraffin supply especially got short, owing to leakage. This was very tiresome as I had to spend more and more time in the dark and the house got considerably colder without the lamp to give heat. The food problem solved itself, since one's appetite becomes very small if one takes no exercise. . . . By the middle of April no more light, luxuries had run out, and the comfort of the house was much reduced. Tobacco was completely exhausted, so tea was used as a substitute. Food consisted of a little oatmeal, just warmed up for breakfast, and thereafter, uncooked pemmican, biscuit and margarine." He tried to approximate a state of hibernation.

His solitary confinement without the consoling presence of those darlings of civilization the radio and the phonograph was a test of his mental, not physical, stamina. Except for the roar of the blizzards, which howled down his shaft, and an occasional subterranean explosion, there was nothing to be heard but the sounds he himself made. "For the first month or so I was very averse to the least noise. The complete silence all around seemed to urge one to keep in tune with it by being silent oneself." [15] He would have the world see him not as a hero but as a rational creature being most rational in adapting himself to unusual conditions. His strength was based on "one fact which I have not yet mentioned, but without which this chapter would not be complete. [It] was the curious growing feeling of security that came to me as time passed. Many doubts presented themselves to me at the start, and for a while they grew in number and weight. But as each month passed without relief I felt more and more certain of its arrival. By the time I was snowed in I had no doubts on the matter, which was a great comfort to my mind. I will not attempt any explanation of this, but leave it as a fact, which was very clear to me at that time, that while powerless to help myself some outer Force was in action on my side, and that I was not destined to leave my bones on the Greenland Ice Cap." [15] This faith was justified. "On May 5 the primus gave its last gasp. A few minutes later an extraordinary scraping and scratching sound was heard overhead, which turned out to be the relief party." [15] May 5! Alone he had held the station for five months.

But meanwhile down at the base Watkins, though he never for a moment doubted Courtauld's ability to "carry on," was eager to relieve him at the earliest possible date, even before the appointed time, May 1. A party of four, leaving the base the 8th of March, traveled to the station. Hampered by appalling storms, they advanced slowly. Finally they reached the vicinity of the station, but, search as they would, they could not locate it. Food was running low, and wisely they decided to hurry back to the base so that a fresh party might set out and still arrive in time. Immediately upon their return a second party, led by Watkins, set out. On May 4 they camped and, after taking observations, found that they were one mile northwest of the station. "We left our tent and walked over to fetch Courtauld. On reaching the summit of a long undulation we made out a black speck in the distance. It was a flag. Could it be the Union Jack of the Ice Cap Station? We went racing towards it at full speed and as we approached we saw a large drift on each side of the flag. It was indeed the Station. But as we got near we began to have certain misgivings. The whole place had a most extraordinary air of desolation. The large Union Jack we had last seen in December was now a mere fraction of its former size. Only the tops of the various survey instruments and the handle of a spade projected through the vast snow drift which submerged the whole tent with its snow houses and surrounding walls. Was it possible that a man could be alive there? As we skied up this gently sloping drift a ray of hope appeared when we saw the ventilator of the tent just sticking through the snow. A moment later Watkins knelt down and shouted down the pipe. Imagine our joy and relief when an answering shout came faintly from the depths of the snow. The voice was tremulous, but it was the voice of a normal man." [16] The superb spirit of Arctic exploration that manifests itself in moments of intense action was in Courtauld displayed in a time of prolonged and intense inaction. No fatalities marred the work of the British Arctic Air Route Expedition. They all returned safely to England in the fall of 1931.

When, the following winter, young Gino Watkins, as the leader of the expedition, gave a report before the Royal Geographical Society, his youthful bearing almost belied the importance and scope of his achievements. At the conclusion Lauge Koch, a veteran of Greenland exploration, said to the assembly: "Take care of Mr. Watkins and his companions. . . . Years are passing rapidly and it is only during a short period of one's life that one is able to carry on the work they have carried on. Employ them while they are still young. Time is short. Let them do what they can do now." Gino Watkins, with some of the members of the expedition, returned to Greenland in 1932. There in a kayak accident he lost his life. He was twenty-five when he died.

But the work, never finished, goes on, and expeditions continue to seek in a study of the great Ice-Cap the clue to world-wide weather conditions.

18

The Northeast and Northwest Passages

NILS ADOLF ERIK, Baron Nordenskiöld, stands out as one of the giants among Arctic explorers, not alone for his varied geographical work but also for his other scientific investigations and his illuminating historical research into early European geography. He may be called Nansen's spiritual father. Born in Helsingfors, Finland, in 1832, the son of a well-known scientist belonging to the large Swedish colony, Adolf Erik was in his middle twenties when, because of his radical activities, he had to leave. Finland at that time was part of Russia. He moved to Stockholm and became interested in Arctic problems. In 1858 he made his first Arctic voyage, serving as geologist in Torell's Spitsbergen Expedition. Returning there three years later as a member of a party measuring an arc of the meridian, he made a boat journey through Hinlopen Strait and discovered new islands in the Northeast Land group. In 1864 he was the leader of a group equipped to winter on Spitsbergen, but he had to return home when his modest supplies were taxed to meet the needs of seven boatloads of walrus-hunters who had been wrecked near by. At that time he made a map of Spitsbergen, compiling all the exact information ascertained so far; it "delineated Spitsbergen with an accuracy hitherto unattained in any Arctic land." [1] He made two attempts to reach the North Pole, both times using Spitsbergen as a base. In 1868 his vessel, the *Sofia*, reached the highest latitude until then attained by a ship; its injury by the ice forced the expedition to return. Four years later Nordenskiöld was back again; after wintering in Mossel Bay he started north with reindeer-drawn sledges. The rough sea ice so smashed his sledges that he had to retreat. On his return journey he crossed the inland Ice-Cap of Northeast Land. Midway between these two North Polar ventures, in 1870, he made his first trip to the Ice-Cap of Greenland. These many expeditions were supported in the main by an enthusiastic patron, Baron Oscar Dickson.

About that time Nordenskiöld's interest was caught by notices that recorded from time to time the voyages made by experienced whaling-ships in the region of Novaya Zemlya and the Kara Sea. More and more he focused his attention on the vast unknown stretch of water along the Siberian coast. He felt that, could he sail past that coast, he would open a trade route that would bring the great natural resources of Siberia directly to the markets and factories of Europe. In his mind the Northeast Passage had ceased to be a romantic highway leading to Cathay; it was to be a trade route with local stops for commerce. With this in mind he made a reconnoitering trip in 1873 across the Kara Sea to the mouth of the Yenisei and there found an ideal shelter, Dickson Harbor. Two years later he again made a voyage to the Yenisei, this time ascending the river far inland to the town of Yeniseisk. By 1878 Nordenskiöld, financed by his King, Oscar Dickson, and the Russian merchant Sibirikov, was ready and prepared to commence his great adventure—the sailing of the Northeast Passage and the circumnavigation of Europe and Asia.

His expedition was to be not merely one of adventure and exploration. He pointed out in a memorandum submitted to the Swedish government "that the ocean from the mouth of the Yenisei to Chaun Bay has never been ploughed by the keel of any proper sea-going vessel, still less has it been traversed by any steamer specially equipped for navigation among ice. . . . That the small vessels with which it has been attempted never ventured far from the coast . . . that an open sea with a fresh breeze was more destructive to them than a sea covered with ice . . . that they always sought some convenient winter harbour just at the season of the year when the sea is freest of ice, namely late summer or autumn. . . . That it would be possible to solve a geographical problem of several centuries' standing and to carry on researches in geography, hydrology, geology, and natural history, to survey an almost unknown sea of enormous extent. That it will have practical importance in demonstrating the utility of communication between the ports of North Scandinavia and the Ob and Yenisei, and the Pacific Ocean and the Lena. That it will make extensive contributions of immense importance, that it will yield a rich reward." [2]

The *Vega*, his stoutly built ship of 300 tons, was driven by steam engines as well as sails. It was provisioned for two years and was to be accompanied by the *Fraser* and the *Express*, two of Sibirikov's cargo boats bound for the Yenisei, and by the *Lena*, whose destination was the river of that name. Lieutenant Louis Palander of the Swedish Navy, who had been with Nordenskiöld to Spitsbergen in 1872, was captain of the *Vega;* the other officers composed a cordial international entente: Lieutenant Brusewitz of the Swedish Navy, Lieutenant Nordqvist of the Russian Army, Lieutenant Hovgaard of the Danish Navy, Lieutenant Bove of the Italian Navy. In addition there were a surgeon, two scientists, two engineers, a boatswain, a crew of fifteen Swedish seamen, and three Norwegian sealers—in all, thirty men. The four ships left Tromsö on July 18, 1878.

The Northeast Passage! For centuries the object of heroic and romantic endeavor, the northern waterway to Cathay whence adventurers had returned telling marvelous and incredible tales! To all this Nordenskiöld fell heir—and yet the romantic and incredible and heroic do not lard the log of the *Vega*. For this trip Nordenskiöld had prepared himself by years of work and study, and his program was carried through as effortlessly as a play acted by a seasoned repertory troupe. There are no crises, no hairbreadth escapes, nothing but the tremendous emotional thrill of standing on the tip of Cape Chelyuskin, the satisfaction of steaming past mile after mile of the vast Siberian coast.

By the end of July the boats were at Yugor Strait; by the 6th of August they were at Dickson Harbor, where they parted, the *Fraser* and *Express* heading up the Yenisei. From there on, Nordenskiöld was in virgin waters. In his account he speaks of fog and ice, but they did not trouble him greatly. Rather he is concerned with the difficulty, when dredging, of bringing up alive the animals that live on the bottom of the sea. The layer of fresh water that the great rivers spread over the areas where they debouch are deadly to those sea animals. He tells of finding a large shoal of fish that had been enclosed by ice in a small hole and, when the surface had frozen over, unable to get oxygen, had literally died by drowning; of fascinating illusions created by mist and ice, where gulls loomed as large as bears, and walruses were seen as mountains; of sailing over waters and past shores fabulously rich in mammoth fossils. They made important longitudinal corrections as they progressed and found several islands previously unknown.

So far the *Vega* and the *Lena* had met with open water. On August 19 they were off Cape Chelyuskin. "It was with a certain amount of veneration that we set foot on the shore of this promontory [the northernmost tip of the Old World] which only once before nearly a century and a half ago had been trodden by man, and which for the first time had been passed by a ship." [8] In the hope of discovering land to the north Palander steamed in that direction until heavy drift ice forced him to steer back to the open coastal lane. On the

28th they were at the mouth of the Lena, and there the last cargo boat left them. Past Cape Shelagski they saw natives for the first time since leaving Yugor Strait. "Every man, with the exception of the cook, who could be induced by no catastrophe to leave his pots and pans, and who circumnavigated Asia and Europe perhaps without once having been on land, rushed on deck to see the two native boats that approached." [2] The Chukchi interested them. They "are shrewd and calculating men of business and have been brought up to this from early childhood through the barter which they carry on between America and Siberia. Many a beaver skin that comes to the market at Irbit belongs to an animal that has been caught in America, whose skin passed from hand to hand among the wild men of America and Siberia, until it finally reaches the Russian merchant. For this barter a sort of market is held on an island in Bering Strait. At the most remote market in Polar America a beaver skin is said, some years ago, to have been exchanged occasionally for a leaf of tobacco. An exceedingly beautiful black fox skin was offered to me by a Chukch for a pot. Unfortunately I had none I could dispense with. Here too prices have risen. When the Russians first came they got eight sable skins for a knife, and 18 for an axe, and [the Chukchi] laughed at the credulous foreigners who were so easily deceived. At Yakutsk a pot was even sold for as many sable skins as it would hold." [2]

So far fine weather had favored them. But with the beginning of September they were increasingly troubled by snow and drift ice, while fogs and shoal water made advance a hazardous procedure. Slowly they crept on, preceded by a steam launch from which soundings were constantly made. Cape Yakan was passed. But the cold grew sharper, the ice heavier and more solid, the days shorter, and navigation more and more difficult. Captain Cook's North Cape was passed; before them lay compact ice-floes. It was the 28th of September. They were 120 miles from their goal. From their ice-quieted spot they could almost see where the free, open water of the Pacific billowed and breathed. Luck was against them. Only 120 miles, and yet the ship was so tightly held that not until July 18, 1879, ten months later, was she released.

During the winter the various observations that had been started were systematically continued, and constant intercourse was kept up with near-by natives. With both the coastal and the inland, or reindeer, Chukchis the men spent much time, establishing friendly relations even at the cost of personal discomfort. "Imagine yourself in an almost hermetically closed little room [the inner tent of the Chukchis] with a temperature of about 100 degrees, while outside the mercury freezes, and filled with a close stinking smoke from train-oil [used for lighting, heating, and cooking] and the perspiration from half a score naked Chukchis of various ages and both sexes, and you will soon understand that it wants a Siberian climate and habit to make one feel at home." [2]

Winter passed and spring came, and the milder weather brought with it the promise of freedom. The months must have seemed uncommonly long-drawn-out as they waited for the opportunity to steam away, but not until July 18 did a strong south wind break up the ice-floes. At last the path lay open to the *Vega*. She steamed past Serdze Kamen, the point to which Bering had sailed, and on July 20 at "eleven o'clock in the forenoon we were right abreast of East Cape, and with colours flying from our masthead we saluted with our little cannon the easternmost point of Asia. As soon as we came out of the ice south of East Cape, we noticed the heavy swell of the Pacific Ocean. The completion of the North-East Passage was celebrated the same day with a grand dinner, when the last of many of our delicacies disappeared." [3]

For his achievement in the *Vega* Nordenskiöld was created Baron in 1880. His work and interest in the Arctic continued for the rest of his life. It will be remembered that he made the second of his two trips to the Ice-Cap of Greenland in 1883—it was the last of his field trips. "His latest labours, in bringing to light and publishing medieval maps and charts and portolans in two splendid volumes, were not the least important. His researches and discoveries threw much new light on the history of cartography. When he died [in 1902] a vast amount of knowledge died with him, and there passed away from among us an illustrious man of science, a great explorer, a great geographer, and a man of whom his countrymen might well be proud." [4]

The Northeast Passage was next attempted by the Russians. In 1913 Commander Vilkitski of the Imperial Navy, commanding the two ice-breakers *Taimyr* and *Vaigach*, left Anadyr Bay. Vilkitski was primarily interested in making hydrographic surveys of the little-known waters of Arctic Siberia. Starting on the 4th of August, he rounded Cape Dezhnev two days later and continued on to Chaun Bay. After surveying it he tried in vain to reach Wrangel Island. He then steered for the New Siberian Islands to continue his oceanographic studies and thence went west to the Taimyr Peninsula. Off Cape Chelyuskin, on the 1st of September, solid ice to the west blocked his way and forced him to go in a northeasterly direction in an effort to get through. Thirty miles to the north he came upon a long, narrow island. Passing this, the vessels steamed on, and after another thirty miles another new island was discovered, a high land with glaciers, Nicholas II Land.* He landed on it on September 4 and surveyed twenty miles of its eastern coastline. Unable to stay longer, because the ice to the west was getting heavier and heavier, Vilkitski turned back to the east. He wintered in Petropavlovsk. Despite the outbreak of the First World War, in which his country was engaged, he was ordered to renew his attack on the Northeast Passage. In 1915 he succeeded. He was the first to sail it from east to west.

If Nordenskiöld and Nansen typify one phase of exploration, the compelling curiosity and scientific interest to study the configuration of the earth and some of the forces governing it, then Amundsen was the other, the adventurous, sporting spirit who is happiest and at his best when facing the unknown. To the latter, living meant doing what had never been done before, no matter how hard. He and Peary are brothers. Adventure comes first and last, and scientific problems are sandwiched in somewhere in the middle.

Roald Amundsen is best known for his exploit in the Antarctic, when he made a magnificent and successful dash for the South Pole, reaching that goal a bare few weeks ahead of the fated Scott expedition. Because his navigation of the Northwest Passage did not involve any such drama and because the navigation of the passage itself had lost its appeal to the general public, that earlier episode is not so widely remembered. The period of intense interest in the Northwest Passage had ended with the tragedy of Franklin, the superb seamanship of Collinson, the technical victory of McClure, and McClintock's last voyage in the *Fox*. The tide of romantic appeal had subsided, yet to the adventurous the challenge still remained to sail the intricate waterways across the top of the Americas.

Amundsen gave up medical studies to train himself to be an explorer, an Arctic explorer. Without funds and with little backing, all his life he was bothered by financial considerations; in his autobiography he tells how he seized the opportunity so financially favorable to Norwegian shipping during World War I to accumulate a tidy fortune for himself. The successful completion of the Northwest

* Since the Russian Revolution it has been known first as Lenin Land and subsequently as Northern Land. In 1930-2 Northern Land was surveyed by a Soviet party of four under the leadership of Ushakov. Using dog-sledges, they mapped in about 18,000 square miles of hitherto unknown land. They found that Northern Land consists of four large islands—Young Communist Leaguer, Young Pioneer, October Revolution, and Bolshevik—with many smaller ones. In addition to the exploration, important scientific observations were made.

Passage was his first goal. In 1900, when he was only twenty-eight, he bought a small herring-boat in which he hoped to navigate it. His boat was called the *Gjoa*. "She was 47 tons and of the same age as myself."[5] Seventy-two feet long, eleven feet wide, of shallow draught, cutter-rigged, with an auxiliary gasoline engine, the *Gjoa*, though neither a beauty nor a giant, was sturdy and seaworthy. To combine scientific study with adventure he planned to make a long stay in the vicinity of the North Magnetic Pole so as to carry out important meteorological observations. The *Gjoa*, carrying provisions for five years, looked like a floating moving-van as Amundsen steered her out of Christiania harbor, June 16, 1903 (a secret, guarded beginning on a rainy midnight so that he and six chosen companions could escape from an important and impatient creditor who was threatening to stop the expedition). Haggling and dour looks were left behind; they were free to follow their fortune. The *Gjoa* danced before the breeze. By the end of July they were at Disko, thence across Melville Bay to Dalrymple Rock, near Cape York, where additional stores, left by Scotch whalers, were picked up. They were at the entrance to Lancaster Sound on August 20, and two days later at Beechey Island, where Franklin had spent his first winter. Following the route of the *Erebus* and the *Terror*, the *Gjoa* sailed down Peel Sound, and Amundsen noticed how, as they neared the vicinity of Bellot Strait near the North Magnetic Pole, their sluggish compass absolutely declined to function at all.

"We were fast approaching the De La Rouquette Islands . . . the point that Sir Allen Young reached with the *Pandora* in 1875 where he encountered an invincible barrier of ice. Were we and the *Gjoa* to meet the same fate? Then as I walked, I felt something like an irregular lurching motion, and I stopped in surprise. The sea all around me was smooth and calm. . . . I continued my walk and there it was again! A sensation as though, in stepping out, my foot touched the deck sooner than it should have done, according to my calculation. . . . I had not gone many steps when the sensation came again. . . . I could not be mistaken, there was a slight irregular motion in the ship. I would not have sold this slight motion for any amount of money. It was a swell under the boat—a message from the open sea. The water to the south was open."[5] Luck was with them, they were to get through. It was a ticklish job navigating the virgin waters of Franklin Strait. Not only was their compass useless, but often they were wrapped up in a heavy fog, which made their advance slow and timorous like that of the newly blind. James Ross Strait lay just ahead of them, the passageway Franklin did not know of when he sailed to the other side, to the west of King William Land. And here was a new danger. The strait was studded with elongated low islands with far-projecting shallows. "The weather was dark and the wind was blowing a stiff gale from abaft, the outlook was most uncertain." [5] A storm was on them. They tried in vain to get through the shoal water to the lee of an island. Soon the gale was blowing harder, whipping the water into choppy, rough waves. Heavy sleet fell. Unable to reach shelter, they suffered a bad beating. In the gray of the morning a shock ran through the boat. They had run aground on a large submerged reef. Which way should they turn to find deep water? The soundings gave them little hope. The distance across the reef was 220 yards, and they had grounded at high tide. They lightened the ship by throwing overboard twenty-five of their heaviest cases. Day came, clear and fine, ideal weather for making progress—but they could not budge the *Gjoa* an inch. And so night found them.

"When I came on deck at 2 a.m. next morning it was blowing fresh from the north. At 3 a.m. the vessel began to move as if in convulsions. I had all hands called. . . . The north wind freshened to a gale, accompanied by sleet. . . . The vessel pitched violently. . . . We decided as a last resort to get her off with the sails. The spray was dashing over the ship, and the wind came in gusts, howling through the rigging, but we struggled and toiled and got the sails set. Then we commenced a method of sailing not one of us is ever likely to forget. The mighty press of sail and the high choppy sea combined, had the effect of lifting the vessel up and pitching her forward again among the rocks, so that we expected at every moment to see her planks scattered on the sea. The false keel was splintered and floated up. . . . I stood on the rigging and followed the dance from one rock to another. . . . If the vessel broke up, what then? . . . The water on the reef got shallower and I noted how the sea broke on its outer edge. It looked as if the raging north wind meant to carry us just to that bitter end. The sails were as taut as drum heads, the rigging trembled. . . . I thought it almost impossible the ship could hold together." [5] To aid the *Gjoa* in her desperate fight Amundsen ordered the rest of the deck cargo thrown overboard. "There was not a boat's length between us and the shallowest part. The spray and the sleet were washing over the vessel, the mast trembled, and the *Gjoa* seemed to pull herself together for one final leap. She was lifted up high and flung bodily down on the bare rocks, bump, bump—with terrific force. . . . Yet another thump, worse than ever, then one more, and we slid off." [5] But before Amundsen could enjoy the warm flood of relief that rushed through his body, he was dismayed to hear the man at the wheel call out sharply: "There's something wrong with the rudder, it will not steer." [5] The boat gave a sudden lurch, and the same voice shouted triumphantly: "The rudder is all right again!" [5] Danger still surrounded them on all sides. "The banks lay all around us. . . . We were drenched to the skin and our teeth chattered with cold. The lead-line was brought into requisition, and from that hour the *Gjoa* did not make another quarter of a mile of the North-West Passage without one man aloft and another plying the lead." [5]

After spending a day repairing the ship, they were pinned down by a five-day gale that boxed the compass. On September 8 they were sailing again, sailing cautiously through a thick snowstorm that hid the land from their sight. And so they came to the mouth of Rae Strait. They breathed easier when their soundings showed no bottom; they were out of the shoals. As they rounded the southeastern point of King William Land, the weather cleared and they could get their bearings. For safety's sake Amundsen decided to put into a sheltered bay and anchor there for the night. "This proved to be a lucky hit. There was perfectly smooth water under the lee. . . . From the deck there was nothing particular to be seen except the wide large bay. But Hansen, who was on the look-out aloft, saw more than we did. He suddenly called out: 'I see the finest little harbour in the world!' I climbed up to him and true enough saw a small harbour quite sheltered from the wind, a veritable haven of rest for us weary travellers" [5]—Gjoahavn—and it proved to be a most perfect spot to winter in. In addition Gjoahavn fulfilled the many prerequisites for a site near the North Magnetic Pole in which to make detailed and exact meteorological observations.

Simpson Strait was ice-free and beckoned to them to sail on and achieve the passage by sea, but they had work to do at Gjoahavn and there they stayed. Only a very short time was left in which to get settled before winter was upon them. They had to hurry and land their stores, build their houses and observatories. By the end of September they were comfortably entrenched and their observations started. Two men were sent to an island in Simpson Strait where it was said reindeer were to be found, and they brought back twenty. Soon reindeer were sighted near their camp, and they knew that they need have no fear of starving. A great thrill came one morning toward the end of October. One of the men sighted reindeer, and the others immediately made preparations to hunt. Only Hansen remained quiet, straining his sharp eyes as he studied the far-off specks. " 'Well, Hansen, have you no mind to shoot reindeer today?' 'Ah, yes,' he said softly, 'but not *that* sort of reindeer, over there—they walk on two legs!' " [5] And so they met their first Eskimos, the little-known inhabitants of King William Land, with whom they remained on cordial terms during their whole stay. That winter a large settlement grew up around them, and with their Eskimo friends they traveled, hunted, and bartered.

The winter passed happily and quickly and profitably. Spring came and soon summer blessed the land. Game was plentiful, flowers and herbs grew and flowered, and millions of insects buzzed and fussed about busily. Then they settled down to a second winter (1904–5). In April two of the men started on a long sledge trip to survey roughly the unmapped stretch along the east coast of Victoria Island. They returned safely to the ship at the end of June, having carried out their mission. Meanwhile those who remained behind had been busy getting ready to sail again. On June 1 the self-registering instruments were stopped after nineteen months of uninterrupted work. By the end of July, Gjoahavn was free from ice, but they had to wait another two weeks before Simpson Strait was open and they could venture out. On August 13 they resumed navigation. "We jumped, so to speak, right into the same doubtful navigation as before, impenetrable fog, no compass, and a very changeable breeze, which was therefore a poor guide. The lead was thrown continually . . . it flew up and down so rapidly that it was almost a wonder that it did not melt. . . . In this manner we groped our way." [5] The channel through Simpson Strait was narrow and shallow and it zigzagged from side to side, but the *Gjoa* found her way through. The stout little herring-ship also went safely through the much more chaotic region between Norden-skiöld Island and the Royal Geographical Society group in the waters south of Victoria Strait (Queen Maud Sea). When they had success-fully negotiated that, they knew the worst was over, for right ahead lay Cambridge Bay, which Collinson had reached from the west in the much larger *Enterprise*. "We anchored on August 17 on the west side of Cape Colborne, and this was a significant day in the history of our Expedition—for we had sailed the *Gjoa* through the hitherto unsolved link in the North West Passage." [5] Before them lay Dease Strait, where Collinson had found deep water a few miles from shore though shallows existed off all points and turnings. The compass was again lively, and "Collinson's description of the waters was very helpful to us. He had throughout done excellent and valuable work." [5] Their troubles were over. On August 26 they sighted Nelson Head, the southern head of Banks Island, and they made for it, going full speed with a fair breeze and advantageous current. And that day came the memorable words: "Vessel in sight, sir." The Northwest Passage had been accomplished, the centuries-long hope had that moment come true—vessel in sight, sir.

"The words were magical. . . . It seemed as if the *Gjoa* understood that the hardest part of the struggle was over, she seemed so wonderfully light in her movements. . . . The only objects between sky and sea that possessed any interest for us were the two mastheads on the horizon. . . ." [5] They had met with the *Charles Hanson*, an American whaler out of San Francisco, the vanguard of the Bering Sea whaling-fleet. From its captain they received handsome and valuable presents—a bag of potatoes, a bag of onions, and, what was more precious for continuing their voyage, a set of American charts with marginal notes and indications of courses. But they did not know that they still had a long way to go. Between them and their goal lay heavy ice and dense fog. At King Point, off the mouth of the Mackenzie River, they encountered such thick pack ice that they could not advance. They waited for the sea to clear and let them through. In vain they waited—and the season ended. They had to spend a third winter in the Arctic before they could reach the Pacific. They had plenty of company: many Eskimos were near by, and only thirty-five miles away, at Herschel Island, five whaling-ships were wintering. It was at King Point that Wiik, the magnetic observer and the youngest member of the expedition, died, apparently of pneumonia.

Just about a year after the *Gjoa* had sailed out of Gjoahavn she resumed her voyage, and by the last day of August 1906 had completed her task and was entering Nome harbor. Amundsen had written *finis* to the search for the Northwest Passage.

In 1923 the Northwest Passage was traversed for the first time by dog-sledge. It was accomplished as a part of the Fifth Thule Expedition of 1921–4, led by Knud Rasmussen. The main work of this expedition lay in ethnological research, and the geographical discoveries, while interesting, were not of primary importance. The route lay overland via Rae Isthmus and Boothia Isthmus to King William Land and from there along the coast of Arctic America to Kotzebue Sound. The party, consisting of Rasmussen, an Eskimo woman, Añarulanguaq, and an Eskimo youth, Miteq, started from Danish Island near Repulse Bay, March 10, 1923, and reached their destination August 21, 1924. By this passage Rasmussen welded together the various sections that had been discovered piece by piece. In one year he traversed the coastline that it had taken Franklin, Back, Richardson, Rae, Simpson, and others more than a quarter of a century to explore.

The Northeast Passage is open to navigation only for the three summer months and yet to the people of the U.S.S.R. it is their Suez * and Panama Canal: it is the shortest water route between Soviet ports in Europe and in the Far East. This imperative geographical fact—at once an inspiration and an incentive to the Soviet peoples—distinguishes the economic and political importance of the Northeast Passage and explains in part why, by comparison, the Northwest Passage and its adjacent lands is disregarded and neglected. Not only is the Northeast Passage the shortest water route; it is the highway along which Siberian timber, furs, and ores can be shipped cheaply to the world markets.

The creation in 1932 of the Main Administration of the Northern Sea Route (known as the G.U.S.M.P.) gave expression to these geographic and economic necessities. This agency co-ordinates the scientific, exploratory, and economic activities of the vast Siberian north; it utilizes powerful technical weapons: ice-breaker fleets cut lanes through the ice and lead caravans of freighters bringing machinery, foodstuffs, consumer goods, and so forth in exchange for Siberian exports; airplanes, scouting for open water, direct the ice-breakers and at the same time locate seal rookeries and thus help the sealing-fleet contribute steadily and substantially to the nation's fat industry; more than fifty meteorological stations regularly radio reports on weather and ice conditions and carry on experimental and theoretical investigations as well. The administration has equipped bases where all kinds of ships can be repaired and supplied. But, most important of all, it trains the thousands of men and women who are eager to work in the Arctic in the special skills needed there. Since World War II the G.U.S.M.P. has expanded its activities. Its daring and successful experiments in growing cereals and legumes and in caring for domesticated animals in the far north were directed primarily toward bettering the physical conditions for those living and working there. Recently it has constructed prefabricated units that can be shipped by boat from Archangel and assembled wherever needed. Each unit has a steam-heated house designed for ten persons—two apartments for families and single rooms for the unmarried, with modern plumbing

---

* It is interesting to recall that Nordenskiöld sailed the Northeast Passage just three years after Britain acquired control of the Suez Canal.

and hot and cold water, a miracle of luxury in the Arctic—a radio station, a pavilion for scientific observations, and hothouses and barns to guarantee a supply of fresh vegetables and meat.

The scientifically and socially imaginative scholar Professor Otto J. Schmidt is head of the Northern Sea Route Administration. He initiated its work in 1932 when, commanding the ice-breaker *Sibiryakov*, he made the run from Archangel to the Bering Strait in two months and four days. The next year he was the hero of the Chelyuskin epic. The specially built *Chelyuskin*, part cargo ship, part icebreaker, tried to explore a section of the northern seas still insufficiently known while engaged in transporting equipment and new personnel to the Wrangel Island Station. Just west of Bering Strait, where the *Vega* had been caught and held by the ice, the *Chelyuskin* was sunk. On the restless, pressure-driven ice-floes, two thousand miles from civilization, 105 persons, including an infant newly born on the ship, built a camp. Their main task, after maintaining their health and hopes, was making a flying-strip and keeping it even and open despite the constant efforts of the hummocks to obliterate the leveled field. Without mishap, airplanes, flown by veteran polar pilots, evacuated everyone.

From the disaster of the *Chelyuskin* as well as the success of the *Sibiryakov* the people of the Soviet Union have learned much about navigating the Northeast Passage, and the bold concepts and unceasing vigilance of the Northern Sea Route Administration have received popular support. Their east-west traffic moves through waters that are as carefully charted and patrolled as the north-south shipping lanes along our own eastern coast. Industrial towns and new river ports on the Ob, the Yenesei, and the Lena have sprung up; modernization and civilization are lifting Arctic Siberia out of its age-old oblivion without submerging the native populations, who have been helped and trained to take an active role in this new world of which they are a part.

Arctic Siberia is being endowed with life. This planned and supervised development is a notable instance of Arctic exploration placed in its true perspective—as a prelude to the utilization of its great resources.

19

Jones Sound and Beaufort Sea

IN THE exploration of both Lancaster and Smith Sounds large unknown tracts of land had been revealed. It was not until the turn of this century that Jones Sound, the last of the three important waterways noted by Baffin almost three hundred years before, was penetrated. And in its exploration the expedition led by Otto Sverdrup was rewarded with the discovery of new lands whose area is greater than that of the combined discoveries of all the Franklin search parties. Sverdrup's rights as explorer were recognized by the Canadian government, under whose jurisdiction all the islands of Arctic America lie, when he was paid $67,000 a few weeks before he died in 1930, and with this sum the Dominion also purchased his original maps, notes, diaries, and other documents relative to his expedition. At the same time an announcement was made that Norway had formally confirmed Canada's title to the islands known as the Sverdrup group.

Nansen, Amundsen, and Sverdrup are the three Norwegians who by their exploits revived the ancient glory of the Vikings. Because of their efforts Norway became one of the leading countries in polar work. And though Sverdrup has been overshadowed by Nansen's genius and Amundsen's spectacular successes, he was for more than forty years one of the outstanding men in Arctic exploration. As Nansen's companion in the first crossing of Greenland and as captain of the *Fram* on her famous drift, he shared in the hazards and plaudits of those ventures; as leader of the Second Fram Expedition, he could boast of having uncovered 100,000 square miles of new land. It is rather interesting that each of the three men sailed to his greatest achievement in the same ship, the *Fram*.*

A few days after the *Fram* had returned from her first voyage, in

* The *Fram* carried Amundsen to the Bay of Whales, his base for his successful dash to the South Pole, 1910–12.

281

1896, Nansen's chief patrons, the consul Axel Heiberg and the Ringnes brothers, wealthy brewers, asked him to lead another Arctic expedition that they were eager to sponsor. Nansen declined the command and suggested that they offer it to Sverdrup. The latter accepted readily, for he felt that "there were still many white spaces on the map which I was glad of an opportunity of colouring with the Norwegian colours." [1] Of the many white spaces, the most engrossing at that time was the unknown coast of northern Greenland, and Sverdrup's plans veered in that direction. Luckily his patrons allowed him a free hand in choosing where he would explore, so that he was not bound to any one locality and was at liberty to change his objective. Preparations for the projected expedition were started at once and the personnel chosen. With Sverdrup went sixteen of his countrymen: Lieutenant Baumann of the Royal Navy was second in command; Lieutenant Isachsen of the army was cartographer; Per Schei was geologist; Simmons, botanist; Bay, zoologist; there were a doctor and ten other men. On June 24, 1898 the *Fram*, reconditioned by Colin Archer, her builder, set forth on her second voyage of discovery.

Her route lay along the west coast of Greenland, as far north up Smith Sound as she could go. But navigation was bad that year, and heavy ice stopped the *Fram* on the Canadian side, just north of Cape Sabine, at Rice Strait. (That very season Peary, on board the *Windward*, was also kept from reaching a high latitude.) By the middle of August, Sverdrup's party began to establish themselves for the winter. Near the spot where Greely and his men had suffered in Starvation Camp, the men of the *Fram* found plenty of game, and seal, bear, and walrus were shot and added to their provisions. They explored the country around Hayes Sound and exchanged visits with Peary, whose ship was a few days' distance from theirs.

It will be remembered that the east coast of Ellesmere Land had been well outlined by the many ships that sailed north via Smith Sound, whereas its western coast had only been touched at twice: Lieutenant Aldrich of the Nares Expedition had reached Cape Alfred Ernest on its northwestern shore, and Lieutenant Lockwood of the Greely Expedition had discovered Greely Fiord. Here, then, was a white space that could be profitably investigated. In the spring of 1899 two parties left the *Fram* to cross Ellesmere Land. Sverdrup and Bay made their way over an ice-free isthmus where herds of musk-oxen fed, and reached a large fiord, which was named after Bay. Bad weather obscured a great part of the fiord from them and forced them to return to the ship. Meanwhile a second party, keeping more to the south along the glaciated region, came to a broad belt of bare ground that stretched away to the sea. As summer approached, both groups were back on the *Fram*. Preparations were made to steam northward. But again, as in the previous season, ice blocked Smith Sound, and Sverdrup, an experienced master of ice-navigation, could not drive his way through. It was then that he altered his plans, changed his course, and headed south for Jones Sound. "We knew there were several extensive stretches of unexplored land lying north of the point where Inglefield turned back in 1852 and thence up to Greely Fiord. Belcher, for instance, saw land due north from Table Island, which he called North Cornwall." [1]

Steaming westward along Jones Sound, Sverdrup noticed the luxuriant Arctic vegetation that graced the southern coast of Ellesmere Island, vegetation that promised abundant game. Soon they were in the vicinity of Inglefield's farthest, where progress was stopped not by ice but by a fog. Cautiously, like blindfolded people, they felt their way into the shelter of Havnefjord, and there they prepared for winter. During the autumn, trips were made to the west to lay down depots, the main one sixty miles away. Again they added to their supplies by killing twenty-six musk-oxen at a near-by fiord, appropriately called Moskusfjord. Early in the spring of 1900 nine men set out on extended sledging-trips. Five were to return when ten days past the main depot, leaving the other four to explore along the unknown western coastline of Ellesmere Island. "It turned out that the coast instead of trending to the north, continued west all the way to North Kent." * [1] When they came to the western reach of the shore they gazed on the swift, whirling current that, laden with hummocks and icebergs, smashes and jams its way through Hell Gate—a fearful stretch, along which they passed. Mad waters on one side, on the other towering precipices and cliffs supporting enormous cornices, which here and there had toppled down, leaving trails of black debris, and between them a crazy path over frenzied masses of pressed-up ice-floes. At last Hell Gate lay behind them, and the going was easier. They worked their way round the deep indentation of Norwegian Bay to its northern side, where the supporting party turned back. With their return the loads of the explorers became bigger and heavier, slowing their advance. The weather was foul, alternating gales and fogs, and the cold was so intense that it froze their brandy solid. Making a line across the ice to the northwest, they reached a

---

* A small island lying between North Devon and Ellesmere Islands, separated from the former by Cardigan Strait, and from the latter by a second, parallel strait, Hell Gate.

high coast—Axel Heiberg Land—along which they sledged. At Cape Southwest, Sverdrup climbed a pressure-ridge. "While I was up there scanning the country, I suddenly became aware of something greyish-blue far away in the west. What could it be? It must be new land. Yes, yes, it was. But the looming was so great it was impossible to gain any idea of what it was like."[1] In order to cover as much territory as possible Sverdrup decided to divide the work: he and a companion continued to the north while Isachsen with one man headed west to investigate the new land.

To the north along the west coast of Heiberg Land, a mountainous coast cut by fiords, valleys, and clefts, the hard going was made almost intolerable by terrible weather. Fog and wind, wind and fog, and snow plagued Sverdrup and his companion until, though eager to reach the northern limits of the land, they were forced on May 5, at 80° 55′ N., to turn back. The same bad weather attended them as they beat their way south. "It often happened that the more violent squalls from the mountains all but overturned the sledges, and the air was frequently so thick that I could hardly see the dogs before my own sledge; but on we drove in spite of all—we were obliged to do so."[1] Not until Cape Southwest did the weather clear and the going become easier. But they still had to pass along Hell Gate, and Sverdrup feared lest, because of the advanced season, it should be impassable. His misgivings disappeared when he saw that where they had had to cut their way foot by foot through blocks of ice, the ice was now smooth—but they only just got off it in time. It was a thin layer, treacherously covered with snow, spread over deep, swift waters. The only alternative was to cross the high, thick neck of land to Gaasefjord (Goose Fiord), the inlet nearest Hell Gate on the south side of Ellesmere Island. They left the ice and climbed up the mainland. The day was warm, the weather delightful, and that night they camped on bare ground. "We pulled off our boots and amused ourselves by walking about in our socks, like children when they are allowed to go barefoot."[1] It was a hard struggle up the steep slopes to the watershed. On the other side the hills slanted down to a pretty valley, through which a lively river ran. Down they went along the valley, which became narrower and narrower. "We began to wonder whether, after all, it was going to end in a cañon. Without any warning we were suddenly stopped by a high wall of ice, which entirely cut off the valley. We made a halt to see if we could find any means of advance, in order to avoid driving the long distance back again; but the ice was absolutely perpendicular and inaccessible to any being without wings. Suddenly it occurred to me that somewhere or other the river must have an outlet; there might be a tunnel through which we might pass, and on looking behind a massive snowdrift I really saw a big hole, which, on investigation, proved to be the beginning of a very large tunnel which pierced the glacier. A journey through it did not seem very alluring; from the roof were suspended big blocks of ice which might fall at any moment; and indeed a good many had already done so . . . which pointed an unequivocal warning to the danger of passing that way. . . . I shall not forget the moment when we entered the tunnel. I was afraid. . . . And yet it was not fear that had most hold on me, but rather an uneasy feeling of awe. . . . Along the walls were grotto after grotto, vault after vault, with pillars and capitals in rows like giants in rank; and over the whole shone a ghost-like bluish-white light . . . it was like driving straight into Soria Moria Castle, the castle 'east of the sun and west of the moon'; the most glorious of all." [1] Safely out on the other side, they made good time and that evening camped at Gaasefjord. From there it was easy going to the *Fram*.

In the meanwhile Isachsen, four days after parting from Sverdrup, had approached the new land sighted to the west, the two Ringnes Islands. Behind a high barrier of pressure-ridges, he saw, "the land rose at a gentle gradient, with higher land north and south, though nothing we could see exceeded a height of 900 feet." [1] This was a different formation from Axel Heiberg Land, whose steep precipices rise to 5,000 feet. A brief visit to this island was all he could allow himself. While Sverdrup and Isachsen had been exploring, notable work had also been done in charting and studying the geological formation of the fiords near Norwegian Bay. But all the men felt that even more important discoveries were waiting to be made the following year.

Summer came, and Sverdrup headed the *Fram* to the west along Jones Sound and then north through Cardigan Strait. There he maneuvered the ship against strong adverse currents, only to get caught by floes that drifted her out of the strait again. For a month she was pushed forward and backward until passage through Cardigan Strait was abandoned and harborage sought at Gaasefjord. The countryside around was covered with grass and moss and flowers and dotted with lakes. Game was everywhere, on the land, in the water, in the air; and the men feasted on walrus meat, musk-ox steaks, and ducks, ptarmigan gulls. The winter passed pleasantly, and with spring the sledging-parties were off. Again Isachsen went west to explore and map the new land he had visited the season before, while Sverdrup with three companions headed for the north. They were anxious to determine if north of Norwegian Bay there was a waterway reaching as far as Greely Fiord. This would make Heiberg Land an island and account for the open water seen from Bay Fiord, discovered the first year. At first the going was fairly good, though great effort and valuable time were lost in exploring fjords which, it was hoped, would connect with Bay Fiord. But again and again they found themselves in blind alleys, forced to retrace their steps. Finally they penetrated into Troldfjord, "an ugly place shut in on both sides by high and gloomy walls of rock." [1] Hopefully they went on, even though the steep dark walls drew closer and closer together, until at last they were in a deep canyon that twisted sharply from right to left. The snow on the floor of the canyon had been beaten into a hard path by millions of hares that hopped all over the place. But Troldfjord did not end in an impassable cliff. A steep slope, over which they could drag their sledges, led up to the watershed. Up they clambered, dogs and men dragging the sledges. And then, when the summit was gained, what joy! Below them lay Bay Fiord. "The waterway was covered with pressed-up autumn ice, horribly difficult to make one's way in, apparently, but little we cared for that. We had looked into the promised land." [1] Beyond Bay Fiord they caught a glimpse of a strip of ice-covered water that ran to the north, Eureka Sound. "For twenty-five days [we had been] searching eagerly for the mysterious sound which now at last lay large and open before us like a broad highroad, leading onward to unknown lands as yet untrodden by a white man's foot." [1]

Sverdrup sent two men to trace Greely Fiord to the east, while he and Schei went north on Eureka Sound until Svartevaeg, which Peary had named Cape Thomas Hubbard, the northernmost point of Heiberg Island, was reached.

Isachsen in the meanwhile had been exploring the new land to the west. It consisted of two large islands, separated by Hassel Sound, which he named in honor of the Ringnes brothers, Amund and Ellef. By June both groups were back at the ship with an enormous amount of work accomplished. Not only had the discoveries been vast, but the geological investigations had been most thorough and illuminating. They were ready to return home.

Soon it was summer, and the men eagerly watched for the ice in Gaasefjord to disappear. Jones Sound was open, but the ice around the *Fram* still held; and, though the men blasted and cut, a strip of solid ice prevented them from reaching the open water only five miles away. Reluctantly they had to prepare to pass a fourth winter in the Arctic. In the early spring more sledge trips were made. Sverdrup again went north, this time tracing the west coast of Ellesmere Land beyond Greely Fiord to Lands Lokk, only sixty miles south of Cape Alfred Ernest. "From a point about three miles north of the camp, the land turned to the northeast. . . . North and west of this land, as far as I could make out, was sea, and again sea with ordinary coarse polar ice. South of us was Axel Heiberg Island,"[1] and between Svartevaeg and Lands Lokk lay Nansen Sound. Sverdrup had practically completed the charting of the unknown west coast of Ellesmere Island. A second party went by sledge along Wellington Channel south to Beechey Island, partly to look at the fifty-year-old depots, relics of the Franklin search, and partly to correct their chronometers according to the place determination of the English. They found the house that had been erected there in ruins, the depot robbed, and the boat left by Sir John Ross broken and useless. A third party went by boat along the north coast of North Devon, charting that unknown shore. All three parties were back on the *Fram* by July. By August 8 the ship was clear of ice and on her way home. Sverdrup was the hero of the hour when the *Fram* reached Christiania harbor. He was a man who wore his laurels modestly, but his patrons could well be proud of an expedition that added so much new land to the maps of the earth and whose scientific studies were extensive and enlightening.

Sverdrup's subsequent work in the Arctic was as head of an expedition sent to search for the lost Russian explorer Brusilov in 1914–15. He failed to find Brusilov, but that expedition was notable for its pioneer use of wireless telegraphy. Sverdrup was able to report to the Russian Admiralty in St. Petersburg the position of Vilkitski's icebreakers, then in winter quarters in their successful attempt of the Northeast Passage. And though he was then in his sixtieth year, he made a long sledge trip along the Siberian coast to meet Vilkitski. The last voyage he made into the Arctic was to the Kara Sea in 1920.

Sverdrup's discoveries received confirmation from an American explorer who crossed and recrossed that area, Donald MacMillan. The MacMillan Crocker Land Expedition of 1913–17 set out "to reach, map the coastline, and explore Crocker Land whose mountains Peary sighted in 1906"[2] to the northwest of Ellesmere Island. MacMillan planned to cross Ellesmere Island to Bay Fiord and thence to go up Eureka Sound to the polar sea, since it promised most in the way of game, thereby eliminating the necessity of laying down depots. Leaving Etah early in February 1914, he arrived at Cape Thomas Hubbard, having covered the 580 miles in thirty-three days of continuous travel. From there his path lay to the north over the ice of the polar sea. Peary had placed Crocker Land about 120 miles to the north-west. For several days, while working his way over the ice of the polar sea, MacMillan and his men saw what Peary had seen—"Hills, valleys, snow-capped peaks extending through at least 120 degrees of the horizon." [2] But it was a mirage, which deceived them as it had Peary and which constantly varied in extent and character until it disappeared completely. In order to make no mistake of omission, however, MacMillan pushed on until he was two hundred miles from land. On all sides lay the frozen sea. He was certain that "Crocker Land" was nothing but a trick of ice and light, for "to see land at a distance of 200 miles from where Peary stood, the land must have reached an altitude of more than 30,000 feet!" [2] And that would be more than five times as high as the highest peak on Elles-mere Island. A second trip in 1916 took MacMillan westward from Heiberg Island to the Ringnes Islands and thence to King Christian Land, identified as the Finlay Island sighted by Osborn in 1853 but never before visited.

At the same time that MacMillan was working to the north and west of Jones Sound, another explorer was investigating the great bight north of Canada and west of the Parry Archipelago. Vilhjal-mur Stefansson is one of the most interesting of Arctic explorers, and one of the greatest alive. He has an abiding curiosity, an inquiring, original mind, and the courage to combat the fallacies contained in the myths—of whatever size, shape, or content—that our society cherishes. Not only have his journeys over unknown lands and seas included an area as great as Sverdrup's, but he is also the expounder and proponent of the theory of "living off the country," and has been the first to apply this method on the deep Arctic Sea far from land. Stefansson today is the prophet of the north. He is on the warpath to wipe out people's foolish preconceived notions of all Arctic lands as being sterile and forever snowbound; he would educate men to the economic value of the tundra, the vast grazing-lands of Arctic America; he stresses the importance of learning all that can be learned of the Arctic regions as the shortest highway between the great centers of population—New York, London, Moscow, Peiping. In his second expedition to the Arctic, in 1908–12, he lived among the natives of Coronation Gulf, doing valuable anthropological work, and achieved some fame when he reported on the little-known tribe of "blond Eskimos." In those four years he mastered the Eskimo way of life, living like the natives, whose existence depends entirely on their hunting ability. It must be said that Stefansson is an unusually keen and well-trained hunter, a most adaptable personality.

Stefansson was commander of the Canadian Arctic Expedition of 1913–18, the main objective of which was the exploration of Beaufort Sea, the last great unknown area, the last remaining problem in North Polar discovery. Dr. R. M. Anderson, who had accompanied him on his earlier venture, was in charge of the scientific research. He is responsible for the wealth of data accumulated in the various scientific fields, which, combined, form one of the outstanding contributions to the knowledge of polar Canada. Captain Bob Bartlett, a master navigator and veteran Arctic sledger, was in command of the expedition's main ship, the *Karluk.*

While about one half of the scientific staff were already established in quarters at Bernard Harbour, a little west of the mouth of the Coppermine River, the other half with Stefansson were aboard the *Karluk,* trying to round Point Barrow in order to join them. Off Point Barrow the ship became fast in the ice, and Stefansson left her, with five others, among whom was Hubert Wilkins, to hunt fresh meat for the autumn and winter. He and his companions never saw the *Karluk* again. Two days after they left, a full-bodied Arctic blizzard swept over the entire region and carried the ship away from the shore ice out into the ice-filled polar sea. To the west she drifted, on the same terrible pack that had killed the *Jeannette.* The *Karluk* "creaked and groaned and, once or twice, actually sobbed as the water oozed through her seams." [3] From the middle of September 1913, when she was beset, until the 10th of January 1914, when she sank, the crew held themselves in readiness to abandon her hourly. Yet throughout those four harrowing months, in which they drifted 1,100 miles to the west, scientific observations of various kinds were carried on. Unfortunately they were lost in the ensuing disaster. When the ship was fatally crushed, nineteen men and one woman—the Eskimo seamstress—had to cross the ever shifting ice-pack to the nearest land, Wrangel Island, sixty miles to the southwest. They had to make their way over incredibly rough ice—high pressure-ridges and impassable debris—in the depth of the winter night when the temperature hovered between 45° and 55° below zero. Of the twenty only nine came through alive: four set out from the main party in an attempt to reach Alaska and were never seen again; four never reached Wrangel Island; and three died there while waiting for help to come to them. Had Bartlett not been there, it is doubtful if any would have come out of that nightmare alive.

Meanwhile Stefansson and his companions, ignorant of the impending tragedy, made their way to Point Barrow and from there went eastward to Bernard Harbour. In addition to the *Karluk* the expedition had two smaller vessels, the *North Star* and the *Mary Sachs*. The *North Star* was to act as a contact ship for Stefansson when he explored north of the mainland, while the other was to be used in coastal surveys, dredging, and so on.

In March 1914 Stefansson began his trip over Beaufort Sea. In accordance with his theory that "a small party of white men with one or two sledges to haul scientific equipment, cooking gear, clothing, arms, ammunition and the like, could travel wherever it listed over the polar sea, no matter what the latitude and remain indefinitely," he started out over the ice.* With him went two men, Storker Storkerson and Ole Andreasen. They had one sledge and six dogs and carried food for only forty days. It was a gesture as daring as Nansen's crossing of Greenland, for few believed it possible to find game on the sea far from land. In fact so certain were people of the impossibility of such a procedure that the party was given up for dead when months passed and they did not return, even though such a quick return was not part of Stefansson's plan; and the *North Star* was not sent to keep her rendezvous.

At first the three men did not stop to hunt more than was necessary, but traveled as far as they could before warm weather disrupted the ice. Their route lay to the northeast. It was hard going, for they had to contend with adverse currents that carried them in the opposite direction. Spring came while they were still on the sea ice, and toward the last it was a matter of going from floe to floe in order to reach land. After ninety-six days on a moving sea they managed to make Norway Island, just west of the northwest tip of Banks Island. There they spent the summer hunting caribou, wind-drying the meat for later use, and curing the skins so that they could be made into clothes. That whole summer they waited for the ship that never came. Fearing lest an accident had overwhelmed the *North Star*, the three men journeyed south to look for her. Thus it was that they found the *Mary Sachs* at Cape Kellett.

In the following years Stefansson roamed over a wide area. He made another sortie out over the moving pack ice, a hundred miles

---

* It was not a purely academic theory even at that time. As long ago as 1853 Dr. John Rae, that remarkable servant of the Hudson's Bay Company, had announced that the custom of carrying great stocks of provisions had been the chief drawback in the land expeditions, and had wintered with eight men at Repulse Bay, relying for food on what he could secure with his gun and fishing-tackle. Also, Nansen and Johansen on their famous sledge trip had fed and clothed and kept themselves warm for an equally long period. Stefansson was merely extending Rae's theory and practice and Nansen's experience to include the Arctic seas as well as the Arctic lands. To Stefansson the only extended "lifeless area" is the Greenland Ice-Cap.

to the west of Prince Patrick Island, and escaped being carried away from land to the southwest only after a terrific struggle. The stretch of coast on the west side of that island between McClintock's and Mecham's farthest was traced. He experienced the same bad weather that had harassed his precursors; but to him it was not a barren land as they had found it. The offshore waters were well stocked with seals, which he shot—game Mecham had not even thought to look for. For the most part he traversed historic country; he found a report McClintock had written sixty-two years before; he revisited McClure's Mercy Bay, where, except for debris and pieces of anchor chains, everything had been salvaged by Eskimos; on the northwest tip of Banks Island he picked up McClure's note announcing his discovery of the Northwest Passage in 1850; he journeyed over to Parry's Rock at Winter Harbour, "the best located spot in the whole archipelago," to take observations for time and latitude; and at Ellef Ringnes Island he found a record left by MacMillan just a few months before. But Stefansson also made discoveries. Between Prince Patrick Island and the Ringnes Islands he found and explored Brock, Borden, Meighen, and Lougheed Islands, probably the last unknown lands in that area. All in all, Stefansson sledged thousands of miles— hard and dangerous miles over drift ice, difficult, bewildering miles along coasts where he found, "as McClintock and Mecham had before us, that in the spring this region is so beset with fogs and he who travels every day is half the time in doubt as to where he is going, and never knows whether he is headed inland or out to sea until he either stumbles against a cut bank or finds himself floundering among the hummocks of the off-shore pack." [4] Often, when the season was warm and he was sledging over ice, he encountered long stretches where the top snow had melted, forming deep pools. "The dogs had to swim now and then and the sledge floated after them. We had in the bottom of the sledge two or three empty tin cans which acted as buoys, and the men walked with the sledge to keep it from capsizing in the water while I waded ahead. This is much more unpleasant work than sledging at 50 below zero."

Stefansson's original party of three was augmented by the crew of the *Mary Sachs*, a fact that necessitated the feeding and housing of a large group. During the winter of 1916–17, spent at Liddon Gulf, seventeen men lived in tents made of musk-ox skins, heated with coal found in a near-by seam and burned in stoves made out of tin cans; they used musk-ox tallow to furnish light; and they were well and suitably clad in garments made from caribou skins. That should be proof to an incredulous world how friendly the Arctic can be! And yet rumor after rumor drifted southward throughout that long period that Stefansson and his men had perished of starvation.

In August 1917 Stefansson started for home. He could review with satisfaction the work he had accomplished: he had made sizable inroads on the unknown Beaufort Sea, he had discovered new land, he had successfully tested his theory of "living off the country." And yet when the schooner was beset near Herschel Island, he could not stay quietly aboard. He decided that here was a proffered opportunity to "camp on an ice-floe" and drift westward in a course parallel to that taken by the ill-starred *Karluk*. Only this time he wanted to be two hundred miles farther north. This drift was to end somewhere off the Siberian coast, the mainland to be reached by walking over the intervening ice. Just as he was about to start out, he contracted typhoid fever at Herschel Island, but his illness did not stop this daring plan from being carried out. The command devolved on Storkerson, who carried on with four companions. Starting north over the ice in March 1918, they established a camp on a floe "about seven miles in diameter and 15 or more miles in length and remained encamped on it for six months." As they drifted with the pack, they made regular observations, noting the depth, currents, and temperature of the frozen sea. Life on the floe was pleasant enough, comfortably housed as they were and with plenty to eat. And though they drifted over 400 miles, they failed to get as far west as they had hoped. Storkerson despaired of ever reaching Siberian waters, and that, together with the fact that he was tormented with asthma—a strange illness to get on an ice-floe!—made him return before he had reached his proposed terminus. In the first week of October, about the worst season of the year for travel over the ice, they started for shore. The young ice that was cementing the old floes together was weak and not discernible under a blanket of snow that covered all danger spots. And yet in less than a month they had crossed the three hundred miles that lay between them and the Alaskan shore. The work of the expedition was brought to a brilliant conclusion. It was a notable achievement, by virtue of both its exploring and its scientific research; it is exceptional because of Stefansson's theories, which were substantiated.

20

To the Pole

The Arctic fever is in our blood, and there is no cure for such patients but to put them on ice.—WALTER WELLMAN.

IN THE RECENT history of Arctic Exploration undue stress was laid on the attainment of the North Pole. In 1896 Nansen showed conclusively by the *Fram's* drift across the polar basin that the Pole lay somewhere on a shifting, ice-covered sea, at a point that had to be mathematically determined. From then on, reaching it became a purely sporting proposition, since the hardiest explorer, the most experienced, and the one with the finest equipment could hope to do no more than dash to the Pole and dash back again to land. To give such a sporting gesture any scientific significance, time would have to be spent at the Pole in order to carry out a series of observations. This is the reason that some of the most distinguished men who have devoted themselves to Arctic research have deplored the energy and money spent on such a polar steeplechase.

In the past the problem of reaching the North Pole had been subordinate to the hope of finding, via that route, a waterway to the East; and though the early North Polar attempts failed in their ultimate purpose, they resulted in the discovery of new lands. But even from the very beginning of polar exploration the ships that sailed with orders to attain the northern axis of the earth have been in number and importance the exception, not the rule.

The first proposal involving a North Polar voyage was made by Robert Thorne, an English merchant residing in Seville, when in 1527 he urged upon Henry VIII the necessity of trying to reach Cathay by way of the Pole. In his letter he argued that, since the way to Cathay and India by the west was barred by Spain and to the east by Portugal, the logical route for the English was by the north, by way of the Pole. For, once the explorers were there, he said, they could "decline to that part which they list." [1] And it was Thorne who made that magnificent reply to the critics who claimed that no ship would be able to penetrate the icy seas, that no man would be able to live in the inhuman cold of these regions: "There is no land unhabitable, nor sea innavigable," [1] a reply that might well serve as the motto of Elizabethan questing. It is in the light, then, of the attempt to reach the East and so to participate in the lucrative Eastern trade that the first North Polar voyages must be viewed. To these explorers and their financial backers the North Pole was a means, not an end. Willoughby in 1553, Barents in 1596, and Hudson in 1607 aimed to reach Cathay by way of the Pole. They failed to attain either the Pole or the East, but they opened the way for the trading-ships of the Russia Company and the whaling-ships that sailed to Spitsbergen waters.

Almost two hundred years passed before expeditions again sailed for the North Pole. Phipps in 1773, Scoresby in 1806, Buchan in 1818, and Parry in 1827 were imbued with the same desire and motivated by the same reason: they wanted a short cut to the East. Again they tried to force sailing-ships through the Arctic pack ice to the north of Spitsbergen—and again the ice defeated them. But with Parry came an important change in the technique of Arctic exploration. He "proposed to attempt to reach the North Pole, by means of travelling with sledge-boats over the ice, or through any spaces of water that might occur." [2] For the first time an expedition planned to use a ship to transport it to a far northern base, and advance from there over the ice on sledges. This method inaugurated by Parry became a commonplace procedure. In his ship, the *Hecla*, he reached Treurenberg Bay on the north coast of Spitsbergen in June 1827. From there, with twenty-seven men, provisioned for seventy-one days, he set out to walk over the ice to the Pole. Their supplies were loaded into two boats equipped with steel runners so that they could be hauled over large ice-floes when necessary.

The men faced a terrific task. It was back-breaking work to drag the unwieldy boats over the hummocky ice. Rain soaked them. The melting ice opened up a series of disconnected pools that necessitated a constant unloading and reloading of the boats, so that four hours of hard work were spent to gain half a mile. They advanced blindly through dense and dismal fogs. They were tormented by snow-blindness. As the days passed they floundered more and more through deep, soft, wet snow, through pools of fresh water that lay knee-deep over the surface of the ice and prevented the runners from sliding easily. They were so wet that the mere wringing out of their stockings became an inexpressible luxury. Against all these miserable conditions they fought, sustained by the hope that soon they would reach the "main ice," which had been described as "one continued plain of smooth, unbroken ice, bounded only by the horizon." [6] It continued to rain, rain, rain.

Despite their heroic efforts they gained surprisingly little. Parry's observations for latitude revealed that they were just barely advancing. Something was carrying them southward almost as fast as they labored in the opposite direction. The pack was drifting and carrying them rapidly southward. Twelve hours a day they toiled to get farther north, and then, while they rested, the drift nullified their labors. Fighting the drift was as futile as trying to get to the end of an endless treadmill. At 82° 45′ N. they turned back. They just failed to reach the eighty-third parallel, for which a prize of one thousand pounds had been offered. Sixty-one days after they had left the ship they were back again, having traveled almost a thousand miles, though their farthest was only 172 miles from the *Hecla*. But Parry had set a record for the highest north that for half a century remained unequaled.

In all the attempts made to reach the North Pole during the nineteenth century the discovery of new lands and the accumulation of important scientific data more than recompensed the explorers for their failure to achieve their goal. The explorations of Kane and Hayes and Hall revealed large stretches of the Greenland and Ellesmere coasts; the same is true of both the Nares and the Greely Expeditions. Koldewey, in the Second German North Polar Expedition, blocked in a large section of the East Greenland coast. Nansen's dash for the Pole was a ribbon of color that heightened the solid worth of his drift in the *Fram*. Peary's first attempt to get to the Pole resulted in the delineation of the northern limits of Greenland. And while the Italian North Polar Expedition led by the Duke of the Abruzzi failed to discover new lands to the north of Franz Josef Land, by their failure they proved that the lands that had been reported there were mirages. Thus, "the actual attainment was of no scientific importance, but it was of value as an ultimate objective and the lure of the pole led men onward into the unknown, and thus served science in its day." [3]

With the beginning of this century a new element crept into the old idea of reaching the North Pole, deflecting it from the field of exploration into the realm of sport. It became a race to see which nation, which man, would be the first to stand on the "top of the world." When members of the Greely Expedition of 1882 stood at their farthest north, 83° 24′, four miles nearer the Pole than had the Englishmen of the Nares Expedition in 1875, those four miles of northing loomed larger in the public imagination than their valuable scientific work. Their record fell when Nansen placed the Norwegian flag at 86° 12′ in 1895. This record was bettered by Cagni six years later when he reached 86° 34′—twenty-two miles nearer the Pole—and unfurled the Italian flag. In 1905 Peary, on his second North Polar trip, reached a new high latitude of 87° 6′. Thus, step by step, they approached that desired point.

Of all these men Peary was the most desirous, the most assiduous, in his efforts to climb the ladder of the latitudes to "ninety north" and there plant his country's colors. He had no hope, no thought, of finding new lands or collecting additional data about the region he was aiming for. It simmered down to a personal struggle between him and his beloved adversary, the Arctic. He wanted to prove that man can conquer the planet he inhabits. He trained for the fight as an athlete trains for a race; he prepared for it as a general prepares for a campaign; and though he was an athlete and a general, he was also a mystic, living a life remote from all mundane matters. His last two polar trips can be understood only if regarded as highly esoteric experiences.

Peary tackled his problem in a very realistic way. Constant planning and long experience finally resulted in a technique that was the key to the solution of the problem. He used Eskimo methods of travel, shelter, and clothing and employed Eskimos as sledge-drivers and igloo-builders. From his land base at Cape Columbia a series of relaying, supporting parties preceded him. They were to clear the trail, erect a series of camps, and lay down the necessary food, so that when all this preliminary work had been done, his party could advance quickly and easily along the prepared highway. Thus he would find himself within striking-distance of the Pole with fully loaded sledges and with his men and dogs comparatively fresh. It is this method that is all-important in considering his dash to the Pole. For, as Stefansson points out, Peary "developed a method by which anyone of good health, sound judgment and a reasonable apprenticeship in polar work could reach the Pole or any other point no farther removed from the nearest land than five or six hundred miles." [4] The North Pole is a little over four hundred miles from Cape Columbia.

In his second North Polar attempt, of 1905, the Peary method was first used. Thanks to strong financial backing, Peary was able to

The Eagle after landing on the ice. FROM *Andrée's Story*—ONE OF THE PHOTOGRAPHS TAKEN BY THE ANDRÉE PARTY AND PRINTED FROM NEGATIVES FOUND IN THE ICE THIRTY YEARS LATER.

Copyright by Albert Bonnier, Stockholm, and in the U.S.A. by Hearst Enterprises, Inc.

Siberia. A SOVIET ICE-BREAKER CUTTING A LANE THROUGH THE ICE FOR A CARAVAN OF FREIGHTERS.

Siberia. A MIRACLE OF LUXURY IN THE ARCTIC: HOTHOUSES AND BARNS THAT GUARANTEE A SUPPLY OF FRESH VEGETABLES AND MEAT.

have the *Roosevelt* built for him, a ship designed and constructed to get through the ice of Smith Sound to the northern end of Ellesmere Island within short distance of his main land base. His equipment, complete in every detail, included more than two hundred dogs and several Eskimo families, men, women, and children. In his plan it was imperative that he have Eskimo men to carry on the routine of living while on the march and Eskimo women to make the clothing for his entire field group. To the Eskimo children it was a grand picnic.

The autumn was spent in transporting several thousand pounds of supplies to Cape Hecla, about ninety miles from the ship and near Cape Columbia. By the end of February the first party was ready to start north over the ice. That Peary failed to reach the Pole on that trip was due to adverse ice conditions. He turned back when the haggard faces of his comrades, his few remaining emaciated dogs and nearly empty sledges, forced him to realize that, with unforeseeable conditions that could fatally delay his homeward dash, he had "cut the margin [of safety] as narrow as could reasonably be expected." It was due to the magnificent seamanship of the skipper of the *Roosevelt*, Captain Bob Bartlett, that the vessel was not smashed to pieces as she steamed southward through the ice of Smith Sound.

The *Roosevelt* was reconditioned and outfitted for Peary's third and last polar venture. A group of patrons organized by Herbert L. Bridgman formed the Peary Arctic Club to help him solve his financial worries. Bartlett was again captain of the ship, and among the twenty-two members of the expedition were Matthew Henson, who had been with Peary on all his previous trips, the surgeon Dr. Goodsell, his secretary Ross Marvin, and two "tenderfeet," Borup and MacMillan. The *Roosevelt* started northward in July 1908. At Etah forty-nine Eskimos and 246 dogs joined the party. By the beginning of September Bartlett had maneuvered the ship to Cape Sheridan, near where the Nares Expedition had wintered on the exposed shore of the polar sea. During the autumn all the supplies needed for the spring drive were moved to the land base at Cape Columbia. From that point the parties started out the last day of February 1909.

Twenty-four men, nineteen sledges, and 133 dogs began the march over the polar ice. The above-mentioned six members of the expedition led the relaying, supporting parties, preparing the way for Peary. From the first the going was hard. Unusually low temperatures—in the minus fifties—caused a great many frost-bites; violent winds swept the snow off the rough ice so that the sledges were constantly in need of repairs; and then they were stopped by a wide, open lane of water.* "Three, four, five days passed in intolerable inaction, and still the broad line of black water spread before us. . . . During those five days I paced back and forth, deploring the luck which, when everything else was favourable, should thus impede our way with open water." [5] The lead closed on the sixth day. One by one the supporting parties turned back. At 87° 46′ N. the last of them, with Bartlett at their head, started for land. It was one month since they had left Cape Columbia. They had gone 280 miles and still had 133 miles to go to reach the Pole.

In five forced marches Peary drove his party—consisting of Henson and four Eskimos—over those 133 miles. That final spurt brought them, on April 6, 1909, to 89° 57′ N. "The Pole at last. The prize of three centuries. My dream and goal for twenty years. Mine at last! I cannot bring myself to realize it. It seems all so simple and commonplace." [5] Six men stood at last at that magical point at which east and west and north disappear and only one direction remains—south; where a year is measured by one day and one night. They stayed there only thirty hours and then raced south for Cape Columbia. Peary knew that if he was to reach land he must do so before the next full moon set the pack in motion and opened leads. In sixteen days he covered the 485 miles lying between him and land, thereby establishing a record surpassing other explorers' as well as his own previous trips for rapid travel.

It is impossible to throw a strong light on Peary without revealing the shadowy figure of Dr. Frederick Cook. The Cook-Peary question was one that divided the world: either you believed that Peary had reached the North Pole or you gave your allegiance to Cook. People with no idea of the real points involved took sides and argued vehemently and bitterly. Investigations were made by geographic societies and by Congress. Dozens of books, thousands of articles, were written to defend one of the men as a hero and to belittle the other. And, to judge by the number of words still being written on the subject after the lapse of these many years, the question would still seem to be unresolved, the issue still alive.

* Ernest Leffingwell in 1906–7 devised a method that solved this very problem. He took a medium-weight sail-canvas and greased it well on both sides with lard. When not needed, it made a roll no larger than a tent; and by being simply wrapped around a sledge it transformed the latter into a boat. The larded surface made it possible to crack and peel off the adhering ice, so that the weight of the canvas remained the same. Peary knew of this method but did not make use of it because he did not believe that the ice would peel off. It remained for Stefansson to make successful use of it in his expedition of 1913–18.

Cook was an extraordinary figure. It is impossible to dismiss him simply by calling him a liar. Rather it may be said that he was a great teller of stories, a fiction-writer who on a certain amount of fact built a vivid and absorbing yarn. For a man of his ability and experience he harbored too puissant an imagination. These qualities emerge from his record prior to his polar attempt: as ethnologist in Peary's expedition to Greenland in 1892 and as surgeon for the Belgian Antarctic Expedition four years later he had done excellent work. But his claim to have ascended Mount McKinley in 1906 has since been invalidated by Archdeacon Hudson Stuck, Bellmore Browne, and others who have established fairly conclusively that Cook climbed only about 11,000 feet of a 21,000-foot mountain.

The following year, 1907, he sailed north on his polar venture in the yacht *John R. Bradley,* named in honor of his sole patron. Only one companion, Rudolf Francke, went with him. The two men, with their modest supplies, were landed at Annoatok, an Eskimo village twenty-five miles from Etah. There they spent the winter, and the inhabitants, men, women, and children, helped Cook get everything in order for his trip. They hunted for him, helped him build sledges, made clothing, supplied him with drivers and dogs. He started from there on February 19, 1908. With him were Francke and nine Eskimos; his equipment included eleven sledges, 103 dogs in prime condition, four thousand pounds of supplies, and a twelve-foot folding canvas boat. He chose Sverdrup's trail—across Smith Sound to Cape Sabine, then across Ellesmere Island to its west coast as far as Cape Thomas Hubbard, the northernmost tip of Axel Heiberg Island. It was the route offering the most abundant game, and he hoped by taking it to keep his provisions intact for the trip over the ice. Within a month he had reached Cape Thomas Hubbard, a distance of 550 miles. By March 18 he was ready to part from his supporting party and begin his trip to the north. At Cape Thomas Hubbard he left a large cache so that he would have a sure food supply for the return trip. With him went two Eskimo youths, each about twenty years old, E-tuk-i-shook and Ah-we-lah. Twenty-six of the best dogs hauled two sledges, on which was loaded everything needed for the venture. Their objective lay five hundred miles to the north.

They struggled northward over the ice, encountering the same conditions, surmounting the same obstacles, tried by the same hardships, as come to all those who venture over the Arctic Sea. On April 21 Cook's reckoning gave him their position as 89° 46′ N. "We all were lifted to the paradise of winners as we stepped over the snows of a destiny for which we had risked life and willingly suffered the tortures of an icy hell. . . . Step by step my heart filled with a strange rapture of conquest . . . we touched the mark . . . there is sunrise within us. . . . We are at the top of the world!" [8] They stayed there but twenty-four hours and then started back. It was imperative that they reach land before the warm weather set in.

Cook then tells how they dashed back for land, of the difficulties they faced: how their food ran low and how the steady drift of the ice to the west carried them farther and farther away from their depot at Cape Thomas Hubbard. Fogs surrounded them. For twenty days they went on, not knowing where they were, enveloped in a gray mystery. Then at last clear weather came. "Land loomed to the west and south of us . . . I took observations. *They gave us latitude 79° 32′, and longitude 101° 22′.** At last I had discovered our whereabouts, and found that we were indeed far from where we ought to be. . . . We were in Crown Prince Gustav Sea. To the east were the low mountains and high valleys of Axel Heiberg Land. . . . Between us and the land lay fifty miles of small crushed ice and impassable lines of open water. . . . The land to the south was nearer. Due south there was a wide gap which we took to be Hassel Sound. . . . The ice southward was tolerably good and the drift was south-south-east." [8] They reached the low-lying Ringnes Islands. They rested there awhile and made their plans for the future. They hoped by pushing southward to reach Lancaster Sound, where there would be a good chance of meeting a whaler. The drift of the ice favored them, and they reached Grinnell Peninsula on North Devon Island. Although the distance to Lancaster Sound was short, the season was too far advanced for land travel, sledging had become quite impossible, and without a reserve of food they could not await the drift of the ice.

Their troubles were increased by the terrifying fact that they had come to the end of their ammunition. Only a handful of cartridges was left. "We fortunately had the material of which these [harpoons and lances] could be made, and the boys possessed the savage genius to shape a new set of weapons." [8] Bows and arrows were fashioned out of the hickory used in the sledge. The sledge also furnished the wood for making the shafts for harpoons and lances. The tips were made out of musk-ox horns and whalebone picked up along the shore. Additional tips were made out of the metal of the sledge shoe. The nails in the cooking-box were used as rivets. The skin of a seal shot with one of the last cartridges was cut into strips for harpoon and lasso lines. Thus equipped they headed eastward along Jones Sound, and

* Italics not in the original. See p. 301 for the significance of this statement.

with these primitive weapons they hunted walrus, bears, and seal. Winter was fast approaching. They still had three hundred miles to go to reach Annoatok. They prepared to winter where they were. A badly ruined, ancient Eskimo stone house offered the most promise of shelter, and they set about to make it habitable. Game was found in abundance, especially musk-ox, which they were able to secure in sufficient numbers. The meat of the musk-ox became their staple food for seven months; the skin, with its remarkable fur, part hair, part wool, made their beds, roofed their igloo, and furnished them with clothes; the bones supplied them with material for harpoon points and knife-handles; and the fat served as both fuel and food.

The winter passed slowly. Their simple life made no demands on their time or energy. They slept for long hours and occupied their waking hours in preparing for their return to Annoatok. On the 11th of February 1909 the sun shone. It was their signal to start for home. At the end of a month their provisions had run out. No game was seen. Several meals were made out of a candle and three cups of hot water. Then a bear was caught, then a seal. Greenland was only thirty miles away, but a wide stretch of open water forced them to make a long detour to cross Smith Sound. "The days were prolonged, the decayed seal food ran low, water was almost impossible. We had eaten the strips of meat and frozen seal cautiously. We had eaten other things—our very boots and leather lashings as a last resort. So weak that we had to climb on hands and knees, we reached the top of an iceberg, and from there we saw Annoatok." [7]

This journey, as told by Cook, is a magnificent adventure. But it is impossible to reconcile his account with certain facts. First, there is the version given by the two Eskimos who accompanied him. They told their own people and Rasmussen, Freuchen, and others that they were never out of sight of land. It was they who pointed out that the picture taken at the "First Camp at the Pole, April 21, 1908" showed them wearing musk-ox pants. On Cook's own word and that of the Eskimos he had no musk-ox pants or skins when they left Annoatok, and they did not kill any musk-ox until after they had returned from the Pole and had gone into winter quarters on Jones Sound. This would confirm the Eskimos' statement that that picture had been taken near their winter camp. They also deny his account of having run out of ammunition. Secondly there is the point of Cook's whereabouts on reaching land again.* If Cook's location and description are checked by Sverdrup's earlier discoveries, *the only other account that existed until 1921*, they are perfectly all right. But Stefansson

---

* See p. 300.

went through that very region in his trip of 1913–18 and discovered small islands. Thus, when we study Cook's location in the light of these subsequent explorations, we find that he was within eight miles of Meighen Island. Had he been where he claims he was, he could not have overlooked Meighen Island, which, rising to a height of about eight hundred feet, would have blotted out his view of Axel Heiberg Island, fifty miles away.

Cook's actual route, therefore, after leaving his supporting party at Cape Thomas Hubbard was probably as follows: he went southward along the west coast of Axel Heiberg Island, keeping close to the shore, and wintered somewhere on Jones Sound. He knew from Sverdrup's account that game there was plentiful. Then the following spring he headed back for Greenland. The story told in Cook's *My Attainment of the Pole* is exciting and well written, but it nevertheless appears to be mainly fiction.

It is many years now since the Pole was reached and, viewing Peary's exploit from such a vantage-point, it would seem fair to say that if any man were to reach the Pole, that man would be Peary. He had the desire, the overwhelming, compelling desire; he had the physical ability and the necessary technique acquired from long experience; and he had the financial backing. But like all deeds whose import is self-contained, it seems a strange goal on which to have lavished so much energy and planning and money. Like so many grand gestures, when seen in retrospect, it does not seem to matter greatly.

Peary's problem had been to get to the North Pole and back; polar problems—the drifting ice and driving winds that he had tried to cope with—had, of necessity, remained unstudied. Not until 1937 was an attempt made by Soviet scientists to investigate conditions at the Pole.

For a year and a half Professor Schmidt and his staff of the Northern Sea Route Administration worked to outline the scope of the research and to plan every detail of the expedition—transportation, equipment, and supplies. The brilliance and care of this preparation was repaid by the importance and variety of the scientific results and the well-being of the four men who spent nine months on the drifting ice-pack. With Ivan Papanin, the leader, went P. Shirshov, a hydrologist and hydrobiologist, Y. Fyodorov, a magnetologist and astronomer, and E. Krenkel, a radio operator. The temporary station they set up was very elaborate: a large black tent was their living-quarters; they had a windmill to generate power for electricity and radio transmission, an assortment of complex and cumbersome apparatus—cables three miles long to lower dredges to the ocean floor, special traps to sample plant and animal life at various depths, instruments to measure the salinity and temperature of the ocean at different levels, and food and fuel for a year and a half. Their clothing included capacious felt boots, ten-gallon galoshes, and fur boots to keep their feet warm, reindeer-fur shirts, sealskin trousers, and wolfskin sleeping-bags lined with eiderdown. Four heavy-engine transport planes ferried the men and their ten tons of equipment from Rudolph Island, in the Fridtjof Nansen Archipelago, to the North Pole.

On May 21, 1937 the first orange-colored plane carrying Schmidt and the four members of the expedition made an easy landing on an open, level ice-field. Several days later the other planes arrived. At the end of a fortnight the station was installed, the planes had left, and the four men had settled down to the work they had begun the very first day.

From the North Pole every direction is south. Toward which land would they go? Slowly at first and then with increasing speed they drifted. By January 1938 their floe arrived off northeastern Greenland and, colliding with grounded ice, split apart. Only a small insecure area was left them. By February 19 they reached 70° 54'— between Scoresby Sound and Jan Mayen. Their work was finished and they and all their equipment were picked up by two ice-breakers that broke a path through the ice to their station.

At the North Pole Peary had taken one sounding, but his line of 7,544 feet had not even touched bottom. The Papanin group found the ocean there to be 14,070 feet deep. Every thirty to thirty-five miles they took soundings—thirty-three in all—from which we know that the ocean bed rises in giant, jagged steps from the Pole to Greenland. They found that at first they drifted only one mile a day, but that as they went farther south their rate increased. Shirshov's analysis of the water showed that the constant presence of plant life indicates the presence of animal life in the far northern areas and that beneath the below-zero Arctic water was a warmer, more saline layer —that water from the Atlantic underlies the entire Arctic basin. Weather and ice reports were radioed daily, and as their investigations began to accumulate, they radioed full monthly reports so that if anything happened to them the work they had done would not be lost.

Guided by their weather reports in the summer of 1937, the Soviet pilots Chkalov and Gromov flew non-stop from Moscow to Portland, Oregon, and from Moscow to San Jacinto, California. Their route lay over the North Pole.

21

Flying in the Arctic

WITH PEARY and Stefansson the technique of Arctic sledging and the art of Arctic living begun less than a hundred years before by Parry, McClintock, and Rae achieved their fullest expression. To-day men do not fear the Arctic. The food problem is so well understood that the phantom of scurvy no longer terrorizes those working and traveling in the far north; instead they utilize its food resources of land and sea. The polar winter, with its cold and darkness, which was first shunned, then passed in dread, then endured stoically, is now appreciated as the most favorable time for sledging, for during those months the surface of the snow and ice is at its best. Thus with the knowledge that has been gained the power of the explorer has increased, and at the present day a member of a well-organized, well-equipped expedition who delights in and is exhilarated by life in the Arctic must regard the stories of old-time hardships as "curious fantasies or epics of heroic men struggling blindly with ignorance." [1]

Since one of the major problems of polar exploration has always been that of travel, it is only to be expected that men would turn to the new means offered by air transport. It was a joyous escape from the long-drawn-out drudgery of traversing, on foot and heavy-laden, the baffling pack ice, the most formidable obstacle the explorer faces in the north.

Several facts must be borne in mind when dealing with flying in the Arctic. First a distinction—real though finely drawn—must be made between aeronautics and exploration.* As Frank Debenham has pointed out, "as soon as the airship or aeroplane is in the air the

---

* The late Robert Marshall, author of *Arctic Village*, expressed this distinction with emotion in a letter to me (December 1934): "From an aesthetic and psychological standpoint I think machine exploration is damnable, and Wilkins and Byrd have been the two chief villains in the outrageous prevalent practice of making exploration chiefly a matter of getting machinery to run a little further than normal from the factory."

problems cease to be polar in any way, and only become so again when it is necessary to find a landing-place." Then, since the problem of exploration today is one of refinement upon earlier pioneer work, patient observation and accurate measurement are required, and these cannot always be accomplished by rapid flights through the air. In winter it is hard to distinguish between land and sea, and in summer the prevalence of fogs may not only blot out the entire panorama but also make flight decidedly hazardous. Amundsen records that "a tremendous sea of fog, in some places of extraordinary density," prevented him from making any observations when over the Beaufort Sea, the last great unexplored area in the north. In its effect upon the problems yet remaining to be solved, flying within the Arctic has done little more than confirm what was already known or deduced. Thus Amundsen in the *Norge* reported land where land was known to be and no land where none was expected.

And yet the airplane has demonstrated its value, especially in aerial survey of difficult stretches. Chukhnovsky, the Soviet flier, has reconnoitered over great areas of the Siberian Arctic in the region of the Yenisei River and in 1930 mapped from the air the unknown delta of the Pyasina River. That same year Major Burwash and Flight-Lieutenant Mawdesley of the Canadian Arctic Patrol similarly photographed thousands of miles of coastline near King William Land that had previously been roughly charted. Donald MacMillan, the American explorer, used an airplane in 1931 to map the unknown, forbidding interior of Labrador. In Greenland this same method has been employed to chart in detail its rocky, indented, dangerous east coast. Aerial surveying of this coast was begun in the vicinity of Angmagssalik by Flight-Lieutenant D'Aeth of the British Arctic Air Route Expedition and was carried forward by those enterprising Danish explorers Mikkelsen, Lauge Koch, and Rasmussen. By the end of 1932 eastern Greenland had been surveyed by air from Cape Farewell to Cape Bismarck. It is such flights, systematically carried on without much publicity, that point the way to the time when the whole of the Arctic will yield its secrets to the explorer in the air.

But the valuable work of aerial survey does not coincide with the most spectacular flights. For the most part the latter have been made either to reach the North Pole or to cross, via the shorter route of the high latitudes, from the Old World to the New. All of the flying in the Arctic has been done since World War I—all except that of the Andrée Expedition.

Salomon August Andrée, a Swedish scientist born in 1854, tried as long ago as 1896 to reach the North Pole by means of a balloon.

In this desire he was doubtless influenced by the tremendous interest evoked by Nansen's transpolar drift on the *Fram*. For a moment the paths of these two men crossed. In 1896 Andrée, waiting at his base at Dane Island, Spitsbergen, for a favorable moment to commence his adventure, met the *Fram* as she was returning to Norway triumphant, her adventure already in the past. And though he was fully prepared to fly that season, Andrée had to postpone his flight because the desired southern wind needed to carry him across the Pole did not blow.

Like Nansen, Andrée planned his entire expedition with meticulous care for detail. Whereas the capacious *Fram* held all the supplies and equipment needed to make that expedition entirely self-sufficing for a period of five years, the *Eagle*, Andrée's balloon, imposed strict limitations of space and weight upon its cargo. His personnel and equipment had to be inclusive but limited. In addition to the balloon paraphernalia he had to have supplies and stores that would enable his party to retreat over the ice were the balloon wrecked. For his base he chose a level sheltered spot at Dane Island, and there the *Eagle* was assembled and filled with gas. The wireless being unknown, he took with him homing-pigeons and special buoys in order to have some communication with the world. Andrée had two companions: Nils Strindberg, twenty-five years old and just recently affianced, was in charge of the cartography and photography, and Knut Frænkel, a twenty-seven-year-old civil engineer and ardent sportsman, served as general assistant. It is well to remember that Andrée was neither an impractical visionary nor a man given to stunts; he was a quiet, studious scientist who was a generation ahead of his time in being "air-minded." He was well aware of the hazards attending his flight, and he faced the possibility of disaster, for he notes in his diary: "Dangerous? Perhaps. But what am I worth?" [2]

Undeterred by his failure to start in 1896, Andrée returned the next year to Dane Island. Again the gas bag was filled and the equipment assembled. By the end of June 1897 all was in readiness, awaiting the right wind. On July 11 the favorable southerly wind blew. "Andrée gave orders; everyone was willing and helpful, and everything went well. . . . The balloon had now risen. . . . The moment had come to attach the car. When this was done and a sufficient number of bags of ballast had been taken on board, it was time to say good-bye. This was done heartily and touchingly but without any signs of weakness. . . . And now the three of them stand there, on top of the car. There is a moment's solemn silence. . . . The right instant has come. 'Cut away everywhere!' cried Andrée. Three knives cut the three lines holding fast the bearing-ring, and the balloon rises amid the hurrahs of those below." [2] Free to float, the *Eagle* rose. Then it sank. Ballast was thrown. Again the car dipped toward the water for a moment. Then it rose. It soared. Again it sank. Then it jerked up. The *Eagle* floated quickly northward. Soon it was out of sight.

From the very start it was made clear to the airmen that the "sensitiveness to temperature conditions, and especially to clouds and mists, displayed by the *Eagle*—as by all other balloons—will play a decisive part during the continuation of the journey." [2] During the first hours the three men were busy noting the speed, the height. Far below them flew a gull, keeping pace with them over the open ice-floes. Soon a mist wiped out the mountains of Spitsbergen. The day passed quickly. Homing-pigeons were sent out with messages. Andrée went inside the car to sleep, leaving the other two to keep watch. After a few hours they ran into a fog, and the balloon lost some altitude. Hours passed. It was Andrée's turn to take the watch. He noted that the balloon had changed its direction and was headed west instead of north. When Strindberg and Frænkel had rested, the three men prepared a light meal. It was seventeen hours since they had started.

Suddenly the balloon sank so low that the car bumped on the ice. It was in danger of being smashed. The situation was critical. Hurriedly they threw overboard as much ballast as they could, but still the *Eagle* struggled to rise against the weight of the thick fog. Matters became worse. Every five hundred feet the car left its mark on the ice. As Andrée expressed it, "the ice is stamped." Finally the *Eagle* stopped altogether. Everything was dripping, the balloon was heavily weighted down. It was in this situation that Andrée, keeping watch alone in the car of the *Eagle*, wrote the following lines:

"Although we have thrown out our ballast, and although the wind might, perhaps, carry us to Greenland, we determined to be content with standing still. We have been obliged to throw out a great deal of ballast today, have not had any sleep or been allowed any rest from the repeated bumpings, and we probably could not have stood it much longer. . . . Is it not a little strange to be floating here above the Polar Sea? To be the first to have floated here in a balloon? How soon, I wonder, shall we have successors? Shall we be thought mad or will our example be followed? I cannot deny that all three of us are dominated by a feeling of pride. We think we can well face death, having done what we have done. Isn't it all, perhaps, the expression of an extremely strong sense of individuality which cannot bear the thought of living and dying like a man in the ranks, forgotten by coming generations? Is this ambition?" [2] Andrée had made his peace with life.

For thirteen hours "the balloon sways, twists, and rises and sinks incessantly. It wishes to be off but cannot." [2] The wind was not strong enough to lift it from the ice. In the morning of July 13 the balloon shook itself free and bumped along. More homing-pigeons were set free. One of these birds, after flying for two days, settled on the masthead of a Norwegian sealer. Hungry and exhausted, it slept with its head under its wing. "The skipper, who thought the bird looked like a ptarmigan, climbed up the rigging and shot it. It fell overboard and it was not thought worth while to lower a boat to get it. But when, later in the day, they met another sealer, they learned that it might have been one of Andrée's homing-pigeons, and, although they were not certain that Andrée had begun his balloon flight, the skipper returned to the place where he had shot the bird and sent two boats out to look for it. And, strangely enough, one of the boats actually found the bird." [2] In this incident was sounded the motif of the whole Andrée story. He was lost, he died, and yet, thanks to the strange accidental discovery of his body and papers, neither his work nor its meaning perished.

Soon after the homing-pigeons had been released the *Eagle*, again weighted down by fog, dipped so low that the car hit the hummocks violently, continually. Andrée's diary noted repetitiously: "fog," "fog," "dense fog," "constant fog," "fog." Then he wrote: "Through the fog the ice and water are visible lifted up along the line of vision and the water is consequently bewilderingly like land. It has deceived me several times." [2] For a few hours the *Eagle* floated. But another dense fog enveloped them, a fog with fine drizzle, which settled in the form of hoarfrost on the ropes. It weighed down the balloon, and the violent bumping began all over again. The first few hours of the new day, July 14, were a monotonous recording of these "touches." The fog held, and the *Eagle* bumped along. Then, when the morning was still young, "the balloon rose to a great height but we opened both valves and were down again. . . . We jumped out of the balloon." [2] Andrée's polar expedition in the *Eagle* was ended. The erratic course of the balloon had taken them to about 82° 56′ N. and 29° 52′ E. They had been in the *Eagle* for sixty-four hours.

The flight over the pack ice was ended. The men now faced the task of reaching the nearest land on foot. Quickly they reorganized their routine and their equipment. A whole week was spent preparing for the march to land. The tent, sleeping-bag, guns and ammunition, sledges, the boat, were put in order and packed with the necessary provisions. On the 23rd they finally broke camp and started for Franz Josef Land, where they knew from Nansen's experience it was possible for human beings to subsist through the Arctic winter. But Andrée did not know when he set the course for southeast that between him and Franz Josef Land flowed an unconquerable ocean current.

Walking across the drifting pack ice, pulling on sledges too heavily loaded, ferrying dangerously across lanes of water, killing and eating bears, making their way laboriously over hummocks, blinded by fogs and plagued by rain and soft, deep snow—the events were common to all such trips over the floating pack during the summer season. But their diaries are enlivened by a constant good humor, as though they were enjoying a camping-trip and were not faced with a desperate struggle for their lives. By August 4 it became apparent that they could "surmount neither the current nor the ice" and had "absolutely no prospect of doing anything by continuing our tramp to E." They decided to march westward in the direction of Spitsbergen. Those first two strenuous weeks had dulled the fine edge of their strength. They still had six weeks of equally hard going before making land. By the middle of September minor ailments further weakened them, and to their dismay they noticed that despite all their efforts "the current and the wind irresistibly carried us down into the jaws between North-East Land and Franz Josef Land and that we had not the least [chance] to reach North-East Land. . . . We at last discovered the necessity of submitting to the inevitable, i.e., wintering on the ice." [2] Though they were troubled by the thought of hunger, they were always able to kill bears, seals, and birds. "We have wandering butcher shops all around us." September 17: "The day has been a remarkable one for us because of our having seen land today for the first time since July 11." [2] It was White Island, or Giles Land. "There is no question of our attempting to go on shore, for the entire island seems to be one single block of ice with glacier cliffs. But it appears to be not absolutely inaccessible on the east and west points." [2]

They were not eager to reach land. The ice was drifting southward and promised to carry them with it to more southerly, frequented land. That prospect seemed more hopeful than the alternative of taking shelter on the ice-shrouded island. In order to be secure and sheltered they built a snow hut "solid and neat" on a large ice-floe. The snow hut gave them neither security nor shelter. They were subjected to the perils of the moving pack. "Our floe is diminishing in a somewhat alarming degree close to our hut. The ice pressure brings the shores closer and closer to us." [2] A few days later, on October 1, "We heard a thunderous crash and water streamed into the hut and when [we] . . . rushed out we found that our large floe had been splintered into a number of little floes and that one fissure had divided the floe just outside the wall of the hut. . . . This was a great reversal in our position and our prospects. The hut and the floe could not give us shelter." [2] And so four days later they moved their camp from the ice and took refuge on White Island. Twelve days after that the entries in their diaries stop. It is possible only to guess the cause of their death. It was not lack of food or shelter, it was not disease. Strindberg died first, perhaps accidentally. Stefansson has pointed out that Andrée and Frænkel were probably poisoned while they slept by carbon-monoxide fumes from their faulty cook stove. Their adventure ended in the same sudden, courageous way it had begun.

Though Professor Nathorst circumnavigated White Island a scant year later,* the fate of Andrée, Strindberg, and Frænkel remained a mystery for thirty-three years. They had literally disappeared into the thin air. But the ice, which had been their worst enemy when they were alive, preserved their bodies in a remarkable way. By an almost miraculous chance these were found by Dr. Gunnar Horn in 1930 lying in their last camp. Enough of their photographs, diaries, notebooks, and other memoranda were intact to give a firsthand account of their life from the time they floated away. Pictures taken by the men thirty-three years before were developed, their written words deciphered. Thus the almost complete story of those pioneers of Arctic flying became known.

Problems of aeronautical interest—the use of the airplane as an aid in Arctic exploration and the feasibility of using airplanes in the Arctic—were those that principally concerned the Oxford University Expedition to Spitsbergen in 1924. Led by Professor George Binney, it had the co-operation of the British Air Ministry, which was alive to the importance of the test flights to be made. Despite the fact that Binney's seaplane was twice disabled and finally wrecked and abandoned, he succeeded in making several flights over parts of Spitsbergen and Northeast Land. Luckily he escaped without suffering any injuries. His results were more valuable aeronautically than geographically. The next year reconnoitering flights were undertaken by Commander Byrd in conjunction with MacMillan's 1925 expedition to Etah. They hoped to be able to explore over the Arctic Sea to the

* See Appendix I.

east of Heiberg Land, but storms and fogs were so frequent that out of the whole season only three or four days were good for flying. The results, from the point of view of exploration, were negligible.

That very year, on May 21, 1925, Amundsen with Lincoln Ellsworth and four other men set out in two Dornier flying-boats, the *N-24* and the *N-25*, to fly to the North Pole. Their jumping-off place was King's Bay, Spitsbergen, where there was a coal-mining village. They carried fuel for twelve hundred miles and food for twenty days. "After a journey lasting eight hours, the time estimated to bring us to the Pole, we came down into the first open 'lead' big enough for our airplanes to land in to take observations as to our exact whereabouts." [3] They found that strong head winds had held them back and that they were 120 miles from the Pole. Then suddenly, before they could get away, the lead closed up. And though the airplanes were only three miles apart, they were hidden from each other by high hummocks. A whole day was spent by the parties in locating each other, and five more days passed before they were reunited. Then they took stock of the situation. Ellsworth's airplane, the *N-24*, was wrecked; the *N-25* was lying in a pool, threatened on all sides by the pack. To get the *N-25* into the air again it was first necessary to construct a level runway on the curdled, moving ice-floes. It was either that or a four-hundred-mile walk to Greenland. They decided to try the first alternative before they were forced to the second. For long hours every day they worked. Three wooden shovels, a two-pound pocket safety-ax, and an ice anchor were the only implements they had with which to move three hundred tons of ice. The cabin of the flying-boat provided them with shelter. "The scanty heat from the 'Primus,' together with that given out by our bodies, was sufficient to raise the temperature above freezing. The hoarfrost [which coated heavily the inside of the metal compartment], melting, dripped down our necks and spattered into our mugs of chocolate. . . . Spitsbergen was but eight hours away; maybe tomorrow we would be on the way! Thus passed our twenty-four ice-bound days, but on the twenty-fifth —the day we had actually set, two weeks previously, to start on foot for the Greenland coast, 400 miles away, which we knew we could not reach—our efforts to free the planes from the ice were rewarded, and one plane with six men in it rose and left that hell, forever." [3]

They reached Spitsbergen with but twenty-three gallons of gasoline left in the tank. "The scientific results, from an expedition that cost $150,000, consisted in the exploration of 120,000 square miles of hitherto unknown regions and the taking of two soundings which showed the depth of the Polar Sea at that latitude to be 12,000 feet, thus precluding the likelihood of any land on the European side of the North Pole." [3]

The next year, on May 9, 1926, Byrd flew from the very same place, King's Bay, Spitsbergen, to the North Pole and back. Despite his success his flight was of little importance in Arctic exploration. Amundsen and Ellsworth had already shown that there was no possibility of land along his track; unlike them, Byrd did not hazard a landing to take soundings. Two days after Byrd had flown to the Pole, Amundsen and Ellsworth, using the same base, started on their second flight. This time they planned to go from Spitsbergen to Alaska. Their craft was the *Norge,* a dirigible, whose designer, Colonel Umberto Nobile, acted as pilot. Their floating storehouse carried a large equipment, including tents, sleeping-bags, snowshoes, skis, arms and ammunition, a sledge, a big canvas boat, and provisions calculated to last the crew of sixteen men two months. Superb weather attended them at the start. "The sun shone brilliantly out of a sky of pure turquoise, and the whale-like shadow that our airship cast beneath us trailed monotonously across a glittering snow-field." [3] They could see whales and polar bears far below them. "Intermittent light fogs hid the ice from our view, rolling beneath us like a great woollen ocean," [3] the same fogs that had been so fatal to Andrée's unpowered airship. After sixteen hours they approached the spot where they had been frozen in the year previous—"what memories!" Soon afterward the navigator suddenly announced: "Here we are! as the sun's image started to cover his sextant bubble. We were over the North Pole! With motors throttled and heads uncovered we descended to within 300 feet of the ice and dropped the three flags [American, Norwegian, and Italian]. As we circled I hung over the side of the fuselage of our floating wings, lost in wonder at the sight of the goal, the attainment of which had acted as the motive force to produce some of the most wonderful journeys, in the face of terrible conditions, in the history of our race." [3]

Ellsworth then quotes Conrad: "There is no more evanescent quality in an accomplished fact than its wonderfulness. Solicited incessantly by the considerations affecting its fears and desires, the human mind turns naturally away from the marvellous side of events." The men squatted down to eat the one and only hot meal on the voyage from Spitsbergen to Alaska. "Hour after hour passed, but there was only the same glittering surface, rifted by wind and tide into cracks and leads of open water. . . . We reached the 'Ice Pole' five and a half hours later. This 'Ice Pole,' so called because it is the center of the Arctic ice mass and therefore the most inaccessible spot in the arctic regions, lies in latitude 86 N. and longitude 157 W. . . . The 16 men that looked down upon the chaos of broken ice-fields and pressure ridges of ice blocks, agreed that it would remain inaccessible except to aircraft." [3] As they approached the Alaskan coast, fog, sleet, and wind assailed them. "Ice coated the aerial wire and froze the windmill driver of our generator, which supplied the electrical energy to operate the transmitter and charge the storage batteries. All our efforts to establish communication with Alaska were of no avail. The last message from Alaska, before the wireless ceased to work, reported a cyclone that seemed to be stationary over Bering Sea. Ice crust formed in the bow of the ship, which was alarming, not only because it loaded her down, but also because it spoiled her trimming. Needless to say, our greatest danger lay in the ice that was torn loose from the sides of the ship by the whirling propellers and thrown against the gas bags. An ice block of the most fantastic shape settled on the sun compass, which stopped the clockwork and put it out of action for the rest of the trip." [3]

Forty-eight hours after starting they first sighted the Alaskan coast near Point Barrow. "Flat and snow covered, it was the most desolate looking coast line imaginable, but it was land and that was enough. Passing over the coast line [toward Nome], the fog became denser and denser . . . at last it became impossible to see any longer, and we rose through fog and cloud into bright sunshine." [3] For the next twenty-four hours, until they were able to find their exact position by identifying a message sent out by the Nome wireless station, they zigzagged around; for twenty-four hours they did not know whether they had gone too far west and were over Bering Strait or too far south and were over the Aleutian Islands. But eventually they found their way out of limbo. "At 3.30 on the morning of May 14, we rounded Cape Prince of Wales, and, tired but happy, brought our airship, coated with a ton of ice, safely to rest at the little trading post of Teller, 91 miles northwest of Nome, after a journey of 3,393 miles, lasting 72 hours, across the Polar Sea from Europe to America." [3]

Two years later, in 1928, the polar sea was again crossed in the opposite direction. George Hubert Wilkins, since knighted, who had received his Arctic training under Stefansson, flew in an airplane from Point Barrow to Deadman's Island, Spitsbergen, in twenty and one half hours. His sole companion was Carl Ben Eielson, the most famous pilot in Alaska. This successful flight was the third Wilkins had made within the Arctic. In 1926 he had made a reconnaissance flight over the Beaufort Sea. No land was sighted. The following year with Eielson he started on another, a longer, scouting flight. After flying 550 miles to the northwest, they were forced by engine trouble to land. This was the first time a land plane equipped with skis made a landing hundreds of miles from the shore on the heavy pack ice. While Eielson made the necessary repairs, Wilkins took two soundings that showed the ocean to be of great depth, precluding the possibility of land. When the temporary repairs were finished they started for home. A second time they had trouble, and again Eielson landed to make repairs. Flying once more, they encountered a blizzard, their speed was greatly reduced, and finally they ran out of gas. For the third time they landed without accident. Now their problems were preaeronautical, and they decided to travel light and fast. Carrying only their rifles and ammunition, cooking-gear, and bedding-rolls, they started walking for the nearest shore, seventy miles away. In this situation Wilkins proved that he had learned the art of "living off the country," and he and Eielson* reached the coast safely. Undaunted by this adventure, Wilkins kept on with his plans to fly from the New World to the Old. Without mishap he spanned the distance in less than a day.

But as if the Arctic resented the speed and certainty with which Wilkins had accomplished his phenomenal flight, within a month after his success there occurred one of the most disastrous of modern Arctic tragedies. The tragedy of the dirigible *Italia*, in which eight of the crew were lost, was immeasurably heightened by the fact that Roald Amundsen, one of the giants of polar exploration, and four companions were killed while aiding in the rescue. Amundsen died in trying to rescue a man with whom he had had a bitter quarrel. For the acrimonious dissension that arose between Amundsen and Nobile after the flight of the *Norge* led directly to the subsequent flight of the *Italia*. It was to validate his side of the argument that Nobile persuaded the Italian government to send out an Italian North Polar Expedition, and to give the expedition some semblance of value three surveys were included in its program. First, it was to fly eastward from Spitsbergen to chart the lands north of Russia; second, it was to fly to the North Pole and moor there for three weeks, landing a party of six men to make observations; and third, by several flights to the west it was to study the islands of the Canadian Archipelago. The crew of sixteen, except for the Swedish Professor Finn Malmgren

* Before his tragic death while on a routine commercial flight over Bering Strait (1929), Eielson had been the first man to pilot an airplane in the Antarctic.

and the Czech Professor Behounek, were all Italians. A hangar was built at King's Bay, Spitsbergen, and the steamer *Città di Milano* was sent there to act as a base ship.

On May 15 the *Italia* carried out the first part of her program and a week later started on the second part of the proposed task—the flight to the Pole. Here the original plans had to be altered. A protracted stay at the Pole was deemed inadvisable because of the way in which the airship became sheathed with ice. The landing-party had to be omitted, since the six men who were to stay at the Pole had taken passage for home after the *Italia's* first flight. A strong favoring wind sped the dirigible, and the flight to the Pole was made in record time. But it was this very wind that proved a terrific obstacle on the return journey. Soon the sun was clouded over. They had to fly low through the fog to determine their speed and drift. Progress was slow. The airship was heavily weighted by ice, and fragments thrown off from the propellers tore little rifts in the gas bag, which required constant patching. They did not know exactly where they were. Then they had trouble with the elevator helm. The engines were stopped, and the ship rose above the fog into strong sunlight. An observation showed that they were then 180 miles northeast of King's Bay. When the elevator had been repaired, they again descended into the fog. At 10 a.m. on the 25th they were flying low with a "bit of a list to bow." At 10.30 the engineer reported that the ship was heavy, down at the stern, and falling rapidly. Three minutes later the *Italia* crashed. Both the stern motor gondola and the pilot cabin were dragged away by the gas bag. Luckily one side of the pilot cabin fell out, strewing its inmates and contents over the floe. Nothing more was ever known of the six men in the gondola, who were carried off with the wrecked ship.

In the pilot cabin with Nobile were the two foreign professors, Captains Mariano and Zappi, the wireless operator Biaggi, Ceccioni the chief mechanic, and three others. Malmgren sustained a broken arm and Ceccioni a broken leg; otherwise all escaped unhurt. Fortunately the equipment that had been dumped with them, while scanty, was remarkably complete. They had a tent, a sleeping-bag, petrol, matches, revolver and cartridges, a Very pistol, a field radio outfit, and 155 pounds of provisions. Biaggi immediately set about getting the wireless in order, so that their rescuers would know where to locate them. For as days passed and the *Italia* failed to return to her base, the attention of all Europe was directed on rescue. And yet, in the absence of definite knowledge of the *Italia's* whereabouts, the disappearance of the airship, the search and rescue assumed, in the year 1928, the same bewildering proportions of the Franklin mystery seventy-five years before.

When the *Italia* had circled over the Pole, messages had been sent out to the King of Italy, the Pope, and Mussolini. Late that night the *Città di Milano* had been wirelessed that head winds were retarding the airship. That was the last message received. And when days had passed and vague apprehensions had crystallized into the certainty of disaster, then the world was faced with the great question: where had the *Italia* landed? Some said the *Italia* had come down near northern Greenland, others located the spot at Spitsbergen, and still others maintained that it was on Franz Josef Land. It began to look as though the rescuers would have to search over an area covering a quarter of the circumference of the earth. Of this uncertainty the survivors were well aware. Within a few hours of the crash Biaggi was able to send and receive messages. Almost at once they heard the San Paolo station near Rome announce anxiety at their failure to return. As the days passed, they learned of the tremendous concentration of relief ships and airplanes. It was maddeningly exasperating. They heard every message the *Città di Milano* sent out to them and to Rome; they heard of every searching-party that was going out; they knew that the search was being directed to the wrong spot—but they could not make themselves heard. To the men on the ice-floe it seemed as if their base ship did not want to hear them. Desperately they continued to send out their message, repeating over and over again S.O.S.F.O.Y.N.C.I.R.C.A.

A Russian peasant living near Archangel, a wireless amateur, was the first to catch the S O S on June 2. He heard it faintly between two concert broadcasts. Immediately the local Soviet notified Moscow. Then for a day confusion reigned. It was deemed impossible for an amateur to get what all the powerful stations had been unable to pick up; it was taken as a bid for notoriety. To add to the bewilderment no one knew what FOYN CIRCA meant. It was curiously misinterpreted to mean Francesco—Franz Josef Land. And the confusion was made grotesque by the fact that the ice-party and the base ship had wirelesses that worked on different wave-lengths. It was Professor Samoilovich, director of the Soviet Institute of Arctic Research, who located Foyn as a small island northeast of Spitsbergen and, from a study of weather conditions, was convinced that it was near there the party was to be found. On June 6 Biaggi received, via San Paolo: "The Soviet Embassy has informed the Italian government . . ." and the survivors knew that their location was known.

Men of five nations joined in the rescue. Two Norwegian sealers, each carrying an aviator—Captain Riiser-Larsen and Lieutenant Holm—were sent out. Sweden sent out two ships, likewise equipped with planes to aid in the search. The Swedish aviators were Lieutenants Lundborg and Schiberd and Captain Tornberg. Italy sent north a big Savoia airplane, piloted by Major Maddalena, to assist the base ship. France put the seaplane *Latham,* with a crew of four, at the disposal of Amundsen. By June 9 the rescue work was started in earnest. By then the base ship was in direct communication with Biaggi. The facts of the disaster were known, and it was also learned that on May 30 three men, Malmgren, Mariano, and Zappi, had started out to reach Northeast Land in the hope of finding a fishing-ship. The aerial rescue work was begun on June 16 on a large scale. The Norwegian aviators were the first to pass near the missing men, but they failed to see them because of the blinding reflection of the ice. Two days later Amundsen and the Frenchmen set out for the ice-fields. On the 20th Maddaléna sighted Nobile's party, and two days later he returned to drop supplies by parachute. Neither time did he risk a landing. By now serious concern was felt for Amundsen's party, who had not been heard from, and rescue work was begun for the rescuers. Nothing more was ever seen of them. But proof that they had all perished came when, at the beginning of September, a float of one of the seaplane's wings was picked up near the Norwegian coast. No other trace has ever been found of Amundsen and his companions.

On June 24 Lundborg, chancing a hazardous landing, brought away Nobile. It was for allowing himself to be rescued before his companions that Nobile was later reduced in rank. The next day Lundborg flew to bring back Ceccioni, who had suffered a fractured leg in the crash. This time the Swedish aviator wrecked his plane beyond repair on the rough ice and found himself stranded with the men he had hoped to rescue. Then for two weeks, though many flights were made, nothing much happened. Time was pressing, for the ice was breaking up, thereby reducing the chance of bringing a plane down. On July 6 Schiberd made a risky landing and carried off his compatriot Lundborg. It was then generally felt that rescuers by air could do no more than drop supplies; there was not the slightest chance of landing to remove the men from the ice-floe. As for the three men who had started for Northeast Land more than a month before, they were given up for dead.

But all this time the Russians had been making their effort toward rescuing the stranded party. Two Russian ice-breakers, the *Krassin* and the *Malygin,* each equipped with a scouting-airplane, had been ordered to Spitsbergen. With scarcely any publicity they had been steadily steaming toward Foyn Island, and it was only the day after the Swedish aviators had declared rescue by plane to be out of the question that all hope centered on the *Krassin.*

Professor Samoilovich was in charge of the operations, and the aviator co-operating with the ship was Chukhnovsky. On July 30 the *Krassin,* her engines working to the limit, was six miles to the north of Spitsbergen. That evening the vessel reached the edge of the pack ice and began cutting her channel. For several days she smashed her way through—a slow, hard, but effective advance. For every foot of those many miles the *Krassin* had to drive her bow into the ice, crack it under her, back off, and drive her bow up again until the ice had split asunder. And the pack was solid, without a single lead to help speed the ship. On July 7 a large level stretch of ice was transformed into a flying-field. The next day Chukhnovsky made his first flight. The day after, a heavy fog fell. But on the 10th Chukhnovsky reported by radio to his ship that he had spied men on the ice and gave their location. It was the ill-fated Malmgren party. Unfortunately a fog blew up, obscured the *Krassin,* and forced Chukhnovsky to land where the visibility was better. He brought his plane down safely near Cape Wrede, on Northeast Land. The *Krassin* went ahead, forcing a way to where the Malmgren party had been reported. On the 12th Zappi and Mariano were rescued. Malmgren was not with them, for he had died, under conditions not made quite clear. It is on account of the grave charge levelled at Zappi—the charge of cannibalism, of killing a man in order to eat him—that the *Italia* Expedition has always been spoken of with horror. In this, Mariano had no part, for he was almost dead of starvation and cold when he was rescued, and he died a few months afterward.

Fourteen miles away the main party was located and taken aboard. Four days later Chukhnovsky and his plane were reached. On July 18 the *Krassin* reached open water and steamed slowly back to King's Bay. There the survivors were transferred to the *Città di Milano.* The chunky, stolid *Krassin* had won in her duel with the pack and had saved the survivors of the *Italia.* Thus was ended a heroic, disastrous flight to the Pole. It has remained a highly controversial episode.

There have been no more flights to the Pole, though flying in the Arctic has continued. In 1931 an American, Parker Cramer, and a German, Captain Wolfgang von Gronau, made separate attempts to test the feasibility of flying from Europe to America by the northern route. Cramer, the first to fly across the Greenland Ice-Cap, was lost at sea; von Gronau, following his trail a month later, reached Chicago safely on a flight from Iceland.

As in Elizabethan times, men are interested in the Arctic as providing the shortest route between the two hemispheres. And lest it be thought that interest in the Arctic or experimenting with new means of transport in that difficult area has ceased, it is well to remember that in 1932 Wilkins, the daring Australian explorer, tried for the first time to cross the Arctic Sea by submarine. Men had walked over the pack, men had flown over the pack; why not try to advance under the pack? His attempt was unsuccessful, handicapped as it was by an old and decrepit submarine, the *Nautilus,* but his spirit was admirable.

Is Arctic exploration a thing of the past? To that question Debenham has given the fitting answer: "In the past the element of romance which is inseparable from polar exploration has been at once a help and a hindrance: a help in that it has attracted at the same time both financial support and the services of men with high ideals; a hindrance in that it has overshadowed the scientific side of exploration and has tended to alienate the interest of those who are proof against sentiment. Discovery in the geographical sense will soon be a thing of the past, for we shall shortly know, at least in outline, the main geographical features in every part of the world. But exploration—the more detailed examination of unfrequented tracts—is likely to provide work for geographical pioneers for the next century or longer."

And so the work will go on, for the Arctic, despite the fact that its main outlines are known and charted, is still a vast "unfrequented tract."

Appendices

APPENDIX I

Further Exploration in Spitsbergen

THIS phase of exploration received its last important addition when Giles Land was added to the maps in 1707. In that year the Dutch whaling-captain, Cornelis Giles, after sailing first to the north, then to the east, and finally to the southeast of the archipelago, sighted very high land. This island, the easternmost one of the Spitsbergen group, was subsequently seen occasionally, but not until 1898 was it circumnavigated and briefly visited by Professor Nathorst. Of it he wrote: "Giles Land was glittering white from its highest summit down to the very edge of the sea. It was covered throughout with its soft mantle of snow; not a rock projected through it to break its spotless purity. The island rose in regular curves to an altitude of 600 or 700 feet, and was one continuous mass of ice and snow. The ice plunges down into the sea all around the island (except at the N.E. and S.W. ends), and is quite inaccessible, being abruptly broken off at the water's edge. With the sun shining upon it White Island [as Giles Land was renamed] must be a fascinating object." It was to this haven that Andrée and his two companions came after they had landed from their balloon. And on that speck of land, shrouded in snow and ice, they died. (See Chapter XXI.)

In 1764 Catherine the Great of Russia sent an expedition to Spitsbergen to determine whether or not an open sea route existed between there and the Far East. An advance party under Lieutenant Nemtinov established a post that same year at Recherche Bay. The following year the main expedition under the command of Captain Chichagov sailed from Archangel. They spent a fortnight at Bell Sound and then headed northward to carry out their instructions. After another fortnight of sailing around through drift ice they turned back for Russia. The expedition tried again the next year, but its results were equally fruitless. The project was abandoned.

It is impossible to write of Spitsbergen without paying tribute to the work of William Scoresby, Jr. The many profitable voyages he made to Spitsbergen waters he described himself in his two great books (see Chapter

XVII). They "summed up the Arctic knowledge of his day and laid a firm foundation for future advance."

If it was the early whalers who first unraveled the outlines of Spitsbergen, it was the Norwegian sealing-captains who played as impressive a role in the later phase of exploration. In 1863 Captain Carlsen circumnavigated the whole of Spitsbergen for the first time. During the last half of the nineteenth century the voyages of Captains Lund, Tobiesen, Aarström, Mathilas, Altman, Johnsen, and Nilsen revealed in detail the northern and eastern coasts. But whereas the successive explorations of the early whalers resulted in a confusion of names and places, the magnificent navigation and valuable data of the sealers was systematically arranged by Professor Mohn. He saw to it that their work was not lost, was not buried in obscure fishing-logs.

The scientific exploration of Spitsbergen was started at the beginning of the last century and in the main was carried out by an important series of Swedish expeditions. In 1827, the very year that Parry tried to reach the Pole from his base at Treurenberg Bay (see Chapter XX), Keilhau, a geologist, modestly began this study. Ten years later Professor Lovén, inspired by Keilhau's work, examined the geology of the west coast. It was Lovén who, twenty years later, induced Torell to extend the scope of the observations. All branches of natural history were to be included. In 1858 and 1861 Torell and Nordenskiöld led expeditions to Spitsbergen. Three years later Nordenskiöld took another group of scientists there, and in 1868 he returned and explored the northern coast and part of Northeast Land. In 1872 Nordenskiöld tried to reach the Pole from his base at Mossel Bay (see Chapter XVIII). The next year he crossed Northeast Land and touched at Seven Islands. During the International Circumpolar Year the Swedes occupied a station at Ice Fiord (see Chapter XV). In 1890 Gustaf Nordenskiöld went overland from Horn Sound to Bell Sound, and from Advent Bay to Coles Bay. He also studied various other harbors. From 1898 to 1900 the Swedes in conjunction with the Russians measured an arc of the meridian.

Thus by the close of the nineteenth century the outlines of Spitsbergen were almost entirely known and had been delineated with great accuracy. But exploration had not pierced deeply beyond the coastal fringe. Not until Sir Martin Conway, leading a small party, crossed Spitsbergen for the first time, was the nature of the interior revealed. The region between Ice and Bell Sounds and Agardh Bay was traversed. The party then headed north, visited some of the bays on that coast, and then went south along the full length of Hinlopen Strait to Wiche Islands. The following season they covered a more northerly section and surveyed Horn Sound. Conway is also the author of *No Man's Land,* the authoritative history of Spitsbergen.

As early as 1871 a tourist steamer called at Spitsbergen. Yachtsmen had been touching there ever since Lord Dufferin visited English Bay in 1856.

The role Spitsbergen has assumed since the beginning of Arctic flying has been told in Chapter XXI.

One of the most unexpected recent developments in Spitsbergen has been the opening and operation of coal mines. In 1900 a shaft was sunk by a Trondheim company on the south shore of Ice Fiord. "After blasting through 40 feet of clear fossil ice, solid rock was reached, and 20 feet lower a seam of coal 10 ft. thick." Near by in Longyear City, a mine started and successfully run by an American, the coal is mined throughout the year. It is stored in great bins until it can be shipped out during the summer. This American venture proved so profitable that other nationalities hastened to exploit the extensive coal beds, of which about three quarters are of an excellent grade. And so a third phase might be said to have begun for Spitsbergen, and once again, as in the beginning, her resources are being carried southward to enrich many nations.

APPENDIX II

List of Franklin Search Parties

1847–50. Sir John Richardson and his second, Dr. Rae. Overland, and along the coast in boats, from the Mackenzie to the Coppermine.

1848–52. Capt. Thomas Moore of H.M.S. *Plover*. To Bering St.

1848–50. Capt. Henry Kellett of H.M.S. *Herald*. To Bering St.

1848–50. Robert Sheldon, in yacht *Nancy Dawson*. To Bering St.

1848–9. Capt. Sir James Clarke Ross of H.M.S. *Enterprise*. To Lancaster Sd.

1848–9. Capt. E. J. Bird of H.M.S. *Investigator*. To accompany the *Enterprise*.

1849–50. James Saunders of H.M.S. *North Star*. To Wolstenholme Sd. and Pond Bay.

1849. Dr. Robert Goodsir in the whaler *Advice*. To Baffin Bay.

1849. Lt. W. J. S. Pullen of H.M.S. *Herald*. Boat voyage from Bering St. to the Mackenzie. Commanded 5 boats from *Herald, Plover,* and *Nancy* in effort to go east.

1850–1. Lt. De Haven, U.S.N., in the *Advance,* fitted at the expense of Henry Grinnell of New York. To Lancaster Sd. and Wellington Ch.

1850–1. S. P. Griffen, U.S.N., in the *Rescue,* at the expense of Mr. Grinnell. To Lancaster Sd. and Wellington Ch.

1850–1. Capt. Horatio Austin of H.M.S. *Resolute*. To Lancaster Sd. and Cornwallis Ld.

1850–1. Capt. Ommanney of H.M.S. *Assistance*. To accompany Capt. Austin.

1850–1.   William Penny, master of the *Lady Franklin* under British Admiralty orders. To Lancaster Sd. and Wellington Ch.

1850–1.   Alex. Stewart, master of the *Sophia,* under British Admiralty orders. To Lancaster Sd. and Wellington Ch.

1850–1.   Rear-Admiral Sir John Ross in the yacht *Felix,* fitted at the expense of Hudson's Bay Co. To Lancaster Sd.

1850.   Capt. C. C. Forsyth, commanding the *Prince Albert,* belonging to Lady Franklin. To Prince Regent Inlet and Beechey I.

1850–4.   Capt. Robert McClure of H.M.S. *Investigator.* To Bering St., Banks I., and Lancaster Sd. The crews were forced to abandon ship and, by walking over the ice to Beechey I., in a strictly technical sense completed the Northwest Passage.

1850–5.   Capt. Richard Collinson of H.M.S. *Enterprise.* To Bering St., Banks I., and along the southern or Continental Ch. to Cambridge Bay, near King William Ld., whence he retraced his course to England. He shares with McClure the honor of having technically achieved the Northwest Passage.

1851.   Dr. Rae, employed by the British Admiralty, descended the Coppermine and traced Wollaston Ld. from its eastern extremity to its junction with Victoria Ld., and up to the parallel of the north end of King William Ld. in Victoria St.

1851–2.   William Kennedy, master of the *Prince Albert,* belonging to Lady Franklin. To Prince Regent Inlet, Bellot St., and Prince of Wales I.

1852.   Capt. Charles Frederick of H.M.S. *Amphitrite.* To Bering St.

1852.   Capt. Edward Inglefield in the *Isabel,* Lady Franklin's vessel. To Smith Sd.

1852–5.   Capt. Rochfort Maguire of H.M.S. *Plover.* To Bering St.

1852.   Dr. R. McCormick. A boat excursion in Wellington Ch.

1852–4.   Capt. Sir Edward Belcher of H.M.S. *Assistance.* To Wellington Ch.

1852–4.   Capt. Henry Kellett of H.M.S. *Resolute.* To Lancaster Sd., Melville and Banks Is.

1852–4.   Lt. Sherard Osborn of H.M.S. *Pioneer.* To Wellington Ch.

1852–4.   Capt. Francis Leopold McClintock of H.M.S. *Intrepid.* To Lancaster Sd. and Prince Arthur I.

1852–4.   Capt. W. S. J. Pullen of H.M.S. *North Star.* To Beechey I.

1853.   William Fawckner, master of *Breadalbone Transport.* To Beechey I. Crushed in the ice and foundered.

1853.   Lt. Elliott, of the store ship *Diligence.*

1853.   Capt. E. A. Inglefield of H.M.S. *Phœnix.* To Beechey I.

1853.   Dr. Rae of the Hudson's Bay Co., acting under British Admiralty orders. By sledge to Wollaston Ld., and boat voyage to Victoria St., between that island and King William Ld.

1853–4.   Dr. Rae, at the expense of the Hudson's Bay Co. To Repulse Bay, and east side of King William Ld., bringing the first intelligence of the loss of the *Erebus* and *Terror* and their crews.

List of Franklin Search Parties

1853–5. Dr. Elisha Kent Kane, U.S.N. To Smith Sd., Humboldt Glacier, and Grinnell Ld.

1854. Capt. E. A. Inglefield of H.M.S. *Phœnix*. To Beechey I.

1854. Commander Jenkins of the *Talbot*. To Beechey I.

1855. John Anderson, chief factor of the Hudson's Bay Co. Canoe voyage down the Great Fish R. to Montreal I. and Pt. Ogle, procuring further relics of the *Erebus* and *Terror*.

1857–9. Capt. Leopold McClintock in the *Fox*, Lady Franklin's yacht. To Peel Sd., Prince Regent Inlet, Bellot St., King William Ld., and Montreal I., bringing precise intelligence of the fate of the *Erebus* and *Terror* and a short record of their proceedings.

1864–9. Charles Francis Hall. Living and traveling with Eskimos, by sledge across Rae Isthmus to King William Ld.; Todd I., where he found relics of the men and learned all the natives had to tell of the disaster.

1878–9. Lt. Schwatka, U.S.A., and W. H. Gilder. By sledge to Back R., across Simpson St. to King William Ld. Five months' extensive search yields relics, traces of McClintock, corroboration of Eskimo stories.

APPENDIX III

Chronology of Northern Exploration

NOTE: *This chronology does not attempt to be all-inclusive. Only the more important expeditions have been listed, as well as those less important ones that were led by outstanding persons.*

330 B. C. *ca.*	Pytheas of Massilia	Britain
870 A. D. *ca.*	Rabna Floki	Iceland
875 *ca.*	Ottar	Kola Peninsula, White Sea
983	Erik the Red	Greenland
1000	Leif Eriksson	America
1360 *ca.*	Nicholas of Lynn	
1497	John Cabot	Newfoundland
1500–1	Cortereals	Labrador
1553	Willoughby, Chancellor	Russia
1556	Borough	Russia
1576–8	Frobisher—three voyages	Baffin Island
1580	Pet, Jackman	Kara Sea
1584	Brunel	Kara Sea

1585–7	Davis—three voyages	Davis Strait
1594–5	Nai, Tetgales, Barents—two voyages	Spitsbergen
1596–7	Ryp, Heemskerck, Barents	Novaya Zemlya
1603–4	Cunningham, Knight, Hall —two voyages	Greenland
1606	Knight	Labrador
1607–10	Hudson—three voyages	Greenland, Spitsbergen, Jan Mayen, Hudson River, Hudson Bay
1609–14	Poole, Marmaduke, Baffin, and others—many voyages	Spitsbergen
1612	Button, Bylot	Hudson Bay
1615–16	Baffin, Bylot—two voyages	Hudson Bay, Baffin Bay
1619–20	Munk	Hudson Bay
1631–2	James	Hudson Bay
1631–2	Fox	Hudson Bay
1648	Dezhnev	Northeastern Siberia
1707	Giles	Spitsbergen
1721	Egede	Greenland
1725–42	Great Northern Expedition: Bering, Chirikov, Khariton and Dmitri Laptev, Chelyuskin, and others	Bering Sea, Arctic Siberia
1730	Gvosdev	Alaska
1741	Middleton	Hudson Bay
1746–7	Moore	Hudson Bay
1751	Wallöe	S.E. Greenland
1760–2	Shalaurov	Arctic Siberia
1761	Christopher	Hudson Bay
1762	Norton	Hudson Bay
1769	Hearne	Coppermine R.
1770–3	Lyakhov—two voyages	New Siberian Is.
1773	Phipps	Spitsbergen
1778	Cook	N.E. Siberia, Alaska
1788	Billings	N.E. Siberia
1789	Mackenzie	Mackenzie R.
1806–13	Giesecke	Greenland
1809–10	Hedenström, Sannikov	Islands N. of Siberia
1818	Buchan, Franklin	Spitsbergen
1818	John Ross, Parry	Baffin Bay
1819–20	Parry	American Arctic Archipelago
1819–22	Franklin and others	N. coastline of America (land)
1820–3	Wrangel, Anjou	N.E. Siberia (land)
1821–3	Parry	American Arctic Archipelago
1822	Scoresby	East Greenland

1823	Clavering, Sabine	East Greenland
1824	Lyon	Hudson Bay
1924–5	Parry	American Arctic Archipelago
1825–6	Beechey	Pt. Barrow
1825–7	Franklin and others	N. coastline of America (land)
1827	Parry	Sea N. of Spitsbergen
1828–9	Graah	E. Greenland
1829–33	John and James C. Ross	N. Magnetic Pole
1833–4	Back	Great Fish River (land)
1836–7	Back	Hudson Bay
1837–9	Dease and Simpson	N. coast of America (land)
1846–7	Rae	N. coast of America (land)
1845–8	Franklin and others	Northwest Passage
1848–51	Kellett	Franklin search
1848–9	James Ross, McClintock	Franklin search
1850–4	Collinson, McClure	Franklin search
1851	Rae	Franklin search
1850–1	De Haven	Franklin search
1850–1	Austin, Ommanney, John Ross, and others	Franklin search
1851–2	Kennedy, Bellot	Franklin search
1852	Inglefield	Franklin search
1852–4	Belcher, McClintock, Kellett, and others	Franklin search
1853–4	Rae	Franklin search
1853–5	Kane	Franklin search (Greenland)
1857–8	McClintock	Franklin search
1858 1861	} Torrell, Nordenskiöld	Spitsbergen
1860–1	Hayes	Greenland
1863	Carlsen	Circumnavigation of Spitsbergen
1864 1868	} Nordenskiöld	Spitsbergen
1869–71	Koldewey, Hegemann	E. Greenland
1870	Nordenskiöld	Greenland Ice-Cap
1871–3	Hall	Smith Sd.
1872–3	Nordenskiöld	Spitsbergen
1872–4	Payer, Weyprecht	Franz Josef Land
1875–7	Nares and others	Northern Ellesmere I., Greenland
1875–6	Young	Lancaster Sd., Smith Sd.
1878–9	Nordenskiöld	Northeast Passage
1879–82	De Long	New Siberian Is.
1880–1	Leigh Smith—two voyages	Spitsbergen, Franz Josef Land

1881–4	Greely	Ellesmere I., Greenland
1882–3	First International Circumpolar Year	
1883–5	Holm, Garde	E. Greenland
1888	Nansen	Crossing Greenland Ice-Cap
1891–2	Peary	N. Greenland
1893–6	Nansen, Sverdrup	Drift across polar basin
1893–5	Peary	N. Greenland
1894–7	Jackson	Franz Josef Land
1896–7	Conway	Spitsbergen
1898–1902	Peary	N. Ellesmere I., N. Greenland
1898–1902	Sverdrup	Sverdrup Archipelago
1899–1900	Duke of the Abruzzi	N. of Franz Josef Land
1900	Amdrup and others	E. Greenland
1903–5	Amundsen	Northwest Passage
1905–6	Peary	N. of Greenland
1906–8	Mylius Erichsen, J. P. Koch, and others	N.E. Greenland
1908–9	Peary	North Pole
1908–9	Cook	
1908–12	Stefansson, Anderson	Victoria Island
1909–12	Mikkelsen	N.E. Greenland
1912	Rasmussen, Freuchen	N.E. Greenland
1912–3	J. P. Koch	N.E. Greenland
1913–5	Vilkitski	Northeast Passage
1913–7	MacMillan	"Crocker Land"
1913–8	Stefansson, Bartlett, Anderson—Canadian Arctic Expedition	Beaufort Sea
1916–9	Rasmussen, Wulff, Lauge Koch	N.W. Greenland
1920–3	Lauge Koch	N. Greenland
1923–4	Rasmussen	Northwest Passage by land
1930–1	British Arctic Air Route Expedition, Wegener, Hobbs	Greenland
1930–2	Ushakov	Northern Land
1932–3	Second International Circumpolar Year	
	Main Administration of the Northern Sea Route	Arctic Siberia
1937–8	Papanin	North Pole

AVIATION

1897	Andrée, Strindberg, Frænkel
1924	Binney
1925	Amundsen, Ellsworth

Chronology of Northern Exploration

1926	Byrd
1926	Amundsen, Ellsworth, Nobile
1928	Wilkins and Eielson, Nobile
1932	Wilkins's attempt in the submarine *Nautilus*
1937	Chkalov and Gromov

References

NOTE: *The following references do not constitute a complete bibliography of all the source material on which this work is based, but are merely a list of those books from which quotations have been taken as indicated by the superior figures at the end of each quotation. Grateful acknowledgment is made to the publishers and authors who have given permission to use copyrighted material from the following list.*

I. Arctic Scenery

1. CHARLES F. HALL: *Arctic Researches, and Life among the Esquimaux.* Harper & Bros., New York, 1865.
2. KNUD RASMUSSEN: *Greenland by the Polar Sea.* W. Heinemann, London, 1921; F. A. Stokes, New York, 1921.

II. Quest and Conquest

1. FRANK DEBENHAM: *The Polar Regions.* Ernest Benn, London, 1930.
2. ROBERT F. SCOTT: *The Voyage of the Discovery.* Smith, Elder & Co., London, 1905; Charles Scribner's Sons, New York, 1928.
3. G. B. PARKS: *Richard Hakluyt and the English Voyages.* American Geographical Society, New York, 1928.
4. JOHN MILTON: *Paradise Lost.*
5. JOHN MILTON: *Samson Agonistes.*
6. JOHN L. LOWES: *The Road to Xanadu.* Houghton, Mifflin Co., Boston, 1927.
7. F. NANSEN: *In Northern Mists, Arctic Exploration in Early Times.* W. Heinemann, London, 1911; F. A. Stokes, New York, 1911.

III. The Greeks and the Vikings

1. F. NANSEN: *In Northern Mists.*
2. SIR CLEMENTS MARKHAM: *The Lands of Silence.* The University Press, Cambridge, 1921.
3. LORD DUFFERIN: *Letters from High Latitudes.* Adams, Stevenson & Co., Toronto, 1873; J. M. Dent & Sons, London, and E. P. Dutton & Co., New York, 1910.
4. JOHN L. LOWES: *The Road to Xanadu.*

References

IV. The Paths to Cathay

1. JOHN L. LOWES: *The Road to Xanadu.*
2. G. B. PARKS: *Richard Hakluyt and the English Voyages.*
3. F. NANSEN: *In Northern Mists.*
4. HARVEY FERGUSSON: *Rio Grande.* Alfred A. Knopf, New York, 1933.
5. F. NANSEN: *Farthest North.* Harper & Bros., New York and London, 1903.
6. SIR JOHN BARROW: *Chronological History of Voyages into the Arctic Regions.* J. Murray, London, 1818.
7. RICHARD HAKLUYT: *Principal Navigations . . . of the English Nation.* London, 1598–1600, and Edinburgh, 1884–90. Edited by Edmund Goldsmid.
8. SIR CLEMENTS MARKHAM: *The Lands of Silence.*

V. The Dutch in the Arctic

1. MILTON WALDMAN: *The Omnibus Book of Travellers' Tales.* L. Stein, London, 1931; Brentano's, New York.
2. GERRIT DE VEER: *The Three Voyages of William Barents to the Arctic Regions.* Printed for the Hakluyt Society, London, 1876.

VI. Smeerenburg and the Whale-Oil Rush

1. EMILY JAMES PUTNAM: *The Lady.* Sturgis & Walton Co., New York, 1910; G. P. Putnam's Sons, New York and London, 1933.
2. G. B. PARKS: *Richard Hakluyt and the English Voyages.*
3. SIR MARTIN CONWAY: *No Man's Land; a History of Spitsbergen.* Cambridge University Press, 1906.
4. *Churchill's Voyages,* Vol. IV. I. Walthoe, London, 1732.
5. LORD DUFFERIN: *Letters from High Latitudes.*

VII. Hudson and His Strait; Baffin and His Bay

1. SIR JOHN BARROW: *Chronological History of Voyages into the Arctic Regions.*
2. CAPTAIN LUKE FOX: *North-West Fox; or Fox from the North-West Passage.* Edited by Miiler Christy. Hakluyt Society, London, 1894.
3. SIR CLEMENTS MARKHAM: *The Lands of Silence.*
4. SAMUEL PURCHAS: *Hakluytus Posthumus or Purchas His Pilgrimes.* T. MacLehose & Sons, Glasgow, 1905–7.

VIII. Russia

1. F. A. GOLDER: *Russian Expansion on the Pacific, 1641–1850.* Arthur H. Clark Co., Cleveland, 1914.

IX. After the Great Northern Expedition

1. BARON A. E. NORDENSKIÖLD: *Voyage of the Vega around Asia and Europe.* Macmillan, London, 1881; New York, 1882.

2. CAPTAIN JAMES COOK: *A Voyage to the Pacific Ocean.* Vol. III by Captain James King. G. Nichol & T. Cadell, London, 1784.

3. FERDINAND WRANGEL: *Narrative of an Expedition to the Polar Sea, 1820–23.* James Madden, London, 1840.

4. L. S. BERG: "Reports on Bering Strait and Its Shores before Bering and Cook," *Journal of Hydrography,* Vol. II (XLIII), No. 2. Petrograd: 10th Government Printing Office of Admiralty, 1920.

5. WALDEMAR JOCHELSON: *Peoples of Asiatic Russia.* American Museum of Natural History, New York, 1928.

6. F. A. GOLDER: *Russian Expansion on the Pacific, 1641–1850.* Arthur H. Clark Co., Cleveland, 1914.

X. The British Attack the Arctic

1. KNUD RASMUSSEN: *Across Arctic America.* G. P. Putnam's Sons, New York and London, 1927.

2. SIR MARTIN CONWAY: *No Man's Land.*

3. CAPTAIN F. W. BEECHEY: *Voyage of Discovery towards the North Pole.* R. Bentley, London, 1843.

4. SIR JOHN ROSS: *Voyage of Discovery in H.M. Ships Isabella and Alexander.* London, 1819.

5. SIR EDWARD PARRY: *Journal of a Voyage for the Discovery of the N.W. Passage in 1819–20.* John Murray, London, 1821.

6. SIR CLEMENTS MARKHAM: *The Lands of Silence.*

7. SIR EDWARD PARRY: *Journal of a Second Voyage in 1821–23.* London, 1824.

8. SIR EDWARD PARRY: *Journal of a Third Voyage in 1824–25.* London, 1826.

9. SIR JOHN ROSS: *Narrative of a Second Voyage in Search of a N.W. Passage.* London, 1835.

10. CAPTAIN GEORGE BACK: *Narrative of an Expedition in H.M.S. Terror in 1836–37.* John Murray, London, 1838.

11. SAMUEL HEARNE: *Journey to the Northern Ocean.*

12. SIR JOHN FRANKLIN: *Narrative of a Journey to the Shores of the Polar Sea, in 1819–22.* John Murray, London, 1823.

13. SIR JOHN FRANKLIN: *Narrative of a Second Expedition . . . 1825–27.* John Murray, London, 1828.

14. SIR GEORGE BACK: *Narrative of the Arctic Land Expedition to the Mouth of the Great Fish River.* John Murray, London, 1836.

15. THOMAS SIMPSON: *Narrative of Discoveries on the North Coast of America.* Richard Bentley, London, 1843.

16. DR. JOHN RAE: *Narrative of an Expedition to the Shores of the Arctic Sea in 1846–47.* London, 1850.

XI. Franklin's Last Voyage

1. SIR ALLEN YOUNG: *Cruise of the Pandora.* W. Clowes & Sons, London, 1876.

References

XII. The Mystery of the Missing Ships

1. SIR CLEMENTS MARKHAM: *The Lands of Silence.*
2. J.-R. BELLOT: *Journal d'un voyage aux mers polaires.* 1851.
3. CAPTAIN SHERARD OSBORN: *The Discovery of the North-West Passage . . . by Captain McClure.* Edinburgh, London, 1865.
4. DR. JOHN RAE: *Report of the Arctic Searching Expedition under His Command.* Parliamentary papers, London, 1855.
5. CAPTAIN LEOPOLD MCCLINTOCK: *Voyage of the Fox in the Arctic Seas.* London, 1859.
6. SIR EDWARD BELCHER: *The Last of the Arctic Voyages . . . 1852–4.* London, 1855.

XIII. The Route to the North

1. WILLIAM ELDER: *Biography of Elisha Kent Kane.* Philadelphia, London, 1858.
2. DR. E. K. KANE: *Arctic Explorations.* Childs & Petersen, Philadelphia, 1856.
3. C. F. HALL: *Arctic Researches.*
4. C. F. HALL: *Narrative of the North Polar Expedition. U.S. Ship Polaris.* Government Printing Office, Washington, 1876.
5. SIR GEORGE NARES: *Narrative of a Voyage to the Polar Sea during 1875–6.* S. Low, Marston, Searle & Rivington, London, 1878.
6. SIR CLEMENTS MARKHAM: *The Lands of Silence.*
7. KNUD RASMUSSEN: *Greenland by the Polar Sea.*

XIV. Franz Josef Land

1. JULIUS VON PAYER: *New Lands within the Arctic Circle.* Macmillan, London, 1876.
2. FREDERICK JACKSON: *A Thousand Days in the Arctic.* Harper & Bros., New York, London, 1899.
3. DUKE OF THE ABRUZZI: *On the Polar Star in the Arctic Sea.* London, 1903.

XV. The International Circumpolar Stations

1. LIEUTENANT A. W. GREELY: *Three Years of Arctic Service.* Charles Scribner's Sons, New York, 1886.
2. MAJOR-GENERAL A. W. GREELY: *Polar Regions in the Twentieth Century.* Little, Brown & Co., Boston, 1928.
3. COMMANDER W. S. SCHLEY: *The Rescue of Greely.* Charles Scribner's Sons, New York, 1885.

XVI. Laying a Ghost

1. EMMA DE LONG: *The Voyage of the Jeannette.* Houghton, Mifflin Co., Boston, 1884.
2. F. NANSEN: *First Crossing of Greenland.* Longmans, Green, London and New York, 1890.

3. F. NANSEN: *Farthest North.*
4. FREDERICK JACKSON: *A Thousand Days in the Arctic.*
5. LEWIS GANNETT, in a review of Sörensen's *Saga of Fridtjof Nansen* in the *Herald Tribune,* New York, October 20, 1932.

XVII. Greenland

1. SIR CLEMENTS MARKHAM: *The Lands of Silence.*
2. F. NANSEN: *Farthest North.*
3. SCORESBY LOG BOOKS. *Seven Log Books Concerning Arctic Voyages of Captain Wm. Scoresby, Sr.* Explorers Club, New York, 1916–17.
4. SIR MARTIN CONWAY: *No Man's Land.*
5. JULIUS VON PAYER: *New Lands within the Arctic Circle.*
6. KARL KOLDEWEY: *The German Arctic Expedition of 1869–70.* Washington, 1871.
7. ROBERT E. PEARY: *Nearest the Pole.* Doubleday, Page, New York, 1907.
8. EINAR MIKKELSEN: *Lost in the Arctic.* G. H. Doran, New York, 1913.
9. KNUD RASMUSSEN: *Greenland by the Polar Sea.*
10. LAUGE KOCH, articles in the *Geographical Journal,* Vols. LXII, LXIV.
11. MARTIN VAHL (editor): *Greenland.* H. Milford, London, 1928.
12. JACOB WASSERMANN: *Bula Matari.* Liveright, New York, 1933.
13. F. NANSEN: *First Crossing of Greenland.*
14. ROBERT E. PEARY: *Northward over the Great Ice.* New York, 1898.
15. F. SPENCER CHAPMAN: *Northern Lights.* Chatto & Windus, London, 1932; Oxford University Press, New York, 1933.

XVIII. The Northeast and Northwest Passages

1. MAJOR-GENERAL A. W. GREELY: *The Polar Regions in the Twentieth Century.*
2. BARON A. E. NORDENSKIÖLD: *The Voyage of the Vega around Asia and Europe.*
3. LIEUTENANT A. HOVGAARD: *Nordenskiöld's Voyage around Asia and Europe.* London, 1882.
4. SIR CLEMENTS MARKHAM: *The Lands of Silence.*
5. ROALD AMUNDSEN: *The Northwest Passage.* A. Constable & Co., London, 1908; E. P. Dutton & Co., New York, 1908.

XIX. Jones Sound and Beaufort Sea

1. OTTO SVERDRUP: *New Land.* Longmans, Green & Co., London, 1904.
2. DONALD MACMILLAN: *Four Years in the White North.* Harper & Bros., New York and London, 1918.
3. CAPTAIN "BOB" BARTLETT: *The Log of "Bob" Bartlett.* G. P. Putnam's Sons, New York and London, 1928.
4. V. STEFANSSON: *The Friendly Arctic.* Macmillan Co., New York, 1921.

References

XX. To the Pole

1. R. HAKLUYT: *Principal Navigations . . . of the English Nation.*
2. SIR WILLIAM EDWARD PARRY: *Narrative of an Attempt to Reach the North Pole.* J. Murray, London, 1928.
3. R. N. RUDMOSE BROWN, in *Smithsonian Institution Report,* 1928, pp. 349–75.
4. V. STEFANSSON: *The Friendly Arctic.*
5. ROBERT E. PEARY: *The North Pole.* F. A. Stokes Co., New York, 1910.
6. CONSTANTINE PHIPPS: *A Voyage towards the North Pole.* 1773.
7. DR. FREDERICK COOK: *My Attainment of the Pole.* Mitchell Kennerley, The Polar Pub. Co., New York, 1911.

XXI. Flying in the Arctic

1. R. N. RUDMOSE BROWN, in *Smithsonian Institution Report,* 1928.
2. *Andrée's Story. The Complete Record 1897–1930.* Viking Press, New York, 1930.
3. L. ELLSWORTH: "At the North Pole," in *Yale Review,* Vol. XVI, No. 4 (July 1927).

Index

Index

Index

Index

Index

Index

Index

Index

Index

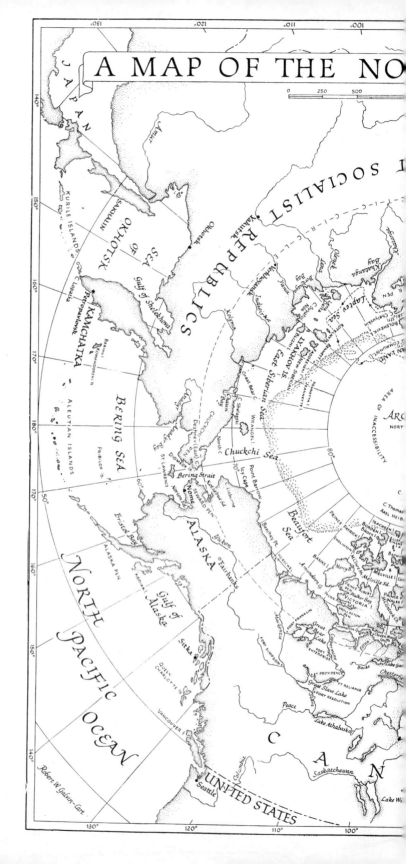

A MAP OF THE NO

Robert W. Galvin—Cart.

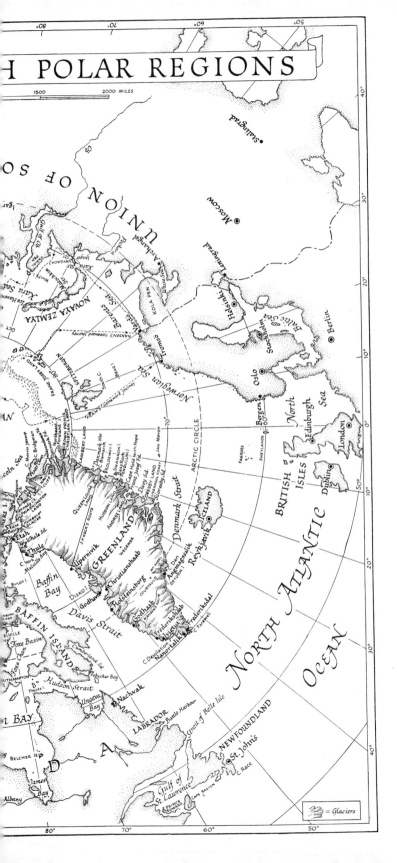

1500   2000 MILES

Spitsbergen

UNION OF SO

Moscow

UNION

White Sea

Archangel

NOVAYA ZEMLYA

Barents Sea

KOLA PEN.

Leningrad

Helsinki

Baltic Sea

Berlin

Tromsö

Stockholm

NANSEN'S Homeward Journey

Oslo

Bergen

Norwegian Sea

North Sea

Edinburgh

BRITISH ISLES

London

Dublin

ARCTIC CIRCLE

Jan Mayen

FAEROES

SHETLANDS

SPITSBERGEN

FRANZ JOSEF LAND

LAMBERT LAND

Denmark Hbr.

C. Bismarck

SHANNON I.

Cape Hold with Hope

King Oscar Fjd.

Davy Sd.

SCORESBY LAND

Scoresby Sd.

Denmark Strait

ICELAND

Reykjavik

Angmagssalik

GREENLAND

Upernivik

Disko I.

Godthaab

Baffin Bay

Christianshaab

Holstensborg

Godthaab

Frederikshaab

Julianehaab

Nanortalik

Frederiksdal

C. Farewell

Davis Strait

BAFFIN ISLAND

Foxe Basin

Cumberland Sd.

Frobisher Bay

Hudson Strait

Nachvak

Ungava Bay

LABRADOR

Battle Harbour

Strait of Belle Isle

NORTH ATLANTIC OCEAN

NEWFOUNDLAND

St. John's

C. Race

Gulf of St. Lawrence

CAPE BRETON

BAY

D A

James Bay

Albany

= Glaciers